# THE EARLY HISTORY OF ROME

# OF ROME

# (BOOKS I-V)

# By LIVY

## Translated by D. SPILLAN

The Early History of Rome (Books I-V)
By Livy (Titus Livius Patavinus)
Translated by D. Spillan

Print ISBN 13: 978-1-4209-5815-7
eBook ISBN 13: 978-1-4209-5816-4

Cover Image: a detail of "The Shepherd Faustulus Bringing Romulus and Remus to his Wife", by Nicolas Mignard, c. 1654, Dallas Museum of Art.

Please visit *www.digireads.com*

# CONTENTS

## *Preface.*

In this new English version of the most elegant of the Roman historians, the object of the translator has been, to adhere as closely to the original text as is consistent with the idioms of the respective languages. But while thus providing more especially for the wants of the classical student, he has not been unmindful of the neatness and perspicuity required to satisfy the English reader.

There have been several previous translations of our author, but the only one now before the public, or deserving of particular mention, is that by Baker, which is undoubtedly a very able performance, and had it been more faithful, would have rendered any other unnecessary.

The edition used for the present translation is that published at Oxford under the superintendence of Travers Twiss, whose carefully revised text is by far the best extant. The few notes and illustrations which the limits of an edition in this popular form permit, are chiefly confined to the explanation of grammatical difficulties. Historical and antiquarian illustration is now so abundantly supplied by excellent Manuals and Dictionaries, that it has been deemed unnecessary to swell the present volumes by additions in that department.

Among the manuals of Roman History which may most advantageously be used by the student, is Twiss's Epitome of Niebuhr, 2 vols. 8vo, a work frequently referred to in these pages.

THE HISTORY OF ROME.

*Book I.*

*The coming of Æneas into Italy, and his achievements there; the reign of Ascanius in Alba, and of the other Sylvian kings. Romulus and Remus born. Amulius killed. Romulus builds Rome; forms a senate; makes war upon the Sabines; presents the* opima spolia *to Jupiter Feretrius; divides the people into* curiæ; *his victories; is deified. Numa institutes the rites of religious worship; builds a temple to Janus; and having made peace with all his neighbours, closes it for the first time; enjoys a peaceful reign, and is succeeded by Tullus Hostilius. War with the Albans; combat of the Horatii and Curiatii. Alba demolished, and the Albans made citizens of Rome. War declared against the Sabines; Tullus killed by lightning. Ancus Marcius renews the religious institutions of Numa; conquers the Latins, confers on them the right of citizenship, and assigns them the Aventine hill to dwell on; adds the hill Janiculum to the city; enlarges the bounds of the empire. In his reign Lucumo comes to Rome; assumes the name of Tarquinius; and, after the death of Ancus, is raised to the throne. He increases the senate, by adding to it a hundred new senators; defeats the Latins and Sabines; augments the centuries of knights; builds a wall round the city; makes the common sewers; is slain by the sons of Ancus after a reign of thirty-eight years; and is succeeded by Servius Tullius. He institutes the census; closes the lustrum, in which eighty thousand citizens are said to have been enrolled; divides the people into classes and centuries; enlarges the Pomœrium, and adds the Quirinal, Viminal, and Esquiline hills to the city; after a reign of forty years, is murdered by L. Tarquin, afterwards surnamed Superbus. He usurps the crown. Tarquin makes war on the Volsci, and, with the plunder taken from them, builds a temple to Jupiter Capitolinus. By a stratagem of his son, Sextus Tarquin, he reduces the city of Gabii; after a reign of twenty-five years is dethroned and banished, in consequence of the forcible violation of the person of Lucretia by his son Sextus. L. Junius Brutus and L. Tarquinius Collatinus first created consuls*

PREFACE.

Whether in tracing the history of the Roman people, from the foundation of the city, I shall employ myself to a useful purpose,[1] I am neither very certain, nor, if I were, dare I say: inasmuch as I observe, that it is both an old and hackneyed practice,[2] later authors always supposing that they will either adduce something more authentic in the facts, or, that they will excel the less polished ancients in their style of writing. Be that as it may, it will, at all events, be a satisfaction to me, that I too have contributed my share[3] to perpetuate the achievements of a people, the lords of the world; and if, amidst so great a number of historians,[4] my reputation should remain in obscurity, I may console myself with the celebrity and lustre of those who shall stand in the way of my fame. Moreover, the subject is both of immense labour, as being one which must be traced back for more than seven hundred years, and which, having set out from small beginnings, has increased to such a degree that it is now distressed by its own magnitude. And, to most readers, I doubt not but that the first origin and the events immediately succeeding, will afford but little pleasure, while they will be hastening to these later times,[5] in which the strength of this overgrown people has

---

[1] "Employ myself to a useful purpose,"—*facere operæ pretium*, "to do a thing that is worth the trouble,"—"to employ oneself to a good purpose."—See Scheller's Lat. Lexicon.

[2] "A practice,"—*rem.*—Some, as Baker, refer it to *res populi* R. Others, as Stroth, to *res pop. Rom. perscribere.*

[3] "My share,"—*pro virili parte*, or, "to the best of my ability."

[4] "Historians."—Those mentioned by Livy himself are Q. Fabius Pictor, Valerius Antias, L. Piso, Q. Ælius Tubero, C. Licinius Macer, Cœlius, Polybius, etc.

[5] "Hastening to these later times."—The history of the recent civil wars would possess a more intense interest for the Romans of the Augustan age.

for a long period been working its own destruction. I, on the contrary, shall seek this, as a reward of my labour, viz. to withdraw myself from the view of the calamities, which our age has witnessed for so many years, so long as I am reviewing with my whole attention these ancient times, being free from every care[6] that may distract a writer's mind, though it cannot warp it from the truth. The traditions which have come down to us of what happened before the building of the city, or before its building was contemplated, as being suitable rather to the fictions of poetry than to the genuine records of history, I have no intention either to affirm or refute. This indulgence is conceded to antiquity, that by blending things human with divine, it may make the origin of cities appear more venerable: and if any people might be allowed to consecrate their origin, and to ascribe it to the gods as its authors, such is the renown of the Roman people in war, that when they represent Mars, in particular, as their own parent and that of their founder, the nations of the world may submit to this as patiently as they submit to their sovereignty.—But in whatever way these and such like matters shall be attended to, or judged of, I shall not deem of great importance. I would have every man apply his mind seriously to consider these points, viz. what their life and what their manners were; through what men and by what measures, both in peace and in war, their empire was acquired[7] and extended; then, as discipline gradually declined, let him follow in his thoughts their morals, at first as slightly giving way, anon how they sunk more and more, then began to fall headlong, until he reaches the present times, when we can neither endure our vices, nor their remedies. This it is which is particularly salutary and profitable in the study of history, that you behold instances of every variety of conduct displayed on a conspicuous monument; that from thence you may select for yourself and for your country that which you may imitate; thence *note* what is shameful in the undertaking, and shameful in the result, which you may avoid. But either a fond partiality for the task I have undertaken deceives me, or there never was any state either greater, or more moral, or richer in good examples, nor one into which luxury and avarice made their entrance so late, and where poverty and frugality were so much and so long honoured; so that the less wealth there was, the less desire was there. Of late, riches have introduced avarice, and excessive pleasures a longing for them, amidst luxury and

---

[6] "From every care,"—the fear of giving offence by expressing his opinions freely, and the sorrow, which, as a patriot, he could not but feel in recording the civil wars of his countrymen.
[7] "Acquired."—This refers to the whole period antecedent to the time when Ap. Claudius carried the Roman arms beyond Italy against the Carthaginians; (2) *extended*, from that time till the fall of Carthage; (3) *sinking*, the times of the Gracchi; (4) *gave way more and more*, those of Sulla; (5) *precipitate*, those of Cæsar; (6) the present times, those of Augustus after the battle of Actium.—*Stocker*.

a passion for ruining ourselves and destroying every thing else. But let complaints, which will not be agreeable even then, when perhaps they will be also necessary, be kept aloof at least from the first stage of commencing so great a work. We should rather, if it was usual with us (historians) as it is with poets, begin with good omens, vows and prayers to the gods and goddesses to vouchsafe good success to our efforts in so arduous an undertaking.

## CHAPTER I.

Now first of all it is sufficiently established that, Troy having been taken, the utmost severity was shown to all the other Trojans; but that towards two, Æneas and Antenor, the Greeks forbore all the rights of war, both in accordance with an ancient tie of hospitality, and because they had ever been the advisers of peace, and of the restoration of Helen—then that Antenor after various vicissitudes came into the innermost bay of the Adriatic Sea, with a body of the Heneti, who having been driven from Paphlagonia in consequence of a civil commotion, were in quest both of a settlement and a leader, their king Pylæmenes having been lost at Troy; and that the Heneti and Trojans, having expelled the Euganei, who dwelt between the sea and the Alps, took possession of the country; and the place where they first landed is called Troy; from whence also the name of Trojan is given to the canton; but the nation in general is called Veneti: that Æneas was driven from home by a similar calamity, but the fates leading him to the founding of a greater empire, he came first to Macedonia: that he sailed from thence to Sicily in quest of a settlement: that from Sicily he made for the Laurentine territory; this place also has the name of Troy. When the Trojans, having disembarked there, were driving plunder from the lands,—as being persons to whom, after their almost immeasurable wandering, nothing was left but their arms and ships,—Latinus the king, and the Aborigines, who then occupied those places, assembled in arms from the city and country to repel the violence of the new-comers. On this point the tradition is two-fold: some say, that Latinus, after being overcome in battle, made first a peace, and then an alliance with Æneas: others, that when the armies were drawn out in battle-array, before the signals were sounded, Latinus advanced to the front of the troops and invited the leader of the adventurers to a conference. That he then inquired who they were, whence (they had come), or by what casualty they had left their home, and in quest of what they had landed on the Laurentine territory: after he heard that the host were Trojans, their chief Æneas, the son of Anchises and Venus, and that, driven from their own country and their homes, which had been destroyed by fire, they were seeking a settlement and a place for building a town, struck with admiration of the noble origin of the nation and of the hero, and their spirit, alike prepared for peace or war, he confirmed the assurance of future friendship by giving his right hand: that upon this a compact was struck between the chiefs, and mutual greetings passed between the armies: that Æneas was hospitably entertained by Latinus: that Latinus, in the presence of his household gods, added a family league to the public one, by giving Æneas his daughter in marriage. This event confirms the Trojans in the hope of at length terminating their wanderings by a fixed and permanent settlement. They build a town. Æneas calls it Lavinium, after the name of his wife. In a short time, too, a son was the issue of the new marriage, to whom his parents gave the name of Ascanius.

The Aborigines and Trojans were soon after attacked together in war. Turnus, king of the Rutulians, to whom Lavinia had been affianced before the coming of Æneas, enraged that a stranger had been preferred to himself, made war on Æneas and Latinus together. Neither side came off from that contest with cause for rejoicing. The Rutulians were vanquished; the victorious Aborigines and Trojans lost their leader Latinus. Upon this Turnus and the Rutulians, diffident of their strength, have recourse to the flourishing state of the Etruscans, and their king Mezentius; who holding his court at Cœre, at that time an opulent town, being by no means pleased, even from the commencement, at the founding of the new city, and then considering that the Trojan power was increasing much more than was altogether consistent with the safety of the neighbouring states, without reluctance joined his forces in alliance with the Rutulians. Æneas, in order to conciliate the minds of the Aborigines to meet the terror of so serious a war, called both nations Latins, so that they might all be not only under the same laws, but also the same name. Nor after that did the Aborigines yield to the Trojans in zeal and fidelity towards their king Æneas; relying therefore on this disposition of the two nations, who were now daily coalescing more and more, although Etruria was so powerful, that it filled with the fame of its prowess not only the land, but the sea also, through the whole length of Italy, from the Alps to the Sicilian Strait, though he might have repelled the war by means of fortifications, yet he led out his forces to the field. Upon this a battle ensued successful to the Latins, the last also of the mortal acts of Æneas. He was buried, by whatever name human and divine laws require him to be called,[8] on the banks of the river Numicius. They call him Jupiter Indiges.

Ascanius, the son of Æneas, was not yet old enough to take the government upon him; that government, however, remained secure for

---

[8] Æneas, being now deified, could not be called by his human name; and in speaking of his being buried, it would be improper to name him by his divine title. ―― *Indigetem.* He is called by Dionysius χθόνιος θεός.

him till the age of maturity. In the interim, the Latin state and the kingdom of his grandfather and father was secured for the boy under the regency of his mother (such capacity was there in Lavinia). I have some doubts (for who can state as certain a matter of such antiquity) whether this was the Ascanius, or one older than he, born of Creusa before the fall of Troy, and the companion of his father in his flight from thence, the same whom, being called Iulus, the Julian family call the author of their name. This Ascanius, wheresoever and of whatever mother born, (it is at least certain that he was the son of Æneas,) Lavinium being overstocked with inhabitants, left that flourishing and, considering these times, wealthy city to his mother or step-mother, and built for himself a new one at the foot of Mount Alba, which, being extended on the ridge of a hill, was, from its situation, called Longa Alba. Between the founding of Lavinium and the transplanting this colony to Longa Alba, about thirty years intervened. Yet its power had increased to such a degree, especially after the defeat of the Etrurians, that not even upon the death of Æneas, nor after that, during the regency of Lavinia, and the first essays of the young prince's reign, did Mezentius, the Etrurians, or any other of its neighbours dare to take up arms against it. A peace had been concluded between the two nations on these terms, that the river Albula, now called Tiber, should be the common boundary between the Etrurians and Latins. After him Sylvius, the son of Ascanius, born by some accident in a wood, ascends the throne. He was the father of Æneas Sylvius, who afterwards begot Latinus Sylvius. By him several colonies, called the ancient Latins, were transplanted. From this time, all the princes, who reigned at Alba, had the surname of Sylvius. From Latinus sprung Alba; from Alba, Atys; from Atys, Capys; from Capys, Capetus; from Capetus, Tiberinus, who, being drowned in crossing the river Albula, gave it a name famous with posterity. Then Agrippa, the son of Tiberinus; after Agrippa, Romulus Silvius ascends the throne, in succession to his father. The latter, having been killed by a thunderbolt, left the kingdom to Aventinus, who being buried on that hill, which is now part of the city of Rome, gave his name to it. After him reigns Proca; he begets Numitor and Amulius. To Numitor, his eldest son, he bequeaths the ancient kingdom of the Sylvian family. But force prevailed more than the father's will or the respect due to seniority: for Amulius, having expelled his brother, seizes the kingdom; he adds crime to crime, murders his brother's male issue; and under pretence of doing his brother's daughter, Rhea Sylvia, honour, having made her a vestal virgin, by obliging her to perpetual virginity he deprives her of all hopes of issue.

But, in my opinion, the origin of so great a city, and the establishment of an empire next in power to that of the gods, was due to the Fates. The vestal Rhea, being deflowered by force, when she had brought forth twins, declares Mars to be the father of her illegitimate offspring, either because she believed it to be so, or because a god was a more creditable author of her offence. But neither gods nor men protect her or her children from the king's cruelty: the priestess is bound and thrown into prison; the children he commands to be thrown into the current of the river. By some interposition of providence,[9] the Tiber having overflowed its banks in stagnant pools, did not admit of any access to the regular bed of the river; and the bearers supposed that the infants could be drowned in water however still; thus, as if they had effectually executed the king's orders, they expose the boys in the nearest land-flood, where now stands the ficus Ruminalis (they say that it was called Romularis). The country thereabout was then a vast wilderness. The tradition is, that when the water, subsiding, had left the floating trough, in which the children had been exposed, on dry ground, a thirsty she-wolf, coming from the neighbouring mountains, directed her course to the cries of the infants, and that she held down her dugs to them with so much gentleness, that the keeper of the king's flock found her licking the boys with her tongue. It is said his name was Faustulus; and that they were carried by him to his homestead to be nursed by his wife Laurentia. Some are of opinion that she was called Lupa among the shepherds, from her being a common prostitute, and that this gave rise to the surprising story. The children thus born and thus brought up, when arrived at the years of manhood, did not loiter away their time in tending the folds or following the flocks, but roamed and hunted in the forests. Having by this exercise improved their strength and courage, they not only encountered wild beasts, but even attacked robbers laden with plunder, and afterwards divided the spoil among the shepherds. And in company with these, the number of their young associates daily increasing, they carried on their business and their sports.

They say, that the festival of the lupercal, as now celebrated, was even at that time solemnized on the Palatine hill, which, from Palanteum, a city of Arcadia, was first called Palatium, and afterwards Mount Palatine. There they say that Evander, who belonged to the tribe of Arcadians,[10] that for many years before had possessed that country, appointed the observance of a feast, introduced from Arcadia, in such manner, that young men ran about naked in sport and wantonness, doing honour to Pan Lycæus, whom the Romans afterwards called Inuus. That the robbers, through rage at the loss of their booty, having lain in wait for them whilst intent on this sport, as the festival was now well known, whilst Romulus vigorously defended himself, took Remus prisoner; that they delivered him up, when taken, to king Amulius, accusing him with the utmost effrontery. They principally alleged it as

---

[9] Forte quâdam divinitus. *θείᾳ τινι τύχῃ*. Plut.
[10] Scil. "The Pallantean."

a charge against them, that they had made incursions upon Numitor's lands, and plundered them in a hostile manner, having assembled a band of young men for the purpose. Upon this Remus was delivered to Numitor to be punished. Now, from the very first, Faustulus had entertained hopes that the boys whom he was bringing up were of the blood royal; for he both knew that the children had been exposed by the king's orders, and that the time at which he had taken them up agreed exactly with that period: but he had been unwilling that the matter, as not being yet ripe for discovery, should be disclosed, till either a fit opportunity or necessity should arise. Necessity came first; accordingly, compelled by fear, he discovers the whole affair to Romulus. By accident also, whilst he had Remus in custody, and had heard that the brothers were twins, on comparing their age, and *observing* their turn of mind entirely free from servility, the recollection of his grand-children struck Numitor; and on making inquiries[11] he arrived at the same conclusion, so that he was well nigh recognising Remus. Thus a plot is concerted for the king on all sides. Romulus, not accompanied by a body of young men, (for he was unequal to open force,) but having commanded the shepherds to come to the palace by different roads at a fixed time, forces his way to the king; and Remus, with another party from Numitor's house, assists his brother, and so they kill the king.

Numitor, at the beginning of the fray, having given out that enemies had invaded the city, and assaulted the palace, after he had drawn off the Alban youth to secure the citadel with a garrison and arms, when he saw the young men, after they had killed the king, advancing to congratulate him, immediately called an assembly of the people, and represented to them the unnatural behaviour of his brother towards him, the extraction of his grand-children, the manner of their birth and education, and how they came to be discovered; then he informed them of the king's death, and that he was killed by his orders. When the young princes, coming up with their band through the middle of the assembly, saluted their grandfather king, an approving shout, following from all the people present, ratified to him both that title and the sovereignty. Thus the government of Alba being committed to Numitor, a desire seized Romulus and Remus to build a city on the spot where they had been exposed and brought up. And there was an overflowing population of Albans and of Latins. The shepherds too had come into that design, and all these readily inspired hopes, that Alba and Lavinium would be but petty places in comparison with the city which they intended to build. But ambition of the sovereignty, the bane of their grandfather, interrupted these designs, and thence arose a

---

[11] By all his inquiries he arrived at the same conclusion as before, viz. that they were his grand-children.

shameful quarrel from a beginning sufficiently amicable. For as they were twins, and the respect due to seniority could not determine the point, they agreed to leave to the tutelary gods of the place to choose, by augury, which should give a name to the new city, which govern it when built.

Romulus chose the Palatine and Remus the Aventine hill as their stands to make their observations. It is said, that to Remus an omen came first, six vultures; and now, the omen having been declared, when double the number presented itself to Romulus, his own party saluted each king; the former claimed the kingdom on the ground of priority of time, the latter on account of the number of birds. Upon this, having met in an altercation, from the contest of angry feelings they turn to bloodshed; there Remus fell from a blow received in the crowd. A more common account is, that Remus, in derision of his brother, leaped over his new-built wall, and was, for that reason, slain by Romulus in a passion; who, after sharply chiding him, added words to this effect: "So shall every one fare, who shall dare to leap over my fortifications."[12] Thus Romulus got the sovereignty to himself; the city, when built, was called after the name of its founder. His first work was to fortify the Palatine hill where he had been educated. To the other gods he offers sacrifices according to the Alban rite; to Hercules, according to the Grecian rite, as they had been instituted by Evander. There is a tradition, that Hercules, having killed Geryon, drove his oxen, which were extremely beautiful, into those places; and that, after swimming over the Tiber, and driving the cattle before him, being fatigued with travelling, he laid himself down on the banks of the river, in a grassy place, to refresh them with rest and rich pasture. When sleep had overpowered him, satiated with food and wine, a shepherd of the place, named Cacus, presuming on his strength, and charmed with the beauty of the oxen, wished to purloin that booty, but because, if he had driven them forward into the cave, their footsteps would have guided the search of their owner thither, he therefore drew the most beautiful of them, one by one, by the tails, backwards into a cave. Hercules, awaking at day-break, when he had surveyed his herd, and observed that some of them were missing, goes directly to the nearest cave, to see if by chance their footsteps would lead him thither. But when he observed that they were all turned from it, and directed him no other way, confounded, and not knowing what to do, he began to drive his cattle out of that unlucky place. Upon this, some of the cows, as they usually do, lowed on missing those that were left; and the lowings of those that were confined being returned from the cave, made Hercules

---

[12] According to Cato, Rome was founded on the day of the *Palilia*, the 11th of the Calends of May, in the first year of the 7th Olympiad, and 751 B.C. This is two years short of Varro's computation.

turn that way. And when Cacus attempted to prevent him by force, as
he was proceeding to the cave, being struck with a club, he was slain,
vainly imploring the assistance of the shepherds. At that time Evander,
who had fled from the Peloponnesus, ruled this country more by his
credit and reputation than absolute sway. He was a person highly
revered for his wondrous knowledge of letters,[13] a discovery that was
entirely new and surprising to men ignorant of every art; but more
highly respected on account of the supposed divinity of his mother
Carmenta, whom these nations had admired as a prophetess, before the
coming of the Sibyl into Italy. This prince, alarmed by the concourse of
the shepherds hastily crowding round the stranger, whom they charged
with open murder, after he heard the act and the cause of the act,
observing the person and mien of the hero to be larger, and his gait
more majestic, than human, asked who he was? As soon as he was
informed of his name, his father, and his native country, he said, "Hail!
Hercules! son of Jupiter, my mother, a truth-telling interpreter of the
gods, has revealed to me, that thou shalt increase the number of the
celestials; and that to thee an altar shall be dedicated here, which some
ages hence the most powerful people on earth shall call Ara Maxima,
and honour according to thy own institution." Hercules having given
him his right hand, said, "That he accepted the omen, and would fulfil
the predictions of the fates, by building and consecrating an altar."
There for the first time a sacrifice was offered to Hercules of a chosen
heifer, taken from the herd, the Potitii and Pinarii, who were then the
most distinguished families that inhabited these parts, having been
invited to the service and the entertainment. It so happened that the
Potitii were present in due time, and the entrails were set before them;
when they were eaten up, the Pinarii came to the remainder of the feast.
From this time it was ordained, that while the Pinarian family
subsisted, none of them should eat of the entrails of the solemn
sacrifices. The Potitii, being instructed by Evander, discharged this
sacred function as priests for many ages, until the office, solemnly
appropriated to their family, being delegated to public slaves, their
whole race became extinct. This was the only foreign religious
institution which Romulus adopted, being even then an abettor of
immortality attained by merit, to which his own destinies were
conducting him.

The duties of religion having been duly performed, and the
multitude summoned to a meeting, as they could be incorporated into
one people by no other means than fixed rules, he gave them a code of
laws, and judging that these would be best respected by this rude class
of men, if he made himself dignified by the insignia of authority, he
assumed a more majestic appearance both in his other appointments,

---

[13] He taught the Italians to read and write.

and especially by taking twelve lictors to attend him. Some think that he chose this number of officers from that of the birds, which in the augury had portended the kingdom to him. I do not object to be of the opinion of those who will have it that the apparitors (in general), and this particular class of them,[14] and even their number, was taken from their neighbours the Etrurians, from whom were borrowed the curule chair, and the gown edged with purple; and that the Etrurians adopted that number, because their king being elected in common from twelve states, each state assigned him one lictor. Meanwhile the city increased by their taking in various lots of ground for buildings, whilst they built rather with a view to future numbers, than for the population[15] which they then had. Then, lest the size of the city might be of no avail, in order to augment the population, according to the ancient policy of the founders of cities, who, after drawing together to them an obscure and mean multitude, used to feign that their offspring sprung out of the earth, he opened as a sanctuary, a place which is now enclosed as you go down "to the two groves."[16] Hither fled from the neighbouring states, without distinction whether freemen or slaves, crowds of all sorts, desirous of change: and this was the first accession of strength to their rising greatness. When he was now not dissatisfied with his strength, he next sets about forming some means of directing that strength. He creates one hundred senators, either because that number was sufficient, or because there were only one hundred who could name their fathers. They certainly were called Fathers, through respect, and their descendants, Patricians.[17]

And now the Roman state was become so powerful, that it was a match for any of the neighbouring nations in war, but, from the paucity of women, its greatness could only last for one age of man; for they had no hope of issue at home, nor had they any intermarriages with their neighbours. Therefore, by the advice of the Fathers, Romulus sent ambassadors to the neighbouring states to solicit an alliance and the privilege of intermarriage for his new subjects. "That cities, like every thing else, rose from very humble beginnings. That those which the gods and their own merit aided, gained great power and high renown. That he knew full well, both that the gods had aided the origin of

---

[14] *Apparitores hoc genus.* There is something incorrect in the language of the original here. In my version I have followed Drakenborch. Walker, in his edition, proposes to read *ut* for *et*; thus, *quibus ut apparitores et hoc genus ab Etruscis —— numerum quoque ipsum ductum placet, "who will have it, that as public servants of this kind, so was their number also, derived from the Etrurians."*

[15] The population at that time consisted of not more than 3,000 foot, and less than 300 horse. At the death of Romulus, it is said to have amounted to 46,000 foot and almost 1,000 horse.

[16] τὸ μεταξὺ χωρίον τοῦ τε Καπιτωλίου καὶ τῆς ἄκρας ὃ καλεῖται νῦν κατὰ τὴν Ῥωμαίων διάλεκτον μεθόριον δυοῖν δρυμῶν. Dio. ii. 15.

[17] *Ex industria—deditâ operâ—* ἀπὸ παρασκευῆς.

Rome, and that merit would not be wanting. Wherefore that, as men, they should feel no reluctance to mix their blood and race with men." No where did the embassy obtain a favourable hearing: so much did they at the same time despise, and dread for themselves and their posterity, so great a power growing up in the midst of them. They were dismissed by the greater part with the repeated question, "Whether they had opened any asylum for women also, for that such a plan only could obtain them suitable matches?" The Roman youth resented this conduct bitterly, and the matter unquestionably began to point towards violence. Romulus, in order that he might afford a favourable time and place for this, dissembling his resentment, purposely prepares games in honour of Neptunus Equestris; he calls them Consualia. He then orders the spectacle to be proclaimed among their neighbours; and they prepare for the celebration with all the magnificence they were then acquainted with, or were capable of doing, that they might render the matter famous, and an object of expectation. Great numbers assembled, from a desire also of seeing the new city; especially their nearest neighbours, the Cæninenses, Crustumini, and Antemnates. Moreover the whole multitude of the Sabines came, with their wives and children. Having been hospitably invited to the different houses, when they had seen the situation, and fortifications, and the city crowded with houses, they became astonished that the Roman power had increased so rapidly. When the time of the spectacle came on, and while their minds and eyes were intent upon it, according to concert a tumult began, and upon a signal given the Roman youth ran different ways to carry off the virgins by force. A great number were carried off at hap-hazard, according as they fell into their hands. Persons from the common people, who had been charged with the task, conveyed to their houses some women of surpassing beauty, destined for the leading senators. They say that one, far distinguished beyond the others for stature and beauty, was carried off by the party of one Thalassius, and whilst many inquired to whom they were carrying her, they cried out every now and then, in order that no one might molest her, that she was being taken to Thalassius; that from this circumstance this term became a nuptial one. The festival being disturbed by this alarm, the parents of the young women retire in grief, appealing to the compact of violated hospitality, and invoking the god, to whose festival and games they had come, deceived by the pretence of religion and good faith. Neither had the ravished virgins better hopes of their condition, or less indignation. But Romulus in person went about and declared, "That what was done was owing to the pride of their fathers, who had refused to grant the privilege of marriage to their neighbours; but notwithstanding, they should be joined in lawful wedlock, participate in all their possessions and civil privileges, and, than which nothing can be dearer to the human heart, in their common children. He begged them only to assuage the fierceness of their anger, and cheerfully surrender their affections to those to whom fortune had consigned their persons." [He added,] "That from injuries love and friendship often arise; and that they should find them kinder husbands on this account, because each of them, besides the performance of his conjugal duty, would endeavour to the utmost of his power to make up for the want of their parents and native country." To this the caresses of the husbands were added, excusing what they had done on the plea of passion and love, arguments that work most successfully on women's hearts.

The minds of the ravished virgins were soon much soothed, but their parents by putting on mourning, and tears and complaints, roused the states. Nor did they confine their resentment to their own homes, but they flocked from all quarters to Titus Tatius, king of the Sabines; and because he bore the greatest character in these parts, embassies were sent to him. The Cæninenses, Crustumini, and Antemnates were people to whom a considerable portion of the outrage extended. To them Tatius and the Sabines seemed to proceed somewhat dilatorily. Nor even do the Crustumini and Antemnates bestir themselves with sufficient activity to suit the impatience and rage of the Cæninenses. Accordingly the state of the Cæninenses by itself makes an irruption into the Roman territory. But Romulus with his army met them ravaging the country in straggling parties, and by a slight engagement convinces them, that resentment without strength is of no avail. He defeats and routs their army, pursues it when routed, kills and despoils their king in battle, and having slain their general takes the city at the first assault. From thence having led back his victorious army, and being a man highly distinguished by his exploits, and one who could place them in the best light, went in state to the capitol, carrying before him, suspended on a frame curiously wrought for that purpose, the spoils of the enemy's general, whom he had slain, and there after he had laid them down at the foot of an oak held sacred by the shepherds, together with the offering, he marked out the bounds for a temple of Jupiter, and gave a surname to the god: "Jupiter Feretrius," he says, "I, king Romulus, upon my victory, present to thee these royal arms, and to thee I dedicate a temple within those regions which I have now marked out in my mind, as a receptacle for the grand spoils, which my successors, following my example, shall, upon their killing the kings or generals of the enemy, offer to thee." This is the origin of that temple, the first consecrated at Rome. It afterwards so pleased the gods both that the declaration of the founder of the temple should not be frustrated, by which he announced that his posterity should offer such spoils, and that the glory of that offering should not be depreciated by the great number of those who shared it. During so many years, and amid so many wars since that time, grand spoils have been only twice gained,[18] so rare has been the successful attainment of that honour.

Whilst the Romans are achieving these exploits, the army of the Antemnates, taking advantage of their absence, makes an incursion into the Roman territories in a hostile manner. A Roman legion being marched out in haste against these also, surprise them whilst straggling through the fields. Accordingly the enemy were routed at the very first shout and charge: their town taken; and as Romulus was returning, exulting for this double victory, his consort, Hersilia, importuned by the entreaties of the captured women, beseeches him "to pardon their fathers, and to admit them to the privilege of citizens; that thus his power might be strengthened by a reconciliation." Her request was readily granted. After this he marched against the Crustumini, who were commencing hostilities; but as their spirits were sunk by the defeat of their neighbours, there was still less resistance there. Colonies were sent to both places, but more were found to give in their names for Crustuminum, because of the fertility of the soil. Migrations in great numbers were also made from thence to Rome, chiefly by the parents and relatives of the ravished women. The last war broke out on the part of the Sabines, and proved by far the most formidable: for they did nothing through anger or cupidity; nor did they make a show of war, before they actually began it. To prudence stratagem also was added. Sp. Tarpeius commanded the Roman citadel; Tatius bribes his maiden daughter with gold, to admit armed soldiers into the citadel: she had gone by chance outside the walls to fetch water for the sacrifice. Those who were admitted crushed her to death by heaping their arms upon her; either that the citadel might seem rather to have been taken by storm, or for the purpose of establishing a precedent, that no faith should, under any circumstances, be kept with a traitor. A story is added, that the Sabines commonly wore on their left arm golden bracelets of great weight, and large rings set with precious stones, and that she bargained with them for what they had on their left hands; hence that their shields were thrown upon her instead of the golden presents. There are some who say that in pursuance of the compact to deliver up what was on their left hands, she expressly demanded their shields, and that appearing to act with treachery, she was killed by the reward of her own choosing.

The Sabines, however, kept possession of the citadel, and on the day after, when the Roman army, drawn up in order of battle, filled up all the ground lying between the Palatine and Capitoline hills, they did not descend from thence into the plain, till the Romans, fired with resentment, and with a desire of retaking the citadel, advanced to attack

---

[18] Two, one by A. Cornelius Cossus for slaying L. Tolumnius, king of Veii, u. c. 318, another by M. Claudius Marcellus, for killing Viridomarus, king of the Gauls, u. c. 532.

them. Two chiefs, one on each side, animated the battle, viz. Mettus Curtius on the part of the Sabines, Hostus Hostilius on that of the Romans. The latter, in the front ranks, supported the Roman cause by his courage and bravery, on disadvantageous ground. As soon as Hostus fell, the Roman line immediately gave way and was beaten to the old gate of the Palatium. Romulus, himself too carried away with the general rout, raising his arms to heaven, says, "O Jupiter, commanded by thy birds, I here laid the first foundation of the city on the Palatine hill. The Sabines are in possession of the citadel, purchased by fraud. From thence they are now advancing hither, sword in hand, having already passed the middle of the valley. But do thou, father of gods and men, keep back the enemy at least from hence, dispel the terror of the Romans, and stop their shameful flight. Here I solemnly vow to build a temple to thee as Jupiter Stator, as a monument to posterity, that this city was saved by thy immediate aid." Having offered up this prayer, as if he had felt that his prayers were heard, he cries out, "At this spot, Romans, Jupiter, supremely good and great, commands you to halt, and renew the fight." The Romans halted as if they had been commanded by a voice from heaven; Romulus himself flies to the foremost ranks. Mettus Curtius, on the part of the Sabines, had rushed down at the head of his army from the citadel, and driven the Romans in disorder over the whole ground now occupied by the forum. He was already not far from the gate of the Palatium, crying out, "We have defeated these perfidious strangers, these dastardly enemies. They now feel that it is one thing to ravish virgins, another far different to fight with men." On him, thus vaunting, Romulus makes an attack with a band of the most courageous youths. It happened that Mettus was then fighting on horseback; he was on that account the more easily repulsed: the Romans pursue him when repulsed: and the rest of the Roman army, encouraged by the gallant behaviour of their king, routs the Sabines. Mettus, his horse taking fright at the din of his pursuers, threw himself into a lake; and this circumstance drew the attention of the Sabines at the risk of so important a person. He, however, his own party beckoning and calling to him, acquires new courage from the affection of his many friends, and makes his escape. The Romans and Sabines renew the battle in the valley between the hills; but Roman prowess had the advantage.

At this juncture the Sabine women, from the outrage on whom the war originated, with hair dishevelled and garments rent, the timidity of their sex being overcome by such dreadful scenes, had the courage to throw themselves amid the flying weapons, and making a rush across, to part the incensed armies, and assuage their fury; imploring their fathers on the one side, their husbands on the other, "that as fathers-in-law and sons-in-law they would not contaminate each other with impious blood, nor stain their offspring with parricide, the one[19] their grandchildren, the other their children. If you are dissatisfied with the affinity between you, if with our marriages, turn your resentment against us; we are the cause of war, we of wounds and of bloodshed to our husbands and parents. It were better that we perish than live widowed or fatherless without one or other of you." The circumstance affects both the multitude and the leaders. Silence and a sudden suspension ensue. Upon this the leaders come forward in order to concert a treaty, and they not only conclude a peace, but form one state out of two. They associate the regal power, and transfer the entire sovereignty to Rome. The city being thus doubled, that some compliment might be paid to the Sabines, they were called Quirites, from Cures. As a memorial of this battle, they called the place where the horse, after getting out of the deep marsh, first set Curtius in shallow water, the Curtian Lake. This happy peace following suddenly a war so distressing, rendered the Sabine women still dearer to their husbands and parents, and above all to Romulus himself. Accordingly, when he divided the people into thirty curiæ, he called the curiæ by their names. Since, without doubt, the number of the Sabine women was considerably greater than this, it is not recorded whether those who were to give their names to the curiæ were selected on account of their age, or their own or their husbands' rank, or by lot. At the same time three centuries of knights were enrolled, called Ramnenses, from Romulus; Tatienses, from Titus Tatius. The reason of the name and origin of the Luceres is uncertain.

Thenceforward the two kings held the regal power not only in common, but in concord also. Several years after, some relatives of king Tatius beat the ambassadors of the Laurentes, and when the Laurentes commenced proceedings according to the law of nations, the influence of his friends and their importunities had more weight with Tatius. He therefore drew upon himself the punishment due to them; for he is slain at Lavinium, in a tumult which arose on his going thither to an anniversary sacrifice. They say that Romulus resented this with less severity than the case required, either by reason of their association in the kingly power being devoid of cordiality, or because he believed that he was justly killed. He therefore declined going to war; in order, however, that the ill-treatment of the ambassadors and the murder of the king might be expiated, the treaty was renewed between the cities of Rome and Lavinium. With this party, indeed, peace continued, contrary to expectation; another war broke out much nearer home, and almost at the very gates. The Fidenates, thinking that a power too near to themselves was growing to a height, resolve to make war, before their strength should become as great as it was apparent it would be. An

---

[19] *Nepotum et liberûm progeniem* = Nepotes et liberos,—υἷς Ἀχαιων = οἶ Ἀχαιοι.

armed body of young men being sent in, all the land is laid waste between the city and Fidenæ. Then turning to the left, because the Tiber confined them on the right, they continue their depredations to the great consternation of the peasantry. The sudden alarm reaching the city from the country, served as the first announcement. Romulus, roused at this circumstance, (for a war so near home could not admit of delay,) leads out his army: he pitches his camp a mile from Fidenæ. Having left there a small garrison, marching out with all his forces, he commanded a party of his soldiers to lie in ambush in a place[20] hidden by thick bushes which were planted around. Then advancing with the greater part of the foot and all the horse, and riding up to the very gates of the city in a disorderly and menacing manner, he drew out the enemy, the very thing he wanted. The same mode of fighting on the part of the cavalry likewise made the cause of the flight, which was to be counterfeited, appear less surprising: and when, the horse seeming irresolute, as if in deliberation whether to fight or fly, the infantry also retreated, the enemy suddenly rushed from the crowded gates, after they had made an impression on the Roman line, are drawn on to the place of ambuscade in their eagerness to press on and pursue. Upon this the Romans, rising suddenly, attack the enemy's line in flank. The standards of those who had been left behind on guard, advancing from the camp, further increase the panic. The Fidenates, thus dismayed with terrors from so many quarters, turn their backs almost before Romulus, and those who had accompanied him on horseback, could wheel their horses round; and those who a little before had pursued men pretending to fly, now ran back to the town in much greater disorder, for their flight was in earnest. They did not however get clear of the enemy: the Romans pressing on their rear rush in as it were in one body before the gates could be shut against them.

The minds of the Veientes being excited by the contagious influence of the Fidenatian war, both from the tie of consanguinity, for the Fidenates also were Etrurians, and because the very proximity of situation, in case the Roman arms should be turned against all their neighbours, urged them on, they made an incursion on the Roman territories, more to commit depredations than after the manner of a regular war. Accordingly, without pitching a camp, or awaiting the approach of the enemy's army, they returned to Veii, carrying with them the booty collected from the lands; the Roman army on the other side, when they did not find the enemy in the country, being prepared for and determined on a decisive action, cross the Tiber. And when the Veientes heard that they were pitching a camp, and intended to advance to the city, they came out to meet them, that they might rather decide

---

[20] The original has undergone various changes here: my version coincides with the reading, *locis circà densa obsita virgulta obscuris.*

the matter in the open field, than be shut up and fight from their houses and walls. Here the Roman king obtained the victory, his power not being aided by any stratagem, merely by the strength of his veteran army: and having pursued the routed enemies to their walls, he made no attempt on the city, strong as it was by its fortifications, and well defended by its situation: on his return he lays waste their lands, rather from a desire of revenge than booty. And the Veientes, being humbled by that loss no less than by the unsuccessful battle, send ambassadors to Rome to sue for peace. A truce for one hundred years was granted them after they were fined a part of their land. These are the principal transactions which occurred during the reign of Romulus, in peace and war, none of which seem inconsistent with the belief of his divine original, or of the deification attributed to him after death, neither his spirit in recovering his grandfather's kingdom, nor his project of building a city, nor that of strengthening it by the arts of war and peace. For by the strength attained from that outset under him, it became so powerful, that for forty years after it enjoyed a profound peace. He was, however, dearer to the people than to the fathers; but above all others he was most beloved by the soldiers. And he kept three hundred of them armed as a body-guard not only in war but in peace, whom he called Celeres.

After performing these immortal achievements, while he was holding an assembly of the people for reviewing his army, in the plain near the lake of Capra, on a sudden a storm having arisen, with great thunder and lightning, enveloped the king in so dense a mist, that it took all sight of him from the assembly. Nor was Romulus after this seen on earth. The consternation being at length over, and fine clear weather succeeding so turbulent a day, when the Roman youth saw the royal seat empty, though they readily believed the fathers who had stood nearest him, that he was carried aloft by the storm, yet, struck with the dread as it were of orphanage, they preserved a sorrowful silence for a considerable time. Then, a commencement having been made by a few, the whole multitude salute Romulus a god, son of a god, the king and parent of the Roman city; they implore his favour with prayers, that he would be pleased always propitiously to preserve his own offspring. I believe that even then there were some, who silently surmised that the king had been torn in pieces by the hands of the fathers; for this rumour also spread, but was not credited; their admiration of the man, and the consternation felt at the moment, attached importance to the other report. By the contrivance also of one individual, additional credit is said to have been gained to the matter. For Proculus Julius, whilst the state was still troubled with regret for the king, and felt incensed against the senators, a person of weight, as we are told, in any matter however important, comes forward to the assembly, "Romans," he says, "Romulus, the father of this city, suddenly descending from heaven, appeared to me this day at day-break. While I stood covered with awe, and filled with a religious dread, beseeching him to allow me to see him face to face, he said, Go tell the Romans, that the gods so will, that my Rome should become the capitol of the world. Therefore let them cultivate the art of war, and let them know and hand down to posterity, that no human power shall be able to withstand the Roman arms. Having said this, he ascended up to heaven." It is surprising what credit was given to the man on his making this announcement, and how much the regret of the common people and army, for the loss of Romulus, was assuaged upon the assurance of his immortality.

Meanwhile ambition and contention for the throne actuated the minds of the fathers; factions had not yet sprung up from individuals, because, among a new people, no one person was eminently distinguished above the rest: the contest was carried on between the different orders. The descendants of the Sabines wished a king to be elected out of their body, lest, because there had been no king on their side since the death of Tatius, they might lose their claim to the crown[21] according to the compact of equal participation. The old Romans spurned the idea of a foreign prince. Amid this diversity of views, however, all were anxious that there should be a king, they not having yet tasted the sweets of liberty. Fear then seized the senators, lest the minds of the surrounding states being incensed against them, some foreign power should attack the state, now without a government, and the army without a leader. It was therefore their wish that there should be some head, but no one could bring himself to give way to another. Thus the hundred senators divide the government among them, ten decuries being formed, and one selected from each decury, who was to have the chief direction of affairs. Ten governed; one only was attended with the insignia of authority and the lictors: their power was limited to the space of five days, and it passed through all in rotation, and the interval between a kingly government lasted a year. From the circumstance it was called an Interregnum, a term which holds good even now. But the people began to murmur, that their slavery was multiplied, and that they had got a hundred sovereigns instead of one, and they seemed determined to bear no authority but that of a king, and that one of their own choosing. When the fathers perceived that such schemes were in agitation, thinking it advisable to offer them, of their own accord, what they were sure to lose; they thus conciliate the favour of the people by yielding to them the supreme power, yet in such a manner as to grant them no greater privilege than they reserved to themselves. For they decreed, that when the people should choose a

---

[21] Although, according to the terms of the alliance, the Sabines and the Romans were to be in all respects on an equal footing.

king, the election should be valid, if the senate approved. And[22] the same forms are observed at this day in passing laws and electing magistrates, though their efficacy has been taken away; for before the people begin to vote, the senators declare their approbation, whilst the result of the elections is still uncertain. Then the interrex, having called an assembly of the people, addressed them in this manner: "Do you, Romans, choose yourselves a king, and may it prove fortunate, happy, and auspicious to you; so the fathers have determined. Then, if you choose a prince worthy to succeed Romulus, the fathers will confirm your choice." This concession was so pleasing to the people, that, not to be outdone in generosity, they only voted, and required that the senate should determine who should be king of Rome.

The justice and piety of Numa Pompilius was at that time celebrated. He dwelt at Cures, a city of the Sabines, and was as eminently learned in all laws human and divine, as any man could be in that age. They falsely represent that Pythagoras of Samos was his instructor in philosophy, because there appears no other person to refer to. Now it is certain that this philosopher, in the reign of Servius Tullius, more than a hundred years after this, held assemblies of young men, who eagerly imbibed his doctrine, in the most distant part of Italy, about Metapontus, Heraclea, and Croton. But[23] from these places, even had he flourished at the same time, what fame of his (extending) to the Sabines could have aroused any one to a desire of learning, or by what intercourse of language (could such a thing have been effected)? Besides, how could a single man have safely passed through so many nations differing in language and customs? I presume, therefore, that his mind was naturally furnished with virtuous dispositions, and that he was not so much versed in foreign sciences as in the severe and rigid discipline of the ancient Sabines, than which class none was in former times more strict. The Roman fathers, upon hearing the name of Numa, although they perceived that the scale of power would incline to the Sabines if a king were chosen from them, yet none of them ventured to prefer himself, or any other of his party, or any of the citizens or fathers, to that person, but unanimously resolved that the kingdom should be conferred on Numa Pompilius. Being sent for, just as Romulus before the building of the city obtained the throne by an augury, he commanded the gods to be consulted concerning himself

---

[22] The order of the people still requires the sanction of the senate for its ratification: but that sanction now being given beforehand, the order of the people is no longer subject to the control of the senate, and therefore not precarious as heretofore.

[23] *Ex quibus locis, quæ fama in Sabinos, aut quo linguæ commercio —— quenquam excivisset.* "From which (remote) places, what high character of him (could have reached) to the Sabines, or by what intercourse of language could such high character of him have aroused any one to become a pupil?" Other editions read *quâ famâ*; thus, from which places by what high character for talent, or by what intercourse of language, could he, Pythagoras, have aroused any one, etc.?

also. Upon this, being conducted into the citadel by an augur, (to which profession that office was made a public one and perpetual by way of honour,) he sat down on a stone facing the south: the augur took his seat on his left hand with his head covered, holding in his light a crooked wand free from knots, which they called *lituus*; then taking a view towards the city and country, after offering a prayer to the gods, he marked out the regions from east to west, the parts towards the south he called the right, those towards the north, the left; and in front of him he set out in his mind a sign as far as ever his eye could reach. Then having shifted the lituus into his left hand, placing his right hand on the head of Numa, he prayed in this manner: "O father Jupiter, if it is thy will that this Numa Pompilius, whose head I hold, should be king of Rome, I beseech thee to give sure and evident signs of it within those bounds which I have marked." Then he stated in set terms the omens which he wished to be sent; and on their being sent, Numa was declared king and came down from the stand.

Having thus obtained the kingdom, he sets about establishing anew, on the principles of laws and morals, the city recently established by violence and arms. When he saw that their minds, as having been rendered ferocious by military life, could not be reconciled to those principles during the continuance of wars, considering that a fierce people should be mollified by the disuse of arms, he erected at the foot of Argiletum a temple of Janus, as an index of peace and war; that when open, it might show the state was engaged in war, and when shut, that all the neighbouring nations were at peace with it. Twice only since the reign of Numa hath this temple been shut; once when T. Manlius was consul, at the end of the first Punic war; and a second time, which the gods granted our age to see, by the emperor Augustus Cæsar, after the battle of Actium, peace being established by sea and land. This being shut, after he had secured the friendship of the neighbouring states around by alliance and treaties, all anxiety regarding dangers from abroad being removed, lest their minds, which the fear of enemies and military discipline had kept in cheek, should become licentious by tranquillity, he considered, that, first of all, an awe of the gods should be instilled into them, a principle of the greatest efficacy with a multitude ignorant and uncivilized as in those times. But as it could not sink deeply into their minds without some fiction of a miracle, he pretends that he holds nightly interviews with the goddess Egeria; that by her direction he instituted the sacred rites which would be most acceptable to the gods, and appointed proper priests for each of the deities. And, first of all, he divides the year into twelve months, according to the course of the moon; and because the moon does not make up thirty days in each month, and some days are wanting to the complete year as constituted by the solstitial revolution, he so portioned it out by inserting intercalary months, that every twenty-fourth year, the lengths of all the intermediate years being completed, the days should correspond to the same place of the sun (in the heavens) whence they had set out.[24] He likewise made a distinction of the days[25] into profane and sacred, because on some it was likely to be expedient that no business should be transacted with the people.

Next he turned his attention to the appointment of priests, though he performed many sacred rites himself, especially those which now belong to the flamen of Jupiter. But, as he imagined that in a warlike nation there would be more kings resembling Romulus than Numa, and that they would go to war in person, he appointed a residentiary priest as flamen to Jupiter, that the sacred functions of the royal office might not be neglected, and he distinguished him by a fine robe, and a royal curule chair. To him he added two other flamines, one for Mars, another for Quirinus. He also selected virgins for Vesta, a priesthood derived from Alba, and not foreign to the family of the founder. That they might be constant attendants in the temple, he appointed them salaries out of the public treasury; and by enjoining virginity, and other religious observances, he made them sacred and venerable. He selected twelve Salii for Mars Gradivus, and gave them the distinction of an embroidered tunic, and over the tunic a brazen covering for the breast. He commanded them to carry the celestial shields called[26] Ancilia, and to go through the city singing songs, with leaping and solemn dancing. Then he chose out of the number of the fathers Numa Marcius, son of

---

[24] Romulus had made his year to consist of ten months, the first month being March, and the number of days in the year being only 304, which corresponded neither with the course of the sun or moon. Numa, who added the two months of January and February, divided the year into twelve months, according to the course of the moon. This was the lunar Greek year, and consisted of 354 days. Numa, however, adopted 355 days for his year, from his partiality to odd numbers. The lunar year of 354 days fell short of the solar year by $11\frac{1}{4}$ days;—this in 8 years amounted to ($11\frac{1}{4} \times 8$) 90 days. These 90 days he divided into 2 months of 22 and 2 of 23 days, ($[2 \times 22] + [2 \times 23] = 90$,) and introduced them alternately every second year for two octennial periods: every third octennial period, however, Numa intercalated only 66 days instead of 90 days, *i. e.* he inserted 3 months of only 22 days each. The reason was, because he adopted 355 days as the length of his lunar year instead of 354, and this in 24 years (3 octennial periods) produced an error of 24 days; this error was exactly compensated by intercalating only 66 days (90-24) in the third octennial period. The intercalations were generally made in the month of February, after the 23rd of the month. Their management was left to the pontiffs—*ad metam eandem solis unde orsi essent*—*dies congruerent*; "that the days might correspond to the same starting-point of the sun in the heavens whence they had set out." That is, taking for instance the tropic of Cancer for the place or starting-point of the sun any one year, and observing that he was in that point of the heavens on precisely the 21st of June, the object was so to dispense the year, that the day on which the sun was observed to arrive at that same *meta* or starting-point again, should also be called the 21st of June:—such was the congruity aimed at by these intercalations.

[25] *Ille nefastus erit per quem tria verba silentur;*
   *Fastus erit, per quem lege licebit agi.*—Ov. F. i. 47.

[26] *Ancilia,* from ἄγκλος.

Marcus, as pontiff,[27] and consigned to him an entire system of religious rites written out and sealed, (showing) with what victims, upon what days, and in what temples the sacred rites were to be performed; and from what funds the money was to be taken for these expenses. He placed all religious institutions, public and private, under the cognisance of the pontiff to the end that there might be some place where the people should come to consult, lest any confusion in the divine worship might be occasioned by neglecting the ceremonies of their own country, and introducing foreign ones. (He ordained) that the same pontiff should instruct the people not only in the celestial ceremonies, but also in (the manner of performing) funeral solemnities, and of appeasing the manes of the dead; and what prodigies sent by lightning or any other phenomenon were to be attended to and expiated. To elicit such knowledge from the divine mind, he dedicated an altar on the Aventine to Jupiter[28] Elicius, and consulted the god by auguries as to what (prodigies) should be expiated.

The whole multitude having been diverted from violence and arms to the considering and adjusting these matters, both their minds had been engaged in doing something, and the constant watchfulness of the gods now impressed upon them, as the deity of heaven seemed to interest itself in human concerns, had filled the breasts of all with such piety, that faith and religious obligations governed the state, no less than fear of the laws and of punishment. And while[29] the people were moulding themselves after the morals of the king, as their best example, the neighbouring states also, who had formerly thought that it was a camp, not a city, situate in the midst of them to disturb the general peace, were brought (to feel) such respect for them that they considered it impious that a state, wholly occupied in the worship of the gods, should be molested. There was a grove, the middle of which was irrigated by a spring of running water, issuing from a dark grotto. As Numa went often thither alone, under pretence of conferring with the goddess, he dedicated the place to the Muses, because their meetings with his wife Egeria were held there. He also instituted a yearly festival to Faith alone, and commanded the priests to be carried to her temple in an arched chariot drawn by two horses, and to perform the divine service with their hands wrapt up to the fingers, intimating that Faith ought to be protected, and that her seat ought to be sacred even in

---

[27] *Pontificem*, scil. Maximum.
[28] *Eliciunt cœlo te, Jupiter: unde minores*
*Nunc quoque te celebrant, Eliciumque vocant.*
Ov. F. iii. 327.
[29] *Cum ipsi se——formarent, tum finitimi etiam*, etc. Some of the editors of Livy have remarked on this passage, that *cum* when answering to *tum* may be joined to a subjunctive, as here; the fact however is, that *cum* here does not answer to *tum* at all; *cum* is here "whilst,"—and so necessarily requires the verb to be in the subjunctive mood.

men's right hands. He instituted many other sacred rites, and dedicated places for performing them, which the priests call Argei. But the greatest of all his works was his maintenance of peace, during the whole period of his reign, no less than of his royal prerogative. Thus two kings in succession, by different methods, the one by war, the other by peace, aggrandized the state. Romulus reigned thirty-seven years, Numa forty-three: the state was both strong and well versed in the arts of war and peace.

Upon the death of Numa, the administration returned again to an interregnum. After that the people appointed as king, Tullus Hostilius, the grandson of that Hostilius who had made the noble stand against the Sabines at the foot of the citadel. The fathers confirmed the choice. He was not only unlike the preceding king, but was even of a more warlike disposition than Romulus. Both his youth and strength, and the renown of his grandfather, stimulated his ambition. Thinking therefore that the state was becoming languid through quiet, he every where sought for pretexts for stirring up war. It happened that some Roman and Alban peasants had mutually plundered each other's lands. C. Cluilius at that time governed Alba. From both sides ambassadors were sent almost at the same time, to demand restitution. Tullus ordered his to attend to nothing before their instructions. He knew well that the Alban would refuse, and that so war might be proclaimed on just grounds. Their commission was executed more remissly by the Albans. For being courteously and kindly entertained by Tullus, they politely avail themselves of the king's hospitality. Meanwhile the Romans had both been first in demanding restitution, and, upon the refusal of the Albans, had proclaimed war after an interval of thirty days: of this they give Tullus notice. Upon this he granted the Alban ambassadors an opportunity of stating what they came to demand. They, ignorant of all, waste some time in making apologies: "That it was with the utmost reluctance they should say any thing which was not pleasing to Tullus; but they were compelled by their orders. That they had come to demand restitution; and if this be not made, they were commanded to declare war." To this Tullus made answer, "Go tell your king, that the king of the Romans takes the gods to witness, which of the two nations hath with contempt first dismissed the ambassadors demanding restitution, that on it they may visit all the calamities of this war." The Albans carry home these tidings.

War was prepared for on both sides with the utmost vigour, very like to a civil war, in a manner between parents and children: both being Trojan offspring; for from Troy came Lavinium, from Lavinium Alba, and the Romans were descended from the race of Alban kings. But the result of the war rendered the quarrel less distressing, for they never came to any action; and, when the houses only of one of the cities had been demolished, the two states were incorporated into one. The

Albans first made an irruption into the Roman territories with a large army. They pitch their camp not above five miles from the city, and surround it with a trench, which, for several ages, was called the Cluilian trench, from the name of the general, till, in process of time, the name, together with the thing itself, were both forgotten. In that camp Cluilius, the Alban king, dies; the Albans create Mettus[30] Fuffetius dictator. In the mean time, Tullus being in high spirits, especially on the death of the king, and giving out that the supreme power of the gods, having begun at the head, would take vengeance on the whole Alban nation for this impious war, having passed the enemy's camp in the night-time, marches with a hostile army into the Alban territory. This circumstance drew out Mettus from his camp likewise; he leads his forces as near as he can to the enemy; from thence he commands a herald, despatched by him, to tell Tullus that a conference was expedient before they came to an engagement; and that if he would give him a meeting, he was certain he should adduce matters which concerned the interest of Rome not less than that of Alba. Tullus not slighting the proposal, though the advances made were of little avail, draws out his men in order of battle; the Albans on their part come out also. As both armies stood in battle-array, the chiefs, with a few of the principal officers, advance into the middle between them. Then the Alban commences thus:[31] "That injuries and the non-restitution of property according to treaty, when demanded, were the cause of this war, methinks I both heard our King Cluilius (assert), and I doubt not, Tullus, but that you state the same thing. But if the truth is to be told, rather than that which is plausible, the desire of dominion stimulates two kindred and neighbouring states to arms. Nor do I take upon myself to determine whether rightly or wrongly: be that his consideration who commenced the war. The Albans have made me their leader for carrying on the war. Of this, Tullus, I would wish to warn you; how powerful the Etruscan state is around us, and round you particularly, you know better (than we), inasmuch as you are nearer them. They are very powerful by land, extremely so by sea. Recollect that, when you shall give the signal for battle, these two armies will presently be a spectacle to them; and they may fall on us wearied and exhausted, victor and vanquished together. Therefore, in the name of heaven, since, not content with certain liberty, we are incurring the dubious risk of sovereignty and slavery, let us adopt some method, whereby, without much loss, without much blood of either nation, it may be decided which shall rule the other."—The proposal is not

---

[30] *Mettus.* Gronovius and Bekker read *Mettius*; Niebuhr also prefers *Mettius*; he conceives that the Latin *prænomina* and the Roman *nomina* terminated in *ius*.

[31] *Injurias et non redditas*, etc. The construction is, *et ego videor audisse regem nostrum Cluilium* (*præ se ferre*) *injurias et non redditas res ... nec dubito te ferre eadem præ te, Tulle.*

displeasing to Tullus, though both from the natural bent of his mind, as also from the hope of victory, he was rather inclined to violence. After some consideration, a plan is adopted on both sides, for which Fortune herself afforded the materials.

It happened that there were in each of the two armies three brothers[32] born at one birth, unequal neither in age nor strength. That they were called Horatii and Curiatii is certain enough; nor is there any circumstance of antiquity more celebrated; yet in a matter so well ascertained, a doubt remains concerning their names, to which nation the Horatii and to which the Curiatii belonged. Authors claim them for both sides; yet I find more who call the Horatii Romans. My inclination leads me to follow them. The kings confer with the three brothers, that they should fight with their swords each in defence of their respective country; (assuring them) that dominion would be on that side on which victory should be. No objection is made; time and place are agreed on. Before they engaged, a compact is entered into between the Romans and Albans on these conditions, that the state whose champions should come off victorious in that combat, should rule the other state without further dispute. Different treaties are made on different terms, but they are all concluded in the same general method. We have heard that it was then concluded as follows, nor is there a more ancient record of any treaty. A herald asked king Tullus thus, "Do you command me, O king, to conclude a treaty with the pater patratus of the Alban people?" After the king had given command, he said, "I demand vervain of thee, O king." To which the king replied, "Take some that is pure." The herald brought a pure blade of grass from the citadel; again he asked the king thus, "Dost thou, O king, appoint me the royal delegate of the Roman people, the Quirites? *including* my vessels and attendants?" The king answered, "That which may be done without detriment to me and to the Roman people, the Quirites, I do." The herald was M. Valerius, who appointed Sp. Fusius pater patratus, touching his head and hair with the vervain. The pater patratus is appointed "ad jusjurandum patrandum," that is, to ratify the treaty; and he goes through it in a great many words, which, being expressed in a long set form, it is not worth while repeating. After setting forth the conditions, he says, "Hear, O Jupiter; hear, O pater patratus of the Alban people, and ye, Alban people, hear. As those (conditions), from first to last, have been recited openly from those tablets or wax without wicked fraud, and as they have been most correctly understood here this day, from those conditions the Roman people will not be the first to swerve. If they first swerve by public concert, by wicked fraud, on that day do thou, O Jupiter, so strike the Roman people, as I shall here this day strike this

---

[32] *Three brothers born at one birth.* Dionys. iii. 14, describes them as cousin-germans. Vid. Wachsmuth, p. 147. Niebuhr, i. p. 342.

swine; and do thou strike them so much the more, as thou art more able and more powerful." When he said this, he struck the swine with a flint stone. The Albans likewise went through their own form and oath by their own dictator and priests. The treaty being concluded, the twin-brothers, as had been agreed, take arms. Whilst their respective friends exhortingly reminded each party "that their country's gods, their country and parents, all their countrymen both at home and in the army, had their eyes then fixed on their arms, on their hands; naturally brave, and animated by the exhortations of their friends, they advance into the midst between the two lines." The two armies sat down before their respective camps, free rather from present danger than from anxiety: for the sovereign power was at stake, depending on the valour and fortune of so few. Accordingly, therefore, eager and anxious, they have their attention intensely riveted on a spectacle far from pleasing. The signal is given: and the three youths on each side, as if in battle-array, rush to the charge with determined fury, bearing in their breasts the spirits of mighty armies: nor do the one or the other regard their personal danger; the public dominion or slavery is present to their mind, and the fortune[33] of their country, which was ever after destined to be such as they should now establish it. As soon as their arms clashed on the first encounter, and their burnished swords glittered, great horror strikes the spectators; and, hope inclining to neither side, their voice and breath were suspended. Then having engaged hand to hand, when not only the movements of their bodies, and the rapid brandishings of their arms and weapons, but wounds also and blood were seen, two of the Romans fell lifeless, one upon the other, the three Albans being wounded. And when the Alban army raised a shout of joy at their fall, hope entirely, anxiety however not yet, deserted the Roman legions, alarmed for the lot of the one, whom the three Curiatii surrounded. He happened to be unhurt, so that, though alone he was by no means a match for them all together, yet he was confident against each singly. In order therefore to separate their attack, he takes to flight, presuming that they would pursue him with such swiftness as the wounded state of his body would suffer each. He had now fled a considerable distance from the place where they had fought, when, looking behind, he perceives them pursuing him at great intervals from each other; and that one of them was not far from him. On him he turned round with great fury. And whilst the Alban army shouts out to the Curiatii to succour their brother, Horatius, victorious in having slain his antagonist, was now proceeding to a second attack. Then the Romans encourage their

---

[33] The order is: *fortuna patriæ deinde futura ea quam ipsi f.* (*animo obvers.*); the fortune of their country, the high or humble character of which for the future depended on their exertions on that occasion.

champion with a shout such as is usually (given) by persons cheering in consequence of unexpected success: he also hastens to put an end to the combat. Wherefore before the other, who was not far off, could come up he despatches the second Curiatius also. And now, the combat being brought to an equality of numbers, one on each side remained, but they were equal neither in hope nor in strength. The one his body untouched by a weapon, and a double victory made courageous for a third contest: the other dragging along his body exhausted from the wound, exhausted from running, and dispirited by the slaughter of his brethren before his eyes, presents himself to his victorious antagonist. Nor was that a fight. The Roman, exulting, says, "Two I have offered to the shades of my brothers: the third I will offer to the cause of this war, that the Roman may rule over the Alban." He thrusts his sword down into his throat, whilst faintly sustaining the weight of his armour: he strips him as he lies prostrate. The Romans receive Horatius with triumph and congratulation; with so much the greater joy, as success had followed so close on fear. They then turn to the burial of their friends with dispositions by no means alike; for the one side was elated with (the acquisition of) empire, the other subjected to foreign jurisdiction: their sepulchres are still extant in the place where each fell; the two Roman ones in one place nearer to Alba, the three Alban ones towards Rome; but distant in situation from each other, and just as they fought.[34]

Before they parted from thence, when Mettus, in conformity to the treaty which had been concluded, asked what orders he had to give, Tullus orders him to keep the youth in arms, that he designed to employ them, if a war should break out with the Veientes. After this both armies returned to their homes. Horatius marched foremost, carrying before him the spoils of the three brothers: his sister, a maiden who had been betrothed to one of the Curiatii, met him before the gate Capena: and having recognized her lover's military robe, which she herself had wrought, on her brother's shoulders, she tore her hair, and with bitter wailings called by name on her deceased lover. The sister's lamentations in the midst of his own victory, and of such great public rejoicings, raised the indignation of the excited youth. Having therefore drawn his sword, he run the damsel through the body, at the same time chiding her in these words: "Go hence, with thy unseasonable love to thy spouse, forgetful of thy dead brothers, and of him who survives, forgetful of thy native country. So perish every Roman woman who shall mourn an enemy." This action seemed shocking to the fathers and to the people; but his recent services outweighed its guilt. Nevertheless he was carried before the king for judgment. The king, that he himself

---

[34] The two Roman champions, we have seen, fell in the one place, *super alium alius*; consequently were buried together; whilst the Curiatii fell in different places, as Horatius contrived to separate them to avoid their joint attack.

might not be the author of a decision so melancholy, and so disagreeable to the people, or of the punishment consequent on that decision, having summoned an assembly of the people, says, "I appoint, according to law, duumvirs to pass sentence on Horatius for[35] treason." The law was of dreadful import.[36] "Let the duumvirs pass sentence for treason. If he appeal from the duumvirs, let him contend by appeal; if they shall gain the cause,[37] cover his head; hang him by a rope from a gallows; scourge him either within the pomœrium or without the pomœrium." When the duumvirs appointed by this law, who did not consider that, according to the law, they could[38] acquit even an innocent person, had found him guilty; one of them says, "P. Horatius, I judge thee guilty of treason. Go, lictor, bind his hands." The lictor had approached him, and was fixing the rope. Then Horatius, by the advice of Tullus,[39] a favourable interpreter of the law, says, "I appeal." Accordingly the matter was contested by appeal to the people. On that trial persons were much affected, especially by P. Horatius the father declaring, that he considered his daughter deservedly slain; were it not so, that he would by his authority as a father have inflicted punishment on his son.[40] He then entreated that they would not render childless him whom but a little while ago they had beheld with a fine progeny. During these words the old man, having embraced the youth, pointing to the spoils of the Curiatii fixed up in that place which is now called Pila Horatia, "Romans," said he, "can you bear to see bound beneath a gallows amidst scourges and tortures, him whom you just now beheld marching decorated (with spoils) and exulting in victory; a sight so shocking as the eyes even of the Albans could scarcely endure. Go, lictor, bind those hands, which but a little while since, being armed, established sovereignty for the Roman people. Go, cover the head of the liberator of this city; hang him on the gallows; scourge him, either within the pomœrium, so it be only amid those javelins and spoils of the enemy; or without the pomœrium, only amid the graves of the Curiatii. For whither can you bring this youth, where his own glories must not redeem him from such ignominy of punishment?" The people could not withstand the tears of the father, or the resolution of the son,

---

[35] *Perduellio*, (duellum, bellum,) high treason against the state or its sovereign; but in those times any offence deserving capital punishment was included under that of treason, *Qui Horatio perduellionem judicent*, to pass sentence on Horatius, as being manifestly guilty of murder; not to try whether he was guilty or not.

[36] Duumviri, etc. Niebuhr considers these to be the very words of the old formula.

[37] If the sentence (of the duumviri) be confirmed by the people.

[38] The letter of the law allowed of no justification or extenuation of the fact. It left no alternative to the judge.

[39] He kindly pointed out the loop-hole in the law, which left an opening for the culprit's acquittal.

[40] By the laws of Romulus, a father had the power of life and death over his children.

so undaunted in every danger; and acquitted him more through admiration of his bravery, than for the justice of his cause. But that so notorious a murder might be atoned for by some expiation, the father was commanded to make satisfaction for the son at the public charge. He, having offered certain expiatory sacrifices, which were ever after continued in the Horatian family, and laid a beam across the street, made his son pass under it as under a yoke, with his head covered. This remains even to this day, being constantly repaired at the expense of the public; they call it Sororium Tigillum. A tomb of square stone was erected to Horatia in the place where she was stabbed and fell.

Nor did the peace with Alba continue long. The dissatisfaction of the populace, because the fortune of the state had been hazarded on three soldiers, perverted the weak mind of the dictator; and because honourable measures had not turned out well, he began to conciliate their affections by perfidious means. Accordingly, as one formerly seeking peace in war, so now seeking war in peace, because he perceived that his own state possessed more courage than strength, he stirs up other nations to make war openly and by proclamation:[41] for his own people he reserves treachery under the mask of alliance. The Fidenates, a Roman colony, having gained over the Veientes as partisans in the confederacy, are instigated to declare war and take up arms under a compact of desertion on the part of the Albans. When Fidenæ had openly[42] revolted, Tullus, after summoning Mettus and his army from Alba, marches against the enemy. When he crossed the Anio, he pitches his camp at the[43] conflux of the rivers. Between that place and Fidenæ, the army of the Veientes had crossed the Tiber. These, in line of battle, occupied the right wing near the river; the Fidenates are posted on the left nearer the mountains. Tullus stations his own men opposite the Veientian foe; the Albans he opposes to the legion of the Fidenates. The Alban had not more courage than fidelity. Neither daring therefore to keep his ground, nor to desert openly, he files off slowly to the mountains. After this, when he supposed he had gone far enough, he[44] halts his entire army; and being still irresolute in mind, in order to waste time, he opens his ranks. His design was, to turn his forces to that side to which fortune should give success. At first the Romans who stood nearest were astonished, when they perceived their flanks were uncovered by the departure of their allies; then a horseman in full gallop announces to the king that the Albans were

---

[41] The part which he reserves for himself and the Albans is to play the traitors to Tullus in the hour of need, wearing meanwhile the mark of friendship to Rome.

[42] The fact is, that the subject population rose up against the Roman colonists, drove them out of the town, and asserted their independence. Nieb. i. 24. 5.

[43] The Tiber and the Anio.

[44] *Erigit*—"he makes it halt," from the French *faire alte*, or formerly *haut*, because soldiers then stand upright and hold their spears erect.

moving off. Tullus, in this perilous juncture, vowed twelve Salii, and temples to Paleness and Panic. Rebuking the horseman in a loud voice, so that the enemy might hear him, he orders him to return to the fight, "that there was no occasion for alarm; that by his order the Alban army was marching round to fall on the unprotected rear of the Fidenates." He likewise commands him to order the cavalry to raise their spears aloft; this expedient intercepted from a great part of the Roman infantry the view of the Alban army retreating. Those who saw it, believing what they had heard the king say, fought with the greater ardour. The alarm is now transferred to the enemy; they had both heard what had been pronounced so audibly, and a great part of the Fidenates, as having been joined as colonists to the Romans, understood Latin. Therefore, that they might not be intercepted from the town by a sudden descent of the Albans from the hills, they take to flight. Tullus presses forward, and having routed the wing of the Fidenates, returned with greater fury against the Veientes, disheartened by the panic of the others: nor did they sustain his charge; but the river, opposed to them behind, prevented a precipitate flight. Whither when their flight led, some, shamefully throwing down their arms, rushed blindly into the river; others, while they linger on the banks, doubting whether to fly or fight, were overpowered. Never before had the Romans a more desperate battle.

Then the Alban army, that had been spectators of the fight, was marched down into the plains. Mettus congratulates Tullus on his defeat of the enemy; Tullus on his part addresses Mettus with great civility. He orders the Albans to unite their camp with the Romans, which he prayed might prove beneficial to both; and prepares a sacrifice of purification for the next day. As soon as it was light, all things being in readiness, according to custom, he commands both armies to be summoned to an assembly. The heralds,[45] beginning at the outside, summoned the Albans first. They, struck[46] too with the novelty of the thing, in order to hear the Roman king harangue, crowded next to him. The Roman legions, under arms, by concert surrounded them; a charge had been given to the centurions to execute their orders without delay. Then Tullus begins as follows: "Romans, if ever before at any other time in any war there was (an occasion) on which you should return thanks, first to the immortal gods, next to your own valour, that occasion was yesterday's battle. For the contest was not more with enemies than with the treachery and perfidy of allies, a contest which is more serious and more dangerous. For that a false opinion may not influence you, the Albans retired to the mountains without my orders,

---

[45] *Præcones ab extremo.* At the farther part of the Roman camp, where it joined that of the Albans.

[46] As well as by the orders issued by Tullus.

nor was that my command, but a stratagem and the pretence of a command: that so your attention might not be drawn away from the fight, you being kept in ignorance that you were deserted, and that terror and dismay might be struck into the enemy, conceiving themselves to be surrounded on the rear. Nor does that guilt, which I now state, extend to all the Albans. They followed their leader; as you too would have done, if I had wished my army to make a move to any other point from thence. Mettus there is the leader of that march, the same Mettus is the contriver of this war; Mettus is the violator of the treaty between Rome and Alba. Let another hereafter attempt the like conduct, unless I now make of him a signal example to mankind." The centurions in arms stand round Mettus, and the king proceeds with the rest as he had commenced: "It is my intention, and may it prove fortunate, auspicious, and happy to the Roman people, to myself, and to you, O Albans, to transplant all the inhabitants of Alba to Rome: to grant your people the rights of citizenship, and to admit your nobles into the rank of senators: to make one city, one republic; that as the Alban state was formerly divided from one people into two, so it may now return into one." On hearing this the Alban youth, unarmed, surrounded by armed men, however divided in their sentiments, yet restrained by the common apprehension, continue silent. Then Tullus proceeded: "If, Mettus Fuffetius, you were capable of learning fidelity, and how to observe treaties, that lesson would have been taught you by me, while still alive. Now, since your disposition is incurable, do you at least by your punishment teach mankind to consider those things sacred which have been violated by you. As therefore a little while since you kept your mind divided between the interest of Fidenæ and of Rome, so shall you now surrender your body to be torn asunder in different directions." Upon this, two chariots drawn by four horses being brought, he ties Mettus extended at full length to their carriages: then the horses were driven on in different directions, carrying off the mangled body on each carriage, where the limbs had been fastened by the cords. All turned away their eyes from so shocking a spectacle. That was the first and last instance of a punishment among the Romans regardless of the laws of humanity. In other cases we may boast that no nation whatever adopted milder forms of punishment.

During these occurrences the cavalry had been despatched onward to Alba to remove the multitude to Rome. The legions were next led thither to demolish the city. When they entered the gates, there was not indeed that tumult nor panic, such as usually takes place with captured cities when the gates being burst open, or the walls levelled by the ram, or the citadel taken by assault, the shouts of the enemy and rush of armed men through the city throws every thing into confusion by fire and sword: but gloomy silence and speechless sorrow so absorbed the minds of all, that, through fear, forgetting what they should leave behind, what they should take with them, all concert failing them, and frequently making inquiries of each other, they now stood at their thresholds, now wandering about they strayed through their houses, doomed to see them for that the last time. But as soon as the shouts of the horsemen commanding them to depart now urged them on, the crashing of the dwellings which were being demolished, was now heard in the remotest parts of the city, and the dust, rising in distant places, had filled every quarter as with a cloud spread over them; hastily snatching up whatever each of them could, whilst they went forth leaving behind them their guardian deity and household gods, and the homes in which each had been born and brought up, a continued train of emigrants soon filled the ways, and the sight of others through mutual commiseration renewed their tears, and piteous cries too were heard, of the women more especially, when they passed by their revered temples now beset with armed men, and left their gods as it were in captivity. After the Albans had evacuated the town, the Roman soldiery level all the public and private edifices indiscriminately to the ground, and one short hour consigned to demolition and ruin the work of four hundred years, during which Alba had stood. The temples of the gods, however, for such had been the orders given by the king, were spared.

In the mean time Rome increases by the demolition of Alba. The number of citizens is doubled. The Cœlian mount is added to the city, and in order that it might be inhabited more populously, Tullus selects that situation for his palace and there took up his abode. The leading persons among the Albans he enrols among the patricians, that that branch of the state also might increase, the Julii, Servilii, Quinctii, Geganii, Curiatii, Clœlii; and as a consecrated place of meeting for the order augmented by him he built a senate-house, which was called Hostilia even down to the age of our fathers. And that every rank might acquire some additional strength from the new people, he formed ten troops of horsemen from among the Albans: he likewise recruited the old, and raised new legions from the same source. Confiding in this increase of strength, Tullus declares war against the Sabines, a nation at that time the most powerful, next to the Etrurians, in men and in arms. Injuries had been done on both sides, and restitution demanded in vain. Tullus complained that some Roman merchants had been seized in an open market near the temple of Feronia; the Sabines, that some of their people had taken refuge in the asylum, and were detained at Rome. These were assigned as the causes of the war. The Sabines, holding in recollection both that a portion of their strength had been fixed at Rome by Tatius, and that the Roman power had also been lately increased by the accession of the Alban people, began, on their part, to look around for foreign aid. Etruria was in their neighbourhood; of the Etrurians the Veientes were the nearest. From thence they drew some volunteers, their minds being stirred up to a revolt, chiefly in consequence of the rankling animosities from (former) wars. And pay also had its weight with some stragglers belonging to the indigent population. They were assisted by no aid from the government, and the faith of the truce stipulated with Romulus was strictly observed by the Veientes (for with respect to the others it is less surprising). While they were preparing for war with the utmost vigour, and the matter seemed to turn on this, which should first commence hostilities, Tullus first passes into the Sabine territory. A desperate battle ensued at the wood called Malitiosa,[47] in which the Roman army was far superior, both by the strength of their foot, and also by the recent augmentation of their cavalry. The Sabine ranks were thrown into disorder by a sudden charge of the cavalry, nor could either the fight be afterwards restored, or a retreat accomplished without great slaughter.

After the defeat of the Sabines, when the government of Tullus and the whole Roman state was in high renown, and in a very flourishing condition, word was brought to the king and senators, that it rained stones on the Alban Mount. As this could scarcely be credited, on persons being sent to inquire into the prodigy, a thick shower of stones fell from heaven in their sight, just as when hail collected into balls is pelted down to the earth by the winds. Besides, they imagined that they heard a loud voice from the grove on the summit of the hill, requiring the Albans to perform their religious service according to the rites of their native country, which they had consigned to oblivion, as if their gods had been abandoned together with their country; and they had either adopted the religion of Rome, or, as may happen, enraged at their evil destiny, had renounced altogether the worship of the gods. A festival of nine days was instituted publicly by the Romans also on account of the same prodigy, either in obedience to the heavenly voice sent from the Alban mount, (for that too is stated,) or by the advice of the aruspices. Certain it is, it continued a solemn observance, that whenever the same prodigy was announced, a festival for nine days was observed. Not long after, they were afflicted with a pestilence; and though from this there arose an aversion to military service, yet no respite from arms was granted by this warlike king, who considered that the bodies of the young men were even more healthy abroad than at home, until he himself also was seized with a lingering disease. Then, together with his body, those fierce spirits became so broken, that he, who formerly considered nothing less worthy of a king than to devote his mind to religion, suddenly became a slave to every form of superstition, important and trifling, and filled the people's minds also with religious scruples. The generality of persons, now wishing to recur to that state of things which had existed under king Numa, thought that

---

[47] *Malitiosam. Τὴν ὕλην καλουμένην Κακοῦργον. Dio. iii.*

the only relief left for their sickly bodies was, if peace and pardon could be obtained from the gods. They say that the king himself, turning over the commentaries of Numa, after he had found therein that certain sacrifices of a secret and solemn nature had been performed to Jupiter Elicius, shut himself up and set about the performance of this solemnity; but that that rite was not duly undertaken or conducted, and that not only no appearance of heavenly notification was presented to him, but that he was struck with lightning and burnt to ashes, together with his house, through the anger of Jupiter, exasperated at the impropriety of the ceremony. Tullus reigned two-and-thirty years with great military renown.

On the death of Tullus the government devolved once more upon the senate, and they nominated an interrex; and on his holding the comitia, the people elected Ancus Marcius king. The fathers confirmed the election. Ancus Marcius was the grandson of king Numa Pompilius by his daughter. As soon as he ascended the throne, reflecting on the renown of his grandfather, and that the late reign, glorious in every other respect, in one particular had not been sufficiently prosperous, the rites of religion having either been utterly neglected, or improperly performed; deeming it of the highest importance to perform the public ceremonies of religion as they had been instituted by Numa, he orders the pontiff, after he had transcribed them all from the king's commentaries on white tables, to expose them to public view. Hence, both his own subjects, desirous of peace, and the neighbouring nations, entertained a hope that the king would conform to the conduct and institutions of his grandfather. Accordingly the Latins, with whom a treaty had been concluded in the reign of Tullus, assumed new courage; and after they had made an incursion upon the Roman lands, return a contemptuous answer to the Romans on their demanding restitution, supposing that the Roman king would spend his reign in indolence among chapels and altars. The genius of Ancus was of a middle kind, partaking both of that of Numa and of Romulus; and, besides that, he thought that peace was more necessary in his grandfather's reign, considering the people were but recent as well as uncivilized, he also (considered) that he could not, without injury, preserve the tranquillity which had fallen to his lot; that his patience was tried, and being tried, was now despised; and that the times were more suited to a king Tullus than to a Numa. In order, however, that as Numa had instituted religious rites in peace, ceremonies relating to war might be transmitted by him, and that wars might not only be waged, but proclaimed also according to some rite, he borrowed from an ancient nation, the Æquicolae, the form which the heralds still preserve, according to which restitution is demanded. The ambassador, when he comes to the frontiers of the people from whom satisfaction is demanded, having his head covered with a fillet, (the fillet is of wool,) says, "Hear, O Jupiter, hear, ye confines, (naming the nation they belong to,) let Justice hear. I am a public messenger of the Roman people; I come justly and religiously deputed, and let my words gain credit." He then makes his demands; afterwards he makes a solemn appeal to Jupiter, "If I unjustly or impiously demand those persons and those goods to be given up to me, the messenger of the Roman people, then never permit me to enjoy my native country." These words he repeats when he passes over the frontiers; the same to the first man he meets; the same on entering the gate; the same on entering the forum, some few words in the form of the declaration and oath being changed. If the persons whom he demands are not delivered up, on the expiration of thirty-three days, for so many are enjoined by the rule, he declares war, thus: "Hear, Jupiter, and thou, Juno, Romulus, and all ye celestial, terrestrial, and infernal gods, give ear! I call you to witness, that this nation (naming it) is unjust, and does not act with equity; but we will consult the fathers in our own country concerning these matters, and by what means we may obtain our right." After that the messenger returns to Rome to consult: the king immediately used to consult the fathers almost in the following words: "Concerning such matters, differences, and quarrels, as the pater patratus of the Roman people, the Quirites, has conferred with the pater patratus of the ancient Latins, and with the ancient Latin people, which matters ought to be given up, performed, discharged, which matters they have neither given up, performed, nor discharged, declare," says he to him, whose opinion he first asked, "what think you?" Then he said, "I think that they should be demanded by a just and regularly declared war, therefore I consent, and vote for it." Then the others were asked in order, and when the majority of those present agreed in the same opinion, the war was resolved on. It was customary for the fecialis to carry in his hand a javelin pointed with steel, or burnt at the end and dipped in blood, to the confines of the enemy's country, and in presence of at least three grown-up persons, to say, "Forasmuch as the states of the ancient Latins, and the ancient Latin people, have offended against the Roman people, the Quirites, forasmuch as the Roman people, the Quirites, have ordered that there should be war with the ancient Latins, and the senate of the Roman people, the Quirites, have given their opinion, consented, and voted that war should be made with the ancient Latins, on this account I and the Roman people declare and make war on the states of the ancient Latins, and on the ancient Latin people." After he had said that, he threw the spear within their confines. After this manner restitution was demanded from the Latins at that time, and war proclaimed: and that usage posterity have adopted.

Ancus, having committed the care of sacred things to the flamines and other priests, set out with a new army, which he had levied, and took Politorium, a city of the Latins, by storm; and following the example of former kings, who had increased the Roman state by taking enemies into the number of the citizens, he transplanted all the people to Rome. And since the Sabines occupied the Capitol and citadel, and the Albans the Cœlian mount around the Palatium, the residence of the old Romans, the Aventine was assigned to the new people; not long after, on Telleni and Ficana being taken, new citizens were added in the same quarter. After this Politorium was taken a second time by force of arms, because the ancient Latins had taken possession of it when vacated. This was the cause of the Romans demolishing that city, that it might not ever after serve as a receptacle to the enemy. At last, the whole war with the Latins being concentrated in Medullia, they fought there with various fortune, sometimes the one and sometimes the other gaining the victory; for the town was both well fortified by works, and strengthened by a strong garrison, and the Latins, having pitched their camp in the open fields, had several times fought the Romans in close engagement. At last Ancus, making an effort with all his forces, obtained a complete victory over them in a pitched battle, and having got a considerable booty, returned thence to Rome; many thousands of the Latins being then also admitted into the city, to whom, in order that the Aventine might be joined to the Palatium, a settlement was assigned near the temple of Murcia. The Janiculum was likewise added, not for want of room, but lest at any time it should become a lodgment for the enemy. It was determined to join it to the city, not only by a wall, but likewise, for the sake of the convenience of passage, by a wooden bridge, then for the first time built across the Tiber. The Fossa Quiritium, no inconsiderable defence against the easy access to the city from the low grounds, is the work of king Ancus. The state being augmented by such great accessions, seeing that, amid such a multitude of persons, the distinction of right and wrong being as yet confounded, clandestine crimes were committed, a prison is built in the heart of the city, overlooking the forum, to intimidate the growing licentiousness. And not only was the city increased under this king, but the territory also and the boundaries. The Mæsian forest was taken from the Veientes, the Roman dominion was extended as far as the sea, and the city of Ostia built at the mouth of the Tiber; salt-pits were formed around it, and, in consequence of the distinguished success achieved in war, the temple of Jupiter Feretrius was enlarged.

In the reign of Ancus, Lucumo, a rich and enterprising man, came to settle at Rome, prompted chiefly by the desire and hope of obtaining great preferment there, which he had no means of attaining at Tarquinii (for there also he was descended from an alien stock). He was the son of Demaratus, a Corinthian, who, flying his country for sedition, had happened to settle at Tarquinii, and having married a wife there, had two sons by her. Their names were[48] Lucumo and Aruns. Lucumo

---

[48] The Lucumones were a class of persons among the Etrurians of a warlike

survived his father, and became heir to all his property. Aruns died before his father, leaving a wife pregnant. The father did not long survive the son, and as he, not knowing that his daughter-in-law was pregnant, died without taking any notice of his grandchild in his will, to the boy that was born after the death of his grandfather, without having any share in his fortune, the name of Egerius was given on account of his poverty. And when his wealth already inspired Lucumo, on the other hand, the heir of all his father's wealth, with elevated notions, Tanaquil, whom he married, further increased such feeling, she being descended from a very high family, and one who would not readily brook the condition into which she had married to be inferior to that in which she had been born. As the Etrurians despised Lucumo, because sprung from a foreign exile, she could not bear the affront, and regardless of the innate love of her native country, provided she might see her husband advanced to honours, she formed the determination to leave Tarquinii. Rome seemed particularly suited for her purpose. In this state, lately founded, where all nobility is recent and the result of merit, there would be room for her husband, a man of courage and activity. Tatius a Sabine had been king of Rome: Numa had been sent for from Cures to reign there: Ancus was sprung from a Sabine mother, and rested his nobility on the single statue of Numa. She easily persuades him, as being ambitious of honours, and one to whom Tarquinii was his country only on the mother's side. Accordingly, removing their effects they set out together for Rome. They happened to have reached the Janiculum; there, as he sat in the chariot with his wife, an eagle, suspended on her wings, gently stooping, takes off his cap, and flying round the chariot with loud screams, as if she had been sent from heaven for the very purpose, orderly replaced it on his head, and then flew aloft. Tanaquil is said to have received this omen with great joy, being a woman well skilled, as the Etrurians generally are, in celestial prodigies, and embracing her husband, bids him hope for high and elevated fortune: that such bird had come from such a quarter of the heavens, and the messenger of such a god: that it had exhibited the omen around the highest part of man: that it had lifted the ornament placed on the head of man, to restore it to the same, by direction of the gods. Carrying with them these hopes and thoughts, they entered the city, and having purchased a house there, they gave out the name of Lucius Tarquinius Priscus. His being a stranger and very rich, caused him to be taken notice of by the Romans. He also promoted his own good fortune by his affable address, by the courteousness of his invitations, and by conciliating those whom he could by acts of kindness; until a report of him reached even to the palace; and by paying court to the king with politeness and address, he in a short time

---

sacerdotal character, patricians, not kings. Vid. Niebuhr, i. p. 372.

so improved the acquaintance to the footing of intimate friendship, that he was present at all public and private deliberations, foreign and domestic; and being now tried in every trust, he was at length, by the king's will, appointed guardian to his children.

Ancus reigned twenty-four years, equal to any of the former kings both in the arts and renown of war and peace. His sons were now nigh the age of puberty, for this reason Tarquin was more urgent that the assembly for the election of a king should be held as soon as possible. The assembly being proclaimed, he sent away the boys to hunt towards the time of their meeting. He is said to have been the first who earnestly sued for the crown, and to have made a set speech for the purpose of gaining the affections of the people: *he said* "that he did not aim at any thing unprecedented; for that he was not the first foreigner, (a thing at which any one might feel indignation or surprise,) but the third who aspired to the sovereignty of Rome. That Tatius not only from being an alien, but even an enemy, was made king: that Numa, unacquainted with the city, and without soliciting it, had been voluntarily invited by them to the throne. That he, as soon as he was his own master, had come to Rome with his wife and whole fortune, and had there spent a greater part of that age, in which men are employed in civil offices, than he had in his native country: that he had both in peace and war thoroughly learned the Roman laws and religious customs, under a master not to be objected to, king Ancus himself; that he had vied with all in duty and loyalty to his prince, and even with the king himself in his bounty to others." While he was recounting these undoubted facts, the people by a great majority elected him king. The same ambition which had prompted Tarquin, in other respects an excellent man, to aspire to the crown, followed him whilst on the throne. And being no less mindful of strengthening his own power, than of increasing that of the commonwealth, he elected a hundred into the fathers, who from that time were called Minorum Gentium, *i. e.* of the younger families: a party hearty in the king's cause, by whose favour they had got into the senate. The first war he waged was with the Latins, from whom he took the town of Apiolæ by storm, and having brought back thence more booty than the character of the war would lead one to expect, he celebrated games with more cost and magnificence than former kings. The place for the circus, which is now called Maximus, was then first marked out, and spaces were parted off for the senators and knights, where they might each erect seats for themselves: they were called fori (benches). They viewed the games from scaffolding which supported seats twelve feet high from the ground. The show took place; horses and boxers were sent for, chiefly from Etruria. These solemn games afterwards continued annual, being variously called the Roman and Great (games). By the same king also spaces round the forum were portioned off for private individuals to build on; porticoes and shops were erected.

He was also preparing to surround the city with a stone wall, when a Sabine war obstructed his designs. The matter was so sudden, that the enemy had passed the Anio before the Roman army could meet and stop them; great alarm therefore was produced at Rome. And at first they fought with dubious success, but with great slaughter on both sides. After this, the enemy's forces being led back into their camp, and the Romans getting time to make new levies for the war, Tarquin, thinking that the weakness of his army lay in the want of horse, determined to add other centuries to the Ramnenses, the Titienses, and Luceres which Romulus had appointed, and to leave them distinguished by his own name. Because Romulus had done this by augury, Attus Navius, at that time a celebrated soothsayer, insisted that no alteration or new appointment of that kind could be made, unless the birds approved of it. The king, enraged at this, and, as it is related, ridiculing the art, said, "Come, thou diviner, tell me, whether what I am thinking on can be done or not?" When he had tried the matter by divination, he affirmed it certainly could. "But I was thinking," says he, "whether you could cut asunder this whetstone with a razor. Take it, and perform what thy birds portend may be done." Upon this, as they say, he immediately cut the whetstone in two. A statue of Attus, with his head veiled, was erected in the comitium, upon the very steps on the left of the senate-house, on the spot where the transaction occurred. They say that the whetstone also was deposited in the same place, that it might remain a monument of that miracle to posterity. There certainly accrued so much honour to augury and the college of augurs, that nothing was undertaken either in peace or war without taking the auspices. Assemblies of the people, the summoning of armies, and affairs of the greatest importance were put off, when the birds would not allow of them. Nor did Tarquin then make any other alteration in the centuries of horse, except doubling the number of men in each of these corps, so that the three centuries consisted of one thousand eight hundred knights. Those that were added were called "the younger," but by the same names with the former; which, now that they have been doubled, they call six centuries.

This part of his forces being augmented, a second battle is fought with the Sabines. But, besides that the Roman army was thus reinforced, a stratagem also is secretly resorted to, persons having been sent to throw into the river a great quantity of timber that lay on the banks of the Anio, it being first set on fire; and the wood being further kindled by favour of the wind, and the greater[49] part of it (being placed)

---

[49] In my version of this passage I have followed the reading, *et pleraque in ratibus, impacta sublicis quum hærerent,* p. i. The burning logs were not sent down the river one by one, but were placed on rafts, so that being incapable of passing on between the piers of the bridge, they firmly stuck there, and burnt the bridge. This mode of interpretation is

on rafts, when it stuck firmly impacted against the piers, sets the bridge on fire. This accident struck terror into the Sabines during the battle, and, after they were routed, impeded their flight; so that many, who had escaped the enemy, perished in the river. Their arms floating down the Tiber, and being recognised at the city, made known the victory, almost before any account of it could be carried there. In that action the glory of the cavalry was prominent: they say that, being posted in the two wings, when the centre of their own infantry was being beaten, they charged so briskly in flank, that they not only checked the Sabine legions who pressed hard on those who retired, but quickly put them to flight. The Sabines made for the mountains with great precipitation, yet few reached them; for, as we said before, the greatest part were driven by the cavalry into the river. Tarquin, thinking it advisable to pursue the enemy closely while in this consternation, after sending the booty and the prisoners to Rome, piling up and burning the spoils which he had vowed to Vulcan, proceeds to lead his army onward into the Sabine territory. And though matters had turned out adversely, nor could they hope for better success; yet, because the occasion did not allow time for deliberation, the Sabines came out to meet him with a hastily raised army; and being again defeated there, and matters having now become desperate, they sued for peace.

Collatia and all the land about it was taken from the Sabines, and Egerius, son to the king's brother, was left there with a garrison. I understand that the people of Collatia were thus surrendered, and that the form of the surrender was as follows: the king asked them, "Are ye ambassadors and deputies sent by the people of Collatia to surrender yourselves and the people of Collatia?" "We are." "Are the people of Collatia their own masters?" "They are." "Do ye surrender yourselves and the people of Collatia, their city, lands, water, boundaries, temples, utensils, and every thing sacred or profane belonging to them, into my power, and that of the Roman people?" "We do." "Then I receive them." The Sabine war being ended, Tarquin returned in triumph to Rome. After that he made war upon the ancient Latins, where they came on no occasion to a general engagement; yet by carrying about his arms to the several towns, he subdued the whole Latin nation. Corniculum, old Ficulea, Cameria, Crustumerium, Ameriola, Medullia, and Nomentum, towns which either belonged to the ancient Latins, or which had revolted to them, were taken. Upon this a peace was concluded. The works of peace were then set about with greater spirit, even than the efforts with which he had conducted his wars; so that the people enjoyed no more ease and quiet at home, than they had done

---

confirmed by Dion. iii. 5, 6. The bridge here meant is the one built by the Sabines at the confluence of the Anio and the Tiber——Another reading is, *pleraque in ratibus impacta subliciis quam hærerent,* "most of them being driven against the boats, resting on piles, stuck there," &c.

abroad: for he both set about surrounding the city with a stone wall, on the side where he had not fortified it, the beginning of which work had been interrupted by the Sabine war, and the lower parts of the city round the forum and the other valleys lying between the hills, because they did not easily carry off the water from the flat grounds, he drains by means of sewers drawn sloping downward into the Tiber. Moreover he levels an area for founding a temple to Jupiter in the Capitol, which he had vowed to him in the Sabine war; his mind even then presaging the future grandeur of the place.

At that time, a prodigy occurred in the palace, wonderful both in its appearance and in its result. They relate, that the head of a boy, called Servius Tullius, as he lay fast asleep, blazed with fire in the sight of many persons. That by the very great noise made at so miraculous a phenomenon, the royal family were awakened; and when one of the servants was bringing water to extinguish the flame, that he was kept back by the queen, and after the confusion was over, that she forbade the boy to be disturbed till he should awake of his own accord. As soon as he awoke the flame disappeared. Then Tanaquil, taking her husband into a private place, said, "Do you observe this boy whom we bring up in so mean a style? Be assured that hereafter he will be a light to us in our adversity, and a protector to our palace in distress. From henceforth let us, with all our care, train up this youth, who is capable of becoming a great ornament publicly and privately." From this time the boy began to be treated as their own son, and instructed in those arts by which men's minds are qualified to maintain high rank. The matter was easily accomplished, because it was agreeable to the gods. The young man turned out to be of a disposition truly royal. Nor, when they looked out for a son-in-law for Tarquin, could any of the Roman youth be compared to him in any accomplishment; therefore the king betrothed his own daughter to him. This high honour conferred upon him, from whatever cause, prevents us from believing that he was the son of a slave, and that he had himself been a slave when young. I am rather of the opinion of those who say that, on the taking of Corniculum, the wife of Servius Tullius, who had been the leading man in that city, being pregnant when her husband was slain, being known among the other female prisoners, and, in consequence of her high rank, exempted from servitude by the Roman queen, was delivered of a child at Rome, in the house of Tarquinius Priscus. Upon this, that both the intimacy between the ladies was improved by so great a kindness, and that the boy, having been brought up in the house from his infancy, was beloved and respected; that his mother's lot, in having fallen into the hands of the enemy, caused him to be considered the son of a slave.

About the thirty-eighth year of Tarquin's reign, Servius Tullius was in the highest esteem, not only with the king, but also with the senate and people. At this time the two sons of Ancus, though they had before that always considered it the highest indignity that they had been deprived of their father's crown by the treachery of their guardian, that a stranger should be king of Rome, who was not only not of a civic, but not even of an Italian family, yet now felt their indignation rise to a still higher pitch at the notion that the crown would not only not revert to them after Tarquin, but would descend even lower to a slave, so that in the same state about the hundredth year[50] after Romulus, descended from a deity, and a deity himself, occupied the throne as long as he lived, a slave, and one born of a slave, should now possess it. That it would be a disgrace both common to the Roman name, and more especially to their family, if, whilst there was male issue of king Ancus still living, the sovereignty of Rome should be accessible not only to strangers, but even to slaves. They determine therefore to prevent that disgrace by the sword. But both resentment for the injury done to them incensed them more against Tarquin himself, than against Servius; and (the consideration) that a king was likely to prove a more severe avenger of the murder, if he should survive, than a private person; and moreover, in case of Servius being put to death, whatever other person he might select as his son-in-law,[51] it seemed likely that he would adopt as his successor on the throne.[52] For these reasons the plot is laid against the king himself. Two of the most ferocious of the shepherds being selected for the daring deed, with the rustic implements to which each had been accustomed, by conducting themselves in as violent a manner as possible in the porch of the palace, under pretence of a quarrel, draw the attention of all the king's attendants to themselves; then, when both appealed to the king, and their clamour reached even the interior of the palace, they are called in and proceed before the king. At first both bawled aloud, and vied in interrupting each other by their clamour, until being restrained by the lictor, and commanded to speak

---

[50] *The hundredth year.* 138 years had elapsed since the death of Romulus: they diminish the number of years designedly, to make the matter appear still worse.

[51] *Son-in-law.* Why not one of his two sons, Lucius and Aruns? Dio. iv. 1. If these were not his grandchildren rather, they must have been infants at the time. Dio. iv. 4, 6.— At this time infants could not succeed to the throne.—*Ruperti.*

[52] This sentence has given some trouble to the commentators.—Some will have it that three distinct reasons are given for assassinating Tarquinius rather than Servius Tullius, and that these are severally marked and distinguished by *et—et—tum*, the second only having *quia*.—Stroth will have it that only two reasons are assigned, one, why the king should be killed, and the other, why Servius Tullius should not be killed, arising from the danger and uselessness of the act—the former has not a *quia*, because it was a fact, (*et injuriæ dolor*, &c.,) while the latter has it in the first part (the danger, *et quia gravior*, &c., *quia* being understood also before the other, the uselessness, *tum, Servio occiso*, &c.) because it contained the reasoning of the youths. Doering says there were only two powerful reasons, revenge and fear, and a ratio probabilis introduced by *tum*; which has the force of insuper. According to Dr. Hunter, there are two formal assertions, one, that resentment stimulated the sons of Ancus against the king himself; the other, that the plot is laid for the king himself upon two considerations, of reason and policy.

in turns, they at length cease railing. According to concert, one begins to state the matter. When the king, attentive to him, had turned himself quite that way, the other, raising up his axe, struck it into his head, and leaving the weapon in the wound, they both rush out of the house. When those who were around had raised up the king in a dying state, the lictors seize on the men who were endeavouring to escape. Upon this followed an uproar and concourse of people, wondering what the matter was. Tanaquil, during the tumult, orders the palace to be shut, thrusts out all who were present: at the same time she sedulously prepares every thing necessary for dressing the wound, as if a hope still remained; at the same time, in case her hopes should disappoint her, she projects other means of safety. Sending immediately for Servius, after she had showed to him her husband almost expiring, holding his right hand, she entreats him not to suffer the death of his father-in-law to pass unavenged, nor his mother-in-law to be an object of insult to their enemies. "Servius," she said, "if you are a man, the kingdom is yours, not theirs, who, by the hands of others, have perpetrated the worst of crimes. Exert yourself, and follow the guidance of the gods, who portended that this head would be illustrious by having formerly shed a blaze around it. Now let that celestial flame arouse you. Now awake in earnest. We, too, though foreigners, have reigned. Consider who you are, not whence you are sprung. If your own plans are not matured by reason of the suddenness of this event, then follow mine." When the uproar and violence of the multitude could scarcely be withstood, Tanaquil addresses the populace from the upper part of the palace through the windows facing the new street (for the royal family resided near the temple of Jupiter Stator). She bids them "be of good courage; that the king was stunned by the suddenness of the blow; that the weapon had not sunk deep into his body; that he was already come to himself again; that the wound had been examined, the blood having been wiped off; that all the symptoms were favourable; that she hoped they would see him very soon; and that, in the mean time, he commanded the people to obey the orders of Servius Tullius. That he would administer justice, and would perform all the functions of the king." Servius comes forth with the trabea and lictors, and seating himself on the king's throne, decides some cases, with respect to others pretends that he will consult the king. Therefore, the death being concealed for several days, though Tarquin had already expired, he, under pretence of discharging the duty of another, strengthened his own interest. Then at length the matter being made public, and lamentations being raised in the palace, Servius, supported by a strong guard, took possession of the kingdom by the consent of the senate, being the first who did so without the orders of the people. The children of Ancus, the instruments of their villany having been already seized, as soon as it was announced that the king still lived, and that the power of Servius was so great, had already gone into exile to Suessa Pometia.

And now Servius began to strengthen his power, not more by public[53] than by private measures; and lest the feelings of the children of Tarquin might be the same towards himself as those of the children of Ancus had been towards Tarquin, he unites his two daughters in marriage to the young princes, the Tarquinii, Lucius and Aruns. Nor yet did he break through the inevitable decrees of fate by human measures, so that envy of the sovereign power should not produce general treachery and animosity even among the members of his own family. Very opportunely for maintaining the tranquillity of the present state, a war was commenced with the Veientes (for the truce had now expired[54]) and with the other Etrurians. In that war, both the valour and good fortune of Tullius were conspicuous, and he returned to Rome, after routing a great army of the enemy, now unquestionably king, whether he tried the dispositions of the fathers or the people. He then sets about a work of peace of the utmost importance; that, as Numa had been the author of religious institutions, so posterity might celebrate Servius as the founder of all distinction among the members of the state, and of those orders by which a limitation is established between the degrees of rank and fortune. For he instituted the census, a most salutary measure for an empire destined to become so great, according to which the services of war and peace were to be performed, not by every person, (indiscriminately,) as formerly, but in proportion to the amount of property. Then he formed, according to the census, the classes and centuries, and the arrangement as it now exists, eminently suited either to peace or war.

Of those who had an estate of a hundred thousand asses or more, he made eighty centuries, forty of seniors and forty of juniors. All these were called the first class, the seniors were to be in readiness to guard the city, the juniors to carry on war abroad. The arms enjoined them were a helmet, a round shield, greaves, and a coat of mail, all of brass; these were for the defence of their body; their weapons of offence were a spear and a sword. To this class were added two centuries of mechanics, who were to serve without arms; the duty imposed upon them was to carry the military engines. The second class comprehended all whose estate was from seventy-five to a hundred thousand asses, and of these, seniors and juniors, twenty centuries were enrolled. The arms enjoined them were a buckler instead of a shield, and except a coat of mail, all the rest were the same. He appointed the property of

---

[53] By *public—private*. The "public" were the steps taken by Servius to establish his political ascendency, whilst the "private" refer to those intended to strengthen his family connexions.

[54] *The truce had now expired.* If the truce concluded with them by Romulus be here meant, it was long since expired, since about 140 years had now elapsed. It is probable, however, that it was renewed in the reign of Tullius.

the third class to amount to fifty thousand asses; the number of centuries was the same, and formed with the same distinction of age, nor was there any change in their arms, only greaves were taken from them. In the fourth class, the property was twenty-five thousand asses, the same number of centuries was formed: the arms were changed, nothing was given them but a spear and a long javelin. The fifth class was increased, thirty centuries were formed; these carried slings and stones for throwing. Among them were reckoned the horn-blowers, and the trumpeters, distributed into three centuries. This whole class was rated at eleven thousand asses. Property lower than this comprehended all the rest of the citizens, and of them one century was made up which was exempted from serving in war. Having thus divided and armed the infantry, he levied twelve centuries of knights from among the chief men of the state. Likewise out of the three centuries, appointed by Romulus, he formed other six under the same names which they had received at their first institution. Ten thousand asses were given them out of the public revenue, for the buying of horses, and widows were assigned them, who were to pay two thousand asses yearly for the support of the horses. All these burdens were taken off the poor and laid on the rich. Then an additional honour was conferred upon them; for the suffrage was not now granted promiscuously to all, as it had been established by Romulus, and observed by his successors, to every man with the same privilege and the same right, but gradations were established, so that no one might seem excluded from the right of voting, and yet the whole power might reside in the chief men of the state. For the knights were first called, and then the eighty centuries of the first class; and if they happened to differ, which was seldom the case, those of the second were called: and they seldom ever descended so low as to come to the lowest class. Nor need we be surprised, that the present regulation, which now exists, since the tribes were increased to thirty-five, should not agree in the number of centuries of juniors and seniors with the amount instituted by Servius Tullius, they being now double of what they were at that time. For the city being divided into four parts, according to the regions and hills which were then inhabited, he called these divisions tribes, as I think, from the tribute.[55] For the method of levying taxes rateably according to the value of estates was also introduced by him; nor had these tribes any relation to the number and distribution of the centuries.

The census being now completed, which he had expedited by the terror of a law passed on those not rated, with threats of imprisonment and death, he issued a proclamation that all the Roman citizens, horse and foot, should attend at the dawn of day in the Campus Martius, each

---

[55] Varro, de L.L. iv. 36, thinks, on the contrary, that *tributum* was so called, as being paid by the *tribes*.

in his century. There he drew up his army and performed a lustration of it by the sacrifices called suovetaurilia, and that was called the closing of the lustrum, because that was the conclusion of the census. Eighty thousand citizens are said to have been rated in that survey. Fabius Pictor, the oldest of our historians, adds, that such was the number of those who were able to bear arms. To accommodate that number the city seemed to require enlargement. He adds two hills, the Quirinal and Viminal; then in continuation he enlarges the Esquiliæ, and takes up his own residence there, in order that respectability might attach to the place. He surrounds the city with a rampart, a moat, and a wall: thus he enlarges the pomœrium. They who regard only the etymology of the word, will have the pomœrium to be a space of ground without the walls; but it is rather a space on each side the wall, which the Etrurians in building cities consecrated by augury, reaching to a certain extent both within and without in the direction they intended to raise the wall; so that the houses might not be joined to it on the inside, as they commonly are now, and also that there might be some space without left free from human occupation. This space, which it was not lawful to till or inhabit, the Romans called the pomœrium, not for its being without the wall, more than for the wall's being without it: and in enlarging the city, as far as the walls were intended to proceed outwards, so far these consecrated limits were likewise extended.

The state being increased by the enlargement of the city, and every thing modelled at home and abroad for the exigencies both of peace and war, that the acquisition of power might not always depend on mere force of arms, he endeavoured to extend his empire by policy, and at the same time to add some ornament to the city.[56] The temple of Diana at Ephesus was at that time in high renown; fame represented it to have been built by all the states of Asia, in common. When Servius, amid some grandees of the Latins with whom he had taken pains to form connexions of hospitality and friendship, extolled in high terms such concord and association of their gods, by frequently insisting on the same subject, he at length prevailed so far as that the Latin states agreed to build a temple to Diana at Rome, in conjunction with the Roman people. This was an acknowledgment that Rome was the head of both nations, concerning which they had so often disputed in arms. Though that object seemed to have been left out of consideration by all the Latins, in consequence of the matter having been so often attempted unsuccessfully by arms, fortune seemed to present one of the Sabines with an opportunity of recovering the superiority to his country by his own address. A cow is said to have been calved to a certain person, the

---

[56] *Temple of Diana.* Built on the summit of the Aventine mount towards the Tiber. On its brazen pillar were engraved the laws of the treaty, and which were still extant in the time of Augustus.

head of a family among the Sabines, of surprising size and beauty. Her horns, which were hung up in the porch of the temple of Diana, remained, for many ages, a monument of this wonder. The thing was looked upon as a prodigy, as it was, and the soothsayers declared, that sovereignty would reside in that state of which a citizen should immolate this heifer to Diana. This prediction had also reached the ears of the high priest of Diana. The Sabine, when he thought the proper time for offering the sacrifice was come, drove the cow to Rome, led her to the temple of that goddess, and set her before the altar. The Roman priest, struck with the uncommon size of the victim, so much celebrated by fame, thus accosted the Sabine: "What intendest thou to do, stranger?" says he. "Is it with impure hands to offer a sacrifice to Diana? Why dost not thou first wash thyself in running water? The Tiber runs along in the bottom of that valley." The stranger, being seized with a scruple of conscience, and desirous of having every thing done in due form, that the event might answer the prediction, from the temple went down to the Tiber. In the mean time the priest sacrificed the cow to Diana, which gave great satisfaction to the king, and to the whole state.

Servius, though he had now acquired an indisputable right to the kingdom by long possession, yet as he heard that expressions were sometimes thrown out by young Tarquin, importing, "That he held the crown without the consent of the people," having first secured their good will by dividing among them, man by man, the lands taken from their enemies, he ventured to propose the question to the people, whether they "chose and ordered that he should be king," and was declared king with such unanimity, as had not been observed in the election of any of his predecessors. But this circumstance diminished not Tarquin's hope of obtaining the throne; nay, because he had observed that the question of the distribution of land to the people[57] was carried against the will of the fathers, he felt so much the more satisfied that an opportunity was now presented to him of arraigning Servius before the fathers, and of increasing his own influence in the senate, he being himself naturally of a fiery temper, and his wife, Tullia, at home stimulating his restless temper. For the Roman palace also afforded an instance of tragic guilt, so that through their disgust of kings, liberty might come more matured, and the throne, which should be attained through crime, might be the last. This L. Tarquinius (whether he was the son or grandson of Tarquinius Priscus is not clear; with the greater number of authorities, however, I would say, his son[58]) had a brother, Aruns Tarquinius, a youth of a mild disposition. To these two, as has been already stated, the two Tulliæ, daughters of the king,

---

[57] This is noticed as the first trace of the Agrarian division by Niebuhr, i. p. 161.

[58] *His son.* Dionysius will have it that he was the grandson. See Nieb. i. p. 367.

had been married, they also being of widely different tempers. It had so happened that the two violent dispositions were not united in marriage, through the good fortune, I suspect, of the Roman people, in order that the reign of Servius might be more protracted, and the morals of the state be firmly established. The haughty Tullia was chagrined, that there was no material in her husband, either for ambition or bold daring. Directing all her regard to the other Tarquinius, him she admired, him she called a man, and one truly descended of royal blood; she expressed her contempt of her sister, because, having got a man, she was deficient in the spirit becoming a woman. Similarity of mind soon draws them together, as wickedness is in general most congenial to wickedness. But the commencement of producing general confusion originated with the woman. She, accustomed to the secret conversations of the other's husband, refrained not from using the most contumelious language of her husband to his brother, of her sister to (her sister's) husband, and contended, that it were better that she herself were unmarried, and he single, than that they should be matched unsuitably, so that they must languish away through life by reason of the dastardly conduct of others. If the gods had granted her the husband of whom she was worthy, that she should soon see the crown in her own house, which she now saw at her father's. She soon inspires the young man with her own daring notions. Aruns Tarquinius and the younger Tullia, when they had, by immediate successive deaths, made their houses vacant for new nuptials, are united in marriage, Servius rather not prohibiting than approving the measure.

Then indeed the old age of Servius began to be every day more disquieted, his reign to be more unhappy. For now the woman looked from one crime to another, and suffered not her husband to rest by night or by day, lest their past murders might go for nothing. "That what she had wanted was not a person whose wife she might be called, or one with whom she might in silence live a slave; what she had wanted was one who would consider himself worthy of the throne; who would remember that he was the son of Tarquinius Priscus; who would rather possess a kingdom than hope for it. If you, to whom I consider myself married, are such a one, I address you both as husband and king; but if not, our condition has been changed so far for the worse, as in that person crime is associated with meanness. Why not prepare yourself? It is not necessary for you, as for your father, (coming here) from Corinth or Tarquinii, to strive for foreign thrones. Your household and country's gods, the image of your father, and the royal palace, and the royal throne in that palace, constitute and call you king. Or if you have too little spirit for this, why do you disappoint the nation? Why do you suffer yourself to be looked up to as a prince? Get hence to Tarquinii or Corinth. Sink back again to your (original) race, more like your brother than your father." By chiding him in these and other terms, she spurs on the young man; nor can she herself rest; (indignant) that when Tanaquil, a foreign woman, could achieve so great a project, as to bestow two successive thrones on her husband, and then on her son-in-law, she, sprung from royal blood, should have no weight in bestowing and taking away a kingdom. Tarquinius, driven on by these frenzied instigations of the woman, began to go round and solicit the patricians, especially those of the younger families;[59] reminded them of his father's kindness, and claimed a return for it; enticed the young men by presents; increased his interest, as well by making magnificent promises on his own part, as by inveighing against the king at every opportunity. At length, as soon as the time seemed convenient for accomplishing his object, he rushed into the forum, accompanied by a party of armed men; then, whilst all were struck with dismay, seating himself on the throne before the senate-house, he ordered the fathers to be summoned to the senate-house by the crier to attend king Tarquinius. They assembled immediately, some being already prepared for the occasion, some through fear, lest their not having come might prove detrimental to them, astounded at the novelty and strangeness of the matter, and considering that it was now all over with Servius. Then Tarquinius, commencing his invectives against his immediate ancestors: "that a slave, and born of a slave, after the untimely death of his parent, without an interregnum being adopted, as on former occasions, without any comitia (being held), without the suffrages of the people, or the sanction of the fathers, he had taken possession of the kingdom as the gift of a woman. That so born, so created king, ever a favourer of the most degraded class, to which he himself belongs, through a hatred of the high station of others, he had taken their land from the leading men of the state and divided it among the very meanest; that he had laid all the burdens, which were formerly common, on the chief members of the community; that he had instituted the census, in order that the fortune of the wealthier citizens might be conspicuous to (excite) public envy, and that all was prepared whence he might bestow largesses on the most needy, whenever he might please."

When Servius, aroused by the alarming announcement, came in during this harangue, immediately from the porch of the senate-house, he says with a loud voice, "What means this, Tarquin? by what audacity hast thou dared to summon the fathers, while I am still alive? or to sit on my throne?" To this, when he fiercely replied "that he, the son of a king, occupied the throne of his father, a much fitter successor to the throne than a slave; that he (Servius) had insulted his masters full long enough by his arbitrary shuffling," a shout arises from the

[59] *Younger families.* These had been brought into the senate, as we have seen, by Tarquinius Priscus, and consequently favoured the Tarquinian interest. Nieb. i. p. 372.

partisans of both, and a rush of the people into the senate-house took place, and it became evident that whoever came off victor would have the throne. Then Tarquin, necessity itself now obliging him to have recourse to the last extremity, having much the advantage both in years and strength, seizes Servius by the middle, and having taken him out of the senate-house, throws him down the steps to the bottom. He then returns to the senate-house to assemble the senate. The king's officers and attendants fly. He himself, almost lifeless, when he was returning home with his royal retinue frightened to death, and had arrived at the top of the Cyprian street, is slain by those who had been sent by Tarquin, and had overtaken him in his flight. As the act is not inconsistent with her other marked conduct, it is believed to have been done by Tullia's advice. Certain it is, (for it is readily admitted,) that driving into the forum in her chariot, and not abashed by the crowd of persons there, she called her husband out of the senate-house, and was the first to style him king; and when, on being commanded by him to withdraw from such a tumult, she was returning home, and had arrived at the top of the Cyprian street, where Diana's temple lately was, as she was turning to the right to the Orbian hill, in order to arrive at the Esquiline, the person who was driving, being terrified, stopped and drew in the reins, and pointed out to his mistress the murdered Servius as he lay. On this occasion a revolting and inhuman crime is stated to have been committed, and the place is a monument of it. They call it the Wicked Street, where Tullia, frantic and urged on by the furies of her sister and husband, is reported to have driven her chariot over her father's body, and to have carried a portion of her father's body and blood to her own and her husband's household gods, herself also being stained and sprinkled with it; through whose vengeance results corresponding to the wicked commencement of the reign were soon to follow. Tullius reigned forty-four years in such a manner that a competition with him would prove difficult even for a good and moderate successor. But this also has been an accession to his glory, that with him perished all just and legitimate reigns. This authority, so mild and so moderate, yet, because it was vested in one, some say that he had it in contemplation to resign,[60] had not the wickedness of his family interfered with him whilst meditating the liberation of his country.

After this period Tarquin began his reign, whose actions procured him the surname of the Proud, for he refused his father-in-law burial, alleging, that even Romulus died without sepulture. He put to death the principal senators, whom he suspected of having been in the interest of Servius. Then, conscious that the precedent of obtaining the crown by

---

[60] *To resign.* Niebuhr is of opinion that what is said regarding the Commentaries of Servius Tullius, chap. 60, has reference to this.

evil means might be adopted from him against himself, he surrounded his person with armed men, for he had no claim to the kingdom except force, inasmuch as he reigned without either the order of the people or the sanction of the senate. To this was added (the fact) that, as he reposed no hope in the affection of his subjects, he found it necessary to secure his kingdom by terror; and in order to strike this into the greater number, he took cognizance of capital cases solely by himself without assessors; and under that pretext he had it in his power to put to death, banish, or fine, not only those who were suspected or hated, but those also from whom he could obtain nothing else but plunder. The number of the fathers more especially being thus diminished, he determined to elect none into the senate, in order that the order might become contemptible by their very paucity, and that they might feel the less resentment at no business being transacted by them. For he was the first king who violated the custom derived from his predecessors of consulting the senate on all subjects; he administered the public business by domestic counsels. War, peace, treaties, alliances, he contracted and dissolved with whomsoever he pleased, without the sanction of the people and senate. The nation of the Latins in particular he wished to attach to him, so that by foreign influence also he might be more secure among his own subjects; and he contracted not only ties of hospitality but affinities also with their leading men. To Octavius Mamilius of Tusculum he gives his daughter in marriage; (he was by far the most eminent of the Latin name, being descended, if we believe tradition, from Ulysses and the goddess Circe, and by this match he attaches to himself his numerous kinsmen and friends).

The influence of Tarquin among the chief men of the Latins was now considerable, when he issues an order that they should assemble on a certain day at the grove of Ferentina; that there was business about which he wished to confer with them touching their common interest. They assemble in great numbers at the break of day. Tarquinius himself observed the day indeed, but he came a little before sun-set. Many matters were there canvassed in the meeting in various conversations. Turnus Herdonius, from Aricia, inveighed violently against Tarquin for his absence. "That it was no wonder the cognomen of Proud was given him at Rome;" for they now called him so secretly and in whispers, but still generally. "Could anything be more proud than thus to trifle with the entire nation of the Latins? After their chiefs had been called at so great a distance from home, that he who summoned the meeting did not attend; that no doubt their patience was tried, in order that if they submitted to the yoke, he may crush them when at his mercy. For to whom did it not plainly appear that he was aiming at sovereignty over the Latins? But if his own countrymen did well in intrusting it to him, or if it was intrusted, and not seized on by means of murder, that the Latins also ought to intrust him (though not even so, inasmuch as he was a foreigner). But if his own subjects are dissatisfied with him, (seeing that they are butchered one upon another, driven into exile, and deprived of their property,) what better prospects are held out to the Latins? If they follow his advice, that they would depart thence, each to his own home, and take no more notice of the day of meeting than the person who appointed it." When this man, turbulent and daring, and one who had attained influence at home by these means, was pressing these and other observations having the same tendency, Tarquin came in. This put a conclusion to his harangue. All turned away from him to salute Tarquin, who, on silence being enjoined, being advised by those next him to apologize for having come at that time, says, that he had been chosen arbiter between a father and a son; that, from his anxiety to reconcile them, he had delayed; and because that circumstance had consumed that day, that on the morrow he would transact the business which he had determined on. They say that he did not make even that observation without a remark from Turnus; "that no controversy was shorter than one between a father and son, and that it might be decided in a few words,—unless he submitted to his father, that he must prove unfortunate."

The Arician withdrew from the meeting, uttering these reflections against the Roman king. Tarquin, feeling the matter much more acutely than he appeared to do, immediately sets about planning the death of Turnus, in order that he might inspire into the Latins the same terror with which he had crushed the spirits of his own subjects at home; and because he could not be put to death openly, by virtue of his authority, he accomplished the ruin of this innocent man by bringing a false accusation against him. By means of some Aricians of the opposite faction, he bribed a servant of Turnus with gold, to suffer a great number of swords to be introduced privately into his lodging. When this had been completed in the course of one night, Tarquin, having summoned the chiefs of the Latins to him a little before day, as if alarmed by some strange occurrence, says, "that his delay of yesterday, having been occasioned as it were by some providential care of the gods, had been the means of preservation to him and them; that it was told to him that destruction was prepared by Turnus for him and the chiefs of the Latins, that he alone might obtain the government of the Latins. That he was to have made the attempt yesterday at the meeting; that the matter was deferred, because the person who summoned the meeting was absent, whom he chiefly aimed at. That thence arose that abuse of him for being absent, because he disappointed his hopes by delaying. That he had no doubt, but that if the truth were told him, he would come at the break of day, when the assembly met, attended with a band of conspirators, and with arms in his hands. That it was said that a great number of swords had been conveyed to his house. Whether that be true or not, might be known immediately. He requested that they would accompany him thence to Turnus." Both the daring temper of Turnus, and his harangue of yesterday, and the delay of Tarquin, rendered the matter suspicious, because it seemed possible that the murder might have been put off in consequence of it. They proceed then with minds inclined indeed to believe, yet determined to consider every thing false, unless the swords were detected. When they arrived there, Turnus is aroused from sleep, and guards are placed around him; and the servants, who, from affection to their master, were preparing to use force, being secured, when the swords, which had been concealed, were drawn out from all parts of the lodging, then indeed the whole matter appeared manifest, and chains were placed on Turnus; and forthwith a meeting of the Latins was summoned amid great confusion. There, on the swords being brought forward in the midst, such violent hatred arose against him, that without being allowed a defence, by a novel mode of death, being thrown into the reservoir of the water of Ferentina, a hurdle[61] being placed over him, and stones being thrown into that, he was drowned.

Tarquin, having recalled the Latins to the meeting, and applauded those who had inflicted well-merited punishment on Turnus, as one convicted of parricide, by his attempting a change of government, spoke as follows: "That he could indeed proceed by a long-established right; because, since all the Latins were sprung from Alba, they were included in that treaty by which the entire Alban nation, with their colonies, fell under the dominion of Rome, under Tullus. However, for the sake of the interest of all parties, he thought rather, that that treaty should be renewed; and that the Latins should, as participators, enjoy the prosperity of the Roman people, rather than that they should be constantly either apprehending or suffering the demolition of their town and the devastations of their lands, which they suffered formerly in the reign of Ancus, afterwards in the reign of his own father." The Latins were persuaded without any difficulty, though in that treaty the advantage lay on the side of Rome; but they both saw that the chiefs of the Latin nation sided and concurred with the king, and Turnus was a recent instance of his danger to each, if he should make any opposition. Thus the treaty was renewed, and notice was given to the young men of the Latins, that, according to the treaty, they should attend in considerable numbers in arms, on a certain day, at the grove of Ferentina. And when they assembled from all the states according to the edict of the Roman king, in order that they should neither have a general of their own, nor a separate command, or their own standards, he compounded companies of Latins and Romans, so as to make one out of two, and two out of one; the companies being thus doubled, he

---

[61] *Hurdle*, a mode of punishment in use among the Carthaginians. See Tac. Germ. 12. Similar to the Greek, καταποντισμός.

appointed centurions over them.

Nor was Tarquin, though a tyrannical prince in peace, a despicable general in war; nay, he would have equalled his predecessors in that art, had not his[62] degeneracy in other respects likewise detracted from his merit here. He began the war against the Volsci, which lasted two hundred years after his time, and took from them Suessa Pometia by storm; and when by the sale of the spoils he had amassed forty talents of silver and of gold, he designed such magnificence for a temple to Jupiter, as should be worthy of the king of gods and men, of the Roman empire, and of the majesty of the place itself: for the building of this temple he set apart the money arising from the spoils. Soon after a war came upon him, more tedious than he expected, in which, having in vain attempted to storm Gabii, a city in his neighbourhood, when being repulsed from the walls all hopes of taking it by siege also was taken from him, he assailed it by fraud and stratagem, arts by no means Roman. For when, as if the war was laid aside, he pretended to be busily taken up with laying the foundation of the temple, and with his other works in the city, Sextus, the youngest of his three sons, according to concert, fled to Gabii, complaining of the inhuman cruelty of his father, "that he had turned his tyranny from others against his own family, and was uneasy at the number of his own children, intending to make the same desolations in his own house which he had made in the senate, in order that he might leave behind him no issue, nor heir to his kingdom. That for his own part, as he had escaped from amidst the swords and other weapons of his father, he was persuaded he could find no safety any where but among the enemies of L. Tarquin. And, that they might not be led astray, that the war, which it is now pretended has been given up, still lies in reserve, and that he would attack them when off their guard on the occurrence of an opportunity. But if there be no refuge for suppliants among them, that he would traverse all Latium, and would apply to the Volscians, and Æquians, and Hernicians, until he should come to those who knew how to protect children from the impious and cruel persecution of parents. That perhaps he would find some ardour also to take up arms and wage war against this proud king and his haughty subjects." As he seemed a person likely to go further onward, incensed with anger, if they paid him no regard, he is received by the Gabians very kindly. They bid him not to be surprised, if he were at last the same to his children as he had been to his subjects and allies;—that he would ultimately vent his rage on himself if other objects failed him;—that his coming was very acceptable to them, and they thought that it would come to pass that by his aid the war would be transferred from the gates of Gabii to the walls

---

[62] *His degeneracy—degeneratum.* This use of the passive participle is of frequent occurrence in Livy.

of Rome.

Upon this he was admitted into their public councils, where though, with regard to other matters, he professed to submit to the judgment of the old inhabitants of Gabii, to whom they were better known, yet he every now and then advised them to renew the war; to that he pretended to a superior knowledge, because he was well acquainted with the strength of both nations, and knew that the king's pride was decidedly become hateful to his subjects, which not even his own children could now endure. As he thus by degrees stirred up the nobles of the Gabians to renew the war, went himself with the most active of their youth on plundering parties and expeditions, and ill-grounded credit was attached to all his words and actions, framed as they were for deception, he is at length chosen general-in-chief in the war. There when, the people being still ignorant of what was really going on, several skirmishes with the Romans took place, wherein the Gabians generally had the advantage, then all the Gabians, from the highest to the lowest, were firmly persuaded, that Sextus Tarquinius had been sent to them as their general, by the special favour of the gods. By his exposing himself to fatigues and dangers, and by his generosity in dividing the plunder, he was so beloved by the soldiers, that Tarquin the father had not greater power at Rome than the son at Gabii. When he saw he had got sufficient strength collected to support him in any undertaking, he sent one of his confidants to Rome to ask his father what he wished him to do, seeing the gods had granted him the sole management of all affairs at Gabii. To this courier no answer by word of mouth was given, because, I suppose, he appeared of questionable fidelity. The king going into a garden of the palace, as it were to consider of the matter, followed by his son's messenger; walking there for some time in silence, he is said to have struck off the heads of the tallest poppies with his staff. The messenger, wearied with demanding and waiting for an answer, returned to Gabii as if without having accomplished his object, and told what he had said himself, and what he had observed, adding, "that Tarquin, either through passion, aversion to him, or his innate pride, had not spoke a word." As soon as it became evident to Sextus what his father wished, and what conduct he recommended by those silent intimations, he put to death the most eminent men of the city, accusing some of them to the people, and others who were exposed by their own unpopularity. Many were executed publicly, and some, against whom an impeachment was likely to prove less specious, were secretly assassinated. Means of escape were to some allowed, and others were banished, and their estates, as well as the estates of those who were put to death, publicly distributed. By the sweets of corruption, plunder, and private advantage resulting from these distributions, the sense of the public calamities became extinguished in them, till the state of Gabii, destitute of counsel and assistance, was delivered without a struggle into the hands of the Roman king.

Tarquin, thus put in possession of Gabii, made peace with the Æquians, and renewed the treaty with the Etrurians. Then he turned his thoughts to the business of the city. The chief whereof was that of leaving behind him the temple of Jupiter on the Tarpeian mount, as a monument of his name and reign; [since posterity would remember] that of two Tarquinii, both kings, the father had vowed, the son completed it. And that the area, excluding all other forms of worship, might be entirely appropriated to Jupiter, and his temple, which was to be erected upon it, he resolved to unhallow several small temples and chapels, which had been vowed first by king Tatius, in the heat of the battle against Romulus, and which he afterwards consecrated and dedicated. In the very beginning of founding this work it is said that the gods exerted their divinity to presage the future greatness of this empire; for though the birds declared for the unhallowing of all the other temples, they did not admit of it with respect to that of Terminus. This omen and augury were taken to import that Terminus's not changing his residence, and being the only one of the gods who was not called out of the places devoted to their worship, presaged the duration and stability of their empire. This being deemed an omen of the perpetuity, there followed another portending the greatness of the empire. It is reported that the head of a man, with the face entire, appeared to the workmen when digging the foundation of the temple. The sight of this phenomenon unequivocally presaged that this temple should be the metropolis of the empire, and the head of the world; and so declared the soothsayers, both those who were in the city, and those whom they had sent for from Etruria, to consult on this subject. The king was encouraged to enlarge the expense; so that the spoils of Pometia, which had been destined to complete the work, scarcely sufficed for laying the foundation. On this account I am more inclined to believe Fabius Pictor, besides his being the more ancient historian, that there were only forty talents, than Piso, who says that forty thousand pounds weight of silver were set apart for that purpose; a sum of money neither to be expected from the spoils of any one city in those times, and one that would more than suffice for the foundation of any structure, even though exhibiting the magnificence of modern structures.

Tarquin, intent upon finishing this temple, having sent for workmen from all parts of Etruria, employed on it not only the public money, but the manual labour of the people; and when this labour, by no means inconsiderable in itself, was added to their military service, still the people murmured less at their building the temples of the gods with their own hands; they were afterwards transferred to other works, which, whilst less in show, (required) still greater toil: such as the erecting benches in the circus, and conducting under ground the principal sewer,[63] the receptacle of all the filth of the city; to which two works even modern splendour can scarcely produce any thing equal. The people having been employed in these works, because he both considered that such a multitude was a burden to the city when there was no employment for them, and further, he was anxious that the frontiers of the empire should be more extensively occupied by sending colonists, he sent colonists to Signia and Circeii, to serve as defensive barriers hereafter to the city by land and sea. While he was thus employed a frightful prodigy appeared to him. A serpent sliding out of a wooden pillar, after causing dismay and a run into the palace, not so much struck the king's heart with sudden terror, as filled him with anxious solicitude. Accordingly when Etrurian soothsayers only were employed for public prodigies, terrified at this as it were domestic apparition, he determined on sending persons to Delphos to the most celebrated oracle in the world; and not venturing to intrust the responses of the oracle to any other person, he despatched his two sons to Greece through lands unknown at that time, and seas still more so. Titus and Aruns were the two who went. To them were added, as a companion, L. Junius Brutus, the son of Tarquinia, sister to the king, a youth of an entirely different quality of mind from that the disguise of which he had assumed. Brutus, on hearing that the chief men of the city, and among others his own brother, had been put to death by his uncle, resolved to leave nothing in his intellects that might be dreaded by the king, nor any thing in his fortune to be coveted, and thus to be secure in contempt, where there was but little protection in justice. Therefore designedly fashioning himself to the semblance of foolishness, after he suffered himself and his whole estate to become a prey to the king, he did not refuse to take even the surname of Brutus, that, concealed under the cover of such a cognomen, that genius that was to liberate the Roman people might await its proper time. He, being brought to Delphos by the Tarquinii rather as a subject of sport than as a companion, is said to have brought with him as an offering to Apollo a golden rod, enclosed in a staff of cornel-wood hollowed out for the purpose, a mystical emblem of his own mind. When they arrived there, their father's commission being executed, a desire seized the young men of inquiring on which of them the sovereignty of Rome should devolve. They say that a voice was returned from the bottom of the cave, "Young men, whichever of you shall first kiss his mother shall enjoy the sovereign power at Rome." The Tarquinii order the matter to be kept secret with the utmost care, that Sextus, who had been

---

[63] *The principal sewer—the cloaca maxima.* This is attributed to Tarquinius Priscus by several writers. Dio. iii. 67, states that it was he who commenced it. See Plin. H. N. xxxvi. Nieb. i. p. 385.

left behind at Rome, might be ignorant of the response, and have no share in the kingdom; they cast lots among themselves, as to which of them should first kiss his mother, after they had returned to Rome. Brutus, thinking that the Pythian response had another meaning, as if he had stumbled and fallen, touched the ground with his lips; she being, forsooth, the common mother of all mankind. After this they all returned to Rome, where preparations were being made with the greatest vigour for a war against the Rutulians.

The Rutulians, a nation very wealthy, considering the country and age they lived in, were at that time in possession of Ardea. Their riches gave occasion to the war; for the king of the Romans, being exhausted of money by the magnificence of his public works, was desirous both to enrich himself, and by a large booty to soothe the minds of his subjects, who, besides other instances of his tyranny, were incensed against his government, because they were indignant that they had been kept so long a time by the king in the employments of mechanics, and in labour fit for slaves. An attempt was made to take Ardea by storm; when that did not succeed, the enemy began to be distressed by a blockade, and by works raised around them. As it commonly happens in standing camps, the war being rather tedious than violent, furloughs were easily obtained, more so by the officers, however, than the common soldiers. The young princes sometimes spent their leisure hours in feasting and entertainments. One day as they were drinking in the tent of Sextus Tarquin, where Collatinus Tarquinius, the son of Egerius, was also at supper, mention was made of wives. Every one commended his own in an extravagant manner, till a dispute arising about it, Collatinus said, "There was no occasion for words, that it might be known in a few hours how far his Lucretia excelled all the rest. If then, added he, we have any share of the vigour of youth, let us mount our horses and examine the behaviour of our wives; that must be most satisfactory to every one, which shall meet his eyes on the unexpected arrival of the husband." They were heated with wine; "Come on, then," say all. They immediately galloped to Rome, where they arrived in the dusk of the evening. From thence they went to Collatia, where they find Lucretia, not like the king's daughters-in-law, whom they had seen spending their time in luxurious entertainments with their equals, but though at an advanced time of night, employed at her wool, sitting in the middle of the house amid her maids working around her. The merit of the contest regarding the ladies was assigned to Lucretia. Her husband on his arrival, and the Tarquinii, were kindly received; the husband, proud of his victory, gives the young princes a polite invitation. There the villanous passion for violating Lucretia by force seizes Sextus Tarquin; both her beauty, and her approved purity, act as incentives. And then, after this youthful frolic of the night, they return to the camp.

A few days after, without the knowledge of Collatinus, Sextus came to Collatia with one attendant only; where, being kindly received by them, as not being aware of his intention, after he had been conducted after supper into the guests' chamber, burning with passion, when every thing around seemed sufficiently secure, and all fast asleep, he comes to Lucretia, as she lay asleep, with a naked sword, and with his left hand pressing down the woman's breast, he says, "Be silent, Lucretia; I am Sextus Tarquin; I have a sword in my hand; you shall die, if you utter a word." When awaking terrified from sleep, the woman beheld no aid, impending death nigh at hand; then Tarquin acknowledged his passion, entreated, mixed threats with entreaties, tried the female's mind in every possible way. When he saw her inflexible, and that she was not moved even by the terror of death, he added to terror the threat of dishonour; he says that he will lay a murdered slave naked by her side when dead, so that she may be said to have been slain in infamous adultery. When by the terror of this disgrace his lust, as it were victorious, had overcome her inflexible chastity, and Tarquin had departed, exulting in having triumphed over a lady's honour, Lucretia, in melancholy distress at so dreadful a misfortune, despatches the same messenger to Rome to her father, and to Ardea to her husband, that they would come each with one trusty friend; that it was necessary to do so, and that quickly.[64] Sp. Lucretius comes with P. Valerius, the son of Volesus, Collatinus with L. Junius Brutus, with whom, as he was returning to Rome, he happened to be met by his wife's messenger. They find Lucretia sitting in her chamber in sorrowful dejection. On the arrival of her friends the tears burst from her eyes; and to her husband, on his inquiry "whether all was right," she says, "By no means, for what can be right with a woman who has lost her honour? The traces of another man are on your bed, Collatinus. But the body only has been violated, the mind is guiltless; death shall be my witness. But give me your right hands, and your honour, that the adulterer shall not come off unpunished. It is Sextus Tarquin, who, an enemy in the guise of a guest, has borne away hence a triumph fatal to me, and to himself, if you are men." They all pledge their honour; they attempt to console her, distracted as she was in mind, by turning away the guilt from her, constrained by force, on the perpetrator of the crime; that it is the mind sins, not the body; and that where intention was wanting guilt could not be. "It is for you to see," says she, "what is due to him. As for me, though I acquit myself of guilt, from punishment I do not discharge myself; nor shall any woman survive her dishonour pleading the example of Lucretia." The knife, which she kept concealed beneath her garment, she plunges into her heart, and falling forward on the wound, she dropped down expiring. The husband and father shriek

---

[64] *To do so, and that quickly,*—a use of the participles *facto* and *maturato* similar to that already noticed in chap. 53, *degeneratum.*

aloud.

Brutus, while they were overpowered with grief, having drawn the knife out of the wound, and holding it up before him reeking with blood, said, "By this blood, most pure before the pollution of royal villany, I swear, and I call you, O gods, to witness my oath, that I shall pursue Lucius Tarquin the Proud, his wicked wife, and all their race, with fire, sword, and all other means in my power; nor shall I ever suffer them or any other to reign at Rome." Then he gave the knife to Collatinus, and after him to Lucretius and Valerius, who were surprised at such extraordinary mind in the breast of Brutus. However, they all take the oath as they were directed, and converting their sorrow into rage, follow Brutus as their leader, who from that time ceased not to solicit them to abolish the regal power. They carry Lucretia's body from her own house, and convey it into the forum; and assemble a number of persons by the strangeness and atrocity of the extraordinary occurrence, as usually happens. They complain, each for himself, of the royal villany and violence. Both the grief of the father moves them, as also Brutus, the reprover of their tears and unavailing complaints, and their adviser to take up arms against those who dared to treat them as enemies, as would become men and Romans. Each most spirited of the youth voluntarily presents himself in arms; the rest of the youth follow also. From thence, after leaving an adequate garrison at the gates at Collatia, and having appointed sentinels, so that no one might give intelligence of the disturbance to the king's party, the rest set out for Rome in arms under the conduct of Brutus. When they arrived there, the armed multitude cause panic and confusion wherever they go. Again, when they see the principal men of the state placing themselves at their head, they think that, whatever it may be, it was not without good reason. Nor does the heinousness of the circumstance excite less violent emotions at Rome than it had done at Collatia; accordingly they run from all parts of the city into the forum, whither, when they came, the public crier summoned them to attend the tribune of the celeres, with which office Brutus happened to be at that time vested. There an harangue was delivered by him, by no means of that feeling and capacity which had been counterfeited up to that day, concerning the violence and lust of Sextus Tarquin, the horrid violation of Lucretia and her lamentable death, the bereavement of Tricipitinus, to whom the cause of his daughter's death was more exasperating and deplorable than the death itself. To this was added the haughty insolence of the king himself, and the sufferings and toils of the people, buried in the earth in cleansing sinks and sewers; that the Romans, the conquerors of all the surrounding states, instead of warriors had become labourers and stone-cutters. The unnatural murder of king Servius Tullius was dwelt on, and his daughter's driving over the body of her father in her impious chariot, and the gods who avenge parents were invoked by him. By stating these and other, I suppose, more exasperating circumstances, which though by no means easily detailed by writers, the heinousness of the case suggested at the time, he persuaded the multitude, already incensed, to deprive the king of his authority, and to order the banishment of L. Tarquin with his wife and children. He himself, having selected and armed some of the young men, who readily gave in their names, set out for Ardea to the camp to excite the army against the king: the command in the city he leaves to Lucretius, who had been already appointed prefect of the city by the king. During this tumult Tullia fled from her house, both men and women cursing her wherever she went, and invoking on her the furies the avengers of parents.

News of these transactions having reached the camp, when the king, alarmed at this sudden revolution, was going to Rome to quell the commotions, Brutus, for he had notice of his approach, turned out of the way, that he might not meet him; and much about the same time Brutus and Tarquin arrived by different routes, the one at Ardea, the other at Rome. The gates were shut against Tarquin, and an act of banishment passed against him; the deliverer of the state the camp received with great joy, and the king's sons were expelled. Two of them followed their father, and went into banishment to Cære, a city of Etruria. Sextus Tarquin, having gone to Gabii, as to his own kingdom, was slain by the avengers of the old feuds, which he had raised against himself by his rapines and murders. Lucius Tarquin the Proud reigned twenty-five years: the regal form of government continued from the building of the city to this period of its deliverance, two hundred and forty-four years. Two consuls, viz. Lucius Junius Brutus and Lucius Tarquinius Collatinus, were elected by the prefect of the city at the comitia by centuries, according to the commentaries of Servius Tullius.

## Book II.

*Brutus binds the people by oath, never to suffer any king to reign at Rome, obliges Tarquinius Collatinus, his colleague, to resign the consulship, and leave the state; beheads some young noblemen, and among the rest his own and his sister's sons, for a conspiracy to receive the kings into the city. In a war against the Veientians and Tarquiniensians, he engages in single combat with Aruns the son of Tarquin the Proud, and expires at the same time with his adversary. The ladies mourn for him a whole year. The Capitol dedicated. Porsena, king of Clusium, undertakes a war in favour of the Tarquins. Bravery of Horatius Cocles, and of Mucius. Porsena concludes a peace on the receipt of hostages. Conduct of Clœlia. Ap. Claudius removes from the country of the Sabines to Rome: for this reason the Claudian tribe is added to the former number, which by this means are increased to twenty-one. A. Posthumius the dictator defeats at the lake Regillus Tarquin the Proud, making war upon the Romans with an army of Latins. Secession of the commons to the Sacred Mount; brought back by Menenius Agrippa. Five tribunes of the people created. Corioli taken by C. Martius; from that he is surnamed Coriolanus. Banishment and subsequent conduct of C. M. Coriolanus. The Agrarian law first made. Sp. Cassius condemned and put to death. Oppia, a vestal virgin, buried alive for incontinence. The Fabian family undertake to carry on that war at their own cost and hazard, against the Veientians, and for that purpose send out three hundred and six men in arms, who were all cut off. Ap. Claudius the consul decimates his army because he had been unsuccessful in the war with the Veientians, by their refusing to obey orders. An account of the wars with the Volscians, Æquians, and Veientians, and the contests of the fathers with the commons.*

The affairs, civil and military, of the Roman people, henceforward free, their annual magistrates, and the sovereignty of the laws, more powerful than that of men, I shall now detail.—The haughty insolence of the late king had caused this liberty to be the more welcome: for the former kings reigned in such a manner that they all in succession might be not undeservedly set down as founders of the parts, at least of the city, which they added as new residences for the population augmented by themselves. Nor is there a doubt but that the very same Brutus who earned so much glory for expelling this haughty monarch, would have done so to the greatest injury of the public weal, if, through an over-hasty desire of liberty, he had wrested the kingdom from any of the preceding kings. For what would have been the consequence if that rabble of shepherds and strangers, fugitives from their own countries, having, under the protection of an inviolable asylum, found liberty, or at least impunity, uncontrolled by the dread of regal authority, had begun to be distracted by tribunician storms, and to engage in contests with the fathers in a strange city, before the pledges of wives and children, and love of the very soil, to which it requires a length of time to become habituated, had united their affections. Their affairs not yet matured would have been destroyed by discord, which the tranquil moderation of the government so cherished, and by proper nourishment brought to such perfection, that, their strength being now developed, they were able to produce the wholesome fruits of liberty. But the origin of liberty you may date from this period, rather because the consular authority was made annual, than that any diminution was made from the kingly prerogative. The first consuls had all their privileges and ensigns of authority, only care was taken that the terror might not appear doubled, by both having the fasces at the same time. Brutus was, with the consent of his colleague, first attended by the fasces, who had not been a more zealous assertor of liberty than he was afterwards its guardian. First of all he bound over the people, whilst still enraptured with their newly-acquired liberty, by an oath that they would suffer no one to be king in Rome, lest afterwards they might be perverted by the importunities or bribes of the royal family. Next in order, that the fulness of the house might produce more of strength in the senate, he filled up the number of the senators, diminished by the king's murders, to the amount of three hundred, having elected the principal men of the equestrian rank; and from thence it is said the custom was derived of summoning into the senate both those who were patres and those who were conscripti.[65] Forsooth they styled those who were elected into the new senate Conscripti. It is wonderful how much that contributed to the concord of the state, and to attach the affection of the commons to the patricians.

Then attention was paid to religious matters, and as some part of the public worship had been performed by the kings in person, that they might not be missed in any respect, they elect a king of the sacrifices. This office they made subject to the pontiff, that honour being added to the name might be no infringement on their liberty, which was now their principal care. And I know not whether by fencing it on every side to excess, even in the most trivial matters, they may not have exceeded bounds. For when there was nothing else to offend, the name of one of the consuls became an object of dislike to the state. "That the Tarquinii had been too much habituated to sovereignty; Priscus first commenced; that Servius Tullus reigned next; that though an interval thus intervened, that Tarquinius Superbus, not losing sight of the kingdom as the property of another, had reclaimed it by crime and violence, as

---

[65] All were called *Patres conscripti.* Scil. Patres et Conscripti, the conjunction being omitted. Nieb. i. p. 517.

the hereditary right of his family. That Superbus being expelled, the government was in the hands of Collatinus: that the Tarquinii knew not how to live in a private station; the name pleased them not; that it was dangerous to liberty."—Such discourses were at first gradually circulated through the entire state by persons sounding their dispositions; and the people, now excited by jealousy, Brutus convenes to a meeting. There first of all he recites the people's oath: "that they would suffer no one to be king, nor any thing to be in Rome whence danger might result to liberty. That it ought to be maintained with all their might, and nothing that could tend that way ought to be overlooked; he said it with reluctance, for the sake of the individual; and would not say it, did not his affection for the commonwealth predominate; that the people of Rome do not believe that entire liberty has been recovered; that the regal family, the regal name, was not only in the state but even in the government; that was unfavourable, that was injurious to liberty. Do you, L. Tarquinius," says he, "do you, of your own accord, remove this apprehension. We remember, we own it, you expelled the royal family; complete your kindness; take hence the royal name—your property your fellow citizens shall not only restore you, by my advice, but if any thing is wanting they will generously supply. Depart in amity. Relieve the state from a dread which is perhaps groundless. So firmly are they persuaded in mind that only with the Tarquinian race will kingly power depart hence." Amazement at so extraordinary and sudden an occurrence at first impeded the consul's utterance; then, when he was commencing to speak, the chief men of the state stand around him, and by many importunities urge the same request. Others indeed had less weight with him. After Sp. Lucretius, superior in age and rank, his father-in-law besides, began to try various methods, by entreating and advising alternately, that he would suffer himself to be prevailed on by the general feeling of the state, the consul, apprehending lest hereafter these same things might befall him, when again in a private station, together with loss of property and other additional disgrace, he resigned his consulship; and removing all his effects to Lavinium, he withdrew from the state.[66] Brutus, according to a decree of the senate, proposed to the people, that all the family of the Tarquins should be banished from Rome; and in an assembly by centuries he elected P. Valerius, with whose assistance he had expelled the kings for his colleague.

Though nobody doubted that a war was impending from the Tarquins, yet it broke out later than was universally expected; but liberty was well nigh lost by treachery and fraud, a thing they had never

---

[66] Collatinus is supposed to have earned the odium of the people, and his consequent expulsion from Rome, by his endeavours to save his nephews, the Aquillii, from punishment.

apprehended. There were, among the Roman youth, several young men of no mean families, who, during the regal government, had pursued their pleasures without any restraint; being of the same age with, and companions of, the young Tarquins, and accustomed to live in princely style. Longing for that licentiousness, now that the privileges of all were equalized, they complained that the liberty of others has been converted to their slavery: "that a king was a human being, from whom you can obtain, where right, or where wrong may be necessary; that there was room for favour and for kindness; that he could be angry, and could forgive; that he knew the difference between a friend and an enemy; that laws were a deaf, inexorable thing, more beneficial and advantageous for the poor than the rich; that they allowed of no relaxation or indulgence, if you transgress bounds; that it was a perilous state, amid so so many human errors, to live solely by one's integrity." Whilst their minds were already thus discontented of their own accord, ambassadors from the royal family come unexpectedly, demanding restitution of their effects merely, without any mention of return. After their application was heard in the senate, the deliberation on it lasted for several days, (fearing) lest the non-restitution might be a pretext for war, and the restitution a fund and assistance for war. In the mean time the ambassadors were planning different schemes; openly demanding the property, they secretly concerted measures for recovering the throne, and soliciting them as if for the object which appeared to be under consideration, they sound their feelings; to those by whom their proposals were favourably received they give letters from the Tarquins, and confer with them about admitting the royal family into the city secretly by night.

The matter was first intrusted to brothers of the name of Vitellii and those of the name of Aquilii. A sister of the Vitellii had been married to Brutus the consul, and the issue of that marriage were young men, Titus and Tiberius; these also their uncles admit into a participation of the plot: several young noblemen also were taken in as associates, the memory of whose names has been lost from distance of time. In the mean time, when that opinion had prevailed in the senate, which recommended the giving back of the property, and the ambassadors made use of this as a pretext for delay in the city, because they had obtained from the consuls time to procure modes of conveyance, by which they might convey away the effects of the royal family; all this time they spend in consulting with the conspirators, and by pressing they succeed in having letters given to them for the Tarquins. For otherwise how were they to believe that the accounts brought by the ambassadors on matters of such importance were not idle? The letters, given to be a pledge of their sincerity, discovered the plot; for when, the day before the ambassadors set out to the Tarquins, they had supped by chance at the house of the Vitellii, and the conspirators there in private discoursed much together concerning their new design, as is natural, one of the slaves, who had already perceived what was going on, overheard their conversation; but waited for the occasion when the letters should be given to the ambassadors, the detection of which would prove the transaction; when he perceived that they were given, he laid the whole affair before the consuls. The consuls, having left their home to seize the ambassadors and conspirators, crushed the whole affair without any tumult; particular care being taken of the letters, lest they should escape them. The traitors being immediately thrown into chains, a little doubt was entertained respecting the ambassadors, and though they deserved to be considered as enemies, the law of nations however prevailed.

The question concerning the restitution of the tyrants' effects, which the senate had formerly voted, came again under consideration. The fathers, fired with indignation, expressly forbad them either to be restored or confiscated. They were given to be rifled by the people, that after being made participators in the royal plunder, they might lose for ever all hopes of a reconciliation with the Tarquins. A field belonging to them, which lay between the city and the Tiber, having been consecrated to Mars, has been called the Campus Martius. It happened that there was a crop of corn upon it ready to be cut down, which produce of the field, as they thought it unlawful to use, after it was reaped, a great number of men carried the corn and straw in baskets, and threw them into the Tiber, which then flowed with shallow water, as is usual in the heat of summer; that thus the heaps of corn as it stuck in the shallows became settled when covered over with mud: by these and the afflux of other things, which the river happened to bring thither, an island was formed by degrees. Afterwards I believe that mounds were added, and that aid was afforded by art, that a surface so well raised might be firm enough for sustaining temples and porticoes. After plundering the tyrants' effects, the traitors were condemned and capital punishment inflicted. Their punishment was the more remarkable, because the consulship imposed on the father the office of punishing his own children, and him who should have been removed as a spectator, fortune assigned as the person to exact the punishment. Young men of the highest quality stood tied to a stake; but the consul's sons attracted the eyes of all the spectators from the rest of the criminals, as from persons unknown; nor did the people pity them more on account of the severity of the punishment, than the horrid crime by which they had deserved it. "That they, in that year particularly, should have brought themselves to betray into the hands of Tarquin, formerly a proud tyrant, and now an exasperated exile, their country just delivered, their father its deliverer, the consulate which took its rise from the family of the Junii, the fathers, the people, and whatever belonged

either to the gods or the citizens of Rome."[67] The consuls seated
themselves in their tribunal, and the lictors, being despatched to inflict
punishment, strip them naked, beat them with rods, and strike off their
heads. Whilst during all this time, the father, his looks and his
countenance, presented a touching spectacle,[68] the feelings of the father
bursting forth occasionally during the office of superintending the
public execution. Next after the punishment of the guilty, that there
might be a striking example in either way for the prevention of crime, a
sum of money was granted out of the treasury as a reward to the
discoverer; liberty also and the rights of citizenship were granted him.
He is said to have been the first person made free by the Vindicta; some
think even that the term vindicta is derived from him. After him it was
observed as a rule, that those who were set free in this manner were
supposed to be admitted to the rights of Roman citizens.[69]

On these things being announced to him, as they had occurred,
Tarquin, inflamed not only with grief for the frustration of such great
hopes, but with hatred and resentment also, when he saw that the way
was blocked up against stratagem, considering that he should have
recourse to war openly, went round as a suppliant to the cities of
Etruria, "that they should not suffer him, sprung from themselves, of
the same blood, exiled and in want, lately in possession of so great a
kingdom, to perish before their eyes, with the young men his sons. That
others had been invited to Rome from foreign lands to the throne; that
he, a king, extending the Roman empire by his arms, was driven out by
those nearest to him by a villanous conspiracy; that they had by
violence divided the parts among themselves, because no one
individual among them was deemed sufficiently deserving of the
kingdom; that they had given up his effects to the people to be pillaged
by them, that no one might be free from that guilt. That he was desirous
to recover his country and his kingdom, and to punish his ungrateful
subjects. That they should bring succour and aid him; that they might
also revenge the injuries done to them of old, their legions so often
slaughtered, their land taken from them." These arguments prevailed on
the people of Veii, and with menaces they declare that now at least,

---

[67] Niebuhr will have it that Brutus punished his children by his authority as a father,
and that there was no appeal to the people from the father. See Nieb. i. p. 488.

[68] *Animo patris*, the strength of his mind, though that of a father, being even more
conspicuous, &c. So Drakenborch understands the passage,—this sternness of mind, he
says, though he was their father, was a more remarkable spectacle than his stern
countenance. This character of Brutus, as inferrible from the words thus interpreted,
coincides with that given of him by Dionysius and others. I prefer understanding the
passage with Crevier, scil. symptoms of paternal affection to his children displaying
themselves during the discharge of his duty in superintending the public punishment
inflicted on them.

[69] Previously, by the institution of Servius, only such manumitted slaves were
admitted to the rights of citizenship as were registered by their masters in the census.

under the conduct of a Roman general, their former disgrace should be wiped off, and what they had lost in war should be recovered. His name and relation to them induced the people of Tarquinii to take part with him; it seemed an honour that their countrymen should reign at Rome. Therefore the two armies of these two states followed Tarquin in order to recover his kingdom, and to take vengeance upon the Romans. When they entered the Roman territories, the consuls marched to meet them. Valerius led up the foot in a square battalion, and Brutus marched before with his horse to reconnoitre (the enemy). Their cavalry likewise came up first; Aruns, Tarquin's son, commanded it; the king himself followed with the legions. Aruns, when he knew at a distance by the lictors that it was a consul, and on coming nigher discovered for certain that it was Brutus by his face, all inflamed with rage, he cried out, "There is the villain who has banished us from our native country! see how he rides in state adorned with the ensigns of our dignity! now assist me, gods, the avengers of kings." He put spurs to his horse and drove furiously against the consul. Brutus perceived the attack made on him; as it was honourable in these days for the generals to engage in combat, he eagerly offered himself to the combat. They encountered one another with such furious animosity, neither mindful of protecting his own person, provided he could wound his adversary; so that both, transfixed through the buckler by the blow from the opposite direction, fell lifeless from their horses, entangled together by the two spears. The engagement between the rest of the horse commenced at the same time, and soon after the foot came up. There they fought with doubtful success, and as it were with equal advantage, and the victory doubtful. The right wings of both armies were victorious and the left worsted. The Veientians, accustomed to be discomfited by the Roman soldiers, were routed and put to flight. The Tarquinienses, who were a new enemy, not only stood their ground, but even on their side obliged the Romans to give way.

After the issue of this battle, so great a terror seized Tarquin and the Etrurians, that both the armies, the Veientian and Tarquinian, giving up the matter as impracticable, departed to their respective homes. They annex strange incidents to this battle,—that in the silence of the next night a loud voice was emitted from the Arsian wood; that it was believed to be the voice of Silvanus: these words were spoken, "that more of the Etrurians by one[70] had fallen in the battle; that the Roman was victorious in the war." Certainly the Romans departed thence as victors, the Etrurians as vanquished. For as soon as it was light, and not one of the enemy was now to be seen, P. Valerius the consul collected the spoils, and returned thence in triumph to Rome. His colleague's funeral he celebrated with all the magnificence then possible. But a far

---

[70] *Uno plus Tuscorum. Ὡς ἑνὶ κλείους ἐν τῇ μάχῃ τεθνήκασι Τυρρηνῶν ἤ Ῥωμαίων.*

greater honour to his death was the public sorrow, singularly remarkable in this particular, that the matrons mourned him a year,[71] as a parent, because he had been so vigorous an avenger of violated chastity. Afterwards the consul who survived, so changeable are the minds of the people, from great popularity, encountered not only jealousy, but suspicion, originating in an atrocious charge. Report represented that he aspired to the crown, because he had not substituted a colleague in the room of Brutus, and was building a house on the summit of Mount Velia, that there would be there an impregnable fortress on an elevated and well-fortified place. When these things, thus circulated and believed, affected the consul's mind with indignation, having summoned the people to an assembly, he mounts the rostrum, after lowering the fasces. It was a grateful sight to the multitude that the insignia of authority were lowered to them, and that an acknowledgment was made, that the majesty and power of the people were greater than that of the consul. When they were called to silence, Valerius highly extolled the good fortune of his colleague, "who after delivering his country had died vested with the supreme power, fighting bravely in defence of the commonwealth, when his glory was in its maturity, and not yet converted into jealousy. That he himself, having survived his glory, now remained as an object of accusation and calumny; that from the liberator of his country he had fallen to the level of the Aquilii and Vitellii. Will no merit then, says he, ever be so tried and approved by you, as to be exempted from the attacks of suspicion. Could I apprehend that myself, the bitterest enemy of kings, should fall under the charge of a desire of royalty? Could I believe that, even though I dwelt in the very citadel and the Capitol, that I could be dreaded by my fellow citizens? Does my character among you depend on so mere a trifle? Is my integrity so slightly founded, that it makes more matter where I may be, than what I may be. The house of Publius Valerius shall not stand in the way of your liberty, Romans; the Velian mount shall be secure to you. I will not only bring down my house into the plain, but I will build it beneath the hill, that you may dwell above me a suspected citizen. Let those build on the Velian mount to whom liberty is more securely intrusted than to P. Valerius." Immediately all the materials were brought down to the foot of the Velian mount, and the house was built at the foot of the hill where the temple of Victory now stands.

After this laws were passed, which not only cleared him of all suspicions of aiming at the regal power, but had so contrary a tendency, that they made him popular. From thence he was surnamed Poplicola. Above all, the laws regarding an appeal to the people against the magistrates, and that devoting the life and property of any one who

---

[71] A year, scil. of ten months.

should form a design of assuming regal authority, were grateful to the people. And after he had passed these while sole consul, so that the merit in them was exclusively his own, he then held an assembly for the election of a new colleague. Sp. Lucretius was elected consul, who being very old, and his strength being inadequate to discharge the consular duties, dies in a few days. M. Horatius Pulvillus was substituted in the room of Lucretius. In some old writers I find no mention of Lucretius as consul; they place Horatius immediately after Brutus. I believe that, because no important event signalized his consulate, it has been unnoticed. Jupiter's temple in the Capitol had not yet been dedicated; the consuls Valerius and Horatius cast lots which should dedicate it. It fell by lot to Horatius. Publicola departed to the war of the Veientians. The friends of Valerius were more annoyed than they should have been, that the dedication of so celebrated a temple should be given to Horatius.[72] Having endeavoured by every means to prevent that, when all other attempts had been tried in vain, when the consul was now holding the door-post during his offering of prayer to the gods, they suddenly announce to him the shocking intelligence that his son was dead, and that his family being defiled[73] he could not dedicate the temple. Whether he did not believe the fact, or possessed such great firmness of mind, is neither handed down for certain, nor is a conjecture easy. Diverted from his purpose at this intelligence in no other way than to order that the body should be buried,[74] he goes through the prayer, and dedicates the temple. These were the transactions at home and abroad the first year after the expulsion of the kings. After this P. Valerius, a second time, and Titus Lucretius, were elected consuls.

By this time the Tarquins had fled to Lars[75] Porsena, king of Clusium. There, mixing advice with their entreaties, "They sometimes besought him not to suffer them, who were descended from the Etrurians, and of the same blood and name, to live in exile and poverty; at other times they advised him not to let this commencing practice of expelling kings pass unpunished. That liberty has charms enough in itself; and unless kings defend their crowns with as much vigour as the people pursue their liberty, that the highest must be reduced to a level with the lowest; there will be nothing exalted, nothing distinguished above the rest; and hence there must be an end of regal government, the most beautiful institution both among gods and men." Porsena,

---

[72] The Horatii being of the *minores patres*. Nieb. i. p. 533.
[73] *Funesta familia*, as having in it an unburied corpse. Thus Misenus, whilst unburied, *incestat funere classem*. Virg. Æn. vi. 150.
[74] He here rejected the omen. Cic. i. 7, 14.; auguria aut *oblativa* sunt, quæ non poscuntur, aut *impetrativa*, quæ optata veniunt. The latter could not be rejected.
[75] *Lar*. This is generally understood to have been a title of honour equivalent to our term *Lord*.

thinking that it would be an honour to the Tuscans both that there should be a king at Rome, and especially one of the Etrurian nation, marched towards Rome with a hostile army. Never before on any other occasion did so great terror seize the senate; so powerful was the state of Clusium at the time, and so great the renown of Porsena. Nor did they only dread their enemies, but even their own citizens, lest the common people, through excess of fear, should, by receiving the Tarquins into the city, accept peace even if purchased with slavery. Many conciliatory concessions were therefore granted to the people by the senate during that period. Their attention, in the first place, was directed to the markets, and persons were sent, some to the Volscians, others to Cumæ, to buy up corn. The privilege[76] of selling salt, also, because it was farmed at a high rent, was all taken into the hands of government,[77] and withdrawn from private individuals; and the people were freed from port-duties and taxes; that the rich, who were adequate to bearing the burden, should contribute; that the poor paid tax enough if they educated their children. This indulgent care of the fathers accordingly kept the whole state in such concord amid the subsequent severities in the siege and famine, that the highest abhorred the name of king not more than the lowest; nor was any single individual afterwards so popular by intriguing practices, as the whole senate then was by their excellent government.

Some parts seemed secured by the walls, others by the interposition of the Tiber. The Sublician bridge well nigh afforded a passage to the enemy, had there not been one man, Horatius Cocles, (that defence the fortune of Rome had on that day,) who, happening to be posted on guard at the bridge, when he saw the Janiculum taken by a sudden assault, and that the enemy were pouring down from thence in full speed, and that his own party, in terror and confusion, were abandoning their arms and ranks, laying hold of them one by one, standing in their way, and appealing to the faith of gods and men, he declared, "That their flight would avail them nothing if they deserted their post; if they passed the bridge and left it behind them, there would soon be more of the enemy in the Palatium and Capitol than in the

---

[76] *Arbitrium* signifies not only the "privilege," but the "rent" paid for such privilege, or right of monopoly.

[77] *Was all taken into the hands of government.* In my version of this passage I have conformed to the emendation of the original first proposed by Gronovius, and admitted by Stroth and Bekker; scil. *in publicum omne sumptum.*—They did not let these salt-works by auction, but took them into their own management, and carried them on by means of persons employed to work on the public account. These salt-works, first established at Ostia by Ancus, were, like other public property, farmed out to the publicans. As they had a high rent to pay, the price of salt was raised in proportion; but now the patricians, to curry favour with the plebeians, did not let the salt-pits to private tenants, but kept them in the hands of public labourers, to collect all the salt for the public use; and appointed salesmen to retail it to the people at a cheaper rate. See Stocker's ed.

Janiculum; for that reason he advised and charged them to demolish the bridge, by their sword, by fire, or by any means whatever; that he would stand the shock of the enemy as far as could be done by one man." He then advances to the first entrance of the bridge, and being easily distinguished among those who showed their backs in retreating from the fight, facing about to engage the foe hand to hand, by his surprising bravery he terrified the enemy. Two indeed a sense of shame kept with him, Sp. Lartius and T. Herminius, men eminent for their birth, and renowned for their gallant exploits. With them he for a short time stood the first storm of the danger, and the severest brunt of the battle. But as they who demolished the bridge called upon them to retire, he obliged them also to withdraw to a place of safety on a small portion of the bridge still left. Then casting his stern eyes round all the officers of the Etrurians in a threatening manner, he sometimes challenged them singly, sometimes reproached them all; "the slaves of haughty tyrants, who, regardless of their own freedom, came to oppress the liberty of others." They hesitated for a considerable time, looking round one at the other, to commence the fight; shame then put the army in motion, and a shout being raised, they hurl their weapons from all sides on their single adversary; and when they all stuck in the shield held before him, and he with no less obstinacy kept possession of the bridge with firm step, they now endeavoured to thrust him down from it by one push, when at once the crash of the falling bridge, at the same time a shout of the Romans raised for joy at having completed their purpose, checked their ardour with sudden panic. Then Cocles says, "Holy father Tiberinus, I pray that thou wouldst receive these arms, and this thy soldier, in thy propitious stream." Armed as he was, he leaped into the Tiber, and amid showers of darts hurled on him, swam across safe to his party, having dared an act which is likely to obtain more fame than credit with posterity. The state was grateful towards such valour; a statue was erected to him in the comitium, and as much land was given to him as he ploughed around in one day. The zeal of private individuals also was conspicuous among the public honours. For, amid the great scarcity, each person contributed something to him according to his supply at home, depriving himself of his own support.

Porsena being repulsed in his first attempt, having changed his plans from a siege to a blockade, after he had placed a garrison in Janiculum, pitched his camp in the plain and on the banks of the Tiber. Then sending for boats from all parts, both to guard the river, so as not to suffer any provision to be conveyed to Rome, and also to transport his soldiers across the river, to plunder different places as occasion required; in a short time he so harassed the entire country round Rome, that not only every thing else from the country, but even their cattle, was driven into the city, and nobody durst venture thence without the gates. This liberty of action was granted to the Etrurians, not more through fear than from policy; for Valerius, intent on an opportunity of falling unawares upon a number of them, and when straggling, a remiss avenger in trifling matters, reserved the weight of his vengeance for more important occasions. Wherefore, to decoy the pillagers, he ordered his men to drive their cattle the next day out at the Esquiline gate, which was farthest from the enemy, presuming that they would get intelligence of it, because during the blockade and famine some slaves would turn traitors and desert. Accordingly they were informed of it by a deserter, and parties more numerous than usual, in hopes of seizing the entire body, crossed the river. Then P. Valerius commanded T. Herminius, with a small body of men, to lie concealed two miles from the city, on the Gabian road, and Sp. Lartius, with a party of light-armed troops, to post himself at the Colline gate till the enemy should pass by, and then to throw himself in their way so that there may be no return to the river. The other consul, T. Lucretius, marched out of the Nævian gate with some companies of soldiers; Valerius himself led some chosen cohorts down from the Cœlian mount, and they were first descried by the enemy. Herminius, when he perceived the alarm, rose out of the ambush and fell upon the rear of the Tuscans, who had charged Valerius. The shout was returned on the right and left, from the Colline gate on the one hand, and the Nævian on the other. By this stratagem the plunderers were put to the sword between both, they not being a match in strength for fighting, and all the ways being blocked up to prevent escape: this put an end to the Etrurians strolling about in so disorderly a manner.

Nevertheless the blockade continued, and there was a scarcity of corn, with a very high price. Porsena entertained a hope that by continuing the siege he should take the city, when C. Mucius, a young nobleman, to whom it seemed a disgrace that the Roman people, when enslaved under kings, had never been confined within their walls in any war, nor by any enemy, should now when a free people be blocked up by these very Etrurians whose armies they had often routed, thinking that such indignity should be avenged by some great and daring effort, at first designed of his own accord to penetrate into the enemy's camp. Then, being afraid if he went without the permission of the consuls, or the knowledge of any one, he might be seized by the Roman guards and brought back as a deserter, the circumstances of the city at the time justifying the charge, he went to the senate: "Fathers," says he, "I intend to cross the Tiber, and enter the enemy's camp, if I can; not as a plunderer, or as an avenger in our turn of their devastations. A greater deed is in my mind, if the gods assist." The senate approved his design. He set out with a sword concealed under his garment. When he came thither, he stationed himself among the thickest of the crowd, near the king's tribunal. There, when the soldiers were receiving their pay, and the king's secretary sitting by him, dressed nearly in the same style, was busily engaged, and to him they commonly addressed themselves, being afraid to ask which of them was Porsena, lest by not knowing the king he should discover on himself, as fortune blindly directed the blow, he killed the secretary instead of the king. When, as he was going off thence where with his bloody dagger he had made his way through the dismayed multitude, a concourse being attracted at the noise, the king's guards immediately seized and brought him back standing alone before the king's tribunal; even then, amid such menaces of fortune, more capable of inspiring dread than of feeling it, "I am," says he, "a Roman citizen, my name is Caius Mucius; an enemy, I wished to slay an enemy, nor have I less of resolution to suffer death than I had to inflict it. Both to act and to suffer with fortitude is a Roman's part. Nor have I alone harboured such feelings towards you; there is after me a long train of persons aspiring to the same honour. Therefore, if you choose it, prepare yourself for this peril, to contend for your life every hour; to have the sword and the enemy in the very entrance of your pavilion; this is the war which we the Roman youth declare against you; dread not an army in array, nor a battle; the affair will be to yourself alone and with each of us singly." When the king, highly incensed, and at the same time terrified at the danger, in a menacing manner, commanded fires to be kindled about him, if he did not speedily explain the plots, which, by his threats, he had darkly insinuated against him; Mucius said, "Behold me, that you may be sensible of how little account the body is to those who have great glory in view;" and immediately he thrusts his right hand into the fire that was lighted for the sacrifice. When he continued to broil it as if he had been quite insensible, the king, astonished at this surprising sight, after he had leaped from his throne and commanded the young man to be removed from the altar, says, "Be gone, having acted more like an enemy towards thyself than me. I would encourage thee to persevere in thy valour, if that valour stood on the side of my country. I now dismiss you untouched and unhurt, exempted from the right of war." Then Mucius, as if making a return for the kindness, says, "Since bravery is honoured by you, so that you have obtained by kindness that which you could not by threats, three hundred of us, the chief of the Roman youth, have conspired to attack you in this manner. It was my lot first. The rest will follow, each in his turn, according as the lot shall set him forward, unless fortune shall afford an opportunity of you."

Mucius being dismissed, to whom the cognomen of Scævola was afterwards given, from the loss of his right hand, ambassadors from Porsena followed him to Rome. The risk of the first attempt, from which nothing had saved him but the mistake of the assailant, and the risk to be encountered so often in proportion to the number of conspirators, made so strong an impression upon him, that of his own accord he made propositions of peace to the Romans. Mention was made to no purpose regarding the restoration of the Tarquinii to the throne, rather because he had been unable to refuse that to the Tarquinii, than from not knowing that it would be refused to him by the Romans. The condition of restoring their territory to the Veientians was obtained by him, and the necessity of giving hostages in case they wished the garrison to be withdrawn from the Janiculum was extorted from the Romans. Peace being concluded on these terms, Porsena drew his troops out of the Janiculum, and marched out of the Roman territories. The fathers gave Mucius, as a reward of his valour, lands on the other side of the Tiber, which were afterwards called the Mucian meadows. By this honour paid to valour the women were excited to merit public distinctions. As the camp of the Etrurians had been pitched not far from the banks of the Tiber, a young lady named Clælia, one of the hostages, deceiving her keepers, swam over the river, amidst the darts of the enemy, at the head of a troop of virgins, and brought them all safe to their relations. When the king was informed of this, at first highly incensed, he sent deputies to Rome to demand the hostage Clælia; that he did not regard the others; and afterwards, being changed into admiration of her courage, he said, "that this action surpassed those of Cocles and Mucius," and declared, "as he would consider the treaty as broken if the hostage were not delivered up, so, if given up, he would send her back safe to her friends." Both sides kept their faith: the Romans restored their pledge of peace according to treaty; and with the king of Etruria merit found not only security, but honour; and, after making encomiums on the young lady, promised to give her, as a present, half of the hostages, and that she should choose whom she pleased. When they were all brought out, she is said to have pitched upon the young boys below puberty, which was both consonant to maiden delicacy, and by consent of the hostages themselves it was deemed reasonable, that that age which was most exposed to injury should be freed from the enemy's hand. The peace being re-established, the Romans marked the uncommon instance of bravery in the woman, by an uncommon kind of honour, an equestrian statue; (the statue representing) a lady sitting on horseback was placed at the top of the Via Sacra.

Inconsistent with this so peaceful a departure of the Etrurian king from the city, is the custom handed down from the ancients, and which continues down to our times among other usages at public sales, (I mean) that of selling the goods of king Porsena; the origin[78] of which custom must either have occurred during the war, and was not relinquished in peace, or it must have increased from a milder source than the form of expression imports, of selling the goods in a hostile manner. Of the accounts handed down, the most probable is, that

---

[78] *The origin.* Niebuhr mentions a more probable one. See Nieb. i. p. 541; ii. p. 204.

Porsena, on retiring from the Janiculum, made a present to the Romans of his camp well stored with provisions conveyed from the neighbouring and fertile fields of Etruria, the city being then exhausted by the long siege; that this, lest it should be carried away in a hostile manner, by the people being admitted in, was then sold, and called the goods of Porsena, the expression rather importing gratitude for the gift, than an auction of the king's property, which never even was in the power of the Roman people. Porsena, after ending the Roman war, that his army might not seem to have been led into these parts without effecting any thing, sent his son Aruns with a part of his forces to besiege Aricia. The matter not being expected, the Aricians were at first terrified; afterwards assistance, which was sent for from the people of Latium and Cumæ, inspired so much hope, that they ventured to meet them in the field. At the commencement of the battle the Etrurians attacked the Aricians so furiously, that they routed them at the first onset. But the Cuman cohorts, opposing stratagem to force, moved off a little to one side, and when the enemy were carried beyond them in great disorder, they faced about and charged them in the rear. By this means the Etrurians, when they had almost got the victory, were enclosed and cut to pieces.[79] A very small part of them, having lost their general, because they had no nearer refuge, came to Rome without their arms, in the condition and with the air of suppliants. There they were kindly received and provided with lodgings. When their wounds were cured, many of them went home and told the kind hospitality they had met with. Affection for their hosts and for the city detained many at Rome; a place was assigned them to dwell in, which they have ever since called the Tuscan Street.

Then P. Lucretius and P. Valerius Publicola were elected consuls. This year ambassadors came from Porsena for the last time, regarding the restoration of Tarquin to the throne. And when they were answered, that the senate would send deputies to the king; some of the principal persons of that order were forthwith despatched to represent to him "that it was not because the answer could not have been given in a few words, that the royal family would not be received, that select members of the senate had been deputed to him, rather than an answer given to his ambassadors at Rome; but (it was done) that all mention of the matter might be put an end to for evermore, and that their minds might not be disturbed amid so many mutual acts of kindness, by his requiring what was adverse to the liberty of the Roman people, and by their denying to him to whom they would willingly deny nothing, unless they would submit to their own ruin. That the Roman people

---

[79] Niebuhr thinks, that from this defeat of the Etrurians may be dated the commencement of the recovery of their liberty by the Romans, and that the flight of the Roman hostages, the sale of Porsena's goods, &c. were subsequent to it.

were not now under a kingly government, but in a state of freedom, and were firmly determined rather to open their gates to enemies than to kings. That it was the wish of all, that their city might have the same period of existence as their freedom in that city. Wherefore, if he wished Rome to be safe, they entreated that he would suffer it to be free." The king, overcome by modesty, says, "Since it is your firm and fixed resolve, I will neither tease you by repeatedly urging these same subjects more frequently, nor will I disappoint the Tarquinii by holding out hopes of aid which it is not in my power to give them; whether they have need of peace, or of war, let them seek another place from here for their exile, that nothing may disturb the peace between you and me." To these kind promises he added actions still more friendly, for he delivered up the remainder of the hostages, and restored to them the land of the Veientians, which had been taken from them by the treaty concluded at Janiculum. Tarquin, all hopes of return being now cut off, went to Tusculum to live in exile with his son-in-law Mamilius Octavius. Thus the peace between Porsena and the Romans was inviolably preserved.

M. Valerius and P. Posthumius were chosen consuls. This year war was carried on successfully against the Sabines; the consuls received the honour of a triumph. Upon this the Sabines made preparations for war on a larger scale. To make head against them, and lest any sudden danger might arise from Tusculum, (whence they suspected a war, though it was not yet declared,) P. Valerius was created consul a fourth time, and T. Lucretius a second time. A disturbance arising among the Sabines, between the advisers of war and of peace, transferred from thence some additional strength to the Romans. For Attus Clausus, afterwards called at Rome Appius Claudius, when he himself, being an adviser of peace, was hard put to it by those who abetted the war, and was not a match for the faction, fled from Regillum to Rome, accompanied by a great number of clients. The rights of citizenship and land on the other side of the Anio were conferred on them. It was called the old Claudian tribe, and was increased by the addition of some tribesmen who had come from that country. Appius, being chosen into the senate, was soon after advanced, to the highest dignity of that order. The consuls having entered the territories of the Sabines with a hostile army, after they had, both by laying waste their country, and afterwards by defeating them in battle, so weakened the power of the enemy, that they had no reason to dread their taking up arms again for a long time, returned to Rome in triumph. The following year, Agrippa Menenius and P. Posthumius being consuls, P. Valerius, allowed by universal consent to be the ablest man in Rome, in the arts both of peace and war, died in the height of glory, but so poor, that means to defray the expenses of his funeral were wanting: he was buried at the public charge. The matrons mourned for him as they had done for Brutus. The same year two Latin colonies, Pometia and Cora, revolted to the Auruncians. War was commenced against the Auruncians, and after defeating a numerous army of them who boldly met the consuls entering their frontiers, the whole Auruncian war was confined to Pometia. Nor, after the battle was over, did they refrain from slaughter more than in the heat of the action; for a greater number were slain than taken, and the prisoners they put to death indiscriminately. Nor did the enemy, in their resentment, spare even the three hundred hostages which they had received. This year also the consuls triumphed at Rome.

The following consuls, Opiter Virginius and Sp. Cassius, first endeavoured to take Pometia by storm, and afterwards by raising vineæ and other works. But the Auruncians, prompted more by an irreconcilable hatred against them, than induced by hopes of success, or by a favourable opportunity, sallied out of the town, and though more of them were armed with lighted torches than swords, filled all places with fire and slaughter. After they had burnt down the vineæ, slain and wounded many of the enemy, they were near killing one of the consuls, who had been thrown from his horse and severely wounded (which of them authors do not mention). Upon this they returned to Rome, foiled in their object; the consul was left among many more who were wounded with very uncertain hopes of his recovery. After a short time, sufficient for curing their wounds and recruiting their army, they marched against Pometia with redoubled fury and augmented strength. When, the vineæ having been repaired and the other apparatus of war, the soldiers were on the point of scaling the walls, the town surrendered. Yet though the town had surrendered, the leading men of the Auruncians, with no less cruelty than if it had been taken by assault, were beheaded indiscriminately; the others who were colonists were sold by auction, the town was razed, and the land sold. The consuls obtained a triumph more from having severely gratified their revenge, than in consequence of the importance of the war thus brought to a close.

The following year had Postumus Cominius and T. Lartius for consuls. On this year, during the celebration of the games at Rome, as some of the courtesans were being carried off by some of the Sabine youth in a frolic, a mob having assembled, a scuffle ensued, and almost a battle; and from this inconsiderable affair the whole nation seemed inclined to a renewal of hostilities. Besides the dread of the Latin war, this accession was further made to their fears; certain intelligence was received that thirty different states had entered into a confederacy against them, at the instigation of Octavius Mamilius. While the city was perplexed amid this expectation of such important events, mention was made for the first time of nominating a dictator. But in what year or who the consuls[80] were in whom confidence was not reposed, because they were of the Tarquinian faction, (for that also is recorded,) or who was elected dictator for the first time, is not satisfactorily established. Among the oldest writers however I find that Titus Lartius was appointed the first dictator, and Spurius Cassius master of the horse. They chose men of consular dignity, for so the law, made for the election of a dictator, ordained. For this reason, I am more inclined to believe that Lartius, who was of consular rank, was annexed to the consuls as their director and master, rather than Manius Valerius, the son of Marcus and grandson of Volesus, who had not yet been consul. For, had they intended to choose a dictator from that family in particular, they would much rather have chosen his father, Marcus Valerius, a consular person, and a man of distinguished merit. On the creation of the dictator first at Rome, when they saw the axes carried before him, great awe struck the common people, so that they became more submissive to obey orders. For neither was there now, as under the consuls who possessed equal power, the assistance of one of the two, nor was there appeal, nor was there any resource any where but in attentive submission. The creation of a dictator at Rome terrified the Sabines, and the more effectually, because they thought he was created on their account.[81] Wherefore they sent ambassadors to sue for peace, to whom, when earnestly entreating the dictator and senate to pardon the young men's offence, an answer was given that the young men could easily be forgiven, but not the old men, who continually raised one war after another. Nevertheless they continued to treat about a peace, and it would have been granted, if the Sabines would bring themselves to make good the expenses incurred on the war (for that was demanded). War was proclaimed; a tacit truce kept the year quiet.

Servius Sulpicius and M. Tullius were consuls the next year: nothing worth mentioning happened. Then T. Æbutius and C. Vetusius. In their consulship, Fidenæ was besieged, Crustumeria taken, and Præneste revolted from the Latins to the Romans. Nor was the Latin war, which had been fomenting for several years, any longer deferred. A. Postumius dictator, and T. Æbutius his master of the horse, marching with a numerous army of horse and foot, met the enemy's forces at the lake Regillus, in the territory of Tusculum, and, because it was heard that the Tarquins were in the army of the Latins, their rage could not be restrained, but they must immediately come to an engagement. Accordingly the battle was more obstinate and fierce than usual. For the generals were present not only to direct matters by their

---

[80] *Nec quibus consulibus parum creditum sit,* scil. fides non habita fuerit. Arnold in his Roman Hist. considers this to have been the true cause of creating a dictator.

[81] *Eo magis quod propter se.* From this one would be disposed to suspect that the dictator was created to take on him the management of war. See Nieb. p. 553, and Niebhr. Epit. by Twiss, Append. p. 355.

orders, but even charged one another, exposing their own persons. And there was hardly any of the principal officers of either side who came off unwounded except the Roman dictator. As Postumius was drawing up his men and encouraging them in the first line, Tarquinius Superbus, though now enfeebled by age, spurred on his horse with great fury to attack him; but being wounded in the side, he was carried off by a party of his own men to a place of safety. In the other wing also, Æbutius, master of the horse, had charged Octavius Mamilius; nor was his approach unobserved by the Tusculan general, who also briskly spurred on his horse to encounter him. And such was their impetuosity as they advanced with hostile spears, that Æbutius was run through the arm and Mamilius struck on the breast. The Latins received the latter into their second line; but as Æbutius was not able to wield his lance with his wounded arm, he retired from the battle. The Latin general, not in the least discouraged by his wound, stirs up the fight; and because he saw his own men begin to give ground, sent for a company of Roman exiles to support them, commanded by Tarquin's son. This body, inasmuch as they fought with greater fury from having been banished from their country, and lost their estates, restored the battle for a short time.

When the Romans were beginning to give ground on that side, M. Valerius, brother to Poplicola, having observed young Tarquin boldly figuring away at the head of his exiles, fired with the renown of his family, that the slaying of the princes might belong to the same family whose glory their expulsion had been, clapped spurs to his horse, and with his javelin presented made towards Tarquin. Tarquin retired from his violent enemy into a battalion of his own men. As Valerius rushed rashly into the line of the exiles, one of them ran him sideways through the body, and as the horse was in no way retarded by the wound of his rider, the expiring Roman fell to the ground, his arms falling over him. Postumius the dictator, on seeing so distinguished a man slain, the exiles advancing boldly in a body, and his own men disheartened and giving ground, gives the signal to his own cohort, a chosen body of men which he kept for the defence of his person, to treat every Roman soldier whom they should see fly from the battle as an enemy. Upon this the Romans, by reason of the danger on both sides, turned from their flight against the enemy, and, the battle being restored, the dictator's cohort now for the first time engaged in the fight, and with fresh vigour and undaunted resolution falling on the wearied exiles, cut them to pieces. Here another engagement took place between the leading officers. The Latin general, on seeing the cohort of the exiles almost surrounded by the Roman dictator, advanced in haste to the front with some companies of the body of reserve. T. Herminius, a lieutenant-general, having seen them moving in a body, and well knowing Mamilius, distinguished from the rest by his armour and dress, encountered the leader of the enemy with a force so much superior to that wherewith the general of the horse had lately done, that at one thrust he ran him through the side and slew him; and while stripping the body of his enemy, he himself received a wound with a javelin; and though brought back to the camp victorious, yet he died during the first dressing of it. Then the dictator flies to the cavalry, entreating them in the most pressing terms, as the foot were tired out with fighting, to dismount from their horses and join the fight. They obeyed his orders, dismounted, flew to the front, and taking their post at the first line, cover themselves with their targets. The infantry immediately recovered courage, when they saw the young noblemen sustaining a share of the danger with them, the mode of fighting being now assimilated. Thus at length were the Latins beaten back, and their line giving way,[82] they retreated. The horses were then brought up to the cavalry that they might pursue the enemy, and the infantry likewise followed. On this, the dictator, omitting nothing (that could conciliate) divine or human aid, is said to have vowed a temple to Castor, and likewise to have promised rewards to the first and second of the soldiers who should enter the enemy's camp. And such was their ardour, that the Romans took the camp with the same impetuosity wherewith they had routed the enemy in the field. Such was the engagement at the lake Regillus. The dictator and master of the horse returned to the city in triumph.

For the next three years there was neither settled peace nor open war. The consuls were Q. Clælius and T. Lartius. After them A. Sempronius and M. Minucius. In their consulship, a temple was dedicated to Saturn, and the Saturnalia appointed to be kept as a festival. Then A. Postumius and T. Virginius were chosen consuls. In some authors I find that the battle at the lake Regillus was not fought till this year, and that A. Postumius, because the fidelity of his colleague was suspected, laid down his office, and thereupon was created dictator. Such great mistakes of dates perplex one with the history of these times, the magistrates being arranged differently in different writers, that you cannot determine what consuls succeeded certain consuls,[83] nor in what particular year every remarkable action happened, by reason of the antiquity, not only of the facts, but also of the historians. Then Ap. Claudius and P. Servilius were elected consuls. This year was remarkable for the news of Tarquin's death. He died at Cumæ, whither he had fled to the tyrant Aristodemus, after the reduction of the power of the Latins. The senate and people were elated by this news. But with the senators their satisfaction was too extravagant, for by the chief men among them oppression began to be

---

[82] By giving up the advantage of their horses, and forgetting their superiority of rank.
    [83] Qui consules secundum quosdam, who were the consuls that came after certain consuls.

practised on the people to whom they had to that day been attentive to the utmost of their power. The same year the colony which king Tarquin had sent to Signia was recruited by filling up the number of the colonists. The tribes at Rome were increased to twenty-one. And the temple of Mercury was dedicated the fifteenth of May.

During the Latin war, there had been neither peace nor war with the nation of the Volscians; for both the Volscians had raised auxiliary troops to send to the Latins had not so much expedition been used by the Roman dictator, and the Roman employed this expedition that he might not have to contend in one and the same battle with the Latin and the Volscian. In resentment of this, the consuls marched their army into the Volscian territory; the unexpected proceeding alarmed the Volscians, who dreaded no chastisement of mere intention; unmindful of arms, they gave three hundred children of the principal men of Cora and Pometia as hostages. Upon this the legions were withdrawn without coming to any action. Not long after their natural disposition returned to the Volscians, now delivered of their fears; they again make secret preparation for war, having taken the Hernicians into an alliance with them. They send ambassadors in every direction to stir up Latium. But the recent defeat received at the lake Regillus, could scarcely restrain the Latins from offering violence to the ambassadors through resentment and hatred of any one who would advise them to take up arms. Having seized the Volscians, they brought them to Rome. They were there delivered up to the consuls, and information was given that the Volscians and Hernicians were making preparations for war against the Romans. The matter being referred to the senate, it was so gratifying to the senators that they both sent back six thousand prisoners to the Latins, and referred to the new magistrates the business regarding the treaty, which had been almost absolutely refused them. Upon this indeed the Latins were heartily glad at what they had done, the advisers of peace were in high esteem. They send a crown of gold to the Capitol as an offering to Jupiter. Along with the ambassadors and the offering there came a great crowd, consisting of the prisoners who had been sent back to their friends. They proceed to the houses of those persons with whom each had been in servitude, and return thanks for their having been generously kept and treated during their calamity. They then form connexions of hospitality. And never at any former time was the Latin name more closely united to the Roman state, either by public or private ties.

But both the Volscian war was threatening, and the state, being disturbed within itself, glowed with intestine animosity between the senate and people, chiefly on account of those confined for debt. They complained loudly, that whilst fighting abroad for liberty and dominion, they were captured and oppressed at home by their fellow citizens; and that the liberty of the people was more secure in war than in peace, among enemies than among their fellow citizens; and this feeling of discontent, increasing of itself, the striking sufferings of an individual still further aggravated. A certain person advanced in years threw himself into the forum with all the badges of his miseries on him. His clothes were all over squalid, the figure of his body still more shocking, being pale and emaciated. In addition, a long beard and hair had impressed a savage wildness on his countenance; in such wretchedness he was known notwithstanding, and they said that he had been a centurion, and compassionating him they mentioned openly other distinctions (obtained) in the service: he himself exhibited scars on his breast, testimonies of honourable battles in several places. To persons repeatedly inquiring, whence that garb, whence that ghastly appearance of body, (the multitude having now assembled around him almost like a popular assembly,) he says, "that whilst serving in the Sabine war, because he had not only been deprived of the produce of his land in consequence of the depredations of the enemy, but also his residence had been burned down, all his effects pillaged, his cattle driven off, a tax imposed on him at a time very distressing to him, he had incurred debt; that this debt, aggravated by usury, had stripped him first of his father's and grandfather's farm, then of his other property; lastly that a pestilence, as it were, had reached his person. That he was taken by his creditor, not into servitude, but into a house of correction and a place of execution." He then showed his back disfigured with the marks of stripes still recent. At the hearing and seeing of this a great uproar takes place. The tumult is now no longer confined to the forum, but spreads through the entire city. Those who were confined for debt, and those who were now at their liberty, hurry into the streets from all quarters and implore the protection of the people. In no place is there wanting a voluntary associate of sedition. They run through all the streets in crowds to the forum with loud shouts. Such of the senators as happened to be in the forum, fell in with this mob with great peril to themselves; nor would they have refrained from violence, had not the consuls, P. Servilius and Ap. Claudius, hastily interfered to quell the disturbance. The multitude turning towards them, and showing their chains and other marks of wretchedness, said that they deserved all this, taunting them (the consuls) each with the military services performed by himself, one in one place, and another in another. They require them with menaces, rather than as suppliants, to assemble the senate, and stand round the senate-house in a body, determined themselves to be witnesses and directors of the public counsels. Very few of the senators, whom chance had thrown in the way, were forced to attend the consuls; fear prevented the rest from coming not only to the house, but even to the forum. Nor could any thing be done by reason of the thinness of the senate. Then indeed the people began to think their demand was eluded, and the redress of their grievances delayed; that such of the senators as had absented themselves did so not through chance or fear, but on purpose to obstruct the business. That the consuls themselves trifled with them, that their miseries were now a mere subject of mockery. By this time the sedition was come to such a height, that the majesty of the consuls could hardly restrain the violence of the people. Wherefore, uncertain whether they incurred greater danger by staying at home, or venturing abroad, they came at length to the senate; but though the house was at length full, a want of agreement manifested itself, not only among the fathers, but even between the consuls themselves. Appius, a man of violent temper, thought the matter was to be done by the authority of the consuls, and that if one or two were seized, the rest would be quiet. Servilius, more inclined to moderate measures, thought that while their minds were in this ferment, it would be both more safe and more easy to bend than to break them. Amidst these debates, another terror of a more serious nature presented itself.

Some Latin horse came full speed to Rome, with the alarming news that the Volscians were marching with a hostile army, to besiege the city, the announcement of which (so completely had discord made the state two from one) affected the senators and people in a far different manner. The people exulted with joy, and said, that the gods were come as avengers of the tyranny of the fathers. They encouraged one another not to enrol their names, that it was better that all should perish together, than that they should perish alone. That the patricians should serve as soldiers, that the patricians should take up arms, so that the perils of war should remain with those with whom the advantages were. But the senate, dejected and confounded by the two-fold terror, that from their own countrymen, and that from the enemy, entreated the consul Servilius, whose temper was more conciliating, that he would extricate the commonwealth beset with such great terrors. Then the consul, dismissing the senate, proceeds into the assembly. There he shows them that the senate were solicitous that care should be taken for the people's interest: but their alarm for the whole commonwealth had interrupted their deliberation regarding that which was no doubt the greatest part, but yet only a part; nor could they, when the enemy were almost at the gates, allow any thing to take precedence of war: nor, if there should be some respite, was it either to the credit of the people not to have taken up arms in defence of their country unless they first receive a recompence, nor consistent with the dignity of the senators that they adopted measures of relief for the distresses of their countrymen through fear rather than afterwards from inclination. He gave additional confidence to the assembly by an edict, by which he ordained that no one "should detain a Roman citizen either in chains or in prison, so as to hinder his enrolling his name under the consuls. And that nobody should either seize or sell the goods of any soldier, while he was in the camp, or arrest his children or grandchildren." This ordinance being published, the debtors under arrest who were present immediately entered their names, and crowds of persons hastening from all quarters of the city from their confinement, as their creditors had no right to detain their persons, ran together into the forum to take the military oath. These made up a considerable body of men, nor was the bravery or activity of the others more conspicuous in the Volscian war. The consul led out his army against the enemy, and pitched his camp at a little distance from them.

The next night the Volscians, relying on the dissension among the Romans, made an attempt on their camp, to see if any desertion or treachery might be resorted to during the night. The sentinels on guard perceived them; the army was called up, and the signal being given they ran to arms. Thus that attempt of the Volscians was frustrated; the remainder of the night was dedicated to repose on both sides. The next morning at daybreak the Volscians, having filled the trenches, attacked the rampart. And already the fortifications were being demolished on every side, when the consul, although all on every side, and more especially the debtors, cried out that he should give the signal, having delayed a little while for the purpose of trying the feelings of the soldiers, when their great ardour became sufficiently apparent, having at length given the signal for sallying forth, he lets out the soldiers now impatient for the fight. At the very first onset the enemy were routed; the rear of them who fled was harassed, as long as the infantry was able to overtake them; the cavalry drove them in consternation to their very camp. In a little time the camp itself was taken and plundered, the legions having surrounded it, as the panic had driven the Volscians even from thence also. On the next day the legions being led to Suessa Pometia, whither the enemy had retreated, in a few days the town is taken; when taken, it was given up for plunder: by these means the needy soldiers were somewhat relieved. The consul leads back his victorious army to Rome with the greatest glory to himself: as he is setting out for Rome, the deputies of the Ecetrans, (a part) of the Volscians, alarmed for their state after the taking of Pometia, come to him. By a decree of the senate peace is granted them, but their land is taken from them.

Immediately after the Sabines also caused an alarm to the Romans; but it was rather a tumult than a war. It was announced in the city during the night that a Sabine army had advanced as far as the river Anio, plundering the country: that the country houses there were pillaged and burnt down indiscriminately. A. Postumius, who had been dictator in the Latin war, was immediately sent against them with all the horse. The consul Servilius followed him with a chosen body of foot. The cavalry cut off most of the stragglers; nor did the Sabine legion make any resistance against the foot when they came up with

them. Being tired both by their march and their plundering the country
in the night, and a great number of them being surfeited with eating and
drinking in the cottages, they had scarcely sufficient strength for flight.
The Sabine war being thus heard of and finished in one night, on the
following day, amid sanguine hope of peace being secured in every
quarter, ambassadors from the Auruncians come to the senate,
proclaiming war unless the troops are withdrawn from the Volscian
territory. The army of the Auruncians had set out from home
simultaneously with the ambassadors; the report of which having been
seen not far from Aricia, excited such a tumult among the Romans, that
neither the senate could be consulted in regular form, nor could they,
while themselves taking up arms, give a pacific answer to those
advancing against them in arms. They march to Aricia with a
determined army, come to an engagement not far from thence, and in
one battle put an end to the war.

After the defeat of the Auruncians, the people of Rome, victorious
in so many wars within a few days, were expecting the promises of the
consul and the engagement of the senate (to be made good). But
Appius, both through his natural pride, and in order to undermine the
credit of his colleague, issued his decrees regarding borrowed money,
with all possible severity. And from this time, both those who had been
formerly in confinement were delivered up to their creditors, and others
also were taken into custody. When this happened to a soldier, he
appealed to the colleague, and a crowd gathered about Servilius: they
represented to him his promises, severally upbraided him with their
services in war, and with the scars they had received. They loudly
called upon him to lay the matter before the senate, and that, as consul,
he would relieve his fellow citizens, as a general, his soldiers. These
remonstrances affected the consul, but the situation of affairs obliged
him to back out; so completely had not only his colleague, but the
whole body of the patricians, adopted an entirely opposite course. And
thus, by acting a middle part, he neither escaped the odium of the
people, nor gained the favour of the senators. The fathers looked upon
him as a weak, popularity-hunting consul, and the people considered
him as a deceiver. And it soon appeared that he was as odious to them
as Appius himself. A dispute had happened between the consuls, as to
which should dedicate the temple of Mercury. The senate referred the
affair from themselves to the people, and ordained that to whichsoever
of them the dedication should be granted by order of the people, he
should preside over the markets, establish a company of merchants, and
perform the functions of a pontifex maximus. The people gave the
dedication of the temple to M. Lætorius, the centurion of the first
legion, that it might plainly appear to have been done not so much out
of respect to a person on whom an honour above his rank had been
conferred, as to affront the consuls. Upon this one of the consuls

particularly, and the senators, were highly incensed. But the people had acquired courage, and proceeded in a manner quite different from what they had at first intended. For when they despaired of redress from the consuls and senate, upon seeing a debtor led to the court, they flew together from all quarters. And neither the decree of the consul could be heard in consequence of the noise and clamour, nor, when he had pronounced the decree, did any one obey it. All was managed by violence, and the entire dread and danger with respect to personal liberty, was transferred from the debtors to the creditors, who were severally abused by the crowd in the very sight of the consul. In addition to all this, the dread of the Sabine war spread, and when a levy was decreed, nobody gave in his name; Appius being enraged, and bitterly inveighing against the ambitious arts of his colleague, who by his popular silence was betraying the republic, and besides his not passing sentence against the debtors, likewise neglected to raise the levies, after they had been voted by the senate. Yet he declared, that "the commonwealth was not entirely deserted, nor the consular authority altogether debased. That he alone would vindicate both his own dignity and that of the senators." When a daily mob, emboldened by licentiousness, stood round him, he commanded a noted ringleader of the sedition to be apprehended. He, as the lictors were carrying him off, appealed to the people; nor would the consul have allowed the appeal, because there was no doubt regarding the judgment of the people, had not his obstinacy been with difficulty overcome, rather by the advice and influence of the leading men, than by the clamours of the people; so much resolution he had to bear the weight of their odium. The evil gained ground daily, not only by open clamours, but, which was far more dangerous, by a secession and by secret meetings. At length the consuls, so odious to the commons, went out of office: Servilius liked by neither party, Appius highly esteemed by the senators.

Then A. Virginius and T. Vetusius enter on the consulship. Upon this the commons, uncertain what sort of consuls they were to have, held nightly meetings, some of them upon the Esquiline, and others upon the Aventine hill, that they might not be confused by hasty resolutions in the forum, or take their measures inconsiderately and without concert. The consuls, judging this proceeding to be of dangerous tendency, as it really was, laid the matter before the senate. But they were not allowed after proposing it to take the votes regularly; so tumultuously was it received on all sides by the clamours and indignation of the fathers, at the consuls throwing on the senate the odium of that which should have been put down by consular authority. "That if there really were magistrates in the republic, there would have been no council in Rome but the public one. That the republic was now divided and split into a thousand senate-houses and assemblies, some of which were held on the Esquiline, others on the Aventine hill. That one man, in truth such as Appius Claudius, for that that was more than a consul, would in a moment disperse these private meetings." When the consuls, thus rebuked, asked them, "What they desired them to do, for that they would act with as much energy and vigour as the senators wished," they resolve that they should push on the levies as briskly as possible, that the people were become insolent from want of employment. When the house broke up, the consuls ascend the tribunal and summon the young men by name. But none of them made any answer, and the people crowding round them, as if in a general assembly, said, "That the people would no longer be imposed on. They should never list one soldier till the public faith was made good. That liberty should be restored to each before arms were given, that they might fight for their country and fellow citizens, and not for arbitrary lords." The consuls fully understood the orders they had received from the senate, but they saw none of those who had talked so big within the walls of the senate-house present themselves to take any share with them in the public odium. A desperate contest with the commons seemed at hand. Therefore, before they would have recourse to extremities, they thought it advisable to consult the senate a second time. Then indeed the younger senators flocked in a hurry round the chairs of the consuls, commanding them to abdicate the consulate, and resign an office which they had not courage to support.

Having sufficiently tried both[84] ways, the consuls at length said, "Conscript fathers, lest you may say that you were not forewarned, a great disturbance is at hand. We require that they who accuse us most severely of cowardice, would assist us in raising the levies; we shall proceed according to the resolution of the most intrepid amongst you, since it so pleases you." They return to their tribunal, and on purpose commanded one of the most factious of the people, who stood in their view, to be called upon by name. When he stood mute, and a number of men stood round him in a ring, to prevent his being seized, the consuls sent a lictor to him. He being repulsed, such of the fathers as attended the consuls, exclaiming against it as an intolerable insult, ran in a hurry from the tribunal to assist the lictor. But when the violence was turned from the lictor, who suffered nothing else but being prevented from seizing him, against the fathers, the riot was quelled by the interposition of the consuls, in which however, without stones or weapons, there was more noise and angry words than mischief done. The senate, called in a tumultuous manner, is consulted in a manner still more tumultuous; such as had been beaten, calling out for an inquiry, and the most violent members declaring their sentiments no less by clamours and noise than by their votes. At length, when their passion had subsided, the consuls

---

[84] The determination of the plebeians and senators.

reproaching them with there being as much disorderly conduct in the
senate as in the forum, the house began to vote in regular order. There
were three different opinions: P. Virginius did not make the[85] matter
general. He voted that they should consider only those who, relying on
the promise of P. Servilius the consul, had served in a war against the
Auruncans and Sabines. Titius Largius was of opinion, "That it was not
now a proper time to reward services only. That all the people were
immersed in debt, and that a stop could not be put to the evil, unless
measures were adopted for all. And that if the condition of different
parties be different, the divisions would rather be thereby inflamed than
composed." Appius Claudius, who was naturally severe, and, by the
hatred of the commons on the one hand, and praises of the senators on
the other, was become quite infuriated, said, "That these riots
proceeded not from distress, but from licentiousness. That the people
were rather wanton than violent. That this terrible mischief took its rise
from the right of appeal; since threats, not authority, was all that
belonged to the consuls, while permission was given to appeal to those
who were accomplices in the crime. Come," added he, "let us create a
dictator from whom there lies no appeal; this madness, which hath set
every thing in a flame, will immediately subside. Let any one dare then
to strike a lictor, when he shall know that his back, and even his life,
are in the power of that person whose authority he has insulted."

To many the opinion of Appius appeared, as it really was, severe
and violent. On the other hand, those of Virginius and Largius were not
safe for the precedent they established; especially they thought that of
Largius so, as it would destroy all credit. The opinion of Virginius was
reckoned to be most moderate, and a happy medium between the other
two. But through the spirit of faction and a regard of private interest,
which always have and always will obstruct the public councils, Appius
prevailed, and was himself near being created dictator; which step
would certainly have alienated the commons at this most dangerous
juncture, when the Volsci, the Æqui, and the Sabines happened to be all
in arms at the same time. But the consuls and elder senators took care
that this office, in its own nature uncontrollable, should be committed
to a man of moderate temper. They choose Manius Valerius, son of
Volesus, dictator. The people, though they saw that this magistrate was
created against themselves, yet as they had got the right of appeal by
his brother's law, dreaded nothing oppressive or tyrannical from that
family. An edict of the dictator's, which was almost the same with that
published by the consul Servilius, afterwards confirmed their minds.
But judging it safer to confide in both the man and in the absolute
power with which he was vested, they gave in their names, desisting
from all contest. Ten legions were levied, a greater army than had ever

---

[85] *rem non vulgabat*, was not for extending the relief to all.

been raised before. Each of the consuls had three legions assigned him, and the dictator commanded four. Nor could the war be deferred any longer. The Æqui had made incursions upon the Latin territory; the deputies of the Latins begged the senate either to send them assistance, or to allow them to arm themselves for the purpose of defending their own frontiers. It seemed safer that the Latins should be defended without arming, than to allow them to take up arms again. Wherefore Vetusius the consul was sent to their assistance; this immediately put a stop to the devastations. The Æqui retired from the plains, and depending more on the advantage of the ground than on their arms, secured themselves on the summits of the mountains. The other consul, having marched against the Volsci, in order that he too might not waste time, challenged the enemy to pitch their camp nigh to his, and to risk an engagement by ravaging their lands. Both armies stood in order of battle before their lines in a plain between the two camps. The Volsci had considerably the advantage in number. Accordingly they rushed on to the fight, in a careless manner, and as if contemptuously. The Roman consul neither advanced his forces, and not suffering the enemy's shouts to be returned, he ordered them to stand still with their spears fixed in the ground, and when the enemy came up, to draw their swords and fall upon them with all their force. The Volsci, wearied with running and shouting, set upon the Romans as if they had been quite benumbed through fear; but when they found the vigorous resistance that was made, and saw their swords glittering before their face, they turned their backs in great disorder, just as if they had fallen into an ambuscade. Nor had they strength sufficient even for flight, as they had advanced to the battle in full speed. The Romans, on the other hand, as they had not stirred from their ground in the beginning of the action, being fresh and vigorous, easily overtook the enemy, who were weary, took their camp by assault, and after driving them thence, pursued them to Velitræ, into which the conquered and conquerors entered in a body. By the promiscuous slaughter which was here made of all ranks, there was more blood spilt than in the battle itself. Quarter was given to a small number of them, who threw down their arms and surrendered.

Whilst these things are going on among the Volsci, the dictator routs, puts to flight, and strips of their camp, the Sabines, where by far the most serious part of the war lay. By a charge of his cavalry he had thrown into confusion the centre of the enemy's line, where, by the wings extending themselves too far, they had not strengthened their line by a suitable depth of files.[86] The infantry fell upon them in this confusion, by one and the same charge their camp was taken and the war concluded. There was no other battle in those times more memorable than this since the action at the lake Regillus. The dictator

---

[86] *i. e.* by deepening the files.

is borne into the city in triumph. Besides the usual honours, a place in the circus was assigned to him and his descendants, to see the public games; a curule chair was fixed in that place. The lands of Velitræ were taken from the conquered Volsci: colonists were sent from the city to Velitræ, and a colony planted there. Soon after there was an engagement with the Æqui, but contrary to the wish of the consul, because they had to approach the enemy by disadvantageous ground. But the soldiers complaining that the war was on purpose spun out, that the dictator might resign his office before they returned home to the city, and so his promises might fall to the ground without effect, as those of the consul had done before, forced him at all hazards to march his army up the hill. This imprudent step, by the cowardice of the enemy, turned out successfully; for before the Romans came within reach of a dart, the Æqui, quite amazed at their boldness, abandoned their camp, which was situated in a very strong position, and ran down into the valleys on the opposite side.[87] In it abundance of booty was found, and the victory was a bloodless one. Matters being thus successfully managed in war in three different directions, anxiety respecting the event of their domestic differences had left neither the senators nor the people. With such powerful influence, and with such art also, had the money-lenders made their arrangements, so as to disappoint not only the people, but even the dictator himself. For Valerius, after the return of the consul Vetusius, first of all matters brought before the senate that relating to the victorious people, and proposed the question, what it was their determination should be done with respect to those confined for debt. And when this motion was rejected, "I am not acceptable," says he, "as an adviser of concord. You will ere long wish, depend on it, that the commons of Rome had patrons similar to me. For my part, I will neither further disappoint my fellow citizens, nor will I be dictator to no purpose. Intestine dissensions, foreign wars, caused the republic to require such a magistrate. Peace has been secured abroad, it is impeded at home. I will be a witness to disturbance as a private citizen rather than as dictator." Then quitting the senate-house, he abdicated his dictatorship. The case appeared to the commons, that he had resigned his office indignant at the treatment shown to them. Accordingly, as if his engagements to them had been fully discharged, since it had not been his fault that they were not made good, they attended him when returning to his home with approbation and applause.

Fear then seized the senators lest, if the army should be dismissed, secret meetings and conspiracies would be renewed; wherefore though the levy had been held by the dictator, yet supposing that, as they had

---

[87] "On the opposite side." Gronovius proposes instead of *adversus* to read *aversas*: scil. the valleys behind them, or in their rear.

sworn obedience to the consuls, the soldiers were bound by their oath, under the pretext of hostilities being renewed by the Æqui, they ordered the legions to be led out of the city; by which proceeding the sedition was hastened. And it is said that at first it was in contemplation to put the consuls to death, that they might be discharged from their oath: but that being afterwards informed that no religious obligation could be dissolved by a criminal act, they, by the advice of one Sicinius, retired, without the orders of the consuls, to the sacred mount, beyond the river Anio, three miles from the city: this account is more general than that which Piso has given, that the secession was made to the Aventine. There without any leader, their camp being fortified with a rampart and trench, remaining quiet, taking nothing but what was necessary for sustenance, they kept themselves for several days, neither being attacked, nor attacking others. Great was the panic in the city, and through mutual fear all was suspense. The people left in the city dreaded the violence of the senators; the senators dreaded the people remaining in the city, uncertain whether they should prefer them to stay or to depart; but how long would the multitude which had seceded, remain quiet? what were to be the consequences then, if, in the mean time, any foreign war should break out? they certainly considered no hope left, save in the concord of the citizens; this should be restored to the state by fair or by unfair means. It was resolved therefore that there should be sent as ambassador to the people, Menenius Agrippa, an eloquent man, and one who was a favourite with the people, because he derived his origin from them. He being admitted into the camp, is said to have related to them merely the following story in that antiquated and uncouth style; "At a time when all the parts in the human body did not, as now, agree together, but the several members had each its own scheme, its own language, the other parts, indignant that every thing was procured for the belly by their care, labour, and service; that the belly, remaining quiet in the centre, did nothing but enjoy the pleasures afforded it. They conspired accordingly, that the hands should not convey food to the mouth, nor the mouth receive it when presented, nor the teeth chew it: whilst they wished under the influence of this feeling to subdue the belly by famine, the members themselves and the entire body were reduced to the last degree of emaciation. Thence it became apparent that the service of the belly was by no means a slothful one; that it did not so much receive nourishment as supply it, sending to all parts of the body this blood by which we live and possess vigour, distributed equally to the veins when perfected by the digestion of the food." By comparing in this way how similar the intestine sedition of the body was to the resentment of the people against the senators, he made an impression on the minds of the multitude.

Then a commencement was made to treat of a reconciliation, and among the conditions it was allowed, "that the commons should have their own magistrates, with inviolable privileges, who should have the power of bringing assistance against the consuls, and that it should not be lawful for any of the patricians to hold that office." Thus two tribunes of the commons were created, Caius Licinius and L. Albinus. These created three colleagues for themselves. It is clear that among these was Sicinius, the adviser of the sedition; with respect to two, who they were is not so clear. There are some who say, that only two tribunes were elected on the sacred mount, and that there the devoting law was passed. During the secession of the commons, Sp. Cassius and Postumus Cominius entered on the consulship. During their consulate, the treaty with the Latin states was concluded. To ratify this, one of the consuls remained at Rome; the other being sent to the Volscian war, routs and puts to flight the Volscians of Antium, and continuing his pursuit of them, now that they were driven into the town of Longula, he takes possession of the town. Next he took Polusca, also belonging to the Volscians; then he attacked Corioli with all his force. There was then in the camp, among the young noblemen, C. Marcius, a youth distinguished both for intelligence and courage, who afterwards attained the cognomen of Coriolanus. When, as the Roman army was besieging Corioli, and was wholly intent on the townspeople, whom they kept shut up, without any apprehension of war threatening from without, the Volscian legion, setting out from Antium, suddenly attacked them, and, at the same time the enemy sallied forth from the town, Marcius happened to be on guard. He with a chosen body of men not only repelled the attack of those who had sallied out, but boldly rushed in through the open gate, and having cut down all in the part of the city nearest him, and having hastily seized some fire, threw it in the houses adjoining to the wall. Upon this the shouts of the townsmen mingling with the wailings of the women and children, occasioned by the first fright,[88] as is usual, both increased the courage of the Romans, and dispirited the Volscians, seeing the city captured to the relief of which they had come. Thus the Volsci of Antium were defeated, the town of Corioli was taken. And so much did Marcius by his valour eclipse the reputation of the consul, that had not the treaty concluded with the Latins by Sp. Cassius alone, because his colleague was absent, served as a memorial of it, it would have been forgotten that Postumus Cominius had conducted the war with the Volscians. The same year dies Agrippa Menenius, a man during all his life equally a favourite with the senators and commons, still more endeared to the commons after the secession. To this man, the mediator and umpire in restoring concord among his countrymen, the ambassador of the senators to the commons, the person who brought back the commons to the city, were

---

[88] I have here adopted the reading of Stacker and others, scil. *ad terrorem, ut solet, primum ortus.*

wanting the expenses of his funeral. The people buried him by the contribution of a sextans from each person.

T. Geganius and P. Minutius were next elected consuls. In this year, when every thing was quiet from war abroad, and the dissensions were healed at home, another much more serious evil fell upon the state; first a scarcity of provisions, in consequence of the lands lying untilled during the secession of the commons; then a famine such as befals those who are besieged. And it would have ended in the destruction of the slaves at least, and indeed some of the commons also, had not the consuls adopted precautionary measures, by sending persons in every direction to buy up corn, not only into Etruria on the coast to the right of Ostia, and through the Volscians along the coast on the left as far as Cumas, but into Sicily also, in quest of it. So far had the hatred of their neighbours obliged them to stand in need of aid from distant countries. When corn had been bought up at Cumæ, the ships were detained in lieu of the property of the Tarquinii by the tyrant Aristodemus, who was their heir. Among the Volsci and in the Pomptine territory it could not even be purchased. The corn dealers themselves incurred danger from the violence of the inhabitants. Corn came from Etruria by the Tiber: by means of this the people were supported. Amid this distressing scarcity they would have been harassed by a very inconvenient war, had not a dreadful pestilence attacked the Volsci when about to commence hostilities. The minds of the enemy being alarmed by this calamity, so that they were influenced by some terror, even after it had abated, the Romans both augmented the number of their colonists at Velitræ, and despatched a new colony to the mountains of Norba, to serve as a barrier in the Pomptine district. Then in the consulship of M. Minucius, and A. Sempronius, a great quantity of corn was imported from Sicily, and it was debated in the senate at what rate it should be given to the commons. Many were of opinion, that the time was come for putting down the commons, and for recovering those rights which had been wrested from the senators by secession and violence. In particular, Marcius Coriolanus, an enemy to tribunitian power, says, "If they desire the former rate of provisions, let them restore to the senators their former rights. Why do I, after being sent under the yoke, after being, as it were, ransomed from robbers, behold plebeian magistrates, and Sicinius invested with power? Shall I submit to these indignities longer than is necessary? Shall I, who would not have endured King Tarquin, tolerate Sicinius. Let him now secede, let him call away the commons. The road lies open to the sacred mount and to other hills. Let them carry off the corn from our lands, as they did three years since. Let them have the benefit of that scarcity which in their frenzy they have occasioned. I will venture to say, that, brought to their senses by these sufferings, they will themselves become tillers of the lands, rather than, taking up arms and seceding, they would prevent them from being tilled." It is not so easy to say whether it should have been done, as I think that it might have been practicable for the senators, on the condition of lowering the price of provisions, to have rid themselves of both the tribunitian power, and all the restraints imposed on them against their will.[89]

This proposal both appeared to the senate too harsh, and from exasperation well nigh drove the people to arms: "that they were now assailed with famine, as if enemies, that they were defrauded of food and sustenance, that the foreign corn, the only support which fortune unexpectedly furnished to them, was being snatched from their mouth, unless the tribunes were given up in chains to C. Marcius, unless he glut his rage on the backs of the commons of Rome. That in him a new executioner had started up, who ordered them to die or be slaves." An assault would have been made on him as he left the senate-house, had not the tribunes very opportunely appointed him a day for trial; by this their rage was suppressed, every one saw himself become the judge, the arbiter of the life and death of his foe. At first Marcius heard the threats of the tribunes with contempt.—"That the right to afford aid, not to inflict punishment, had been granted to that office; that they were tribunes of the commons and not of the senators." But the commons had risen with such violent determination, that the senators were obliged to extricate themselves from danger by the punishment of one.[90] They resisted however, in spite of popular odium, and employed, each individual his own powers, and all those of the entire order. And first, the trial was made whether they could upset the affair, by posting their clients (in several places), by deterring individuals from attending meetings and cabals. Then they all proceeded in a body (you would suppose that all the senators were on their trial) earnestly entreating the commons, that if they would not acquit as innocent, they would at least pardon as guilty, one citizen, one senator. As he did not attend on the day appointed, they persevered in their resentment. Being condemned in his absence, he went into exile to the Volsci, threatening his country, and even then breathing all the resentment of an enemy. The Volsci received him kindly on his arrival, and treated him still more kindly every day in proportion as his resentful feelings towards his countrymen became more striking, and one time frequent complaints, another time threats were heard. He lodged with Attius Tullus. He was

---

[89] *i. e.* I think it might have been done; whether it would have been right to do so, it is not so easy to decide. Livy means to say that it was possible enough for the senators, by lowering the price of corn, to get rid of the tribunes, &c. Such a judgment is easily formed; it is not, however, he says, so easy to determine, whether it would have been expedient to follow the advice of Coriolanus.

[90] *i. e.* the senate found themselves reduced to the necessity of delivering one up to the vengeance of the people, in order to save themselves from the further consequences of plebeian rage.

then the chief man of the Volscian people, and always a determined enemy of the Romans. Thus, when old animosity stimulated the one, recent resentment the other, they concert schemes for (bringing about) a war with Rome. They did not at once believe that their people could be persuaded to take up arms, so often unsuccessfully tried. That by the many frequent wars, and lastly, by the loss of their youth in the pestilence, their spirits were now broken; that they must have recourse to art, in a case where animosity had become blunted from length of time, that their feelings might become exasperated by some fresh cause of resentment.

It happened that preparations were being made at Rome for a repetition of the[91] great games; the cause of repeating them was this: on the morning of the games, the show not yet being commenced, a master of a family, after flogging his slave loaded with a neck-yoke, had driven him through the middle of the circus; after this the games were commenced, as if that circumstance bore no relation to religion. Not long after Tit. Atinius, a plebeian, had a dream. Jupiter seemed to him to say; "that the person who danced previous to the games had displeased him; unless these games were renewed on a splendid scale, that the city would be in danger; that he should go and announce these things to the consuls." Though his mind was not altogether free from superstitious feelings, his respectful awe of the dignity of the magistrates overcame his religious fear, lest he might pass into the mouths of people as a laughing-stock. This delay cost him dear; for he lost his son within a few days; and lest the cause of this sudden calamity should be doubtful, that same phantom, presenting itself to him sorrowful in mind, seemed to ask him, whether he had received a sufficient requital for his contempt of the deity; that a still heavier one awaited him, unless he went immediately and delivered the message to the consuls. The matter was now still more pressing. Hesitating, however, and delaying he was at length overtaken by a severe stroke of disease, a sudden paralysis. Then indeed the anger of the gods aroused him. Wearied out therefore by his past sufferings and by those threatening him, having convened a meeting of his friends, after he had detailed to them all he had seen and heard, and Jupiter's having so often presented himself to him in his sleep, the threats and anger of heaven realized[92] in his own calamities, by the unhesitating assent of all who were present he is conveyed in a litter into the forum to the consuls; from thence being conveyed into the senate-house, after he had stated those same particulars to the senators, to the great surprise of all, behold another miracle: he who had been conveyed into the senate-

---

[91] The same as the Circenses.

[92] *Realized—repræsentatas*—quasi præsentes factas, oculis subjectas—presented as it were to the sight.—*Rasch.*

house deprived of the use of all his limbs, is recorded to have returned home on his own feet after he discharged his duty.

The senate decreed that the games should be celebrated on as grand a scale as possible. To these games a great number of Volscians came by the advice of Attius Tullus. Before the games were commenced, Tullus, as had been concerted at home with Marcius, comes to the consuls. He tells them that there were matters on which he wished to treat with them in private concerning the commonwealth. All witnesses being removed, he says, "With reluctance I say that of my countrymen which is rather disparaging.[93] I do not however come to allege against them any thing as having been committed by them, but to guard against their committing any thing. The minds of our people are far more fickle than I could wish. We have felt that by many disasters; seeing that we are still preserved, not through our own deserts, but through your forbearance. There is now here a great multitude of Volscians. The games are going on; the city will be intent on the exhibition. I remember what has been committed in this city on a similar occasion by the youth of the Sabines. My mind shudders lest any thing should be committed inconsiderately and rashly. I considered, that these matters should be mentioned before-hand to you, consuls. With regard to myself, it is my determination to depart hence home immediately, lest, if present, I may be affected by the contagion of any word or deed." Having said this, he departed. When the consuls laid before the senate the matter, doubtful with respect to proof, though from credible authority, the authority more than the thing itself, as usually happens, urged them to adopt even needless precautions; and a decree of the senate being passed, that the Volscians should quit the city, criers are sent in different directions to order them all to depart before night. A great panic struck them at first as they ran about to their lodgings to carry away their effects. Afterwards, when setting out, indignation arose in their breasts: "that they, as if polluted with crime and contaminated, were driven away from the games, on festival days, from the converse in a manner of men and gods."

As they went along in an almost continuous body, Tullus having preceded them to the fountain of Ferentina, accosting the chiefs among them according as each arrived, by asking questions and expressing indignation, he led both themselves, who greedily listened to language congenial[94] to their angry feelings, and through them the rest of the multitude, into a plain adjoining to the road. There having commenced an address after the manner of a public harangue, he says, "Though you were to forget the former ill treatment of the Roman people and the

---

[93] *Sequius sit*—otherwise than as it should be.

[94] *Audientes secunda iræ verba*—attentively listening to words which fanned (or chimed in with) their anger.—St.

calamities of the nation of the Volsci, and all other such matters, with what feelings do you bear this outrage offered you to-day, whereon they have commenced their games by insulting us? Have you not felt that a triumph has been had over you this day? that you, when departing, were a spectacle to all, citizens, foreigners, so many neighbouring states? that your wives, your children were exhibited before the eyes of men? What do you suppose to have been the sentiments of those who heard the voice of the crier? what of those who saw you departing? what of those who met this ignominious cavalcade? what, except that we are identified with some enormous guilt by which we should profane the games, and render an expiation necessary; that for this reason we are driven away from the residences of these pious people, from their converse and meeting? what, does it not strike you that we still live because we hastened our departure? if this is a departure and not a flight. And do you not consider this to be the city of enemies, where if you had delayed a single day, you must have all died? War has been declared against you; to the heavy injury of those who declared it, if you are men." Thus, being both already charged with resentment, and incited (by this harangue) they went severally to their homes, and by instigating each his own state, they succeeded in making the entire Volscian nation revolt.

The generals selected for that war by the unanimous choice of all the states were Attius Tullus and Caius Marcius; in the latter of whom their chief hope was reposed. And this hope he by no means disappointed: so that it clearly appeared that the Roman commonwealth was more powerful by reason of its generals than its army. Having marched to Circeii, he expelled from thence the Roman colonists, and delivered that city in a state of freedom to the Volscians. From thence passing across the country through by-roads into the Latin way, he deprived the Romans of their recently acquired towns, Satricum, Longula, Polusca, Corioli. He next retook Lavinium: he then took in succession Corbio, Vitellia, Trebia, Lavici, and Pedum: Lastly he marches from Pedum to the city,[95] and having pitched his camp at the Cluilian trenches five miles from the city, he from thence ravages the Roman territory, guards being sent among the devastators to preserve the lands of the patricians intact; whether as being incensed chiefly against the plebeians, or in order that dissension might arise between the senators and the people. And this certainly would have arisen, so powerfully did the tribunes, by inveighing against the leading men of the state, incite the plebeians, already sufficiently violent of

---

[95] Scil. Rome. Dionysius narrates the expedition of Coriolanus in a different order from that given by Livy, and says that he approached the city twice. Niebuhr, ii. p. 94, n. 535, thinks that the words "passing across the country into the Latin way" (in Latinam viam transversis itineribus transgressus) have been transposed from their proper place, and that they should come in after "he then took," &c. (tunc deinceps).

themselves; but their apprehensions of the foe, the strongest bond of concord, united their minds, distrustful and rancorous though they were. The only matter not agreed on was this, that the senate and consuls rested their hopes on nothing else than on arms; the plebeians preferred any thing to war. Sp. Nautius and Sex. Furius were now consuls. Whilst they were reviewing the legions, posting guards along the walls and other places where they had determined that there should be posts and watches, a vast multitude of persons demanding peace terrified them first by their seditious clamour; then compelled them to convene the senate, to consider the question of sending ambassadors to C. Marcius. The senate entertained the question, when it became evident that the spirits of the plebeians were giving way, and ambassadors being sent to Marcius concerning peace, brought back a harsh answer: "If their lands were restored to the Volscians, that they might then consider the question of peace; if they were disposed to enjoy the plunder of war at their ease, that he, mindful both of the injurious treatment of his countrymen, as well as of the kindness of strangers, would do his utmost to make it appear that his spirit was irritated by exile, not crushed." When the same persons are sent back a second time, they are not admitted into the camp. It is recorded that the priests also, arrayed in their insignia, went as suppliants to the enemy's camp; and that they did not influence his mind more than the ambassadors.

Then the matrons assemble in a body around Veturia, the mother of Coriolanus, and his wife, Volumnia: whether that was the result of public counsel, or of the women's fear, I cannot ascertain. They certainly carried their point that Veturia, a lady advanced in years, and Volumnia, leading her two sons by Marcius, should go into the camp of the enemy, and that women should defend by entreaties and tears a city which men were unable to defend by arms. When they reached the camp, and it was announced to Coriolanus, that a great body of women were approaching, he, who had been moved neither by the majesty of the state in its ambassadors, nor by the sanctity of religion so strikingly addressed to his eyes and understanding in its priests, was much more obdurate against the women's tears. Then one of his acquaintances, who recognised Veturia, distinguished from all the others by her sadness, standing between her daughter-in-law and grand-children, says, "Unless my eyes deceive me, your mother, children, and wife, are approaching." When Coriolanus, almost like one bewildered, rushing in consternation from his seat, offered to embrace his mother as she met him, the lady, turning from entreaties to angry rebuke, says, "Before I receive your embrace, let me know whether I have come to an enemy or to a son; whether I am in your camp a captive or a mother? Has length of life and a hapless old age reserved me for this—to behold you an exile, then an enemy? Could you lay waste this land, which gave you birth and nurtured you? Though you had come with an incensed and vengeful mind, did not your resentment subside when you entered its frontiers? When Rome came within view, did it not occur to you, within these walls my house and guardian gods are, my mother, wife, and children? So then, had I not been a mother, Rome would not be besieged: had I not a son, I might have died free in a free country. But I can now suffer nothing that is not more discreditable to you than distressing to me; nor however wretched I may be, shall I be so long. Look to these, whom, if you persist, either an untimely death or lengthened slavery awaits." Then his wife and children embraced him: and the lamentation proceeding from the entire crowd of women, and their bemoaning themselves and their country, at length overcame the man; then, after embracing his family, he sends them away; he moved his camp farther back from the city. Then, after he had drawn off his troops from the Roman territory, they say that he lost his life, overwhelmed by the odium of the proceeding: different writers say by different modes of death: I find in Fabius, far the most ancient writer, that he lived even to old age; he states positively, that advanced in years he made use of this phrase, "That exile bore much heavier on the old man." The men of Rome were not remiss in awarding their praises to the women, so truly did they live without detracting from the merit of others; a temple was built also and dedicated to female Fortune, to serve as a monument. The Volscians afterwards returned in conjunction with the Æqui into the Roman territory: but the Æqui would no longer have Attius Tullus as their leader; hence from dispute, whether the Volscians or the Æqui should give a general to the allied army, a sedition, and afterwards a furious battle arose. There the good fortune of the Roman people destroyed the two armies of the enemy, by a contest no less bloody than obstinate. T. Sicinius and C. Aquillius were made consuls. The Volsci fell as a province to Sicinius; the Hernici (for they too were in arms) to Aquillius. That year the Hernici were defeated; they came off with respect to the Volscians on equal terms.

Sp. Cassius and Proculus Virginius were next made consuls; a treaty was struck with the Hernici; two-thirds of their land were taken from them: of this the consul Cassius was about to distribute one half among the Latins, the other half among the commons. To this donation he was adding a considerable portion of land, which, though public property, he alleged was possessed by private individuals. This proceeding alarmed several of the senators, the actual possessors, at the danger of their property; the senators felt, moreover, a solicitude on public grounds, that the consul by his donation was establishing an influence dangerous to liberty. Then, for the first time, the Agrarian law was proposed, which even down to our own recollection was never agitated without the greatest commotions in the state. The other consul resisted the donation, the senators seconding him, nor were all the commons opposed to him; they had at first begun to despise a gift which was extended from citizens to allies: in the next place they frequently heard the consul Virginius in the assemblies as it were prophesying—"that the gift of his colleague was pestilential—that those lands were sure to bring slavery to those who should receive them; that the way was paving to a throne." For why was it that the allies were included, and the Latin nation? What was the object of a third of the land that had been taken being given back to the Hernici so lately our enemies, except that instead of Coriolanus being their leader they may have Cassius? The dissuader and opposer of the agrarian law now began to be popular. Both consuls then vied with each other in humouring the commons. Virginius said that he would suffer the lands to be assigned, provided they were assigned to no one but to a Roman citizen. Cassius, because in the agrarian donation he sought popularity among the allies, and was therefore lowered in the estimation of his countrymen, in order that by another donation he might conciliate their affections, ordered that the money received for the Sicilian corn should be refunded to the people. That indeed the people rejected as nothing else than a present bribe for regal authority: so strongly were his gifts spurned in the minds of men, as if they possessed every thing in abundance, in consequence of their inveterate suspicions of his aiming at sovereign power. As soon as he went out of office, it is certain that he was condemned and put to death. There are some who represent his father as the person who inflicted the punishment: that he, having tried him at home, scourged him and put him to death, and consecrated his son's private property to Ceres; that out of this a statue was set up and inscribed, "given from the Cassian family." In some authors I find it stated, and that is more probable, that a day of trial was assigned him for high treason, by the questors, Kæso Fabius and Lucius Valerius; and that he was condemned by the decision of the people; that his house was demolished by a public decree: this is the area before the temple of Tellus. But whether that trial was private or public, he was condemned in the consulship of Ser. Cornelius and Q. Fabius.

The resentment of the people against Cassius was not of long duration. The allurements of the agrarian law, now that its proposer was gone, were of themselves gaining ground in their minds; and this feeling was further heightened by the parsimonious conduct of the senators, who, the Volsci and Æqui having been defeated that year, defrauded the soldiers of the booty; whatever was taken from the enemy, the consul Fabius sold, and lodged the proceeds in the treasury. The Fabian name was odious to the commons on account of the last consul: the senate however succeeded in having Kæso Fabius elected consul with L. Æmilius. The commons, still further incensed at this, stirred up foreign war by exciting disturbance at home; civil dissensions were then interrupted by war. The senators and commons uniting, under the conduct of Æmilius, conquered in battle the Volsci and Æqui who renewed hostilities. The retreat, however, destroyed more of the enemy than the battle; so perseveringly did the horse pursue them when routed. During the same year, on the ides of July, the temple of Castor was dedicated: it had been vowed during the Latin war in the dictatorship of Posthumius: his son, who was elected duumvir for that special purpose, dedicated it. In that year also the minds of the people were excited by the charms of the agrarian law. The tribunes of the people were for enhancing the popular power (vested in them) by promoting the popular law. The senators, considering that there was enough and more than enough of frenzy in the multitude without any additional incitement, viewed with horror largesses and all inducements to temerity: the senators found in the consuls most energetic abettors in making resistance. That portion of the commonwealth therefore prevailed; and not for the present only, but for the forthcoming year they succeeded in bringing in M. Fabius, Kæso's brother, as consul, and one still more detested by the commons for his persecution of Sp. Cassius, L. Valerius. In that year also there was a contest with the tribunes. The law proved to be a vain project, and the abettors of the law mere boasters, by their holding out a gift that was not realized. The Fabian name was from thence held in high repute, after three successive consulates, and all as it were uniformly exercised in contending with the tribunes; accordingly, the honour remained for a considerable time in that family, as being right well placed. A Veientian war was then commenced; the Volscians, too, renewed hostilities; but for foreign wars their strength was almost more than sufficient, and they abused it by contending among themselves. To the distracted state of the public mind were added prodigies from heaven, exhibiting almost daily threats in the city and in the country, and the soothsayers, consulted by the state and by private individuals, one while by means of entrails, another by birds, declared that there was no other cause for the divine anger, but that the ceremonies of religion were not duly attended to. These terrors, however, terminated in this, that Oppia, a vestal virgin, being found guilty of a breach of chastity, was made to suffer punishment.

Quintus Fabius and C. Julius were then made consuls. During this year the dissension at home was not abated, and the war abroad was more desperate. Arms were taken up by the Æquans; the Veientes also entered the territory of the Romans committing devastations; the solicitude about which wars increasing, Kæso Fabius and Sp. Fusius are created consuls. The Æqui were laying siege to Ortona, a Latin city. The Veientes, now satiated with plunder, threatened that they would besiege Rome itself. Which terrors, when they ought to assuage, increased still further the bad feelings of the commons: and the custom of declining the military service was now returning, not of their own accord; but Sp. Licinius, a tribune of the people, thinking that the time was come for forcing the agrarian law on the patricians by extreme necessity, had taken on him the task of obstructing the military preparations. But all the odium of the tribunitian power was turned on the author; nor did the consuls rise up against him more zealously than his own colleagues; and by their assistance the consuls hold the levy. An army is raised for the two wars at the same time; one is given to Fabius to be led against the Æqui, the other to Furius against the Veientians. And with respect to the Veientians, nothing was done worthy of mention. Fabius had much more trouble with his countrymen than with the enemy: that one man himself, as consul, sustained the commonwealth, which the army was betraying, far as in them lay, through their hatred of the consul. For when the consul, in addition to his other military talents, which he exhibited amply in his preparations for and conduct of war, had so drawn up his line that he routed the enemy's army solely by a charge of his cavalry, the infantry refused to pursue them when routed: and though the exhortation of their general, whom they hated, could not move them, neither could even their own infamy, and the present public disgrace and subsequent danger, if the enemy should recover courage, oblige them to quicken their pace, or even to stand in order of battle, if nothing else. Without orders they face about, and with a sorrowful air (you would suppose them beaten) they return to the camp, execrating at one time their general, at another time the services rendered by the cavalry. Nor were any remedies sought by the general for this so pestilent an example; so true is it that the most distinguished talents are more likely to be deficient in the tact of managing their countrymen than in that of conquering an enemy. The consul returned to Rome, not having so much increased his military glory as irritated and exasperated the hatred of his soldiers towards him. The patricians, however, succeeded in having the consulship remain in the Fabian family. They elect M. Fabius consul: Cn. Manlius is assigned as a colleague to Fabius.

This year also had a tribune as a proposer of the agrarian law. It was Titus Pontificius: he pursuing the same course, as if it had succeeded with Sp. Licinius, obstructed the levy for a little time. The patricians being once more perplexed, Appius Claudius asserts "that the tribunitian power was put down last year: for the present by the very act, for the future by the precedent established, and since it was found that it could be rendered ineffective by its own strength; for that there never would be wanting a tribune who would both be willing to obtain a victory for himself over his colleague, and the favour of the better party by advancing the public weal. That both a plurality of tribunes, if there were need of such plurality, would be ready to assist the consuls; and that even one would be sufficient against all. Only let the consuls and leading members of the senate take care to gain over, if not all, at least some of the tribunes, to the commonwealth and the senate." The senators, convinced by the counsels of Appius, both collectively addressed the tribunes with kindness and civility, and the men of consular rank, according as each possessed personal influence over them individually, partly by conciliation, partly by authority, prevailed so far as to make them consent that the powers of the tribunitian office should be beneficial to the state; and by the aid of four tribunes against one obstructor of the public good, the consuls complete the levy. They then set out to the Veientian war, to which auxiliaries had flocked from all parts of Etruria, collected not so much for the sake of the Veientians, as because they had formed a hope that the Roman state might be destroyed by internal discord. And in the councils of all the states of Etruria the leading men openly stated, "that the Roman power was eternal, unless they were distracted by disturbances among themselves. That this was the only poison, this the bane discovered for powerful states, to render great empires mortal. That this evil, a long time retarded, partly by the wise measures of the patricians, partly by the forbearance of the commons, had now proceeded to extremities. That two states were now formed out of one: that each party had its own magistrates, its own laws. That though at first they were accustomed to be turbulent during the levies, still that these same individuals had ever been obedient to their commanders during war; that military discipline being still retained, no matter what might be the state of the city, it had been possible to withstand the evil; that now the custom of not obeying their superior followed the Roman soldier even to the camp. That in the last war in the very field, in the very heat of battle, by consent of the army the victory was voluntarily surrendered to the vanquished Æqui: that the standards were deserted, the general abandoned on the field, and that the army had returned to the camp without orders. That without doubt, if perseverance were used, Rome might be conquered by her own soldiery. That nothing else was necessary than to declare and make a show of war: that the fates and the gods would of themselves manage the rest." These hopes had armed the Etrurians, who in many vicissitudes had been vanquished and victors.

The Roman consuls also dreaded nothing else, than their own strength, and their own arms. The recollection of the destructive precedent set in the last war, deterred them from bringing matters to such a pass as that they should have to fear two armies at the same time. Accordingly they kept within their camp, avoiding this double danger: "that delay and time itself would soften down resentment, and bring a right way of thinking to their minds." The Veientian enemy and the Etrurians proceeded with so much the greater precipitation; they provoked them to battle, first riding up to the camp and challenging them; at length, when they produced no effect by reviling as well the consuls themselves as the army, they stated, "that the pretence of

internal dissension was assumed as a cloak for this cowardice; and that
the consuls distrusted as much the courage as the obedience of their
soldiers. That silence and inaction among men in arms were a novel
form of sedition." Besides this they threw out reproaches, both true as
well as false, on the upstart quality of their race and origin. Whilst they
vociferated these reproaches beneath the very rampart and gates, the
consuls bore them without impatience: but at one time indignation, at
another time shame, distracted the breasts of the ignorant multitude,
and diverted their attention from intestine evils; they were unwilling
that the enemy should come off unpunished; they were unwilling that
success should accrue to the patricians or the consuls; foreign and
domestic hatred struggled for mastery in their breasts; at length the
former prevail, so haughtily and insolently did the enemy revile them;
they crowd in a body to the general's tent; they demand battle, they
require that the signal be given. The consuls confer together as if to
deliberate; they continue the conference for a long time; they were
desirous of fighting, but that desire must be checked and concealed,
that by opposition and delay they might increase the ardour of the
soldiery once roused. An answer is returned, "that the matter in
question was premature, that it was not yet time for fighting: that they
should keep within their camp." They then issue a proclamation, "that
they should abstain from fighting; that if any one fought without orders,
they should punish him as an enemy." When they were thus dismissed,
their eagerness for fighting increases in proportion as they think that the
consuls were less disposed for it; the enemies moreover come up much
more insolently, as soon as it was known that the consuls had
determined not to fight. For they supposed "that they might insult them
with impunity; that their arms were not intrusted to the soldiery. That
the matter would explode in a violent mutiny; that a termination had
come to the Roman empire." Relying on these hopes, they run up to the
gates, heap reproaches on them, with difficulty refrain from assaulting
the camp. Now indeed the Romans could no longer endure these
insults; they crowd from every quarter of the camp to the consuls: they
no longer, as formerly, make their demand with reserve, through the
mediation of the centurions of the first rank; but all proceed
indiscriminately with loud clamours. The affair was now ripe; still they
put it off. Fabius then, his colleague giving way in consequence of his
dread of mutiny being now augmented by the uproar, after he had
commanded silence by sound of trumpet, says, "that these men are able
to conquer, Cneius Manlius, I know; that they are willing they
themselves have prevented me from knowing. It is therefore resolved
and determined not to give the signal, unless they swear that they will
return victorious from this battle. The soldier has once deceived the
Roman consul in the field, the gods he never will deceive." There was a
centurion, Marcus Flavoleius, one of the foremost in demanding battle;

he says, "M. Fabius, I will return victorious from the field." If he deceived, he invokes the anger of father Jove, Mars Gradivus, and of the other gods. After him the entire army severally take the same oath. The signal is given to them when sworn; they take up arms, go into battle, full of rage and of hope. They bid the Etrurians now to cast their reproaches; they severally require that the enemy, once so ready with the tongue, should now stand before them armed as they were. On that day the bravery of all, both commons and patricians, was extraordinary: the Fabian name, the Fabian race shone forth most conspicuous: they are determined to recover in that battle the affections of the commons, which during many civil contests had been alienated from them. The line of battle is formed; nor do the Veientian foe and the Etrurian legions decline the contest.

An almost certain hope was entertained that they would no more fight with them than they had done with the Æqui; that even some more serious attempt was not to be despaired of, considering the irritated state of their feelings, and the very critical occasion. The affair turned out altogether differently; for never before in any other war did the Roman soldiers enter the field with more determined minds (so much had the enemy exasperated them by taunts on the one hand, and the consuls by delay on the other). The Etrurians had scarcely time to form their ranks, when the javelins having been thrown away at random, in the first hurry, rather than discharged with aim, the battle had now come to close fighting, even to swords, where the fury of war is most desperate. Among the foremost the Fabian family was distinguished for the sight it afforded and the example it presented to their fellow citizens; one of these, Q. Fabius, (he had been consul two years before,) as he was advancing at the head of his men against a dense body of Veientians, and whilst engaged amid numerous parties of the enemy, and therefore not prepared for it, was transfixed with a sword through the breast by a Tuscan who presumed on his bodily strength and skill in arms: on the weapon being extracted, Fabius fell forward on the wound. Both armies felt the fall of this one man, and the Roman began in consequence to give way, when the consul Marcus Fabius leaped over the body as it lay, and holding up his buckler, said, "Is this what you swore, soldiers, that you would return to the camp in flight? are you thus more afraid of your most dastardly enemies, than of Jupiter and Mars, by whom you have sworn? But I who have not sworn will either return victorious, or will fall fighting here beside thee, Q. Fabius." Then Kæso Fabius, the consul of the preceding year, says to the consul, "Brother, is it by these words you think you will prevail on them to fight? the gods by whom they have sworn will prevail on them. Let us also, as men of noble birth, as is worthy of the Fabian name, enkindle the courage of the soldiers by fighting rather than by exhorting." Thus the two Fabii rush forward to the front with presented spears, and brought on with them the whole line.

The battle being restored on one side, Cn. Manlius, the consul, with no less ardour, encouraged the fight on the other wing. Where an almost similar result took place; for as the soldiers undauntedly followed Q. Fabius on the one wing, so did they follow Manlius on this, as he was driving the enemy now nearly routed, and when he, having received a severe wound, retired from the battle, they fell back, supposing that he was slain, and would have given way, had not the other consul, galloping at full speed to that quarter with some troops of horse, supported their drooping energies, crying out that his colleague was still alive, that he himself was now come victorious, having routed the other wing. Manlius also shows himself to restore the battle. The well-known voices of the two consuls rekindle the courage of the soldiers; at the same time too the enemy's line was now weakened, whilst, relying on their superior numbers, they draw off their reserve and send them to storm the camp. This being assaulted without much resistance, whilst they lose time in attending to plunder rather than to fighting, the Roman triarii,[96] who had not been able to sustain the first shock, having sent an account to the consuls of the present position of affairs, return in a compact body to the Prætorium, and of themselves renew the battle. The consul Manlius also having returned to the camp, and posted soldiers at all the gates, had blocked up every passage against the enemy. This desperate situation aroused the fury rather than the bravery of the Etrurians; for when rushing on wherever hope held out the prospect of escape, they had frequently advanced with fruitless efforts; one body of young men makes an attack on the consul himself, conspicuous from his arms. The first weapons were intercepted by those who stood around him; afterwards their force could not be sustained. The consul falls, having received a mortal wound, and all around him are dispersed. The courage of the Etrurians rises. Terror drives the Romans in dismay through the entire camp; and matters would have come to extremities, had not the lieutenant-generals, hastily seizing the body of the consul, opened a passage for the enemy at one gate. Through this they rush out; and going away in the utmost disorder, they fall in with the other consul who had been victorious; there again they are slain and routed in every direction. A glorious victory was obtained, saddened however by two so illustrious deaths. The consul, therefore, on the senate voting him a triumph, replied, that "if the army could triumph without their general, he would readily accede to it in consideration of their distinguished behaviour in that war: that for his own part, his family being plunged in grief in consequence of the death of his brother Q. Fabius, and the

---

[96] The triarii were veteran soldiers of approved valour: they formed the third line, whence their name.

commonwealth being in some degree bereaved by the loss of one of her consuls, he would not accept the laurel blasted by public and private grief." The triumph thus resigned was more distinguished than any triumph actually enjoyed; so true it is, that glory refused in due season sometimes returns with accumulated lustre. He next celebrates the two funerals of his colleague and brother, one after the other, he himself acting as panegyrist in the case of both, when by ascribing to them his own deserts, he himself obtained the greatest share of them. And not unmindful of that which he had conceived at the commencement of his consulate, namely, the regaining the affection of the people, he distributes the wounded soldiers among the patricians to be cured. Most of them were given to the Fabii: nor were they treated with greater attention in any other place. From this time the Fabii began to be popular, and that not by any practices except such as were beneficial to the state.

Accordingly Kæso Fabius, having been elected consul with T. Virginius not more with the zealous wishes of the senators than of the commons, attended neither to wars, nor levies, nor any other object, until the hope of concord being now in some measure commenced, the feelings of the commons might be consolidated with those of the senators as soon as possible. Wherefore at the commencement of the year he proposed: "that before any tribune should stand forth as an abettor of the agrarian law, the patricians themselves should be beforehand with them in performing their duty; that they should distribute among the commons the land taken from the enemy in as equal a proportion as possible; that it was but just that those should obtain it, by whose blood and sweat it was obtained." The patricians rejected the proposal with scorn; some even complained that the once brilliant talents of Kæso were now becoming wanton, and were waning through excess of glory. There were afterwards no factions in the city. The Latins were harassed by the incursions of the Æqui. Kæso being sent thither with an army, passes into the very territory of the Æqui to depopulate it. The Æqui retired into the towns, and kept themselves within the walls: on that account no battle worth mentioning was fought. But a blow was received from the Veientian foe through the temerity of the other consul; and the army would have been all cut off, had not Kæso Fabius come to their assistance in time. From that time there was neither peace nor war with the Veientians; their proceedings had now come very near to the form of that of brigands. They retired from the Roman troops into the city; when they perceived that the troops were drawn off, they made incursions into the country, alternately evading war by quiet, quiet by war. Thus the matter could neither be dropped altogether, nor brought to a conclusion; and other wars were impending either at the moment, as from the Æqui and Volsci, who remained inactive no longer than until the recent smart of their late disaster should pass away; or it was evident that the Sabines, ever hostile, and all Etruria would put themselves in motion: but the Veientians, a constant rather than a formidable enemy, kept their minds in constant uneasiness by their insults more frequently than by any danger apprehended from them; a matter which could at no time be neglected, and which suffered them not to direct their attention to any other object. Then the Fabian family addressed the senate; the consul speaks in the name of the family: "Conscript fathers, the Veientian war requires, as you know, a constant rather than a strong force. Do you attend to other wars: assign the Fabii as enemies to the Veientians. We pledge ourselves that the majesty of the Roman name shall be safe in that quarter. That war, as the property of our family, it is our determination to conduct at our own private expense. Let the republic be spared the expense of soldiers and money there." The warmest thanks were returned to them. The consul, leaving the senate-house, accompanied by the Fabii in a body, who had been standing in the porch of the senate-house, returned home. Being ordered to attend on the following day in arms at the consul's gate, they retire to their homes.

The rumour spreads through the entire city; they extol the Fabii to the skies by their encomiums. "That a single family had taken on them the burden of the state: that the Veientian war had now become a private concern, a private quarrel. If there were two families of the same strength in the city, let them demand, the one the Volsci for itself, the other the Æqui; that all the neighbouring states might be subdued, the Roman people all the time enjoying profound peace." The day following, the Fabii take up arms; they assemble where they had been ordered. The consul coming forth in his paludamentum,[97] beholds his entire family in the porch drawn up in order of march; being received into the centre, he orders the standards to be carried forward. Never did an army march through the city, either smaller in number, or more distinguished in fame and in the admiration of all men. Three hundred and six soldiers, all patricians, all of the one stock, not one of whom the senate would reject as a leader in its palmiest days, proceeded on their march, menacing destruction to the Veientian state by the prowess of a single family. A crowd followed, partly belonging to their kinsmen and friends, who contemplated in mind no moderation either as to their hopes or anxiety, but every thing on the highest scale; partly consisting of individuals not connected with their family, aroused by solicitude for the public weal, all enraptured with esteem and admiration. They bid them "proceed in the brave resolve, proceed with happy omens, bring

---

[97] Before a consul set out on any expedition, he offered sacrifices and prayers in the Capitol; and then, laying aside his consular gown, marched out of the city, dressed in a military robe of state, called Paludamentum.

back results proportioned to their undertaking: thence to expect consulships and triumphs, all rewards, all honours from them." As they passed the Capitol and the citadel, and the other sacred edifices, they offer up prayers to all the gods that presented themselves to their sight, or to their mind: that "they would send forward that band with prosperity and success, and soon send them back safe into their country to their parents." In vain were these prayers sent up. Having set out on their luckless road by the right-hand postern of the Carmental gate, they arrive at the river Cremera: this appeared a favourable situation for fortifying a post. L. Æmilius and C. Servilius were then created consuls. And as long as there was nothing else to occupy them but mutual devastations, the Fabii were not only sufficiently able to protect their garrison, but through the entire tract, as far as the Etrurian joins the Roman territory, they protected all their own districts and ravaged those of the enemy, spreading their forces along both frontiers. There was afterwards an intermission, though not of long duration, to these depredations: whilst both the Veientians, having sent for an army from Etruria, assault the post at the Cremera, and the Roman troops, led thither by L. Æmilius the consul, come to a close engagement in the field with the Etrurians; although the Veientians had scarcely time to draw up their line: for during the first alarm, whilst the ranks are posting themselves behind their respective banners and they are stationing their reserves, a brigade of Roman cavalry charging them suddenly in flank, took away all opportunity not only of commencing the fight, but even of standing their ground. Thus being driven back to the Red Rocks, (there they pitched their camp,) they suppliantly sue for peace; for the obtaining of which they were sorry, from the natural inconsistency of their minds, before the Roman garrison was drawn off from the Cremera.

Again the Veientian state had to contend with the Fabii without any additional military armament [on either side]; and there were not merely incursions into each other's territories, or sudden attacks on those making the incursions, but they fought repeatedly in the open field, and in pitched battles: and one family of the Roman people oftentimes gained the victory over an entire Etrurian state, one of the most powerful at that time. This at first appeared mortifying and humiliating to the Veientians: then (they formed) a design, suggested by the circumstance, of surprising their daring enemy by an ambuscade; they were even glad that the confidence of the Fabii was increasing by their great success. Wherefore cattle were frequently driven in the way of the plundering parties, as if they had come there by mere accident, and tracts of land were abandoned by the flight of the peasants; and troops of armed men sent to prevent the devastations retreated more frequently from pretended than from real fear. And now the Fabii had such a contempt for the enemy, as to believe that their invincible arms could not be withstood either in any place or on any occasion: this presumption carried them so far, that at the sight of some cattle at a distance from Cremera, with an extensive plain lying between, they ran down to it (although few troops of the enemy were observed); and when incautious and in disorderly haste they had passed the ambuscade placed on either side of the very road; and when dispersed in different directions they began to carry off the cattle straying about, as is usual when they are frightened, the Veientians rise up suddenly from their ambuscade, and the enemy were in front and on every side. At first the shout that was raised terrified them; then weapons assailed them from every side; and, the Etrurians closing, they also were compelled, hemmed in as they now were by a compact body of soldiers, to contract their own circle within a narrower compass; which circumstance rendered striking both their own paucity of numbers, and the superior numbers of the enemy, the ranks being crowded in a narrow space. Then the plan of fighting, which they had directed equally against every part, being now relinquished, they all incline their forces towards one point; in that direction straining every effort both with their bodies and arms, they forced a passage by forming a wedge. The way led to a hill of moderate acclivity; here they first halted: presently, as soon as the higher ground afforded them time to gain breath, and to recover from so great a panic, they repulsed them as they advanced up; and the small band by the advantage of the ground was gaining the victory, had not a party of the Veientians, sent round the ridge of the hill, made their way to the summit; thus again the enemy obtained the higher ground; all the Fabii were killed to a man, and the fort was taken: it is agreed on all hands that the three hundred and six were cut off; that one[98] only, who nearly attained the age of puberty, was left as a stock for the Fabian race; and that he was destined to prove the greatest support in the dangerous emergencies of the Roman people both at home and in war.

At the time when this disaster was received, C. Horatius and T. Menenius were consuls. Menenius was immediately sent against the Etrurians, elated with victory. Then too an unsuccessful battle was fought, and the enemy took possession of the Janiculum: and the city would have been besieged, scarcity of provisions bearing hard upon them in addition to the war, (for the Etrurians had passed the Tiber,) had not the consul Horatius been recalled from the Volsci; and so closely did that war approach the very walls, that the first battle was fought near the temple of Hope with doubtful success, and a second time at the Colline gate. There, although the Romans had the advantage in a slight degree only, yet that contest rendered the soldiers better for future battles by restoring to them their former courage. Aulus

---

[98] This statement is rejected by Niebuhr entirely.

Virginius and Sp. Servilius are created consuls. After the defeat sustained in the last battle, the Veientians declined an engagement. Ravages were committed, and they made incursions in every direction on the Roman territory from the Janiculum as if from a fortress; no where were the cattle or the husbandmen safe. They were afterwards entrapped by the same stratagem as that by which they had entrapped the Fabii: having pursued some cattle that had been driven on designedly for the purpose of decoying them, they fell into an ambuscade; in proportion as they were more numerous, the slaughter was greater. The violent resentment resulting from this disaster was the cause and commencement of one still greater: for having crossed the Tiber by night, they attempted to assault the camp of the consul Servilius; being repulsed from thence with great slaughter, they with difficulty made good their retreat into the Janiculum. The consul himself also crosses the Tiber, fortifies his camp at the foot of the Janiculum: at break of day on the following morning, both from being somewhat elated by the success of the battle of the day before, more however because the scarcity of corn forced him into measures which, though dangerous, (he adopted) because they were more expeditious, he rashly marched his army up the steep of the Janiculum to the camp of the enemy, and being repulsed from thence with more disgrace than he had repulsed them on the preceding day, he was saved, both himself and his army, by the intervention of his colleague. The Etrurians (hemmed in) between the two armies, when they presented their rear to the one and the other by turns, were entirely cut off. Thus the Veientian war was crushed by a fortunate act of temerity.

Together with the peace, provisions returned to the city in greater abundance, both by reason of corn having been brought in from Campania, and, as soon as the fear felt by each of future famine left them, that corn being brought forward which had been hoarded up. Then their minds once more became licentious from their present abundance and ease, and their former subjects of complaint, now that there were none abroad, they sought for at home; the tribunes began to excite the commons by their poison, the agrarian law: they roused them against the senators who opposed it, and not only against them as a body, but also against particular individuals. Q. Considius and T. Genucius, the proposers of the agrarian law, appoint a day of trial for T. Menenius: the loss of the fort of Cremera, whilst the consul had his standing camp at no great distance from thence, was the charge against him. They crushed him, though both the senators had exerted themselves in his behalf with no less earnestness than in behalf of Coriolanus, and the popularity of his father Agrippa was not yet forgotten. The tribunes, however, went no further than a fine: though they had arraigned him for a capital offence, they imposed on him, when found guilty, a fine of two thousand *asses*. This proved fatal.

They say that he could not submit to the disgrace, and to the anguish of mind (occasioned by it): that, in consequence, he was taken off by disease. Another senator, Sp. Servilius, being soon after arraigned, as soon as he went out of office, a day of trial having been appointed for him by the tribunes, L. Cædicius and T. Statius, at the very commencement of the year, in the consulship of C. Nautius and P. Valerius, did not, like Menenius, meet the attacks of the tribunes with supplications from himself and the patricians, but with firm reliance on his own integrity, and his personal influence. The battle with the Etrurians at the Janiculum was the charge against him also: but being a man of an intrepid spirit, as he had formerly acted in the case of public peril, so now in that which was personal to himself, he dispelled the danger by boldly facing it, by confuting not only the tribunes but the commons also, by a bold speech, and upbraiding them with the condemnation and death of T. Menenius, by the good offices of whose father the commons were formerly re-established, and were now in possession of those laws and those magistrates, by means of which they then exercised their insolence; his colleague Virginius also, who was brought forward as a witness, aided him by assigning to him a share of his own deserts; the condemnation of Menenius however was of greater service to him (so much had they changed their minds).

The contests at home were now concluded. A Veientian war broke out, with whom the Sabines had united their forces. The consul P. Valerius, after auxiliaries were sent for from the Latins and Hernicians, being despatched to Veii with an army, immediately attacks the Sabine camp, which had been pitched before the walls of their allies: and occasioned such great consternation, that while, dispersed in different directions, they sally forth to repel the assault of the enemy, the gate which the Romans first attacked was taken; then within the rampart there was rather a carnage than a battle. From the camp the alarm spreads into the city; the Veientians run to arms in as great a panic as if Veii had been taken: some come up to the support of the Sabines, others fall upon the Romans, who had directed all their force against the camp. For a little while they were disconcerted and thrown into confusion; then they too forming two fronts make a stand: and the cavalry, being commanded by the consul to charge, routs the Etrurians and puts them to flight; and in the same hour two armies and two of the most influential and powerful of the neighbouring states were vanquished. Whilst these transactions are going on at Veii, the Volsci and Æqui had pitched their camp in the Latin territory, and laid waste their frontiers. The Latins, by their own exertions, being joined by the Hernicians, without either a Roman general or Roman auxiliaries, stripped them of their camp. Besides recovering their own effects, they obtained immense booty. The consul C. Nautius, however, was sent against the Volsci from Rome. The custom, I suppose, was not pleasing for allies to carry on wars with their own forces and under their own direction without a Roman general and troops. There was no kind of injury or indignity that was not practised against the Volsci; nor could they be prevailed on however to come to an engagement in the field.

Lucius Furius and Caius Manlius were the next consuls. The Veientians fell to Manlius as his province. War however did not take place: a truce for forty years was granted them at their request, corn and pay for the soldiers being demanded of them. Disturbance at home immediately succeeds to peace abroad: the commons were goaded by the tribunes with the excitement of the agrarian law. The consuls, nothing intimidated by the condemnation of Menenius, nor by the danger of Servilius, resist with their utmost might; Cn. Genucius, a tribune of the people, arraigned the consuls on their going out of office. Lucius Æmilius and Opiter Virginius enter on the consulate. Instead of Virginius I find Vopiscus Julius consul in some annals. In this year (whatever consuls it had) Furius and Manlius, being summoned to trial before the people, go about in suppliant garb not more to the commons than to the younger patricians; they advise, they caution them "to keep themselves from honours and the administration of public affairs, and that they would consider the consular fasces, the prætexta and curule chair, as nothing else than the decorations of a funeral; that when covered with these fine insignia, as with fillets, they were doomed to death. But if the charms of the consulate were so great, they should rest satisfied that the consulate was held in captivity and crushed by the tribunitian power; that every thing was to be done at the nod and command of the tribune by the consul, as if he were a tribune's beadle. If he stir, if he have reference to the patricians, if he should think for a moment that there existed any other party in the state but the commons, let him place before his eyes the banishment of Caius Marcius, the condemnation and death of Menenius." Fired by these discourses, the patricians from that time held their consultations not in public, but in private, and withdrawn from the knowledge of the many; where when this one point was agreed on, that the accused must be rescued whether by just or unjust means, every proposition that was most desperate was most approved; nor was an actor wanted for any deed however daring. Accordingly on the day of trial, when the people stood in the forum in anxious expectation, they at first began to feel surprised that the tribune did not come down; then when the delay was now becoming more suspicious, they considered that he was deterred by the nobles, and they complained that the public cause was abandoned and betrayed. At length those who had been waiting before the gate of the tribune's residence, bring word that he was found dead in his house. As soon as rumour spread this through the whole assembly, just as an army disperses on the fall of its general, so did they separate in different directions. The principal panic seized the tribunes, now warned by their colleague's death what little aid the devoting laws afforded them. Nor did the patricians bear their joy with sufficient moderation; and so far was any of them from feeling compunction at the guilty act, that even those who were innocent wished to be considered to have perpetrated it, and it was openly declared that the tribunitian power should be subdued by chastisement.

Immediately after this victory of a most ruinous precedent a levy is proclaimed; and the tribunes being now overawed, the consuls accomplish the matter without any opposition. Then indeed the commons became enraged more on account of the silence of the tribunes than the command of the consuls: and they said "there was an end of their liberty; that they were come back again to the old condition of things; that the tribunitian power had died along with Genucius and was buried with him; that other means must be devised and practised, by which to resist the patricians; and that the only method for that was that the people should defend themselves, since they now had no other aid. That four-and-twenty lictors waited on the consuls; and that these very individuals were from among the commons; that nothing could be more despicable, nor weaker, if there were only persons who could despise them; that each person magnified those things and made them objects of terror to himself." When they had excited each other by these discourses, a lictor was despatched by the consuls to Volero Publilius, a man belonging to the commons, because he stated, that having been a centurion he ought not to be made a common soldier. Volero appeals to the tribunes. When one came to his assistance, the consuls order the man to be stripped and the rods to be got ready. "I appeal to the people," says Volero, "since tribunes had rather see a Roman citizen scourged before their eyes, than themselves be butchered by you in their bed." The more vehemently he cried out, the more violently did the lictor tear off his clothes and strip him. Then Volero, being both himself of great bodily strength, and being aided by his partisans, having repulsed the lictor, when the shouts of those indignant in his behalf became very intense, betook himself into the thickest part of the crowd, crying out, "I appeal, and implore the protection of the commons; assist me, fellow citizens; assist me, fellow soldiers; there is no use in waiting for the tribunes, who themselves stand in need of your aid." The men, being much excited, prepare as it were for battle; and it became manifest that there was urgent danger, that nothing would be held sacred by any one, that there would no longer exist any public or private right. When the consuls faced this so violent storm, they soon experienced that majesty without strength had but little security; the lictors being maltreated, the fasces broken, they are driven from the forum into the senate-house, uncertain how far Volero would push his victory. After that, the disturbance subsiding, when they had ordered the senate to be convened, they complain of the outrages committed on themselves, of the violence of the people, the daring of Volero. Many violent measures having been proposed, the elder members prevailed, who recommended that the unthinking rashness of the commons should not be met by the passionate resentment of the patricians.

The commons having espoused the interest of Volero, with great warmth choose him, at the next election, tribune of the people for that year, which had Lucius Pinarius and Publius Furius for consuls; and, contrary to the opinion of all men, who thought that he would let loose his tribuneship in harassing the consuls of the preceding year, postponing private resentment to the public interest, without assailing the consuls even by a single word, he proposed a law to the people that plebeian magistrates should be elected at the comitia by tribes. A matter of no trifling moment was now being brought forward, under an aspect at first sight by no means alarming; but one which in reality deprived the patricians of all power to elect whatever tribunes they pleased by the suffrages of their clients. The patricians used all their energies in resisting this proposition, which was most pleasing to the commons; and though none of the college could be induced by the influence either of the consuls or of the chief members of the senate to enter a protest against it, the only means of resistance which now existed; yet the matter, important as it was by its own weight, is spun out by contention till the following year. The commons re-elect Volero as tribune. The senators, considering that the question would be carried to the very extreme of a struggle, elect to the consulate Appius Claudius, the son of Appius, who was both hated by and hated the commons, ever since the contests between them and his father. Titus Quintius is assigned to him as his colleague. In the very commencement of the year no other question took precedence of that regarding the law. But though Volero was the inventor of it, his colleague, Lætorius, was both a more recent abettor of it, as well as a more energetic one. Whilst Volero confined himself to the subject of the law, avoiding all abuse of the consuls, he commenced with accusing Appius and his family, as having ever been most overbearing and cruel towards the Roman commons, contending that he had been elected by the senators, not as consul, but as executioner, to harass and torture the people; his rude tongue, he being a military man, was not sufficient to express the freedom of his sentiments. Language therefore failing him, he says, "Romans, since I do not speak with as much readiness as I make good what I have spoken, attend here to-morrow. I will either die here before your eyes, or will carry the law." On the following day the tribunes take possession of the temple; the consuls and the nobility take their places in the assembly to obstruct the law. Lætorius orders all persons to be removed, except those going to vote; the young nobles kept their places, paying no regard to the officer; then Lætorius orders some of them to be seized. The consul Appius insisted "that the tribune had no jurisdiction over any one except a plebeian; for that he was not a magistrate of the people in general, but only of the commons; for that even he himself could not, according to the usage of their ancestors, by virtue of his authority remove any person; because the words run thus, *if ye think proper, depart, Romans.*" He was able to disconcert Lætorius by arguing fluently and contemptuously concerning the right. The tribune therefore, burning with rage, sends his beadle to the consul; the consul sends his lictor to the tribune, exclaiming that he was a private individual, without power and without magistracy; and the tribune would have been roughly treated, had not both the entire assembly risen up with great warmth in behalf of the tribune against the consul, and a rush of persons belonging to the multitude, which was now much excited, taken place from the entire city into the forum. Appius, however, withstood so great a storm with obstinacy, and the contest would have ended in a battle, not without blood, had not Quintius, the other consul, after giving it in charge to the men of consular dignity to remove his colleague from the forum by force, if they could not do it otherwise, himself assuaged the enraged people by entreaties, and implored the tribunes to dismiss the assembly. "That they should give their passion time to cool; that delay would not deprive them of their power, but would add prudence to strength; and that the senators would be under the control of the people, and the consul under that of the senators."

With difficulty the people were pacified by Quintius: with much more difficulty was the other consul by the patricians. The assembly of the people being at length dismissed, the consuls convene the senate; where, though fear and resentment by turns had produced a diversity of opinions, the more they were recalled, after the lapse of time, from violence to reflection, the more averse did they become to a continuance of the dispute, so that they returned thanks to Quintius, because by his exertions the disturbance had been quieted. Appius is requested "to consent that the consular dignity should be merely so great as it could be in a peaceably conducted state; that as long as the tribune and consuls were drawing all power, each to his own side, no strength was left between; that the object aimed at was in whose hands the commonwealth should be, distracted and torn as it was, rather than that it should be safe." Appius, on the contrary, called gods and men to witness that "the commonwealth was betrayed and abandoned through cowardice; that it was not the consul that was wanting to the senate, but the senate to the consul; that more oppressive laws were now being submitted to than were sanctioned on the sacred mount." Overcome however by the unanimous feeling of the senators, he desisted: the law is carried without opposition.

Then for the first time the tribunes were elected in the comitia by tribes. Piso said that three were added to the number, whereas there had been only two before. He names the tribunes also, Caius Sicinius, Lucius Numitorius, Marcus Duilius, Spurius Icilius, Lucius Mecilius. During the disturbance at Rome, a war with the Volscians and Æquans broke out; they had laid waste the lands, so that if any secession of the people should take place, they might find a refuge with them. The differences being afterwards settled, they removed their camp backwards. Appius Claudius was sent against the Volscians; the Æquans fell to Quintius as his province. The severity of Appius was the same in war as at home, being more unrestrained because he was free from tribunitian control. He hated the commons with more than his father's hatred: he had been defeated by them: when he was set up as the only consul to oppose the tribunitian influence, a law was passed, which former consuls obstructed with less effort, amid hopes of the senators by no means so great (as those formed of him). His resentment and indignation at this, excited his imperious temper to harass the army by the rigour of his command; nor could it (the army) however be subdued by any means; such a spirit of opposition had they imbibed. They executed every measure slowly, indolently, negligently, and with stubbornness: neither shame nor fear restrained them. If he wished the army to move on with expedition, they designedly went more slowly: if he came up to them to encourage them in their work, they all relaxed the energy which they before exerted of their own accord: when he was present they cast down their eyes, they silently cursed him as he passed by; so that his mind, invulnerable to plebeian hatred, was sometimes moved. All kind of harsh treatment being tried in vain, he no longer held any intercourse with the soldiers; he said the army was corrupted by the centurions; he sometimes gibingly called them tribunes of the people and Voleros.

None of these circumstances were unknown to the Volscians, and they pressed on with so much the more vigour, hoping that the Roman army would entertain the same spirit of opposition against Appius, which they had formerly entertained against the consul Fabius. But they were much more violent against Appius than against Fabius. For they were not only unwilling to conquer, like Fabius' army, but they wished to be conquered. When led out to the field, they made for their camp in an ignominious flight, nor did they stand their ground until they saw the Volscians advancing to their fortifications, and making dreadful havoc on the rear of their army. Then the obligation to fight was wrung from them, in order that the victorious enemy should be dislodged from their lines; yet it was sufficiently plain that the Roman soldiers were only unwilling that their camp should be taken; some of them gloried in their own defeat and disgrace. When the determined spirit of Appius, undaunted by these things, wished to exercise severity still further, and he summoned a meeting, the lieutenant-generals and tribunes flock around him, advising him "that he would not determine on venturing a trial of an authority, the entire strength of which lay in the acquiescence of those who were to obey. That the soldiers generally refused to come to the assembly, and that their clamours were heard in every direction demanding that the camp should be removed from the Volscian territory. That the victorious enemy were but a little time ago almost at the very gates and rampart; and that not merely a suspicion, but a manifest indication of a grievous disaster presented itself to their eyes." Yielding at length, (since they would gain nothing save a delay of punishment,) having prorogued the assembly, after he had given orders that their march should be proclaimed for the following day, he, at the first dawn, gave the signal for departure by sound of trumpet. When the army, having just got clear of the camp, were forming themselves, the Volscians, as being aroused by the same signal, fall upon those in the rear; from whom the alarm spreading to the van, confounded both the battalions and ranks with such consternation, that neither the generals' orders could be distinctly heard, nor the lines be drawn up, no one thinking of any thing but flight. In such confusion did they make their way through heaps of dead bodies and of arms, that the enemy ceased to pursue sooner than the Romans to fly. The soldiers being at length collected from their scattered rout, the consul, after he had in vain followed his men for the purpose of rallying them, pitched his camp in a peaceful part of the country; and an assembly being convened, after inveighing not without good reason against the army, as traitors to military discipline, deserters of their posts, frequently asking them, one by one, where were their standards, where their arms; he first beat with rods and then beheaded those soldiers who had thrown down their arms, the standard-bearers who had lost their standards, and moreover the centurions, and those with the double allowance, who had left their ranks. With respect to the rest of the multitude, every tenth man was drawn by lot for punishment.

In a contrary manner to this, the consul and soldiers in the country of the Æquans vied with each other in courtesy and acts of kindness: both Quintius was naturally milder in disposition, and the ill-fated severity of his colleague caused him to indulge more in his own good temper. This, such great cordiality between the general and his army, the Æquans did not venture to meet; they suffered the enemy to go through their lands committing devastations in every direction. Nor were depredations committed more extensively in that quarter in any preceding war. Praises were also added, in which the minds of soldiers find no less pleasure than in rewards. The army returned more reconciled both to their general, and also on account of the general to the patricians; stating that a parent was assigned to them, a master to the other army by the senate. The year now passed, with varied success in war, and furious dissensions at home and abroad, was rendered memorable chiefly by the elections by tribes; the matter was more important from the victory in the contest entered into, than from any real advantage; for there was more of dignity abstracted from the elections themselves by the exclusion of the patricians, than there was influence either added to the commons or taken from the patricians.

A more turbulent year[99] next followed, Lucius Valerius, Tiberius Æmilius being consuls, both by reason of the struggles between the different orders concerning the agrarian law, as well as on account of the trial of Appius Claudius; for whom, as a most active opposer of the law, and as one who supported the cause of the possessors of the public land, as if a third consul, Marcus Duilius and Caius Sicinius appointed a day of trial.[100] Never before was an accused person so hateful to the commons brought to trial before the people; overwhelmed with their resentment on his own account,[101] and also on account of his father. The patricians too seldom made equal exertions in behalf of any one: "that the champion of the senate, and the assertor of their dignity, opposed to all the storms of the tribunes and commons, was exposed to the resentment of the commons, merely for having exceeded bounds in the contest." Appius Claudius himself was the only one of the patricians who made light both of the tribunes and commons and his own trial. Neither the threats of the commons, nor the entreaties of the senate, could ever persuade him not only to change his garb, or address persons as a suppliant, but not even so far as to soften or relax any thing from the usual asperity of his style, when his cause was to be pleaded before the people. The expression of his countenance was the same; the same stubbornness in his looks, the same spirit of pride in his language; so that a great part of the commons felt no less awe of Appius when arraigned, than they had felt of him when consul. He pleaded his cause once, and with the same spirit of an accuser which he had been accustomed to adopt on all occasions: and he so far astounded both the tribunes and the commons by his intrepidity, that, of their own accord, they postponed the day of trial; then they allowed the matter to be protracted. Nor was the time now very distant; before, however, the appointed day came, he dies of some disease; and when the tribunes of the people endeavoured to impede his funeral panegyric,[102] the

---

[99] Niebuhr, ii. p. 231, thinks that it was in this year the Icilian law was passed, according to which, any person interrupting the proceedings of the tribunes, rendered himself liable to capital punishment.—*Twiss.*

[100] Several charges were brought against Appius, according to Dion. ix. 54, who also states that he did not die of any disease, but that he laid violent hands on himself.—*Ruperti.*

[101] The original has *plenus suarum—irarum,*—that is, the anger not of Appius against the commons, but of the commons against him.

[102] Conf. Nieb. ii. n. 754. It may be well to mention that Niebuhr considered that this account regarding the death of Appius was all fictitious. The Greek writers, scil. Dion. ix. 54, Zonar. vii. 17, state that he laid violent hands on himself.

commons would not allow that the last day of so great a man should be defrauded of the usual honours; and they listened to the panegyric of him when dead with as patient ears, as they had listened to the charges brought against him when living, and attended his funeral in vast numbers.

In the same year the consul Valerius, having marched an army against the Æquans, when he could not entice the enemy to an engagement, set about assaulting their camp. A violent storm sent down from heaven with thunder and hail prevented him. Then, on a signal for a retreat being given, their surprise was excited by the return of such fair weather, that they felt a scruple a second time to attack a camp which was defended as it were by some divine power; all the rage of war was turned on the devastation of the land. The other consul, Æmilius, conducted the war against the Sabines. There also, because the enemy confined themselves within their walls, the lands were laid waste. Then, by the burning not only of the country-houses, but of the villages also, which were thickly inhabited, the Sabines being aroused, after they met the depredators, on retreating from an engagement left undecided, on the following day removed their camp into a safer situation. This seemed a sufficient reason to the consul why he should leave the enemy as conquered, departing thence the war being still unfinished.

During these wars, whilst dissensions still continued at home, Titus Numicius Priscus, Aulus Virginius, were elected consuls. The commons appeared determined no longer to brook a delay of the agrarian law, and extreme violence was on the eve of being resorted to, when it was ascertained from the burning of the country-houses and the flight of the peasants that the Volscians were at hand: this circumstance checked the sedition that was now ripe and almost breaking out. The consuls, having been instantly forced to the war by the senate,[103] after leading forth the youth from the city, rendered the rest of the commons more quiet. And the enemy indeed, having done nothing else except alarming the Romans by groundless fear, depart with great precipitation. Numicius marched to Antium against the Volscians, Virginius against the Æquans. Here a signal overthrow being well nigh received from an ambuscade, the bravery of the soldiers restored (the Roman) superiority, which had been endangered through the carelessness of the consul. The general conducted affairs better against the Volscians. The enemy were routed in the first engagement, and forced to fly into the city of Antium, a very wealthy place considering those times; the consul, not venturing to attack it, took from the people

---

[103] In the original we read *coacti extemplo ab senatu*. Niebuhr considers this reading to be corrupt, and is satisfied that the correct reading is *coacto extemplo senatu*. See ii. n. 555.

of Antium another town, Ceno, which was by no means so wealthy. Whilst the Æquans and Volscians engage the attention of the Roman armies, the Sabines advanced in their devastations even to the gates of the city: then they themselves, a few days after, received from the two armies heavier losses than they had occasioned, the two consuls having entered their territories under exasperated feelings.

Towards the close of the year there was some peace, but, as frequently at other times, disturbed by contests between the patricians and commons. The exasperated commons refused to attend the consular elections: Titus Quintius, Quintus Servilius, were elected consuls by the patricians and their dependents: the consuls have a year similar to the preceding, the commencement embroiled, and afterwards tranquil by external war. The Sabines marching across the plains of Crustuminum with great rapidity, after carrying fire and sword along the banks of the Anio, being repulsed when they had come up nearly to the Colline gate and the walls, drove off however great booty of men and cattle: the consul Servilius, having pursued them with a determined army, was unable to come up with the main body itself on the campaign country; he carried his devastation however so extensively, that he left nothing unmolested by war, and returned after obtaining plunder much exceeding that carried off by the enemy. The public interest was supported extremely well against the Volscians also by the exertions as well of the general as of the soldiers. First they fought a pitched battle, on equal ground, with great slaughter and much bloodshed on both sides: and the Romans, because the fewness of their numbers was more likely to make the loss felt, would have given way, had not the consul, by a well-timed fiction, re-animated the army, crying out that the enemy were flying on the other wing; making a charge, they, by supposing that they were victorious, became so. The consul, fearing lest by pressing too far he might renew the contest, gave the signal for a retreat. A few days intervened; rest being taken on both sides as if by a tacit suspension of arms; during these days a vast number of persons from all the states of the Volscians and Æquans came to the camp, certain that the Romans would depart during the night, if they should perceive them. Accordingly about the third watch they come to attack the camp. Quintius having allayed the confusion which the sudden panic had occasioned, after ordering the soldiers to remain quiet in their tents, leads out a cohort of the Hernicians for an advance guard: the trumpeters and horneteers he mounts on horseback, and commands them to sound their trumpets before the rampart, and to keep the enemy in suspense till daylight: during the rest of the night every thing was so quiet in the camp, that the Romans had even the advantage of sleep. The sight of the armed infantry, whom they both considered to be more numerous than they were, and to be Romans, the bustle and neighing of the horses, which became restless, both from the strange riders placed on them, and moreover from the sound of the trumpets frightening them, kept the Volscians intently awaiting an attack of the enemy.

When day dawned, the Romans, invigorated and refreshed with sleep, on being marched out to battle, at the first onset overpowered the Volscians, wearied from standing and want of rest; though the enemy rather retired than were routed, because in the rear there were hills to which there was a secure retreat, the ranks behind the first line being unbroken. The consul, when they came to the uneven ground, halts his army; the soldiers were kept back with difficulty; they cried out and demanded to be allowed to pursue the enemy now discomfited. The cavalry, crowding around the general, proceed more violently: they cry out that they would proceed before the first line. Whilst the consul hesitates, relying on the valour of his men, yet having little confidence in the place, they all cry out that they would proceed; and execution followed the shout. Fixing their spears in the ground, in order that they may be lighter to ascend the steeps, they run upwards. The Volscians, having discharged their missile weapons at the first onset, fling the stones lying at their feet on them as they advanced upwards, and having thrown them into confusion by incessant blows, they drove them from the higher ground: thus the left wing of the Romans was nearly overborne, had not the consul dispelled their fear by exciting a sense of shame as they were just retreating, chiding at the same time their temerity and their cowardice. At first they stood their ground with determined firmness; then, according as their strength carried them against those in possession of the ground, they venture to advance themselves; and by renewing the shout they encourage the whole body to move on; then again making a new effort, they force their way up and surmount the disadvantage of the ground. They were on the point of gaining the summit of the eminence, when the enemy turned their backs, and the pursued and pursuers with precipitate speed rushed into the camp almost in a body. In this consternation the camp is taken; such of the Volscians as were able to make their escape, take the road to Antium. The Roman army also was led to Antium; after being invested for a few days it surrenders without any additional force of the besiegers,[104] but because their spirits had sunk ever since the unsuccessful battle and the loss of their camp.

---

[104] *Additional force of the*, &c. Crovier understands this to signify that the Romans did not employ a greater force for besieging Antium, than they had employed the preceding year, and which at that time seemed insufficient for the purpose. Others understand the words to signify that they surrendered without waiting for the Romans to make any additional efforts to take the town.

## Book III.

*Disturbances about the agrarian laws. The Capitol surprised by
exiles and slaves. Quintius Cincinnatus called from the cultivation of
his farm in the country, made dictator, and appointed to conduct the
war against the Æquans. He conquers the enemy, and makes them pass
under the yoke. The number of the tribunes increased to ten.
Decemvirs, appointed for the purpose of digesting and publishing a
body of laws. These having promulgated a code of laws contained in
ten tables, obtain a continuation of their authority for another year,
during which they add two more to the former ten tables. Refusing to
resign their office, they retain it a third year. Their conduct at first
equitable and just; afterwards arbitrary and tyrannical. The commons,
in consequence of the base attempt of Appius Claudius, one of them, to
debauch the daughter of Virginius, seize on the Aventine mount, and
oblige them to resign. Appius and Oppius, two of the most obnoxious,
are thrown into prison, where they put an end to their own lives; the
rest are driven into exile. War with the Sabines, Volscians, and
Æquans.—Unfair decision of the Roman people, who being chosen
arbitrators between the people of Ardea and Aricia concerning some
disputed lands, adjudge them to themselves.*

After the taking of Antium, Titus Æmilius and Quintus Fabius are
elected consuls. This was the Fabius Quintus who alone had survived
the family cut off at Cremera. Already, in his former consulate,
Æmilius had been an adviser of giving land to the people. Accordingly
in his second consulate also both the abettors of the agrarian law had
raised themselves to the hope of carrying the measure, and the tribunes,
supposing that a matter frequently attempted in opposition to both
consuls might be obtained with the assistance at least of one consul,
take it up, and the consul remained stedfast in his sentiments. The
possessors and a considerable part of the patricians complaining that a
person at the head of the state was recommending himself by his
tribunitial proceedings, and that he was making himself popular by
giving away other persons' property, had transferred the odium of the
entire affair from the tribunes to the consul. A violent contest was at
hand, had not Fabius set the matter straight, by an expedient
disagreeable to neither party, "that under the conduct and auspices of
Titus Quintius, there was a considerable tract of land taken the
preceding year from the Volscians; that a colony might be sent to
Antium, a neighbouring, convenient, and maritime city; that the
commons might come in for lands without any complaints of the
present occupiers, that the state might remain in quiet." This
proposition was accepted. He appoints as triumvirs for distributing the

land, Titus Quintius, Aulus Virginius, and Publius Furius: those who wished to obtain land were ordered to give in their names. The gratification of their aim begat disgust, as usually happens; so few gave in their names that Volscian colonists were added to fill up the number: the rest of the people preferred clamouring for land in Rome, rather than receive it elsewhere. The Æquans sued for peace from Quintus Fabius, (he was sent thither with an army,) and they themselves broke it by a sudden incursion into the Latin territory.

In the following year Quintus Servilius, (for he was consul with Spurius Posthumius,) being sent against the Æquans, fixed his camp in the Latin territory: inaction necessarily kept the army within the camp, involved as they were in a distemper. The war was protracted to the third year, Quintus Fabius and Titus Quintius being consuls. To Fabius, because he, as conqueror, had granted[105] peace to the Æquans, that province was assigned by an extraordinary commission: who, setting out with certain hope that the fame of his name would reduce the Æquans to submission, sent ambassadors to the council of the nation, and ordered them to say "that Quintus Fabius, the consul, stated that he had brought peace to Rome from the Æquans, that from Rome he now brought war to the Æquans, that same right hand being armed, which he had formerly given to them in amity; that the gods were now witnesses, and would presently be avengers of those by whose perfidy and perjury that was brought to pass. That he, however, be matters as they might, would even now prefer that the Æquans should repent of their own accord than be subject to the vengeance of an enemy. If they repent, that there would be a safe retreat in that clemency already experienced; but if they still delighted in perjury, they would wage war with the angry gods rather than with enemies." This statement had so little effect on any of them, that the ambassadors were near being ill-treated, and an army was sent to Algidum against the Romans. When these tidings were brought to Rome, the indignity of the affair, rather than the danger, called out the other consul from the city; thus two consular armies advanced against the enemy in order of battle, so that they might at once engage. But as it so happened that much of the day did not now remain, a person from the advanced guard of the enemy cries out, "This is making a display of war, Romans, not waging it; you draw up your army in line of battle, when night is at hand; we require a greater length of day-light for the contest which is to come on. To-morrow by sun-rise return to the field: you shall have an opportunity of fighting, never fear." The soldiers, stung by these threats, are marched back into the camp till the following day; thinking that the approaching night was tedious, which would cause delay to the contest. Then indeed

---

[105] *Dederat.* The *oratio obliqua* would require *dederit* here, but such instances of the indicative being used for the subjunctive are by no means infrequent.

they refresh their bodies with food and sleep: on the following day, when it was light, the Roman army took their post considerably sooner. At length the Æquans also came forward. The battle was obstinate on both sides, because both the Romans fought under the influence of resentment and hatred; and a consciousness of danger brought on by misconduct, and despair of obtaining future confidence afterwards, obliged the Æquans to exert and have recourse to the most desperate efforts. The Æquans however did not withstand the Roman troops, and when on being beaten they had betaken themselves to their own territories, the outrageous multitude, with dispositions not at all more disposed to peace, began to chide their leaders: "that their interest was committed to the hazard of a pitched battle, in which mode of fighting the Romans were superior. That the Æquans were better fitted for depredations and incursions, and that several parties acting in different directions conducted wars more successfully than the unwieldy mass of one single army."

Having left therefore a guard on the camp, they marched out and attacked the Roman frontiers with such fury, as to carry terror even to the city: the unexpected nature of the thing also caused more alarm, because nothing could be less apprehended, than that an enemy, vanquished and almost besieged in their camp, should entertain a thought of depredation: and the peasants, in a panic pouring in at the gates, cried out, that it was not mere plundering, nor small parties of depredators, but, exaggerating every thing through groundless fear, that whole armies and legions of the enemy were advancing, and that they were pushing forward to the city determined for an assault. Those who were nearest (the gates) carried to others the accounts heard from these, uncertain as they were, and therefore the more groundless; and the hurry and confused clamour of those calling to arms bore no distant resemblance to the panic of a city taken by storm. It so happened that the consul Quintius had returned to Rome from Algidum; this was some relief for their terror; and the tumult being calmed, and after chiding them for being in dread of a vanquished enemy, he posted a guard on the gates. Then having convened the senate, when he set out to defend the frontiers, a suspension[106] of civil business having been proclaimed by a decree of the senate, leaving Quintus Servilius behind as prefect of the city, he found no enemy in the country. Matters were conducted with distinguished success by the other consul; who having attacked the enemy, wherever he knew that they were to come, laden with booty, and proceeding therefore with their army the more encumbered, made their depredation prove fatal to them. Few of the enemy escaped from the ambuscade; all the booty was recovered; thus the return of the consul Quintius to the city put a termination to the

---

[106] *Justitium*—a jure sistendo.

justitium, which lasted only four days. A census was then held, and the lustrum was closed by Quintius: the number of citizens rated are said to have been one hundred and twenty-four thousand two hundred and fourteen, besides orphans of both sexes. Nothing memorable occurred afterwards among the Æquans; they betook themselves into their towns, suffering their possessions to be consumed by fire and to be devastated. The consul, after he had repeatedly carried depredation through the entire country of the enemy, returned to Rome with great glory and booty.

Then Aulus Posthumius Albus and Spurius Furius Fusus were consuls. Furii some writers have written Fusii; this I mention, lest any one may imagine that the change, which is only in the names, may be in the persons themselves. There was no doubt but that one of the consuls would commence hostilities against the Æquans. The Æquans accordingly sought aid from the Volscians of Ecetra; which being granted readily, (so keenly did these states vie in inveterate hatred against the Romans,) preparations for war were made with the utmost vigour. The Hernicians came to the knowledge of it, and warned the Romans that the Ecetrans had revolted to the Æquans; the colony of Antium also was suspected, because when the town was taken, a great number of the inhabitants had fled thence for refuge to the Æquans: and these proved the bravest soldiers during the war with the Æquans. Afterwards the Æquans being driven into the towns, this rabble withdrawing privately, when they returned to Antium, seduced from the Romans the colonists who were already disposed to treachery of their own accord. The matter not being yet ripe, when it was announced to the senate that a defection was intended, the consuls were charged to inquire into the business by summoning to Rome the leading men of the colony. When those persons attended without reluctance, being conducted to the senate by the consuls, they so answered to the questions put to them, that they were dismissed more suspected than they had come. Upon this war was considered as inevitable. Spurius Fusius, one of the consuls to whom that province had fallen, having marched against the Æquans, found the enemy committing depredations in the country of the Hernicians; and being ignorant of their numbers, because they had never been seen all together, he rashly hazarded an engagement with an army not a match for their forces. Being beaten from his ground at the first onset, he betook himself to his camp: nor was that an end of the danger: for both on the next night and the following day, his camp was beset and assaulted with such vigour, that not even a messenger could be sent from thence to Rome. The Hernicians brought an account both that a defeat had taken place, and that the army was besieged: and they struck such terror into the senate, that a charge was given to the other consul Posthumius, that he should "take care that the commonwealth sustained no injury,"[107] which form of a decree has ever been deemed to be one of extreme exigency. It seemed most advisable that the consul himself should remain at Rome to enlist all who were able to bear arms: that Titus Quintius should be sent as pro-consul[108] to the relief of the camp with the army of the allies: to complete that army the Latins and Hernicians, and the colony of Antium, were ordered to supply Quintius with subitary soldiers (so they then called auxiliaries raised for sudden emergencies).

During those days many movements and many attempts were made on either side, because the enemy, having the advantage in numbers, attempted to weaken the Roman strength by dividing it into many parts, as not being likely to suffice for all points of attack. At the same time the camp was besieged, at the same time a part of the army was sent to devastate the Roman territory, and to attempt the city itself, if fortune should favour. Lucius Valerius was left to guard the city: the consul Postumius was sent to repel the attacks on the frontiers. There was no abatement in any part either in vigilance or activity; watches in the city, out-posts before the gates, and guards stationed along the walls: and a justitium was observed for several days (a thing which was necessary in such general confusion). In the mean time the consul Furius, after he had at first passively endured the siege in his camp, burst forth from the Decuman gate on the enemy when off their guard; and though he might have pursued them, he stopped through fear, lest an attack should be made on the camp from the other side. The lieutenant-general Furius (he was the consul's brother) was carried away too far by his ardour; nor did he, from his eagerness to pursue, observe his own party returning, nor the attack of the enemy on his rear: thus being shut out, after repeatedly making many unavailing efforts to force his way to the camp, he fell, fighting bravely. And the consul, turning about to renew the fight, on hearing the account that his brother was surrounded, rushing into the thick of the fight rather rashly than with sufficient caution, received a wound, and was with difficulty rescued by those around him. This both damped the courage of his own men, and rendered the enemy more daring; who, being encouraged by the death of the lieutenant-general, and by the consul's wound, could not afterwards be withstood by any force, so as to prevent the Romans from being driven within their camp and again submitting to a siege, as being a match for them neither in hopes nor in strength; and every thing would have been endangered, had not T. Quintius come to their relief with foreign troops from the Latin and Hernician army. He attacked the Æquans on their rear whilst intent on the Roman camp, and insultingly

---

[107] According to Stroth, this is the first instance we have of a decree of the senate arming the consul with almost dictatorial power.

[108] *Pro-consul*:—the first mention of a pro-consul in Livy.

displaying the head of the lieutenant-general, and, a sally being made at the same time from the camp on a signal given at a distance by him, he surrounded a great number of the enemy. Of the Æquans on the Roman territory the slaughter was less, their dispersion was more complete. On these as they straggled in different directions, and were driving plunder before them, Postumius made an attack in several places, where he had posted convenient detachments; these straying about and pursuing their flight in great disorder, fell in with the victorious Quintius as he was returning with the wounded consul. Then did the consular army by their distinguished bravery take ample vengeance for the consul's wound, and for the death of the lieutenant-general and the cohorts; heavy losses were both inflicted and received on both sides during those days. In a matter of such antiquity it is difficult to state with certainty the exact number of those who fought or fell: Antias Valerius, however, ventures to sum them up; that in the Hernician territory there fell five thousand three hundred Romans; that of the predatory parties of the Æquans, who strayed through the Roman frontiers for the purpose of plundering, two thousand four hundred were slain by the consul Postumius; that the rest of the body that were driving booty before them, and which fell in with Quintius, by no means got off with so light a loss: that of these four thousand, and by way of stating the number exactly, two hundred and thirty, were slain. After this they returned to Rome; the order for the justitium was discharged. The sky seemed to be all on fire; and other prodigies either actually presented themselves to their sight, or exhibited imaginary appearances to their affrighted minds. To avert these terrors, a solemn festival of three days was proclaimed, during which, all the temples were filled with a crowd of men and women, earnestly imploring the protection of the gods. After this the Latin and Hernician cohorts were sent back to their respective homes, thanks having been returned to them for their spirited military services. The thousand soldiers from Antium were dismissed almost with disgrace, because they had come after the battle with assistance then too late.

The elections were then held: Lucius Æbutius and Publius Servilius being elected consuls, enter on their office on the calends of August, which was then considered as the commencement of the year.[109] This was a distressing time, and it so happened that the season was pestilential to the city and country, and not more to men than to cattle; and they increased the malignity of the distemper, by admitting[110] the cattle and the peasants into the city through dread of devastation. This collection of animals of every kind mixed together, distressed both the citizens by the unusual stench, and the peasants

---

[109] Of the year,—i.e. the consular year, not the civil one, which commenced in January.

[110] A similar measure was adopted at Athens. See Thucyd. ii. 52.

crowded together into their close apartments, with heat, want of sleep, and their attendance on each other, and contact itself propagated the disease. Whilst with difficulty sustaining these calamities, ambassadors from the Hernicians suddenly bring word that the Æquans and Volscians, having united their forces, had pitched their camp in their territory, that from thence they were depopulating their frontiers with an immense army. Besides that the thinness of the senate was a proof to the allies that the state was prostrated by the pestilence, they further received this melancholy answer: "That the Hernicians, with the Latins, must now defend their possessions by their own exertions. That the Roman city, through the sudden anger of the gods, was now depopulated by disease. If any respite from that calamity should come, that they would afford aid to their allies, as they had done the year before, and always on other occasions." The allies departed, carrying home, instead of the melancholy news (they had brought), news still more melancholy, as being persons who were now obliged to sustain by their own means a war, which they had sustained with difficulty when backed by the power of Rome. The enemy did not confine themselves any longer to the Hernician territory. They proceed thence with determined hostility into the Roman territories, which were already devastated without the injuries of war. Where, when there was no one to meet them, not even an unarmed person, and they passed through every place destitute not only of troops, but even of the cultivation of the husbandman, they reached as far as the third stone on the Gabinian road. Æbutius, the Roman consul, was dead; his colleague, Servilius, was dragging out life with slender hope of recovery; most of the leading men, the chief part of the patricians, all of the military age, were lying sick, so that strength was wanting not only for the expeditions, which, amid such an alarm the conjuncture required, but scarcely had they sufficient even for quietly mounting guard. The senators whose age and health permitted them, discharged personally the duty of sentinels. The going around[111] and attending to these was assigned to the ædiles of the people; on them devolved the chief administration of affairs and the majesty of the consular authority.

The commonwealth thus desolate, without a head, without strength, the guardian gods and good fortune of the city saved, which inspired the Volscians and Æquans with the disposition of banditti rather than of enemies; for so far was any hope not only of taking but even of approaching the walls of Rome[112] from taking possession of their minds, and so thoroughly did the sight of the houses in the distance, and the adjacent hills, divert their thoughts, (from such an attempt,) that, a murmur having arisen in every direction throughout the

---

[111] *Circuitio.* Stroth observes, that this is what we understand by 'the Round.'

[112] According to Dionysius, the Volsci attacked Rome on this occasion.

entire camp, "why they should waste time in indolence without booty in a wild and desert land, amid the putrid decay of cattle and of human beings, when they might repair to places uninjured by infection, the Tusculan territory abounding in wealth?" they suddenly tore up their standards, and by journeys across the country, they passed through the Lavican territory to the Tusculan hills; and to that quarter was the whole violence and storm of the war directed. In the mean time the Hernicians and Latins, influenced not only by compassion but by shame, if they neither gave opposition to the common enemy, when making for the city of Rome with a hostile army, nor afforded any aid to their allies when besieged, march to Rome with their forces united. Where, when they did not find the enemy, following their tracks as indicated by rumour, they meet them as they are coming down from the Tusculan territory into the Alban valley: there a battle was fought under circumstances by no means equal; and their fidelity proved by no means favourable to the allies for the present. The mortality at Rome by disease was not less than that of the allies by the sword (of the enemy); the only surviving consul dies; other eminent characters also died, Marcus Valerius, Titus Virginius Rutilus, the augurs; Servius Sulpicius, principal curio; and through persons of inferior note the virulence of the disease spread extensively: and the senate, destitute of human aid, directed the people's attention to the gods and to prayers; they were ordered to go to supplicate with their wives and children, and earnestly to implore the protection of heaven. Besides that their own sufferings obliged each to do so, when called on by public authority, they fill all the shrines; the prostrate matrons in every quarter sweeping the temples with their hair, beg for a remission of the divine displeasure, and a termination to the pestilence.

From this time, whether it was from the favour of the gods being obtained, or that the more unhealthy season of the year was now passed, the bodies of the people having shaken off disease, gradually began to be more healthy, and their attention being now directed to public concerns, when several interregna had expired, Publius Valerius Publicola, on the third day after he had entered on his office of interrex, causes Lucretius Tricipitinus, and Titus Veturius Geminus, (or Velusius,) to be elected consuls. They enter on their consulship on the third day of the Ides of August, the state being now sufficiently strong, not only to repel a hostile attack, but even to act itself on the offensive. Therefore when the Hernicians brought an account that the enemy had made an incursion into their frontiers, assistance was readily promised; two consular armies were enlisted. Veturius was sent against the Volscians to carry on an offensive war. Tricipitinus being appointed to protect the territory of the allies from devastation, proceeds no further than into the country of the Hernicians. Veturius routs and puts to flight the enemy in the first engagement. A party of plunderers which had marched over the Prænestine mountains, and from thence descended into the plains, escaped the notice of Lucretius, whilst he lay encamped amongst the Hernicians. These laid waste all the country around Præneste and Gabii: from the Gabinian territory they turn their course towards the heights of Tusculum; great alarm was excited in the city of Rome also, more from the suddenness of the affair, than that there was not sufficient strength to repel violence. Quintus Fabius had the command in the city;[113] he, by arming the young men and posting guards, rendered things secure and tranquil. The enemy therefore carrying off plunder from the adjacent places, not venturing to approach the city, when they were returning by a circuitous route, their caution being now more relaxed, in proportion as they removed to a greater distance from the enemy's city, fall in with the consul Lucretius, who had already explored their motions, drawn up in battle-array and determined on an engagement. Accordingly having attacked them with predetermined resolution whilst struck with sudden panic, though considerably fewer in numbers, they rout and put to flight their numerous army, and having driven them into the deep valleys, when an egress from thence was not easy, they surround them. There the Volscian nation was almost entirely cut off. In some histories I find that thirteen thousand four hundred and seventy fell in the field and in the pursuit, that one thousand two hundred and fifty were taken alive, that twenty-seven military standards were carried off; where, though there may have been some exaggeration in the number, there certainly was great slaughter. The victorious consul having obtained immense booty returned to the same standing camp. Then the consuls join their camps. The Volscians and Æquans also unite their shattered strength. This was the third battle on that year; the same good fortune gave them victory; the enemy being beaten, their camp was also taken.

Thus affairs at Rome returned to their former state; and successes abroad immediately excited commotions in the city. Caius Terentillus Arsa[114] was tribune of the people in that year: he, considering that an opportunity was afforded for tribunitian intrigues during the absence of the consuls, after railing against the arrogance of the patricians for several days before the people, inveighed chiefly against the consular authority, as being exorbitant and intolerable in a free state: "for that, in name only, it was less invidious, in reality almost more oppressive than that of kings. For that two masters had been adopted instead of one, with unbounded, unlimited power; who, themselves unrestrained and unbridled, directed all the terrors of the law, and all kinds of severity against the commons." Now, in order that this licentious power might

---

[113] As *præfectus urbis.*

[114] Niebuhr n. 24, 634, would have us read *Terentilius,* the Roman family names always, he says, ending in *ius.* He also thinks that for *Arsa,* we should read *Harsa.*

not continue perpetual, he would propose a law, that five persons be appointed to draw up laws regarding the consular power. That the consul should use that right which the people may give him over them; that they should not hold their own caprice and licentiousness as law. This law being published, when the patricians became afraid, lest, in the absence of the consuls, they should be subjected to the yoke, the senate is convened by Quintus Fabius, præfect of the city, who inveighed so vehemently against the bill and the author of it, that nothing was omitted of threats and intimidation, even though both the consuls in all their exasperation surrounded the tribune, "that he had lain in wait, and, watching his opportunity, he made an attack on the commonwealth. If the gods in their anger had given them any tribune like him on the preceding year, during the pestilence and war, he could not have been withstood. Both the consuls being dead, and the exhausted state lying enfeebled in universal confusion, that he would have proposed laws to abolish the consular government altogether from the state; that he would have headed the Volscians and Æquans to attack the city. What? if the consuls adopted any tyrannical or cruel proceedings against any of the citizens, was it not competent to him to appoint a day of trial for him; to arraign him before those very judges against any one of whom severity may have been exercised? That it was not the consular authority but the tribunitian power that he was rendering hateful and insupportable: which having been peaceable and reconciled to the patricians, was now about to be brought back anew to its former mischievous habits. Nor would he entreat him not to go on as he commenced. Of you, the other tribunes, says Fabius, we request, that you will first of all consider that that power was provided for the aid of individuals, not for the ruin of the community: that you were created tribunes of the commons, not enemies of the patricians. To us it is distressing, to you a source of odium, that the republic, now bereft of its chief magistrates, should be attacked; you will diminish not your rights, but the odium against you. Confer with your colleague, that he may postpone this business till the arrival of the consuls; even the Æquans and the Volscians, when our consuls were carried off by pestilence last year, did not press on us with a cruel and tyrannical war." The tribunes confer with Terentillus, and the bill being to all appearance deferred, but in reality abandoned, the consuls were immediately sent for.

Lucretius returned with immense spoil, and much greater glory; and this glory he increased on his arrival, by exposing all the booty in the Campus Martius, so that each person might, during three days, recognise his own and carry it away; the remainder was sold, for which no owners appeared. A triumph was by universal consent due to the consul: but the matter was deferred, the tribune still pressing his law; this to the consul seemed of greater importance. The business was discussed for several days, both in the senate and before the people: at length the tribune yielded to the majesty of the consul, and desisted; then the due honour was rendered to the general and his army. He triumphed over the Volscians and Æquans: his troops followed him in his triumph. The other consul was allowed to enter the city in ovation without his soldiers. On the following year the Terentillian law having been taken up by the entire college, assailed the new consuls; the consuls were Publius Volumnius and Servius Sulpicius. On that year the sky seemed to be on fire; a violent earthquake also occurred; it was now believed that an ox spoke, which circumstance had not obtained credit on the year before; among other prodigies it rained flesh also;[115] which shower a great number of birds is reported to have carried off by flying so as to intercept it; that which did fall, is said to have lain scattered about for several days, so that its smell evinced no change. The books[116] were consulted by the duumviri for sacred rites: dangers of attacks being made on the highest parts of the city, and of bloodshed thence resulting, were predicted as about to come from an assemblage of strangers; among other things, an admonition was given that all intestine disturbances should be abandoned. The tribunes alleged that that was done to obstruct the law, and a desperate contest was at hand. Lo! (that the same circle of events may revolve every year) the Hernicians bring word that the Volscians and the Æquans, though their strength was much impaired, were recruiting their armies: that their chief dependence was Antium; that the inhabitants of Antium openly held councils at Ecetra: that that was the source—there the strength—for the war. As soon as this announcement was made in the senate, a levy was ordered: the consuls were commanded to divide the management of the war between them; that the Volscians should be the province of the one, the Æquans that of the other. The tribunes cried out to their faces in the forum, "That the Volscian war was all a concerted farce: that the Hernicians were instructed to act their parts; that the liberty of the Roman people was now no longer crushed by manly efforts, but that it was baffled by cunning; because all probability was now gone that the Volscians, who were almost exterminated, and the Æquans, would of themselves commence hostilities, new enemies were sought for: that a loyal colony, and one in their very vicinity, was being rendered infamous: that war was proclaimed against the unoffending people of Antium, and in reality waged with the commons of Rome, which after loading them with arms they were determined to drive out of the city with precipitous haste, wreaking their vengeance on the tribunes, by the exile and expulsion of their fellow-citizens. That by these means, and let them not think that

[115] Niebuhr, ii. n. 631, asks whether it was worms. Σαρκῶν θραύσματα. Dion. x. 2.
[116] The Sibylline books.

there was any other object contemplated, the law was defeated; unless, whilst the matter was still in abeyance, whilst they were still at home and in the garb of citizens, they would take precaution that they may not be driven out of possession of the city, and be subjected to the yoke. If they only had spirit, that support would not be wanting; that all the tribunes were unanimous; that there was no apprehension from abroad, no danger. That the gods had taken care, on the preceding year, that their liberty could now be defended with safety." Thus far the tribunes.

But, on the other side, the consuls, having placed their chairs within view of them, were proceeding with the levy; thither the tribunes hasten, and draw the assembly along with them; a few were cited, by way of making an experiment, and instantly violence commenced. Whomsoever the lictor laid hold of by order of the consul, him the tribune ordered to be discharged; nor did his own proper jurisdiction set a limit to each, but whatever you set your mind upon, was to be attained by the hope of strength and by force. Just as the tribunes had behaved in impeding the levy, in the same manner did the consuls conduct themselves in obstructing the law which was brought on every assembly day. The commencement of the riot was, when the tribunes ordered the people to proceed to the vote, because the patricians refused to withdraw. The elder citizens scarcely attended the contest, inasmuch as it was one likely not to be directed by prudence, but abandoned to temerity and daring. The consuls also generally kept out of the way, lest in the general confusion they should expose their dignity to any insult. There was a young man, Cæso Quintius, a daring youth, as well by the nobility of his descent, as by his personal size and strength; to those endowments granted by the gods he himself had added many military honours, and eloquence in the forum; so that no person in the state was considered more efficient either in speaking or in acting. When this person took his place in the centre of a body of the patricians, conspicuous above the rest, carrying as it were in his eloquence and bodily strength dictatorships and consulships combined, he alone withstood the storms of the tribunes and the populace. Under his guidance the tribunes were frequently driven from the forum, the commons routed and dispersed; such as came in his way, went off after being ill-treated and stripped; so that it became sufficiently evident, that, if he were allowed to proceed in this way, the law would be defeated. Then the other tribunes being now almost thrown into despair, Aulus Virginius, one of the college, institutes a criminal prosecution on a capital charge against Cæso. By this proceeding he rather irritated than intimidated his violent temper: so much the more vigorously did he oppose the law, annoyed the commons, and persecuted the tribunes, as it were by a regular war. The prosecutor suffered the accused to rush on headlong, and to heighten the charges against him by the flame and material of the popular odium thus incurred: in the mean time he proceeded with the law, not so much in the hope of carrying it through, as to provoke the temerity of Cæso. There many inconsiderate expressions and actions passing among the young men, are charged on the temper of Cæso, through the prejudice raised against him; still the law was resisted. And Aulus Virginius frequently remarks to the people, "Are you even now sensible that you cannot have Cæso, as a fellow-citizen, with the law which you desire? Though why do I say law? he is an opponent of your liberty; he surpasses all the Tarquins in arrogance. Wait till he is made consul or dictator, whom, though but a private citizen, you now see exercising kingly sway over you by his strength and audacity." Many assented, complaining that they had been beaten by him: and strongly urged on the tribune to go through with the prosecution.

The day of trial now approached, and it was evident that persons in general considered that their liberty depended on the condemnation of Cæso: then, at length being forced to it, he addressed the commons individually, though with a strong feeling of indignation; his relatives followed him, the principal members of the state. Titus Quintius Capitolinus, who had been thrice consul, after he recounted many splendid achievements of his own, and of his family, stated, that neither in the Quintian family, nor in the Roman state, had there appeared such promising genius of such early valour. "That he had first been his soldier, that he had often in his sight fought against the enemy." Spurius Furius declared, that "he having been sent to him by Quintius Capitolinus, had come to his aid when in the midst of danger; that there was no individual by whose exertions he considered the common weal more effectually re-established." Lucius Lucretius, the consul of the preceding year, in the full splendour of recent glory, shared his own services with Cæso; he recounted his battles, detailed his distinguished exploits, both on expeditions and in the field; he advised and recommended that they would prefer this extraordinary young man, endowed with all the advantages of nature and of rank, and (one who would prove) of the utmost importance to the interest of that state into which he should come, to be their fellow-citizen, rather than the citizen of a foreign state. "That with respect to that which may be offensive in him, heat and vehemence, time would diminish daily; that the prudence, which may be wanting in him, was increasing daily; that as his faults were declining and his virtues ripening to maturity, they should allow so distinguished a man to become old in their state." Among these his father, Lucius Quintius, who bore the surname of Cincinnatus, without dwelling on his merits, lest he should heighten public hatred, but soliciting pardon for his errors and his youth, implored of them to forgive his son for his sake, who had not given offence to any one by either word or deed. But some, through respect or fear, turned away from listening to his entreaties; others complaining that themselves and their friends had been ill-treated, by the harshness of their answer declared their sentence beforehand.

Independently of the general odium, one charge bore heavily on the accused; that Marcus Volscius Fictor, who some years before had been tribune of the people, had come forward as a witness: "that not long after the pestilence had been in the city, he had fallen in with a party of young men rioting in the Suburra; that a scuffle arose there; and that his elder brother, not yet perfectly recovered from his illness, had fallen down almost dead, being struck with the fist by Cæso; that he was carried home between the hands of some persons, and that he considered that he died from that blow; and that it had not been permitted to him by the consuls of former years to follow up the matter." In consequence of Volscius vociferating these charges, the people became so excited, that Cæso was near being killed through the violence of the people. Virginius orders him to be seized and carried to prison. The patricians oppose force to force. Titus Quintius exclaims, "that a person for whom a day of trial for a capital offence has been appointed, and whose trial was now at hand, ought not to be outraged before trial and without sentence being passed." The tribune says, "that he would not inflict punishment[117] on him before condemnation, that he would however keep him in prison until the day of trial; that the Roman people may have an opportunity of inflicting punishment on one who had killed a man." The tribunes being appealed to, secure their prerogative by adopting a middle course;[118] they forbid his being thrown into confinement, and declare it to be their wish that the accused should appear on his trial, and that a sum of money should be promised to the people, in case he should not appear. How large a sum of money ought to be promised, came under discussion: that is referred to the senate. The accused was detained in the public assembly, until the patricians should be consulted: it was determined that he should give bail:[119] each bail they bound to the amount of three thousand *asses*; how many should be given, was left to the tribunes; they limited the number to ten; for ten sureties the prosecutor discharged the accused. He was the first who gave public sureties. Being discharged

---

[117] Niebuhr denies that the tribunes had the power before the establishment of the decemviri to commit patricians to prison. See however Dion. vii. 17.

[118] In the original the words are, *Medio decreto jus auxilii sui expediunt*. The tribunes were afraid lest, if they allowed Cæso to go entirely at large, the commons might become irritated; whilst if they refused to listen to the application of a patrician when he craved their assistance, they feared lest they should lose an excellent opportunity of establishing their influence and increasing their power. By adopting a line of conduct then which conceded something both to the commons and to Cæso, they as it were *extricate* (expediunt) their power from this double danger.

[119] *Vadis publicos.* According to Gronovius, *publico*, scil. *plebi.* Niebuhr prefers this reading.

from the forum, he went the following night into exile among the Etrurians. When on the day of trial it was pleaded that he had quitted his home in order to go into exile, Virginius notwithstanding holding the comitia, his colleagues when appealed to dismissed the assembly: the fine was rigorously exacted[120] from the father; so that after selling all his effects, he lived for a considerable time in a solitary cottage on the other side of the Tiber, as if in exile. This trial and the proposing of the law gave full employment to the state: there was quiet from foreign arms.

When the tribunes, flushed as it were with victory, imagined that the law was in a manner passed, the patricians being now dismayed by the banishment of Cæso, and when, with respect to the seniors of the patricians, they had relinquished all share in the administration of the commonwealth; the juniors, more especially those who were the intimate friends of Cæso, redoubled their resentful feelings against the commons, and suffered not their spirits to droop; but the greatest improvement was made in this particular, that they tempered their animosity by a certain degree of moderation. When for the first time after Cæso's banishment the law began to be brought forward, arrayed and well prepared with a numerous body of clients, they attacked the tribunes, on their affording a pretext for it by attempting to remove them, in such a manner, that no one individual carried home from thence any prominent share either of glory or ill-will; the people complained that for one Cæso a thousand had started up. During the intermediate days, when the tribunes made no stir regarding the law, nothing could be more mild or peaceable than those same persons; they saluted the plebeians courteously, entered into conversation, and invited them home; they attended the forum, and suffered the tribunes themselves to hold their meetings without interruption: they never were uncivil to any one either in public or in private, unless when the business respecting the law began to be agitated. On other occasions the young men were popular. And not only did the tribunes transact all their other affairs without disturbance, but they were even re-elected for the following year, without one offensive expression, much less any violence being employed. By soothing and managing the commons they gradually rendered them tractable. By these methods the law was evaded for the entire year.

The consuls Caius Claudius, the son of Appius, and Publius Valerius Publicola, found the state in a more tranquil condition. The new year had brought with it nothing new; the thoughts about carrying the law, or submitting to it, engrossed all the members of the state. The more the younger members of the senate endeavoured to insinuate

---

[120] *Rigorously exacted.* See Niebuhr ii. p. 289, who expresses a different opinion on the matter.

themselves into favour with the commons, the more strenuously did the tribunes strive to thwart them, so that they rendered them suspicious in the eyes of the commons by alleging: "that a conspiracy was formed; that Cæso was in Rome; that plans were concerted for assassinating the tribunes, and butchering the commons. That the commission assigned by the elder members of the patricians was, that the young men should abolish the tribunitian power from the state, and the form of government should be the same as it had been before the sacred mount had been taken possession of." Both a war from the Volsci and Æqui, which was now a stated thing, and one that was a regular occurrence for almost every year, was apprehended, and another evil nearer home started up unexpectedly. The exiles and slaves to the number of four thousand and five hundred men took possession of the Capitol and citadel during the night, under the command of Appius Herdonius, a Sabine. Immediately a massacre took place in the citadel of those who had evinced an unwillingness to enter into the conspiracy and to take up arms. Some, during the alarm, run down to the forum, driven precipitately through the panic; the cries, "to arms," and "the enemy are in the city," were heard alternately. The consuls were both afraid to arm the commons, and to suffer them to remain unarmed; uncertain what sudden calamity had assailed the city, whether external or intestine, whether from the hatred of the commons or the treachery of the slaves: they were for quieting the tumults, by such endeavours they sometimes exasperated them; for the populace, panic-stricken and terrified, could not be directed by authority. They give out arms, however, not indiscriminately; only so that, the enemy being still uncertain,[121] there might be a protection sufficient to be relied on for all emergencies. The remainder of the night they passed in posting guards through proper places through the entire city, anxious and uncertain, as to who the persons might be, and how great the number of the enemy was. Daylight then disclosed the war and the leader of the war. Appius Herdonius summoned the slaves to liberty from the Capitol: "that he had espoused the cause of every most unfortunate individual, in order to bring back to their country those driven out by oppression, and to remove the grievous yoke from the slaves. That he had rather that were done under the authority of the Roman people. If there be no hope in that quarter, that he would rouse the Volscians and Æqui, and would try all extremities."

The matter began to disclose itself more clearly to the patricians and the consuls; besides those things, however, which were openly declared, they dreaded lest this might be a scheme of the Veientes or Sabines; and, as there were so many of the enemy in the city, lest the Sabine and Etrurian troops might come on according to a concerted

---

[121] *Incerto hoste*, it being as yet uncertain who the enemy was.

plan; and then lest their eternal enemies, the Volscians and Æqui, should come, not to ravage their territories, as before, but to their very city, already in part taken. Many and various were their fears; among others, the most prominent was their dread of the slaves, lest each might harbour an enemy in his own house, one whom it was neither sufficiently safe to trust, nor to deny[122] confidence to him lest, by not trusting him, he might become more incensed. And (the evil) seemed scarcely capable of being resisted by perfect harmony (between the different orders of the state); only no one apprehended the tribunes or commons, other evils predominating and constantly starting up; that appeared an evil of a mild nature, and one always arising during the cessation of other evils, and it then appeared to be lulled to rest by external terror. Yet that was almost the only one that most aggravated their distressing circumstances: for such madness took possession of the tribunes, that they contended that not war, but the empty appearance of war had taken possession of the Capitol, to avert the people's minds from attending to the law; that these friends and clients of the patricians would depart in greater silence than they came, if they once perceived that, by the law being passed, they had raised these tumults in vain. They then held a meeting for passing the law, having called away the people from their arms. In the mean time, the consuls convene the senate, another dread presenting itself on the part of the tribunes, greater than that which the nightly foe had occasioned.

When it was announced that their arms were being laid aside, and that the men were quitting their posts, Publius Valerius, his colleague still detaining the senate, hastens from the senate-house; he comes thence into the meeting to the tribunes: "What is all this," says he, "tribunes? Are you determined to overthrow the commonwealth under the guidance and auspices of Appius Herdonius? Has he been so successful in corrupting you, who, by his authority, has not influenced your slaves? When the enemies are over our heads, is it your pleasure that arms should be given up, and laws be proposed?" Then directing his discourse to the populace: "If, Romans, no concern for your city, for yourselves, moves you, at least revere the gods of your country, now made captive by the enemy. Jupiter, the best and greatest, Queen Juno, and Minerva, the other gods and goddesses, are besieged; the camp of slaves now holds the tutelary gods of the state. Does this seem to you the form of a state in its senses? Such a crowd of enemies is not only within the walls, but in the citadel, commanding the forum and senate-house: in the mean while meetings are being held in the forum; the senate is in the senate-house, just as when perfect tranquillity prevails; the senator gives his opinion, the other Romans give their votes. Would

---

[122] *Fidem abrogare,*—non habere fidem, non credere. *Non credendo* here seems superfluous.

it not behove all the patricians and commons, consuls, tribunes, citizens, and all classes of persons, to bring aid with arms in their hands, to run into the Capitol, to liberate and restore to peace that most august residence of Jupiter, the best and greatest? O Father Romulus! do thou infuse into thy progeny that determination of thine, by which you once recovered from these same Sabines the citadel, when obtained by gold. Order them to pursue this same path, which thou, as leader, and thy army, pursued. Lo! I, as consul, shall be the first to follow thee and thy footsteps, as far as a mortal can follow a god." The close of his speech was: "That he would take up arms, that he invited every citizen of Rome to arms; if any one should oppose, that he,[123] forgetful of the consular authority, the tribunitian power, and the devoting laws, would consider him as an enemy, whoever he may, wheresoever he may, in the Capitol, or in the forum. That the tribunes might order arms to be taken up against Publius Valerius the consul, since they forbid it against Appius Herdonius; that he would venture to act in that manner in the case of the tribunes, in which the founder of his family had ventured to act in the case of kings." It now became apparent that extreme violence was about to take place, and that a disturbance among the Romans would be exhibited as a sight to the enemy; the law, however, could neither be prepared, nor could the consul proceed to the Capitol: night quashed the contest that had commenced; the tribunes yielded to the night, dreading the arms of the consuls. The fomenters of the disturbances being removed from thence, the patricians went about among the commons, and introducing themselves into their circles of conversation, they introduced observations suited to the occasion: they advised them "to beware into what hazard they were bringing the commonwealth; that the contest was not between the patricians and commons, but that patricians and commons together, the fortress of the city, the temples of the gods, the guardian gods of the state and of private families, were being delivered up to the enemy." Whilst these affairs are going on in the forum for the purpose of appeasing the disturbances, the consuls in the mean time had armed the several gates and the walls, lest the Sabines or the Veientian enemy should make any move.

On the same night, messengers come to Tusculum announcing that the citadel was taken, and the Capitol seized, and the other state of disturbance in the city. Lucius Mamilius was at that time dictator at Tusculum; he, having immediately convoked the senate and introduced the messengers, earnestly advises: "That they should not wait until ambassadors came from Rome, suing for assistance; that the very

---

[123] *Forgetful of the consular,* &c.—i.e. forgetful of the limits of the consular authority; acting in the same manner as if its power were unbounded, and admitted no appeal.

danger and risk, and the social gods, and the faith of treaties, demanded it; that the gods would never afford them an equal opportunity of obliging so powerful a state and so near a neighbour." It is determined that assistance should be sent: the young men are enrolled; arms are given to them. Coming to Rome at break of day, they at a distance exhibited the appearance of enemies. The Æqui or Volscians appeared to be coming. Then when the groundless alarm was removed, they are admitted into the city, and descend in a body into the forum. There Publius Valerius, having left his colleague to guard the gates, was now drawing up in order of battle. The great influence of the man had produced an effect, when he affirmed that, "the Capitol being recovered, and the city restored to peace, if they would allow themselves to be convinced what lurking fraud was concealed under the law proposed by the tribunes, that he would offer no obstruction to the meeting of the people, mindful of his ancestors, mindful of his surname, and that the province of protecting the people had been handed down to him as hereditary by his ancestors." Following him as their leader, notwithstanding the tribunes cried out against it, they direct their march up the Capitoline hill. The Tusculan troops also joined them. Allies and citizens vied with each other which of them should appropriate to themselves the honour of recovering the citadel. Each leader encourages his own men. Then the enemy became terrified, and placed no dependence on any but the place. The Romans and allies advance on them whilst in this state of alarm. They had now broken into the porch of the temple, when Publius Valerius is slain animating the fight at the head of his men. Publius Volumnius, a man of consular rank, saw him falling. Having directed his men to cover the body, he rushes forward to the place and office of consul. Through their ardour and impetuosity the perception of so heavy a blow did not reach the soldiers; they conquered before they perceived that they conquered without a leader. Many of the exiles defiled the temple with their blood; many were taken alive; Herdonius was slain. Thus the Capitol was recovered. With respect to the prisoners,[124] punishment was inflicted on each according to his station, whether he was a freeman or a slave. The commons are stated to have thrown farthings into the consul's house, that he might be buried with greater solemnity.

Peace being established, the tribunes then pressed on the patricians to fulfil the promise of Publius Valerius; they pressed on Claudius, to free the shade of his colleague from breach of faith, and to allow the business of the law to proceed. The consul asserted that he would suffer the discussion on the law to go on, till he had a colleague appointed in

---

[124] Niebuhr thinks that Cæso was among the number. See cap. 25, where we read "Cæsonem neque Quintiæ familiæ, neque reipublicæ restitui posse." Comp. Niebuhr ii. n. 673, Wachsmuth, p. 347.

the room of the deceased. These disputes held on until the elections for substituting a consul. In the month of December,[125] by the most zealous exertions of the patricians, Lucius Quintius Cincinnatus, Cæso's father, is elected consul to enter on his office without delay. The commons were dismayed at their being about to have as consul a man incensed against them, powerful by the support of the patricians, by his own merit, and by three sons, not one of whom yielded to Cæso in greatness of spirit; "whilst they were superior to him by their exercising prudence and moderation, when the occasion required." When he entered on his office, in his frequent harangues from the tribunal, he was not more vehement in restraining the commons than in reproving the senate, "by the listlessness of which body the tribunes of the commons, now become perpetual, by means of their tongues and prosecutions exercised regal authority, not as in a republic of the Roman people, but as if in an ill-regulated family. That with his son Cæso, fortitude, constancy, all the splendid qualifications of youth in war or in peace, had been driven and exiled from the city of Rome: that talkative and turbulent men, sowers of discord, twice and even thrice re-elected tribunes, lived in the most destructive practices with regal tyranny. Did that Aulus Virginius," says he, "deserve less punishment than Appius Herdonius, because he was not in the Capitol? considerably more, by Jove, (in the mind of any one) who would judge the matter fairly. Herdonius, if nothing else, by avowing himself an enemy, in a manner gave you notice to take up arms: this man, by denying the existence of war, took arms out of your hands, and exposed you defenceless to your slaves and exiles. And did you, (without any offence to Caius Claudius and to Publius Valerius, now no more let me say it,) did you advance against the Capitoline hill before you expelled those enemies from the forum. It is shameful before gods and men. When the enemy were in the citadel, in the very Capitol, when the leader of the exiles and slaves, after profaning every thing, took up his residence in the shrine of Jupiter, the best and greatest, arms were taken up in Tusculum sooner than in Rome. It was a matter of doubt whether Lucius Mamilius, the Tusculan leader, or Publius Valerius and Caius Claudius, the consuls, recovered the Roman citadel, and we, who formerly did not suffer the Latins to touch arms, even in their own defence, when they had the enemy in their very frontiers, should have been taken and destroyed now, had not the Latins taken up arms of their own accord. Tribunes, is this bringing aid to the commons, to expose them in a defenceless state to be butchered by the enemy. Now, if any one, even the humblest individual of your commons, (which portion you have as it were broken off from the rest of the state, and made it your country and peculiar

---

[125] The consuls under ordinary circumstances used to commence their office at this time on the Calends of August.

commonwealth,) if any one of these persons were to bring word that his house was beset by an armed band of slaves, you would think that assistance should be afforded to him. Was Jupiter, the best and greatest, when surrounded by the arms of exiles and of slaves, deserving of no human aid? And do these persons require that they be considered sacred and inviolable,[126] with whom the gods themselves are neither sacred nor inviolable? But, steeped as ye are in crimes against both gods and men, do ye say that you will pass your law this year? Verily then the day on which I was created consul was a disastrous day for the commonwealth, much more so even than that on which Publius Valerius the consul fell, if ye should carry it. Now, first of all," says he, "Romans, it is the intention of myself and of my colleague to march the legions against the Volsci and the Æqui. I know not by what fatality we find the gods more propitious when we are at war than in peace. How great the danger from those states would have been, had they known that the Capitol was besieged by exiles, it is better to conjecture from the past, than to feel from actual experience."

The consul's harangue had a great effect on the commons; the patricians, recovering their spirits, considered the state as re-established. The other consul, more eager as a seconder than as the first mover (of a measure), readily suffering his colleague to take the first lead in a matter of so much importance, claimed to himself his share of the consular duty in executing the plan. Then the tribunes, mocking these declarations as empty, went on inquiring "by what means the consuls would lead out the army, as no one would allow them to hold a levy?" "But," says Quintius, "we have no occasion for a levy; since at the time Publius Valerius gave arms to the commons to recover the Capitol, they all took an oath to him, that they would assemble on an order from the consul, and would not depart without an order. We therefore publish our order that all of you, who have sworn, attend to-morrow under arms at the lake Regillus." The tribunes then began to cavil, and wished to absolve the people from their obligation; that Quintius was a private person at the time at which they were bound by the oath. But that disregard of the gods which prevails in the present age had not yet arrived; nor did every one, by his own interpretation, accommodate oaths and laws to his own purposes, but rather adapted his conduct to them. Wherefore the tribunes, as there was no hope of obstructing the matter, attempted to delay the departure (of the army) the more earnestly on this account, because a report had gone out "both that the augurs had been ordered to attend at the lake Regillus, and to consecrate a place, where business might be transacted with the people with the benefit of auspices; that whatever had been passed at Rome by

---

[126] *Neque sacri neque sancti.* Whatever is consecrated by religion is said to be *sacrum*; whilst *sanctum* is said of that which the law states to be inviolable.

tribunitian violence, might be repealed there in an assembly. That all would agree to that which the consuls wished; for that there was no appeal at a distance greater than that of a mile from the city: and that the tribunes, if they should come there, would, among the rest of the crowd, be subjected to the consular authority." These matters alarmed them; but the greatest terror which acted on their minds was, that Quintius frequently said, "that he would not hold an election of consuls. That the state was affected with such a disease, as could not be stopped by the ordinary remedies. That the commonwealth required a dictator, so that whoever should stir a step to disturb the peace of the state, might feel that the dictatorship was without appeal."

The senate was assembled in the Capitol. Thither the tribunes come with the commons in great consternation: the populace, with loud clamours, implore the protection now of the consuls, now of the patricians: nor could they make the consul recede from his determination, until the tribunes promised that they would be under the direction of the patricians. Then on the consul's laying before them the demands of the tribunes and commons, decrees of the senate are passed, "That neither the tribunes should propose the law during that year, and that the consuls should not lead the army from the city—that for the time to come, the senate decided that it was to the injury of the commonwealth, that the same magistrates should be continued, and the same tribunes be re-appointed." The consuls conformed to the authority of the senate, the tribunes were re-appointed notwithstanding the remonstrances of the consuls. The patricians also, that they might not yield to the commons in any particular, re-elected Lucius Quintius consul. No proceeding of the consul was urged with more warmth during the entire year. "Can I be surprised," says he, "if your authority is of little weight, conscript fathers? yourselves are disparaging it. Forsooth, because the commons have violated a decree of the senate, by re-appointing their magistrates, you yourselves also wish it to be violated, lest ye should yield to the populace in rashness; as if to possess greater power in the state consisted in having more of inconstancy and irregularity; for it is certainly more inconstant and greater folly, to do away with one's own decrees and resolutions, than those of others. Imitate, conscript fathers, the inconsiderate multitude; and ye, who should be an example to others, transgress by the example of others, rather than others should act correctly by yours, provided I imitate not the tribunes, nor suffer myself to be re-elected consul, contrary to a decree of the senate. But I advise you, Caius Claudius, that both you on your part restrain the Roman people from this licentiousness, and that you be persuaded of this on my part, that I shall so take it, as not to consider that my honour has been obstructed by you, but that the glory of declining the honour has been augmented, and the odium, which would hang over me from its being continued, has been lessened." Upon this they issue this order jointly: "That no one should attempt to make Lucius Quintius consul: if any one should do so, that they would not allow that vote."

The consuls elected were Quintus Fabius Vibulanus, a third time, and Lucius Cornelius Maluginensis. The census was performed that year; it was a matter of religious scruple that the lustrum should be closed, on account of the Capitol having been taken and the consul slain. In the consulate of Quintus Fabius and Lucius Cornelius, disturbances broke out immediately at the commencement of the year. The tribunes were urging on the commons. The Latins and Hernici brought word that a formidable war was in preparation on the part of the Volscians and Æqui; that the troops of the Volscians were now at Antium. Great apprehension was also entertained, that the colony itself would revolt: and with difficulty were the tribunes prevailed on to allow the war to take precedence. The consuls then divided the provinces between them. It was assigned to Fabius to march the legions to Antium; to Cornelius, to protect the city; lest any part of the enemy, as was the practice of the Æqui, should come to commit depredations. The Hernici and Latins were ordered to supply soldiers in conformity to the treaty; and in the army two parts consisted of allies, one part of natives. When the allies came to the day already appointed, the consul pitches his camp outside the Capuan gate. Then, after the army was purified, he set out for Antium, and encamped not far from the town, and standing camp of the enemy. Where, when the Volscians, not venturing to risk an engagement, were preparing to protect themselves quietly within their ramparts, on the following day Fabius drew up not one mixed army of allies and citizens, but three separate bodies of the three states around the enemy's works. He himself was in the centre with the Roman legions. He ordered them to watch for the signal from thence, so that the allies might both commence the action together, and retire together, if he should sound a retreat. He placed their cavalry in the rear of each division. Having thus assailed the camp in three different points, he surrounds it; and when he pressed on from every side, he dislodges from the rampart the Volscians, not able to sustain his attack. Having then crossed the fortifications, he expels from the camp the crowd who were dismayed and inclining towards one direction. Upon this the cavalry, who could not easily pass over the rampart, having stood by up to that period mere spectators of the fight, having come up with them whilst flying in disorder on the open plain, enjoys a share of the victory, by cutting down the affrighted troops. The slaughter of them as they fled was great, both in the camp and outside the lines; but the booty was still greater, because the enemy were scarcely able to carry off their arms with them; and their entire army would have been destroyed, had not the woods covered them in their flight.

Whilst these transactions are taking place at Antium, the Æqui, in the mean while, sending forward the main strength of their youth, surprise the citadel of Tusculum by night, and with the rest of their army they sit down at no great distance from the walls of Tusculum, so as to divide the forces of the enemy. This account being quickly brought to Rome, and from Rome to Antium, affect the Romans not less than if it was told them that the Capitol was taken; so recent were both the services of the Tusculans, and the very similitude of the danger seemed to require a return of the aid that had been afforded. Fabius, giving up every other object, removes the booty hastily from the camp to Antium. Having a small garrison there, he hurries on his army by forced marches to Tusculum. The soldiers were allowed to carry nothing but their arms, and whatever dressed provision was at hand. The consul Cornelius sends provisions from Rome. The war was carried on at Tusculum for several months. With one part of his army the consul assailed the camp of the Æqui; a part he had given to the Tusculans to recover their citadel. They never could have made their way to it by force. Famine at length withdrew the enemy from it. And when they came to this at last, they were all sent under the yoke by the Tusculans, unarmed and naked. These, when betaking themselves home by an ignominious flight, were overtaken by the Roman consul on Algidum and cut off to a man. After this victory, having marched back[127] his army to Columen, (that is the name of the place,) he pitches his camp. The other consul also, as soon as the Roman walls ceased to be in danger, the enemy being defeated, set out from Rome. Thus the consuls, having entered the territories of the enemies on two different sides, strenuously vie with each other in depopulating the Volscians on the one hand, the Æqui on the other. I find in some writers that the people of Antium revolted[128] the same year. That Lucius Cornelius, the consul, conducted that war and took the town, I would not venture to affirm for certain, because no mention is made of the matter among the older writers.

This war being concluded, a tribunitian war at home alarms the senate. They exclaim, "that the detaining the army abroad was done for a fraudulent motive: that such frustration was for the purpose of doing away with the law; that they, however, would go through with the matter undertaken by them." Publius Lucretius, however, the præfect of the city, so far prevailed that the proceedings of the tribunes were postponed till the arrival of the consuls. A new cause of disturbance also arose. Aulus Cornelius and Quintus Servilius, quæstors, appoint a day of trial for Marcus Volscius, because he had come forward as a

---

[127] *Exercitu relicto* is the ordinary reading. Crevier observes that *reducto* is the more correct.

[128] This account does not seem to be correct. See Niebuhr ii. p. 254.

manifestly false witness against Cæso. For it appeared by many proofs, that the brother of Volscius, from the time he first became ill, not only never appeared in public, but that he had not even arisen from his sick bed, and that he died of an illness of several months' standing; and that at the time to which the witness had referred the commission of the crime, Cæso had not been seen at Rome: those who served in the army with him, positively stating that at that time he had constantly attended at his post with them without any leave of absence. Many persons proposed on their own private responsibility to Volscius to have a judicial decision on the matter.[129] As he would not venture to go to trial, all these matters coinciding rendered the condemnation of Volscius no less certain than that of Cæso had been on the testimony of Volscius. The tribunes occasioned a delay, who said that they would not suffer the quæstors to hold the assembly[130] concerning the accused, unless it was first held concerning the law. Thus both matters were spun out till the arrival of the consuls. When they entered the city in triumph with their victorious army, because silence was (observed) with regard to the law, many thought that the tribunes were struck with dismay. But they, (for it was now the close of the year,) desirous of obtaining a fourth tribuneship, had turned away their efforts from the law to canvassing for the elections; and when the consuls strove with no less strenuousness than if the law in question were proposed for the purpose of lessening their own dignity, the victory in the contest was on the side of the tribunes. On the same year peace was granted to the Æqui on their suing for it. The census, a matter commenced on the preceding year, is completed. The number of citizens rated were one hundred and seventeen thousand three hundred and nineteen. The consuls obtained great glory this year both at home and in war, because they both re-established peace abroad and at home; though the state was not in a state of absolute concord, yet it was less disturbed than at other times.

Lucius Minucius and Caius Nautius being next elected consuls, took up the two causes which lay over since the preceding year. The

---

[129] *Ni ita esset*, a legal form of expression, amounting in this place to "if Volscius attempted to deny it." *Privatim*. Besides the quæstors who by virtue of their office were to prosecute Volscius, many persons on their own account, and on their private responsibility, cited him into court, and challenged him to discuss the case before a judge. A prosecutor was said *ferre judicem res*, when he proposed to the accused person some one out of the *judices selecti*, before whom the case might be tried; if the accused person consented to the person named by prosecutor, then the judge was said *convenisse*, to have been agreed on. Sometimes the accused was allowed to select his own judge, *judicem dicere*. When both the prosecutor and the accused agreed as to the judge, they presented a joint petition to the prætor that he would appoint (*ut daret*) that person to try the cause; at the same time they both bound themselves to pay a certain sum, the one if he did not establish his charge, ni ita esset; the other if he did not prove his innocence.

[130] *Comitia*, i. e. *curiata*, which exercised authority in the cases of persons accused of inflicting injuries on the patricians.

consuls obstructed the law, the tribunes the trial of Volscius in the same manner: but in the new quæstors there was greater power, and greater influence. With Marcus Valerius, son of Valerius and grandson of Volesus, Titus Quintius Capitolinus, who had been thrice consul, was appointed quæstor. Since Cæso could neither be restored to the Quintian family, nor could he, though a most promising young man, be restored to the state, he justly, and as in duty bound, prosecuted the false witness who had deprived an innocent person of the power of pleading his cause. When Virginius in particular and the (other) tribunes were promoting the passing of the law, the space of two months was allowed to the consuls to examine into the law: so that, when they had satisfied the people, as to what secret designs were concealed under it, they should then allow them to give their votes. The granting this respite established tranquillity in the city. The Æqui however did not allow them long rest; who, in violation of the treaty which had been made with the Romans the year before, confer the chief command on Gracchus Clælius. He was then the leading man amongst the Æqui. Under the command of Gracchus they carry hostile depredations into the district of Lavici, from thence into that of Tusculum, and laden with booty they pitch their camp at Algidum. To that camp Quintus Fabius, Publius Volumnius, Aulus Posthumius, come to complain of the wrongs committed, and to demand restitution in accordance with the treaty. The general of the Æqui commands them "to deliver to the oak whatever instructions they brought from the Roman senate; that he in the mean time should attend to other matters." A large oak tree hung over the prætorium, the shade of which constituted a pleasant seat. Then one of the ambassadors, when departing, says, "Let both this consecrated oak and all the gods hear the treaty violated by you, and favour both our complaints now, and our arms presently, when we shall simultaneously avenge the rights of gods and men as violated by you." As soon as the ambassadors returned to Rome, the senate ordered one of the consuls to lead his army against Gracchus at Algidum, to the other they assigned as his province the laying waste of the country of the Æqui. The tribunes, according to their practice, attempted to obstruct the levy; and probably would have eventually prevented it, but a new cause of alarm was suddenly added.

A large body of Sabines, committing dreadful devastation, approached very close to the walls of the city. The fields were laid waste, the city was struck with terror. Then the commons cheerfully took up arms; two large armies were raised, the tribunes remonstrating to no purpose. Nautius led the one against the Sabines; and having pitched his camp at Eretum, by small detachments, generally by nightly incursions, he effected such desolation in the Sabine land, that, when compared to it, the Roman territories seemed intact by an enemy. Minucius had neither the same success nor the same energy of mind in conducting his business; for after he had pitched his camp at no great distance from the enemy, without having experienced any considerable loss, he kept himself through fear within the camp. When the enemy perceived this, their boldness increased, as sometimes happens, from others' fears; and having attacked his camp by night, when open force did not succeed well, they on the following day drew lines of circumvallation around it. Before these could close up all the passes, by a vallum being thrown up on all sides, five horsemen being despatched between the enemies' posts, brought the account to Rome, that the consul and his army were besieged. Nothing could have happened so unexpected, nor so unlooked-for. Accordingly the panic and the alarm was as great as if the enemy besieged the city, not the camp. They send for the consul Nautius; in whom when there seemed to be but insufficient protection, and they were determined that a dictator should be appointed to retrieve their embarrassed affairs, Lucius Quintius Cincinnatus is appointed by universal consent. It is worth those persons' while to listen, who despise all things human in comparison with riches, and who suppose "that there is no room for exalted honour, nor for virtue, unless where riches abound in great profusion." Lucius Quintius, the sole hope of the Roman people, cultivated a farm of four acres, at the other side of the Tiber, which are called the Quintian meadows, opposite to the very place where the dock-yard now is. There, whether leaning on a stake in a ditch which he was digging, or in the employment of ploughing, engaged at least on some rural work, as is certain, after mutual salutations had passed, being requested by the ambassadors to put on his gown, and listen to the commands of the senate, (with wishes) that it might be happy both to him and to the commonwealth, being astonished, and asking frequently "whether all was safe," he bids his wife Racilia immediately to bring his toga from his hut. As soon as he put this on and came forward, after first wiping off the dust and sweat, the ambassadors, congratulating him, unite in saluting him as dictator: they call him into the city; explain to him what terror now exists in the army. A vessel was prepared for Quintius by order of government, and his three sons having come out to meet him, receive him on his landing at the other side; then his other relatives and friends; then the greater part of the patricians. Accompanied by this numerous attendance, and the lictors going before him, he was conducted to his residence. There was a numerous concourse of the commons also; but they by no means looked on Quintius with equal pleasure, considering both the extent of his authority as too great, and the man vested with such authority rather arbitrary. And during that night indeed nothing was done in the city besides posting guards.

On the next day the dictator, after he had come into the forum before day-light, names a master of the horse, Lucius Tarquitius, a man of patrician family, but one who, though he had served his campaigns among the foot by reason of his scanty means, was yet considered by many degrees the first in military skill among the Roman youth. With his master of the horse he came into the assembly, proclaims a suspension of civil business, orders the shops to be closed throughout the city, and forbids any one to attend to any private affairs. Then he commands that all, whoever were of the military age, should attend under arms, in the Campus Martius, before sun-set, with dressed provisions for five days and twelve palisades, and he commanded that whose age was too far advanced for military service, should dress their victuals for the soldiers in their vicinity, whilst the latter were preparing arms, and procuring the palisade. Accordingly, the young men run in different directions to procure the palisades; they took them wherever they were nearest to them; no one was prevented, and they all attended punctually according to the dictator's order. Then the troops being formed, not more fitted for the march than for an engagement, should the occasion require it, the dictator himself marches at the head of the legions, the master of the horse at the head of his cavalry. In both bodies there were such exhortations as the juncture itself required; that "they should quicken their pace; that there was need of expedition, that they might reach the enemy by night; that the consul and the Romans were besieged; that they had been shut up now three days: that it was uncertain what each day or night might bring with it; that the issue of the most important affairs often depended on a moment of time." They, to please their leaders, exclaimed among themselves, "Standard-bearer, hasten on; follow, soldier." At midnight they reach Algidum: and, as soon as they perceived that they were near the enemy, they halted.

There the dictator, having rode about, and having observed, as far as could be ascertained by night, what the situation of the camp was, and what its form, commanded the tribunes of the soldiers to order the baggage to be thrown into one place, and that the soldiers with their arms and palisades should return to their ranks. What he commanded was executed. Then, with the regularity which they had observed on the march, he draws the entire army in a long column around the enemies' camp, and directs that, when the signal was given, they should all raise a shout; and that on the shout being raised, each man should throw up a trench before his post, and fix his palisade. The orders being issued, the signal followed: the soldiers perform what they were commanded; the shout resounds around the enemy: it then passes beyond the camp of the enemy, and reaches the consul's camp: it occasions panic in one place, great joy in another. The Romans, observing to each other with exultation, "that this was the shout of their countrymen, and that aid was at hand," from their watch-guards and out-posts intimidate the enemy on their part. The consul says, that there must be no delay: "that by that shout not only their arrival was intimated, but that proceedings were already commenced by their friends; and that it would be a wonder if the enemies' camp were not attacked on the outside." He therefore orders his men to take up arms and follow him. The battle was commenced by the legions during the night: they give notice to the dictator by a shout, that on that side also the action was commenced. The Æquans were now preparing to prevent the works from being brought around them,[131] when, the battle being commenced by the enemy from within, turning their attention from those employed on the fortifications to those who were fighting on the inside, lest a sally should be made through the centre of their camp, they left the night to remain without interruption for the finishing of the work; and they continued the fight with the consul till daylight. At the break of day they were now encompassed by the dictator's works, and were scarcely able to maintain the fight against one army. Then their lines were attacked by Quintius's army, who immediately after completing their work returned to their arms. Here a new fight pressed on them: the former one had suffered no relaxation. Then the twofold peril pressing hard on them, turning from fighting to entreaties, they implored the dictator on the one hand, the consul on the other, not to make the victory consist in their general slaughter, that they would suffer them to depart without arms. When they were bid by the consul to go to the dictator, he, incensed against them, added ignominy (to defeat). He orders Gracchus Cloelius, their general, and other leaders to be brought to him in chains, and that they should evacuate the town of Corbio; "that he wanted not the blood of the Æquans: that they were allowed to depart; but that the confession may be at length extorted, that their nation was defeated and subdued, that they should pass under the yoke." The yoke is formed with three spears, two fixed in the ground, and one tied across between the upper ends of them. Under this yoke the dictator sent the Æquans.

The enemy's camp being taken, which was full of every thing, (for he had sent them away naked,) he distributed all the booty among his own soldiers only: chiding the consul's army and the consul himself, he says, "Soldiers, ye shall do without any portion of the spoil taken from that enemy to which you were well nigh becoming a spoil: and you, Lucius Minutius, until you begin to assume the spirit of a consul, shall command these legions as lieutenant-general." Minutius accordingly resigns his office of consul, and remains with the army, as he had been commanded. But so meekly obedient were the minds of men at that time to authority combined with superior merit, that this army, mindful of the kindness (conferred) rather than of the slur (cast on them), both voted a golden crown of a pound weight to the dictator, and saluted him as their patron when setting out. The senate at Rome, being convened

---

[131] *Ad prohibenda circumdari opera.* Stroth observes that it should be more properly *ad prohibenda circumdanda opera*, i. e. ad prohibendum, ne opera circumdarentur.

by Quintus Fabius, præfect of the city, ordered Quintius to enter the city in triumph, in the order of march in which he was coming. The leaders of the enemy were led before his car: the military standards were carried before him: his army followed laden with spoil. Tables with provisions are said to have been laid out before the houses of all, and (the soldiers) partaking of the entertainment, followed the car with the triumphal hymn and the usual jests, after the manner of revellers. On that day the freedom of the state was granted to Lucius Mamilius of Tusculum, with universal approbation. The dictator would have laid down his office, had not the assembly for the trial of Marcus Volscius, the false witness, detained him; the fear of the dictator prevented the tribunes from obstructing it. Volscius was condemned and went into exile to Lanuvium. Quintius laid down his dictatorship on the sixteenth day, having received it for six months. During those days the consul Nautius engages the Sabines at Eretum with distinguished success. Besides the devastation of their lands, this additional blow also befell the Sabines. Fabius Quintus was sent to Algidum as successor to Minucius. Towards the end of the year the tribunes began to agitate the question of the law; but because two armies were abroad, the patricians carried the point, that no business should be proposed to the people. The commons succeeded in electing the same tribunes for the fifth time. They report that wolves seen in the Capitol were driven away by dogs; that on account of that prodigy the Capitol was purified. Such were the transactions in that year.

Quintus Minucius and Caius Horatius Pulvillus follow as the next consuls. At the commencement of this year, when there was peace abroad, the same tribunes and the same law occasioned disturbances at home; and parties would have proceeded further, (so highly were their passions inflamed,) had not, as if for the very purpose, news been brought, that by an attack of the Æquans the garrison at Corbio had been cut off. The consuls convene the senate; they are ordered to raise a hasty levy and to proceed to Algidum. Then the contest about the law being given up, a new dispute arose regarding the levy. And the consular authority[132] was about to be overpowered by tribunitian influence, when an additional cause of alarm comes on them: that the Sabine army had made a descent into the Roman lands to commit depredations; that from thence they were advancing to the city. This fear influenced the tribunes to allow the levy to proceed, not without a stipulation, however, that since they had been foiled for five years, and as that was but little protection to the commons, ten tribunes of the people should henceforward be elected. Necessity wrung this from the

---

[132] *Consulare, imperium tribunicio auxilio.*—The consuls possessed *imperium*. The tribunes could not be said to possess it. Their province was confined to *auxilii latio*, sc. adversus consules.

patricians; this exception only they made, that they should not hereafter re-elect the same tribunes. The election for the tribunes was held immediately, lest that measure also, like others, might prove a delusion after the war. On the thirty-sixth year after the first tribunes, ten were elected, two from each class; and provision was made that they should be elected in this manner for the future. The levy being then held, Minucius marched out against the Sabines, and found no enemy. Horatius, after the Æquans, having put the garrison at Corbio to the sword, had taken Ortona also, fights a battle at Algidum; he slays a great number; drives the enemy not only from Algidum, but from Corbio and Ortona also. Corbio he razed to the ground for their having betrayed the garrison.

Marcus Valerius and Spurius Virginius are next elected consuls. Quiet prevailed at home and abroad. They laboured under a scarcity of provisions on account of the excessive rains. A law was proposed regarding the making Mount Aventine public property. The same tribunes of the people being re-elected on the following year, Titus Romilius and Caius Veturius being consuls, strongly recommended the law[133] in all their harangues, "That they were ashamed of their number increased to no purpose, if that question should lie for their two years in the same manner as it had lain for the whole preceding five." Whilst they were most busily employed in these matters, an alarming account comes from Tusculum, that the Æquans were in the Tusculan territory. The recent services of that state made them ashamed of delaying relief. Both the consuls were sent with an army, and find the enemy in their usual post in Algidum. A battle was fought there; upwards of seven thousand of the enemy were slain; the rest were routed; immense booty was obtained. This the consuls sold on account of the low state of the treasury; the proceeding was the cause of dissatisfaction to the army, and it also afforded to the tribunes materials for bringing a charge against the consuls before the commons. Accordingly, as soon as they went out of office, in the consulship of Spurius Tarpeius and Aulus Aterius, a day was appointed for Romilius by Caius Claudius Cicero, tribune of the people; for Veturius, by Lucius Alienus, plebeian ædile. They were both condemned, to the great mortification of the patricians; Romilius to pay ten thousand *asses*; Veturius, fifteen thousand. Nor did this misfortune of their predecessors render the new consuls more remiss. They said that they too might be condemned, and that the commons and tribunes could not carry the law. Then having thrown up the law, which, in its repeated publication, had now grown old, the tribunes adopted a milder mode of proceeding with the patricians.

---

[133] It is extraordinary that Livy makes no mention here of Siccius Dentatus, and his strenuous exertions in endeavouring to carry the agrarian law, as well as of his angry contentions with the consuls. For his character, see Dion. x. 31, 32.

"That they should at length put an end to their disputes. If plebeian laws displeased them, at least they should suffer legislators (chosen) in common, both from the commons and from the patricians, who would propose measures advantageous to both parties, and such as might tend to the equalization of liberty." This proposal the patricians did not reject. They said that "no one should propose laws, except some of the patricians." When they agreed with respect to the laws, and differed only with respect to the proposer; ambassadors were sent to Athens, Spurius Posthumius Albus, Aulus Manlius, Publius Sulpicius Camerinus; and they were ordered to copy out the celebrated laws of Solon, and to become acquainted with the institutions, customs, and laws of the other states of Greece.

The year was undisturbed by foreign wars; the following one was still more quiet, Publius Curiatius and Sextus Quintilius being consuls, the tribunes observing uninterrupted silence, which was occasioned in the first place by their waiting for the ambassadors who had gone to Athens, and for the foreign laws; in the next place, two heavy calamities arose at the same time, famine and pestilence, (which proved) destructive to man, and equally so to cattle. The lands were left desolate; the city exhausted by a constant succession of deaths. Many and illustrious families were in mourning. The Flamen Quirinalis, Servilius Cornelius, died; as also the augur, Caius Horatius Pulvillus; into whose place the augurs elected Caius Veturius, the more eagerly, because he had been condemned by the commons. The consul Quintilius died, and four tribunes of the people. The year was rendered a melancholy one by these manifold disasters; but from an enemy there was perfect quiet. Then Caius Menenius and Publius Sestius Capitolinus were elected consuls. Nor was there in that year any external war: disturbances arose at home. The ambassadors had now returned with the Athenian laws; the tribunes pressed the more urgently, that a commencement should at length be made of compiling the laws. It was resolved that decemvirs should be elected without appeal, and that there should be no other magistrate during that year. There was, for a considerable time, a dispute whether plebeians should be admitted among them: at length the point was given up to the patricians, provided that the Icilian law regarding the Aventine and the other devoting laws were not repealed.

In the three hundred and first year after Rome was built, the form of the government was a second time changed, the supreme power being transferred from consuls to decemvirs, as it had passed before from kings to consuls. The change was less remarkable, because not of long duration; for the joyous commencement of that government became too licentious. So much the sooner did the matter fall, and (the usage) was recurred to, that the name and authority of consuls was committed to two persons. The decemvirs appointed were, Appius

Claudius, Titus Genucius, Publius Sestius, Lucius Veturius, Caius Julius, Aulus Manlius, Servius Sulpicius, Publius Curiatius, Titus Romilius, Spurius Postumius. On Claudius and Genucius, because they had been elected consuls for that year, the honour was conferred in compensation for the honour (of the consulate); and on Sestius, one of the consuls of the former year, because he had proposed that matter to the senate against the will of his colleague. Next to these were considered the three ambassadors who had gone to Athens; at the same time that the honour might serve as a recompence for so distant an embassy; at the same time they considered that persons acquainted with the foreign laws would be of use in digesting the new code of regulations. Other persons made up the number. They say that persons advanced in years were appointed by the last suffrages, in order that they might oppose with less warmth the opinions of others. The direction of the entire government was rested in Appius through the favour of the commons, and he had assumed a demeanour so new, that from a severe and harsh reviler of the people, he became suddenly a protector of the commons, and a candidate for popular favour. They administered justice to the people one every tenth day. On that day the twelve fasces attended the præfect of justice; one beadle attended each of his nine colleagues, and in the singular harmony among themselves, which unanimity might sometimes prove prejudicial to private persons, the strictest equity was shown to others. It will suffice to adduce a proof of their moderation by instancing one matter. Though they had been appointed without (the privilege of) appeal, yet a dead body having been found buried in the house of Publius Sestius, a man of patrician rank, and this having been brought forward in an assembly, in a matter equally clear and atrocious, Caius Julius, a decemvir, appointed a day of trial for Sestius, and appeared before the people as prosecutor (in a matter) of which he was legally a judge; and relinquished his right, so that he might add what had been taken from the power of the office to the liberty of the people.

Whilst the highest and lowest alike experienced from them this prompt administration of justice, impartial, as if from an oracle, then their attention was devoted to the framing of laws; and the ten tables being proposed amid the intense expectation of all, they summoned the people to an assembly: and "what may prove favourable, advantageous, and happy to the commonwealth themselves, and to their children, ordered them to go and read the laws that were exhibited." "That they had equalized the rights of all, both the highest and the lowest, as far as could be devised by the abilities of ten men; that the understanding and counsels of a greater number might prove more successful; that they should turn in their minds each particular within themselves, canvass it in conversation; and bring together under public discussion whatever might seem an excess or deficiency under each particular. That the

Roman people should have such laws, as the general consent might appear not so much to have ratified when proposed, as to have proposed from themselves." When they appeared sufficiently corrected according to public opinion (as expressed) regarding each chapter of the laws as it was published, the laws of the ten tables were passed at the assembly voting by centuries; which, even at the present time, amid this immense heap of laws crowded one upon the other, still remain the source of all public and private jurisprudence. A rumour was then spread that two tables were wanting; on the addition of which a body, as it were, of the whole Roman law might be completed. The expectation of this, as the day of election approached, created a desire to appoint decemvirs again. The commons now, besides that they detested the name of consuls as much as that of kings, required not even the tribunitian aid, as the decemvirs in turn submitted to appeal.

But when the assembly for electing decemvirs was proclaimed for the third market-day, so strong a flame of ambition blazed forth, that the first men of the state began to canvass individuals, (through fear, I suppose, lest the possession of such high authority might become accessible to persons not sufficiently worthy, if the post were left unoccupied by themselves,) suppliantly soliciting for an honour, which had been opposed by them with all their might, from that commons with whom they had so often contended. Their dignity now lowered to the risk of a contest, at such an age, and after passing through such honours, stimulated the exertions of Appius Claudius. You would not know whether to reckon him among the decemvirs or the candidates; he resembled more closely one canvassing for the office than one invested with it; he aspersed the nobility, extolled every most insignificant and humble candidate; surrounded by the Duilii and Icilii who had been tribunes, he bustled about the forum, through their means he recommended himself to the commons; until his colleagues even, who till then had been extremely devoted to him, turned their eyes on him, wondering what he meant. It was evident to them, that there was no sincerity in it; "that certainly such affability amid such pride would not be for nothing. That this excessive lowering of himself, and putting himself on a level with private citizens, was not so much the conduct to be expected from one hastening to go out of office, as of one seeking the means of continuing that office." Not daring openly to oppose his wishes, they set about baffling his ardour by humouring it. They by common consent confer on him, as being the youngest, the office of presiding at the elections. This was an artifice, that he might not appoint himself; which no one ever did, except the tribunes of the people, and that too with the very worst precedent. He, however, declaring that with the favour of fortune he would preside at the elections, seized on the (intended) obstacle[134] as a happy occasion; and having by a coalition foiled the two Quintii, Capitolinus and Cincinnatus, and his own uncle, Caius Claudius, a man most stedfast in the interest of the nobility, and other citizens of the same eminence, he appoints as decemvirs men by no means equal in rank of life: himself in the first instance, which proceeding honourable men disapproved so much the more, as no one had imagined that he would have the daring to act so. With him were elected Marcus Cornelius-Maluginensis, Marcus Sergius, Lucius Minutius, Quintus Fabius Vibulanus, Quintus Pœtelius, Titus Antonius Merenda, Cæso Duilius, Spurius Oppius Cornicen, Manius Rabuleius.[135]

This was the end of Appius's assumption of a character not his own. Henceforward he began to live according to his own natural disposition, and to mould to his own temper his new colleagues before they should enter on their office. They held daily meetings remote from witnesses: then, furnished with their schemes of tyranny,[136] which they digested apart from others, no longer dissembling their arrogance, difficult of access, morose to all who addressed them, they carried out the matter to the ides of May. The ides of May were at that time the usual period for commencing office. At the commencement then of their magistracy, they rendered the first day of their office remarkable by making an exhibition of great terror. For when the preceding decemvirs had observed the rule, that only one should have the fasces, and that this emblem of royalty should pass through all in rotation, to each in his turn, they all suddenly came forth with the twelve fasces. One hundred and twenty lictors filled the forum, and carried before them the axes tied up with the fasces: and they explained that it was of no consequence that the axe should be taken away, as they had been appointed without the privilege of appeal.[137] There was the appearance of ten kings, and terrors were multiplied not only in the humblest individuals, but even in the principal men among the patricians, who thought that a pretext and commencement of bloodshed were sought for; so that if any one should utter a word favourable to liberty, either in the senate or in a meeting of the people, the rods and axes would be instantly brought forward, even to intimidate the rest. For besides that

---

[134] *Impedimentum.* The fact of his presiding at the meeting should have been a bar to his being elected a decemvir.

[135] Niebuhr will have it that five of these were of plebeian rank.

[136] *Impotentibus,* sc. immoderatis—*rari aditus,* the genitive singular.—Stroth.

[137] *Nec attinuisse demi securim, quum sine provocatione creati essent, interpretabantur.* Valerius Publicola had introduced the custom of not having the axes tied up with the fasces when carried before the consuls in the city. But the decemvirs said that this was, because an appeal from the consuls to the people was allowed. Whence, since their jurisdiction allowed of no appeal, they *interpreted,* i. e. by interpreting the meaning or intention of this custom, they concluded that they were not bound by it, and that there was no reason why they should remove the axes from the fasces.—*Crev.*

there was no protection in the people, the right of appeal being done away with, they had also by mutual consent prohibited interference with each other:[138] whereas the preceding decemvirs had allowed the points of law decided by themselves to be amended by appeal to a colleague, and had referred to the people some points which might seem to come within their own jurisdiction. For a considerable time the terror seemed equalized among all ranks; gradually it began to turn entirely on the commons. They spared the patricians; arbitrary and cruel treatment was shown to the humbler classes: they were wholly respective of the person, not of the cause: as being persons with whom interest usurped the force of justice. Their decisions they concerted at home, and pronounced in the forum. If any person appealed to a colleague, he left the one to whom he had appealed in such a manner as to regret that he had not abided by the sentence of the former. An opinion also had gone abroad without an authority, that they had conspired in their tyranny not only for the present time, but that a clandestine league had been struck among them (accompanied) with an oath, that they would not hold the comitia, and that by perpetuating the decemvirate they would retain the power now in their possession.

The plebeians then began to watch narrowly the countenances of the patricians, and (hoped) to catch the breeze of liberty from that quarter, by apprehending slavery from which, they had brought the republic into its present condition. The leading members of the senate detested the decemvirs, detested the commons; they neither approved of what was going on, and they considered that what befell the latter was not without their deserving it. They were unwilling to assist men who, by rushing too eagerly towards liberty, had fallen into slavery: they even heaped injuries on them, that, from their disgust at the present state of things, two consuls and the former mode of government may at length become desirable. The greater part of the year was now passed, and two tables of laws had been added to the ten tables of the former year; and if these laws also were once passed in an assembly of the centuries, there now remained no reason why the republic should require that form of government. They were anxiously waiting to see how soon the assembly would be proclaimed for the election of consuls. The commons were only devising by what means they should re-establish the tribunitian power, that bulwark of their liberty, a thing now so long discontinued. When in the mean time no mention was made of the elections, and the decemvirs, who had at first exhibited themselves to the people, surrounded by men of tribunitian rank, because that was deemed popular, now guarded themselves by collecting young patricians; troops of these beset the tribunals. These

---

[138] *Provocatione—intercessionem.* The *provocatio* was to the people, whilst the *intercessio* referred to the decemvirs against a colleague.

seized and drove about the commons, and the effects of the commons; when success attended the more powerful individual, as far as obtaining any thing he might covet.[139] And now they spared not even their backs. Some were beaten with rods; others had to submit to the axe; and lest such cruelty might go for nothing, a grant of his effects followed the punishment of the owner. Corrupted by such bribes, the young nobility not only made no opposition to oppression, but openly avowed their preference of their own gratification to the general liberty.

The ides of May came. No new election of magistrates having taken place, private persons came forth as decemvirs, without any abatement either in their determination to enforce their authority,[140] or any diminution in the emblems employed to make a parade of their station. This indeed seemed to be regal tyranny. Liberty is now deplored as lost for ever; nor does any champion stand forth, or appear likely to do so. And not only they themselves sunk into despondence, but they began to be looked down upon by the neighbouring states; and they felt indignant that dominion should exist where liberty was lost. The Sabines with a numerous body of men made an incursion on the Roman territory; and having committed extensive devastations, after they had driven with impunity booty of men and cattle, they recalled their troops which had been dispersed in different directions to Eretum, and pitch their camp there, grounding their hopes on the dissensions at Rome; (and trusting) that they would prove an obstruction to the levy. Not only the couriers, but the flight of the country people through the city, occasioned alarm. The decemvirs consult what should be done. Whilst they were thus left destitute between the hatred of the patricians and people, fortune added, moreover, another cause of alarm. The Æquans on the opposite side pitch their camp at Algidum; and ambassadors from Tusculum, imploring relief, bring accounts that the Tusculan land was ravaged by detachments from thence. The panic occasioned hereby urged the decemvirs to consult the senate, two wars at the same time surrounding the city. They order the patricians to be summoned into the senate-house, well aware what a storm of resentment was ready to break upon them; that all would heap on them the causes of the land laid waste, and of the dangers which threatened them; and that that would occasion an attempt to abolish their office, if they did not unite in resisting, and by enforcing their authority with severity on a few of an intractable spirit repress the efforts of others.

---

[139] *Quum fortuna, qua quicquid cupitum foret, potentioris esset.* Stroth considers this passage to be corrupt: he proposes to read *cum fortuna*, so that *portentioris esset* may refer to *quicquid cupitum foret*, i. e. with such favourable success, that every thing which the more powerful person might covet, became his.

[140] *Inhibendum*, sc. *adhibendum*—the term *inhibeo* occurs frequently in this sense, as below, *imperioque inhibendo.* The adjective *imminutis* also refers evidently to *honoris insignibus.*—*Stroth.*

When the voice was heard in the forum of the crier summoning the senators into the senate-house before the decemvirs; as a matter altogether new, because they had long since laid aside the custom of consulting the senate, it attracted the attention of the people, who expressed their surprise: "What could have happened, that after so long an interval they should revive a practice now discontinued. That they had reason to return thanks to the enemy and to war, that any thing was done that used to be done when their state was free." They looked around for a senator through all parts of the forum, and seldom recognised one any where: they then directed their attention to the senate-house, and to the solitude around the decemvirs: whilst both they themselves referred the non-assembling of the patricians to their own universally detested government, and the commons (would have it, that the cause of the non-assembling was) because, being but private citizens, they (the decemvirs) had no right to convene the senate;[141] "that a head was now formed of those who would demand back their liberty, if the commons would but accompany the senate, and as the patricians, when summoned, did not attend the senate, so the commons also should refuse to enlist." Such were the remarks of the commons. There was scarcely any of the patricians in the forum, and but very few in the city. In disgust with the state of affairs, they had retired into the country, and were attending to their own affairs, renouncing all public concerns, considering that they themselves were aloof from ill-treatment in proportion as they should remove themselves from the meeting and converse of their imperious masters. When those who had been summoned did not assemble, apparitors were despatched to their houses, both to levy the penalties,[142] and to ascertain whether they declined attendance through design? They bring back word that the senate was in the country. This was more pleasing to the decemvirs, than if they brought word that they were present and refused obedience to their commands. They command them all to be sent for, and proclaim a meeting of the senate for the following day; which congregated together in much greater numbers than they themselves had expected. By which proceeding the commons considered that their liberty was betrayed by the patricians, because the senate had obeyed

---

[141] The words are, *quum et ipsi invisum consensu imperium, et plebs, quid privatis jus non esset vocandi senatum, non convenire patres interpretarentur*, i. e. while, on the one hand, the decemvirs themselves accounted for the staying away of the senators from the meeting, by the fact of their (the decemvirs') government being disliked by them; whilst, on the other hand, the commons accounted for the non-appearance of the senators by the fact, that being now mere private citizens, their time of office being passed, they (the decemvirs) had no right whatever to convene the senate.—*Stroth.*

[142] The senators were obliged to attend the meeting of the senate when convened by the magistrate; otherwise a fine was imposed, to insure the payment of which pledges were exacted, which were sold in case of non-payment. See Cicero de Orat. iii. 1. Philip. i. 5.

those persons, as if they had a right to compel them, who had already gone out of office; and were but private individuals, were it not for the violence employed by them.[143]

But they showed more obedience in coming into the senate than servility in the sentiments expressed by them, as we have learned. It is recorded that, after Appius's stating the subject of the meeting, and before the opinions were demanded in order, Lucius Valerius Potitus excited a commotion, by demanding permission to express his sentiments concerning the state, and when the decemvirs were prohibiting him with threats, declaring that he would present himself before the people. (We have also heard) that Marcus Horatius Barbatus entered the lists with no less boldness, calling them "ten Tarquins," and reminding them, "that under the leadership of the Valerii and Horatii[144] the kings had been expelled. Nor was it of the mere name that men were then tired, it being that by which it was usual to style Jupiter, and by which Romulus, the founder of the city, and his successors were also styled; a name too which has been retained even in the ceremonies of religion, as a solemn one; that it was the tyranny and arrogance of a king they then detested, which if they were not to be tolerated in one who was both a king himself and the son of a king, who was to tolerate it in so many private citizens? that they should beware lest, by preventing persons from speaking their sentiments freely in the senate, they might oblige them to raise their voice outside the senate-house. Nor could he see how it was less allowable for him, a private citizen, to summon the people to an assembly, than for them to convene the senate. They might try, whenever they pleased, how much more determined a sense of wrong will be found to be in vindicating one's own liberty, than ambition in (vindicating) usurped domination. That they proposed the question concerning the Sabine war, as if the Roman people had any more important war on hand, than that against those who, having been elected for the purpose of framing laws, had left no law in the state; who had abolished elections, annual magistrates, the regular change of rulers, which was the only means of equalizing liberty; who, though private citizens, still possess the fasces and regal dominion. That on the expulsion of the kings, patrician magistrates were appointed, and subsequently, after the secession of the people, plebeian magistrates. To which party, he asked, did they belong? To the

---

[143] In the original the words are: *quod iis qui jam magistratu abissent, privatisque, si vis abesset,* &c., i. e. who differed in no other respect from mere private citizens, except that they had recourse to violence, which it was competent for the magistrate only to do.

[144] Livy's own account of the matter does not justify this claim of the Horatii to having been at the head of the revolution which banished the kings. But Dionysius of Halicarnassus informs us that it was Marcus Horatius who made the army revolt against Tarquinius Superbus, and that the same in his second consulate rendered unavailing all the efforts of Porsenna to restore the Tarquins.

popular party? What had they ever done with the concurrence of the people? were they nobles? who for now nearly an entire year have not held a meeting of the senate; and then hold one in such a manner, that they actually prevent numbers from expressing their sentiments regarding the commonwealth; that they should not place too much hope in the fears of others; that the grievances which they are suffering now appear to men more oppressive than any they may have to apprehend."

Whilst Horatius was exclaiming in this manner, "and the decemvirs could not discover any limit either to their anger or forbearance, nor could they see to what the thing would come, Caius Claudius, who was uncle to Appius the decemvir, delivered an address more like entreaties than reproach, beseeching him by the shade of his own brother and of his father, that he would hold in recollection the civil society in which he had been born rather than the confederacy nefariously entered into with his colleagues; that he besought this much more on Appius's own account, than for the sake of the commonwealth. For that the commonwealth would assert its rights in spite of them, if it could not obtain them with their consent. But that from great contests great animosities arise; the result of the latter he dreads." Though the decemvirs forbad them to speak on any other subject than that which they had submitted to them, they felt too much respect for Claudius to interrupt him. He therefore concluded his address by moving that it was their wish that no decree of the senate should be passed. And all understood the matter thus, that they were judged by Claudius to be private citizens; and many of the men of consular standing expressed their assent. Another measure proposed, more harsh in appearance, possessed much less efficacy; one which ordered the patricians to assemble to elect an interrex; for by passing any resolution they judged, that those persons who convened the senate were magistrates of some kind or other, whilst the person who recommended that no decree of the senate should be passed, had thereby declared them private citizens. When the cause of the decemvirs was now sinking, Lucius Cornelius Maluginensis, brother of Marcus Cornelius the decemvir, having been purposely reserved from among the consular men to close the debate, by affecting an anxiety about the war, defended his brother and his colleagues thus: saying, "he wondered by what fatality it had occurred, that those who had been candidates for the decemvirate, should attack the decemvirs, either as secondaries,[145] or as principals: or when no one disputed for so many months whilst the state was disengaged, whether legal magistrates had the management of affairs, why do they now sow discord, when the enemies are nearly at the gate; unless that in a state of confusion they

---

[145] The original here is rather obscure. *Aut socii, aut hi maxime.* Crevier prefers to read *aut soli aut hi maxime.* Stroth explains *socii, se socios præbendo.*

think that what they are aiming at will be less seen through." But that it was not just that any one should prejudice so important a cause, whilst our minds are occupied with a more momentous concern. It was his opinion, that the point which Valerius and Horatius urged, viz. that the decemvirs had gone out of office before the ides of May, should be discussed in the senate, when the wars which are now impending are over, and the commonwealth has been restored to tranquillity: and that Appius Claudius should now prepare to take notice that an account is to be rendered by him of the comitia which he himself held for electing decemvirs, whether they were elected for one year, or until the laws which were wanting were ratified. It was his opinion that all other matters should be laid aside for the present, except the war; and if they thought that the reports regarding it were propagated without foundation, and that not only the couriers, but the ambassadors of the Tusculans also had stated what was false, he thought that scouts should be despatched to bring back more certain information; but if credit were given both to the couriers and the ambassadors, that the levy should be held at the very earliest opportunity; that the decemvirs should lead the armies, whither it may seem proper to each; and that no other matter should take precedence.

The junior patricians succeeded in having this opinion carried. Valerius and Horatius rising again with greater vehemence demanded aloud, "that it should be allowed them to express their sentiments concerning the republic; that they would address the people, if by a faction they were not allowed to do so in the senate. For that private individuals, either in the senate or in a general assembly, could not prevent them; nor would they yield to their imaginary fasces." Appius then considering that the crisis was now nigh at hand, when their authority would be overpowered, unless their violence were resisted with equal boldness: "It will be better," says he, "not to utter a word on any subject, except that which we are now considering: and to Valerius, when he refused to be silent for a private individual, he commands a lictor to proceed." When Valerius, on the threshold of the senate-house, now craved the protection of the citizens, Lucius Cornelius, embracing Appius, put an end to the dispute, not consulting the interest of him whose interest he affected to consult; and permission to speak his sentiments being obtained for Valerius through Cornelius, when this liberty did not extend beyond words, the decemvirs obtained their object. The consulars also and senior members, from the hatred of tribunitian power still rankling in their bosoms, the desire of which they considered was much more keenly felt by the commons than that of the consular power, almost had rather that the decemvirs themselves should voluntarily resign their office at some future period, than that the people should rise once more into consequence through their unpopularity. If the matter, conducted with gentleness, should again return to the consuls without popular turbulence, that the commons might be induced to forget their tribunes, either by the intervention of wars or by the moderation of the consuls in exercising their authority. A levy is proclaimed amid the silence of the patricians; the young men answer to their names, as the government was without appeal. The legions being enrolled, the decemvirs set about arranging among themselves who should set out to the war, who command the armies. The leading men among the decemvirs were, Quintus Fabius and Appius Claudius. There appeared a more serious war at home than abroad. They considered the violence of Appius as better suited to suppress commotions in the city; that Fabius possessed a disposition rather inconstant in good pursuits than strenuous in bad ones. For this man, formerly distinguished at home and abroad, his office of decemvir and his colleagues had so changed, that he chose rather to be like to Appius than like himself. To him the war against the Sabines was committed, his colleagues, Manius Rabuleius and Quintus Pætelius, being sent with him. Marcus Cornelius was sent to Algidum with Lucius Menucius and Titus Antonius, and Cæso Duilius and Marcus Sergius: they determine on Spurius Oppius as an assistant to Appius Claudius to protect the city, their authority being equal to that of all the decemvirs.

The republic was managed with no better success in war than at home. In this the only fault in the generals was, that they had rendered themselves objects of hatred to their fellow citizens: in other respects the whole fault lay with the soldiers; who, lest any enterprise should succeed under the conduct and auspices of the decemvirs, suffered themselves to be beaten, to their own disgrace, and that of them (the generals). Their armies were routed by the Sabines at Eretum, and in Algidum by the Æquans. Having fled from Eretum during the silence of the night, they fortified their camp nearer to the city, on an elevated situation between Fidenæ and Crustumeria; no where encountering the enemy, who pursued them, on equal ground, they protected themselves by the nature of the place and a rampart, not by valour or arms. Greater disgrace and greater loss were sustained in Algidum, their camp also was lost; and the soldiers, stripped of all their utensils, betook themselves to Tusculum, determined to procure the means of subsistence from the good faith and compassion of their hosts; which, however, did not disappoint them. Such alarming accounts were brought to Rome, that the patricians, having laid aside their hatred of the decemvirs, passed an order that watches should be held in the city; commanded that all who were able by reason of their age to carry arms, should mount guard on the walls, and form out-posts before the gates; they also voted arms to be sent to Tusculum, besides a reinforcement; that the decemvirs also should come down from the citadel of Tusculum and keep their troops encamped; that the other camp should be removed from Fidenæ into the Sabine territory; and that the enemy might be deterred, by thus attacking them first, from entertaining any intentions of attacking the city.

To the calamities received from the enemy, the decemvirs add two flagitious deeds, one abroad, and the other in the city. In the Sabine district, Lucius Siccius, who, during the unpopularity of the decemvirs, introduced, in secret conversation with the common soldiers, mention of electing tribunes and of a secession, was sent forwards to select a place for a camp: instructions were given to the soldiers whom they had sent to accompany him in that expedition, to attack him in a convenient place and slay him. They did not kill him with impunity; for several of the assassins fell around him resisting them, whilst, possessing great personal strength and with a courage equal to that strength, he was defending himself against them, now surrounded as he was. The rest bring an account into the camp that Siccius, when fighting bravely, had fallen into an ambush, and that some soldiers were lost with him. At first the narrators were believed; afterwards a cohort, which went by permission of the decemvirs to bury those who had fallen, when they observed that none of the bodies there were stripped, that Siccius lay in the middle with his arms, all the bodies being turned towards him, whilst there was neither any body of the enemy, nor even any traces of them as going away; they brought back his body, saying, that he had certainly been slain by his own men. The camp was now filled with indignation, and it was being determined that Siccius should be forthwith brought to Rome, had not the decemvirs hastened to perform a military funeral for him at the public expense. He was buried amid the great grief of the soldiery, and with the worst possible reputation of the decemvirs among the common people.

Another atrocious deed follows in the city, originating in lust, attended with results not less tragical than that deed which drove the Tarquins from the city and the throne through the injured chastity and violent death of Lucretia: so that the decemvirs not only had the same end as the kings had, but the same cause also of losing their power. Appius Claudius was seized with a criminal passion for violating the person of a young woman of plebeian condition. Lucius Virginius, the girl's father, held an honourable rank among the centurions at Algidum, a man of exemplary good conduct both at home and in the service. His wife had been educated in a similar manner, as also were their children. He had betrothed his daughter to Lucius Icilius, who had been a tribune, a man of spirit and of approved zeal in the interest of the people. This young woman, in the bloom of youth, distinguished for beauty, Appius, burning with desire, attempted to seduce by bribes and promises; and when he perceived that all the avenues (to the possession of her) were barred by modesty, he turned his thoughts to cruel and tyrannical violence. He instructed a dependent of his, Marcus Claudius, to claim the girl as his slave, and not to yield to those who might demand her interim retention of liberty; considering that, because the girl's father was absent, there was an opportunity for committing the injury. The tool of the decemvir's lust laid hands on the girl as she was coming into the forum (for there in the sheds the literary schools were held); calling her "the daughter of his slave and a slave herself," he commanded her to follow him; that he would force her away if she demurred. The girl being stupified with terror, a crowd collects at the cries of the girl's nurse, who besought the protection of the citizens. The popular names of her father, Virginius, and of her spouse, Icilius, are in the mouths of every one. Their regard for them gains over their acquaintances, whilst the heinousness of the proceeding gains over the crowd. She was now safe from violence, when the claimant says, "that there was no occasion for raising a mob; that he was proceeding by law, not by force." He cites the girl into court. Those who stood by her advising her to follow him, they now reached the tribunal of Appius. The claimant rehearses the farce well known to the judge, as being the author of the plot, "that a girl born in his house, and clandestinely transferred from thence to the house of Virginius, had been fathered on the latter." That he stated a thing ascertained by certain evidence, and would prove it to the satisfaction even of Virginius himself, whom the principal portion of that loss would concern. That it was but just that in the interim the girl should accompany her master. The advocates for Virginia, after they had urged that Virginius was absent on business of the state, that he would be here in two days if word were sent to him, that it was unfair that in his absence he should run any risk regarding his children, demand that he adjourn the whole matter till the arrival of the father; that he should allow the claim for her interim liberty according to the law passed by himself, and not allow a maiden of ripe age to encounter the risk of her reputation before that of her liberty.

Appius prefaced his decree by observing that the very law, which Virginius's friends were putting forward as the ground of their demand, clearly showed how much he favoured liberty. But that liberty would find secure protection in it on this condition, that it varied[146] neither

---

[146] Appius here contrasts two classes of persons, one consisting of individuals, who are in their own power; the other, of those who are not *sui juris*, but are under the control either of a parent, or some other person. If the question arise concerning a person who is *sui juris*, whether he is to be consigned to slavery, or to be restored to liberty, then "*id juris esse*," sc. that he remain free till the decision is made, *because any person*, as being homo *sui juris*, and consequently he himself, "may proceed by law;" but he says, that this does not hold good with respect to a person who is not *sui juris*, but is in the hands of others; such a person, he says, cannot be pronounced free, but must be subject to the power, either of the parent or master, so that no injury be done to either. Wherefore, since the girl is not *sui juris*, she must be in the power, either of Virginius, who says he is her father, or of Claudius, who says he is her master. But since Virginius is not present, that she can be in the power of no one but Claudius, until Virginius arrive.

with respect to cases or persons.[147] For with respect to those individuals who were claimed as free, that point of law was good, because[148] any person may proceed by law (and act for them); with respect to her who is in the hands of her father, that there was no other person (than her father) to whom her master need relinquish his right of possession. That it was his determination, therefore, that her father should be sent for: in the mean time, that the claimant should suffer no loss of his right, but that he should carry off the girl with him, and promise that she should be produced on the arrival of him who was called her father. When many rather murmured against the injustice of this decision than any one individual ventured to protest against it, the girl's uncle, Publius Numitorius, and her betrothed spouse, Icilius, just come in; and way being made through the crowd, the multitude thinking that Appius might be most effectually resisted by the intervention of Icilius, the lictor declares that "he had decided the matter," and removes Icilius, when he attempted to raise his voice. Injustice so atrocious would have fired even a cool temper. "By the sword, Appius," says he, "I must be removed hence, that you may carry off in silence that which you wish to be concealed. This young woman I am about to marry, determined to have a lawful and chaste wife. Wherefore call together all the lictors even of your colleagues; order the rods and axes to be had in readiness; the betrothed wife of Icilius shall not remain without her father's house. Though you have taken from us the aid of our tribunes, and the power of appeal to the commons of Rome, the two bulwarks for maintaining

---

I cannot resist the temptation of giving in full Mr. Gunn's note on the passage, as found in his very neat edition of our author.

"Appius for his own purposes, in interpreting his own law, introduces a distinction betwixt those who were *sui juris*, entirely free, and those who were subject to the *patria potestas*. The law, according to him, can apply only to the former, because in them only is there a true claim for liberty, and in them only could a judge give an interim decision *secundum libertatem*. To give such a decision in favour of Virginia, would be a *variatio personarum*; it would be introducing as entitled to the benefit of the law a class of persons, who were, even according to their own statements, not entitled to *vindiciæ secundum libertatem*. Besides, and most important of all, the law could act in the former, as any citizen was entitled to plead the cause of one presumptively free. But in this case no one could plead, but either the father as master on the one hand, or the alleged master on the other: as the father was not present, consequently no one had any legal claim to urge the law."

[147] *Si nec causis nec personis variet.* Sc. lex variet. Some understand *libertas* as the nominative to variet.

[148] *Because any person.* "As the law permits any strangers to interpose in vindicating an individual's liberty, they have an undoubted right so to do. But the question is not whether this maiden is free: that she cannot be in any case; for she belongs either to her father or her master. Now as her father is not present to take charge of her, no one here but her master can have any title to her." Appius argues that he could not pronounce in favour of her temporary liberty, without prejudice to her father's right and power over her: as there was no one present, who claimed a legal right to the possession of her but M. Claudius, the judge had no alternative but to award her during the interim to his safe keeping.—*Stocker.*

our liberty, absolute dominion has not therefore been given to you over
our wives and children. Vent your fury on our backs and necks; let
chastity at least be secure. If violence be offered to her, I shall implore
the protection of the citizens here present in behalf of my spouse;
Virginius will implore that of the soldiers in behalf of his only
daughter; we shall all implore the protection of gods and men, nor shall
you carry that sentence into effect without our blood. I demand of you,
Appius, consider again and again to what lengths you are proceeding.
Let Virginius, when he comes, consider what conduct he should pursue
with respect to his daughter. Let him only be assured of this, that if he
yield to the claims of this man, he will have to seek out another match
for his daughter. As for my part, in vindicating the liberty of my
spouse, life shall leave me sooner than my honour."

The multitude was now excited, and a contest seemed likely to
ensue. The lictors had taken their stand around Icilius; nor did they,
however, proceed beyond threats, when Appius said, "that it was not
Virginia that was defended by Icilius, but that, being a restless man,
and even now breathing the spirit of the tribuneship, he was seeking an
occasion for a disturbance. That he would not afford him material on
that day; but in order that he may now know that the concession has
been made not to his petulance, but to the absent Virginius, to the name
of father and to liberty, that he would not decide the cause on that day,
nor interpose a decree: that he would request of Marcus Claudius to
forego somewhat of his right, and suffer the girl to be bailed till the
next day. But unless the father attended on the following day, he gave
notice to Icilius and to men like Icilius, that neither the founder would
be wanting to his own law, nor firmness to the decemvir; nor would he
assemble the lictors of his colleagues to put down the promoters of
sedition; that he would be content with his own lictors." When the time
of this act of injustice was deferred, and the friends of the maiden had
retired, it was first of all determined, that the brother of Icilius and the
son of Numitorius, both active young men, should proceed thence
straightforward to the gate, and that Virginius should be brought from
the camp with all possible haste. That the safety of the girl depended on
his being present next day at the proper time, as her protector from
injury. They proceed according to directions and with all speed carry
the account to her father. When the claimant of the maiden was
pressing Icilius to become defendant, and give sureties,[149] and Icilius
said that that was the very thing he was doing, designedly spinning out
the time, until the messengers sent to the camp might gain time for their
journey, the multitude raised their hands on all sides, and every one
showed himself ready to go surety for Icilius. And he with tears in his
eyes says, It is very kind of you; on to-morrow I will avail myself of

---

[149] *Sureties*—sponsores. The preliminary bail.

your assistance; at present I have sufficient sureties. Thus Virginia is bailed on the security of her relations. Appius having delayed a short time, that he might not appear to have sat on account of the present case, when no one applied, all other concerns being given up by reason of their solicitude about the one, betook himself home, and writes to his colleagues to the camp, "not to grant leave of absence to Virginius, and even to keep him in confinement." This wicked scheme was late, as it deserved to be; for Virginius, having already obtained his leave, had set out at the first watch, while the letter regarding his detention was delivered on the following morning to no purpose.

But in the city, when the citizens were standing in the forum erect with expectation, Virginius, clad in mourning, by break of day conducts his daughter, also attired in weeds, attended by some matrons, into the forum, with a considerable body of advocates. He then began to go round and to solicit individuals; and not only to entreat their aid as a boon to his prayers, but demanded it as due to him: "that he stood daily in the field of battle in defence of their children and wives, nor was there any other man, to whom a greater number of brave and intrepid deeds in war can be ascribed than to him. What availed it, if, whilst the city was still secure, their children would be exposed to suffer the severest hardships which would have to be dreaded if it was taken?" Delivering these observations like one haranguing in an assembly, he solicited them individually. Similar arguments were used by Icilius: the female attendants produced more effect by their silent tears than any language. With a mind utterly insensible to all this, (such, a paroxysm of madness, rather than of love, had perverted his mind,) Appius ascended the tribunal; and when the claimant began to complain briefly, that justice had not been administered to him on the preceding day through a desire to please the people, before either he could go through with his claim, or an opportunity of reply was afforded to Virginius, Appius interrupts him. The preamble with which he prefaced the sentence, ancient authors may have handed down perhaps with truth; because I no where find any one that was likely (to have been used) on so scandalous a business, it seems, that the naked fact should be stated as being a point which is agreed on, viz. that he passed a sentence[150] consigning her to slavery. At first all were astounded with amazement at so heinous a proceeding; then silence prevailed for some time. Then when Marcus Claudius proceeded to seize the maiden, the matrons standing around her, and was received with piteous lamentation of the women, Virginius, menacingly extending his hands towards Appius, says, To Icilius, and not to you, Appius, have I

---

[150] *He passed a sentence*, &c. In the original it is, "decresse vindicias secundum servitutem." This decision relates to the definitive bail. Appius the day before had made up his mind to this decision. He had calculated, however, on the non-appearance of the father; yet did not now choose to be foiled by his unexpected presence.—*Stocker.*

betrothed my daughter, and for matrimony, not prostitution, have I brought her up. Do you wish men to gratify their lust promiscuously, like cattle and wild beasts? Whether these persons will endure such things, I know not; I hope that those will not who have arms in their hands. When the claimant of the girl was repulsed by the crowd of women and advocates who were standing around her, silence was commanded by the crier.

The decemvir, engrossed in mind by his lustful propensities, states that not only from the abusive language of Icilius yesterday, and the violence of Virginius, of which he had the entire Roman people as witnesses, but from authentic information also he ascertained, that cabals were held in the city during the whole night to stir up a sedition. Accordingly that he, being aware of that danger, had come down with armed soldiers; not that he would molest any peaceable person, but in order to punish suitably to the majesty of the government persons disturbing the tranquillity of the state. It will, therefore, be better to remain quiet. Go, lictor, says he, remove the crowd; and make way for the master to lay hold of his slave. When, bursting with passion, he had thundered out these words, the multitude themselves voluntarily separated, and the girl stood deserted a prey to injustice. Then Virginius, when he saw no aid any where, says, I beg you, Appius, first pardon a father's grief, if I have said any thing too harsh against you: in the next place, suffer me to question the nurse before the maiden, what all this matter is? that if I have been falsely called her father, I may depart hence with a more resigned mind. Permission being granted, he draws the girl and the nurse aside to the sheds near the temple of Cloacina, which now go by the name of the new sheds: and there snatching up a knife from a butcher, "In this one way, the only one in my power, do I secure to you your liberty." He then transfixes the girl's breast, and looking back towards the tribunal, he says, "With this blood I devote thee, Appius, and thy head." Appius, aroused by the cry raised at so dreadful a deed, orders Virginius to be seized. He, armed with the knife, cleared the way whithersoever he went, until, protected by the crowd of persons attending him, he reached the gate. Icilius and Numitorius take up the lifeless body and exhibit it to the people: they deplore the villany of Appius, the fatal beauty of the maiden, and the dire necessity of the father. The matrons who followed exclaim, "Was this the condition of rearing children? were these the rewards of chastity?" and other things which female grief on such occasions suggests, when their complaints are so much the more affecting, in proportion as (their grief) is more intense from the natural tenderness of their minds. The voice of the men, and more especially of Icilius, entirely turned on the tribunitian power, on the right of appeal to the people which had been taken from them, and on the indignities thrown upon the state.

The multitude was excited partly by the atrocious nature of the deed, partly by the hope of recovering their liberty through a favourable opportunity. Appius now orders Icilius to be summoned before him, now on refusing to come to be seized; at length, when an opportunity of approaching him was not afforded to the beadles, he himself proceeding through the crowd with a body of young patricians, orders him to be taken into confinement. Now not only the multitude, but Lucius Valerius and Marcus Horatius, the leaders of the multitude, stood around Icilius: who, having repulsed the lictor, stated, that "if he meant to proceed by law, they would protect Icilius from one who was but a private citizen; if he desired to employ force, that they would be no bad match for him even then." Hence arises a furious scuffle. The decemvir's lictor attacks Valerius and Horatius: the fasces are broken by the people. Appius ascends the tribunal; Horatius and Valerius follow him. To them the assembly pays attention, they drown with clamour the voice of the decemvir. Now Valerius authoritatively ordered the lictors to depart from one who was but a private citizen: when Appius, whose spirits were now broken, being alarmed for his life, betook himself into a house in the vicinity of the forum, unknown to his enemies, with his head covered up. Spurius Oppius, in order to assist his colleague, rushes into the forum from the opposite side; he sees their authority overpowered by force. Distracted then by various counsels between which he wavered, by assenting to several advisers from every side, he eventually ordered the senate to be convened. Because the proceedings of the decemvirs seemed to be displeasing to the greater portion of the patricians, this step quieted the people with the hope that the government would be abolished through the senate. The senate gave their opinion that neither the commons should be exasperated, and much more that care should be taken that the arrival of Virginius should not occasion any commotion in the army.

Accordingly some of the junior patricians, being sent to the camp which was at that time on Mount Vecilius, announce to the decemvirs "that by every means in their power they should keep the soldiers from mutinying." Where Virginius occasioned greater commotion than he had left behind him in the city. For besides that he was seen coming with a body of near four hundred men, who, fired at the heinous enormity of the occurrence, had accompanied him from the city; the unsheathed weapon and himself besmeared with blood, attracted to him the entire camp; and the gowns[151] seen in the different parts of the camp, had caused the number of people from the city to appear much greater than it really was. When they asked him what was the matter, in consequence of his weeping he uttered not a word. At length, as soon as the crowd of those running together became still, and silence took

---

[151] The dress of the citizens.

place, he related every thing in order as it occurred. Then extending his hands towards heaven, addressing his fellow soldiers, he begged of them, "not to impute to him that which was the crime of Appius, not to abhor him as the murderer of his children." To him the life of his daughter was dearer than his own, if she had been allowed to live in freedom and chastity. When he beheld her dragged to prostitution as if a slave, thinking it better that his child should be lost by death than by dishonour, through compassion for her he fell into an appearance of cruelty. Nor would he have survived his daughter, had he not placed hope of avenging her death in the aid of his fellow soldiers. For that they too had daughters, sisters, and wives; nor was the lust of Appius Claudius extinguished with his daughter; but in proportion as it escaped with impunity, so much the more unbridled would it be. That in the calamities of others a warning was given to them to guard against a similar injury. That for his own part, his wife had been taken from him by fate; his daughter, because she no longer could live in chastity, died an unfortunate but honourable death; that there was no longer in his house an opportunity for Appius's lust; that from any other violence of his he would defend his person with the same spirit with which he vindicated that of his daughter. That others should take care of themselves and of their children. To Virginius, uttering these words in a loud voice, the multitude responded with a shout, "that they would not be backward, with respect either to his wrongs or their own liberty. And the gown-men mixing with the crowd of soldiers, both by narrating with sorrow those same circumstances, and by showing how much more shocking they must have appeared when seen than when merely heard, and also by telling them that matters were now desperate at Rome; those also who followed (the persons that accompanied Virginius from Rome) and alleged that Appius, having with difficulty escaped with life, had gone into exile;[152] all these individuals so far influenced them that there was a general cry to arms, they snatched up their standards, and set out for Rome." The decemvirs, being alarmed at the same time both by what they now saw, as well as by those things which they had heard had taken place at Rome, ran about to different parts of the camp to quell the commotion. Whilst they proceeded with mildness no answer was returned to them. If any of them attempted to exert authority over them, the answer given was, that "they were men and had arms." They go in a body to the city and post themselves on the Aventine; encouraging the commons, according as each person met them, to reassume their liberty, and elect tribunes of the people; no other violent expression was heard. Spurius Oppius holds a meeting of the senate; it is resolved that no harsh proceedings should be adopted,

---

[152] Two classes of persons are here intended: 1. Those who accompanied Virginius into the camp. 2. Others who followed them subsequently.

as occasion for the sedition had been given by themselves. Three men of consular rank, Spurius Tarpeius, Caius Julius, Publius Sulpicius, are sent as ambassadors, to inquire, in the name of the senate, by whose orders they had deserted the camp? or what they intended in posting themselves on the Aventine in arms, and in turning away their arms from the enemy and taking their own country? They were at no loss for an answer; they wanted some one to give the answer, there being as yet no certain leader, and individuals not being forward enough to expose themselves to the invidious office. The multitude only called out with one voice, that they should send Lucius Valerius and Marcus Horatius to them: that to them they would give their answer.

The ambassadors being dismissed, Virginius reminds the soldiers "that a little time before they had been embarrassed in a matter of no very great difficulty, because the multitude was without a head; and that the answer given, though not inexpedient, was the result rather of an accidental concurrence than of a concerted plan. His opinion was, that ten persons be elected, who should preside in the management of their affairs, and, in the style of military dignity, that they should be called tribunes of the soldiers." When that honour was offered to himself in the first instance, he replied, "Reserve for an occasion more favourable to you and to me those your kind opinions of me. My daughter being unavenged, neither allows any honour to be satisfactory to me, nor in the disturbed state of things is it useful that those should be at your head who are most obnoxious to party malice. If there will be any use of me, such use will be derived not in a less degree from me in a private station." They then elect military tribunes ten in number. Nor was the army among the Sabines inactive. There also, at the instance of Icilius and Numitorius, a secession from the decemvirs took place, the commotion of men's minds on recollecting the murder of Siccius being not less than that, which the recent account of the barbarous attempt made on the maiden to gratify lust had enkindled. When Icilius heard that tribunes of the soldiers were elected on Mount Aventine, lest the election-assembly in the city might follow the precedent of the military assembly, by electing the same persons tribunes of the commons, being well versed in popular intrigues and having an eye to that office, he also takes care, before they proceeded to the city, that the same number be elected by his own party with an equal power. They entered the city through the Colline gate in military array, and proceeded in a body to the Aventine through the middle of the city. There, joined to the other army, they commissioned the twenty tribunes of the soldiers to select two out of their number, who should hold the command in chief. They choose Marcus Oppius and Sextus Manilius. The patricians, alarmed for the general safety, though there was a meeting every day, waste the time in wrangling more frequently than in deliberation. The murder of Siccius, the lust of Appius, and the disgraces incurred in war were urged as charges against the decemvirs. It was resolved that Valerius and Horatius should proceed to the Aventine. They refused to go on any other conditions, than that the decemvirs should lay down the badges of that office, which had expired the year before. The decemvirs, complaining that they were now being degraded, stated that they would not resign their office, until those laws were passed on account of which they had been appointed.

The people being informed through Marcus Duilius, who had been tribune of the people, that by reason of their continual contentions no business was transacted, passes from the Aventine to the Sacred mount; Duilius affirming that serious concern for business would not enter the minds of the patricians, until they saw the city deserted. That the Sacred mount would remind them of the people's firmness; that they would then know, that matters could not be restored to concord without the restoration of (the tribunitian) power. Having set out along the Nomentan way, which was then called the Ficulnean, they pitched their camp on the Sacred mount, imitating the moderation of their fathers by committing no violence. The commons followed the army, no one whose age would permit him declining to go. Their wives and children attended their steps, piteously asking to whom would they leave them, in a city in which neither chastity nor liberty were respected? When the unusual solitude rendered every place in Rome void; when there was in the forum no one but a few old men; when, the patricians being convened into the senate, the forum appeared deserted; more now besides Horatius and Valerius began to exclaim, "What will ye now wait for, conscript fathers? If the decemvirs do not put an end to their obstinacy, will ye suffer all things to go to wreck and ruin? What power is that, decemvirs, which ye embrace and hold so firmly? do you mean to administer justice to walls and mere houses? Are you not ashamed that an almost greater number of your lictors is to be seen in the forum than of the other citizens? What are ye to do, in case the enemy should approach the city? What, if the commons should come presently in arms, if we seem not to be moved by their secession? do you mean to conclude your power by the fall of the city? But (the case is this,) either we must not have the commons, or they must have their tribunes. We would sooner dispense with our patrician magistrates, than they with their plebeian. That power, when new and untried, they wrested from our fathers; much less will they, now that they have tested the sweets of it, endure its loss: more especially since we make not a moderate use of our power, so that they may not stand in need of (tribunitian) aid." When these arguments were thrown out from every quarter, the decemvirs, overpowered by the united opinions of all, declare that, since such seems to be the feeling, they would submit to the authority of the patricians. All they ask is, that they may be protected from popular rage; they give a warning, that they should not through shedding their blood habituate the people to inflict punishment on the patricians.

Then Valerius and Horatius, having been sent to bring back the people on such terms as might seem fit, and to adjust all differences, are directed to make provision also for the decemvirs from the resentment and violence of the multitude. They set forward and are received into the camp with great joy by the people, as being their liberators beyond all doubt, both at the commencement of the disturbance and at the termination of the matter. In consideration of these things, thanks were returned to them on their arrival. Icilius speaks in the name of the people. When the terms came to be considered, the ambassadors inquiring what were the demands of the people, the same individual, having already concerted the plan before the arrival of the ambassadors, stated demands of such a nature, that it became evident, that more hope was placed in the justice of their case than in arms. For they demanded back the tribunitian office and the right of appeal, which, before the appointment of decemvirs, had been the props of the people, and that it should not be visited with injury to any one, to have instigated the soldiers or the commons to seek back their liberty by a secession. Concerning the punishment only of the decemvirs was their demand immoderate; for they thought it but just that they should be delivered up to them; and they threatened that they would burn them alive. In answer the ambassadors say, the demands which have been the result of deliberation are so reasonable, that they should be voluntarily offered to you; for you seek them as safeguards to your liberty, not as means of licentious power to assail others. Your resentment we must rather pardon than indulge; seeing that from your hatred of cruelty ye rush into cruelty, and almost before you are free yourselves, you wish already to lord it over your enemies. Shall our state never enjoy rest from punishments, either of the patricians on the Roman commons, or of the commons on the patricians? you have occasion for a shield rather than for a sword. He is sufficiently and abundantly humble, who lives in a state on an equal footing, neither inflicting nor suffering injury. Moreover, "should you feel disposed to render yourselves formidable, when, having recovered your magistrates and laws, decisions on our lives and fortunes shall be in your hands; then you shall determine according to the merits of each case; now it is sufficient that your liberty be restored."

All permitting them to act just as they think proper, the ambassadors assure them that they would speedily return, having completed every matter. When they went and laid before the patricians the message of the commons, the other decemvirs, since, contrary to their own expectation, no mention was made of their punishment, raised no objection. Appius, being of a truculent disposition and a particular object of detestation, measuring the rancour of others towards him by his own towards them, says, "I am aware of the fate which hangs over me. I see that the contest against us is deferred, until our arms are delivered up to our adversaries. Blood must be offered up to popular rage. Not even do I demur to resign my decemvirate." A decree of the senate is then passed, "that the decemvirs should without delay resign their office; that Quintus Furius, chief pontiff, should hold an election of plebeian tribunes, and that the secession of the soldiers and commons should not be visited on any one." These decrees being finished, the senate being dismissed, the decemvirs come forth into the assembly, and resign their office, to the great joy of all. News of this is carried to the commons. All the people remaining in the city escort the ambassadors. This crowd was met by another joyous body from the camp; they congratulate each other on the restoration of peace and concord to the state. The deputies address the assembly: "Be it advantageous, fortunate, and happy for you and the republic, return into your country to your household gods, your wives and children; but carry into the city the same modesty which you observed here, where, amid the consumption of so many matters necessary for so large a number of persons, no man's field has been injured. Go to the Aventine, whence ye set out. In that auspicious place, where ye took the first step towards liberty, ye shall elect tribunes of the people. The chief pontiff will be at hand to hold the elections." Great was their assent and joy, as evinced in their approbation of every measure. They then hastily raise their standards, and having set out for Rome, vie in exultation with all they met. There, the chief pontiff holding the meeting for the elections, they elected as their tribunes of the people, first of all A. Virginius, then Lucius Icilius, and Publius Numitorius the uncle of Virginia, the advisers of the secession. Then Caius Sicinius, the offspring of him who is recorded to have been elected first tribune of the commons on the Sacred mount; and Marcus Duilius, who had passed through a distinguished tribuneship before the creation of the decemvirs, and was never wanting to the commons in their contests with the decemvirs. Marcus Titinius, Marcus Pomponius, Caius Apronius, Publius Villius, and Caius Oppius, were elected more from hope (entertained of them) than from any services (performed). When he entered on his tribuneship, Lucius Icilius proposed to the commons, and the commons ordered, that the secession from the decemvirs which had taken place should not prove detrimental to any individual. Immediately after Duilius carried a proposition for electing consuls, with right of appeal. All these things were transacted in an assembly of the commons in the Flaminian meadows, which they now call the Flaminian circus.

Then through an interrex Lucius Valerius and Marcus Horatius were elected consuls, who immediately entered on their office; whose consulship was popular without any actual injury to the patricians, though not without their displeasure; for whatever provision was made for securing the liberty of the commons, that they considered to be a diminution made in their own power. First of all, when it was as it were a point in controversy, whether patricians were bound by regulations enacted in an assembly of the commons, they proposed a law in the assembly of the centuries, that whatever the commons ordered collectively, should bind the entire people; by which law a most keen-edged weapon was given to motions introduced by tribunes. Then another law made by a consul concerning the right of appeal, a singular security to liberty, and subverted by the decemviral power, they not only restore, but guard it also for the time to come, by enacting a new law, "that no one should appoint any magistrate without a right of appeal; if any person should so elect, it would be lawful and right that he be put to death; and that such killing should not be deemed a capital offence." And when they had sufficiently secured the commons by the right of appeal on the one hand, by tribunitian aid on the other, they renewed for the tribunes themselves (the privilege) that they should be held sacred and inviolable, the memory of which matter had now been almost lost, reviving certain ceremonies which had been long disused; and they rendered them inviolable both by the religious institution, as well as by a law, enacting, that "whoever should offer injury to tribunes of the people, ædiles, judges, decemvirs, his person should be devoted to Jupiter, and his property be sold at the temple of Ceres, Liber and Libera." Commentators deny that any person is by this law sacrosanct; but that he who may do an injury to any of them, is deemed to be devoted; therefore that an ædile may be arrested and carried to prison by superior magistrates, which, though it be not expressly warranted by law, for an injury is done to a person to whom it is not lawful to do an injury according to this law, yet it is a proof that an ædile is not considered as sacred; that the tribunes were sacred and inviolable by an ancient oath of the commons, when first they created that office. There have been persons who supposed that by this same Horatian law provision was made for the consuls also and the prætors, because they were elected under the same auspices as the consuls; for that a consul was called a judge. Which interpretation is refuted, because at this time it was not yet the custom for the consul to be styled judge, but the prætor. These were the laws proposed by the consuls. It was also regulated by the same consuls, that decrees of the senate should be deposited with the ædiles of the commons in the temple of Ceres; which before that used to be suppressed and altered at the pleasure of the consuls. Marcus Duilius then, tribune of the commons, proposed to the people, and the people ordered, that "whoever left the people without tribunes, and whoever caused a magistrate to be elected without the right of appeal, should be punished with stripes and beheaded." All these matters, though against the feelings of the patricians, passed off without opposition from them, because no severity was aimed at any particular individual.

Then both the tribunitian power and the liberty of the commons being firmly established, the tribunes now deeming it both safe and seasonable to attack individuals, single out Virginius as the first prosecutor and Appius as defendant. When Virginius appointed a day for Appius, and Appius came down to the forum, accompanied by some young patricians, the memory of his most profligate exercise of power was instantly revived in the minds of all, as soon as they beheld himself and his satellites. Then Virginius says, "Long speeches have been invented for matters of a doubtful nature. Accordingly I shall neither waste time in dwelling on the guilt of this man before you, from whose cruelty ye have rescued yourselves by force of arms, nor shall I suffer him to add impudence to his other enormous crimes in defending himself. Wherefore, Appius Claudius, I remit to you the accumulated impious and nefarious deeds you have had the effrontery to commit for the last two years; with respect to one charge only, unless you will appoint a judge, (and prove) that you have not, contrary to the laws, sentenced a free person to be a slave, I order that you be taken into custody." Neither in the aid of the tribunes, nor in the judgment of the people, could Appius place any hope: still he both appealed to the tribunes, and, when no one regarded him, being seized by the bailiff, he exclaims, "I appeal." The hearing of this one expression, that safeguard of liberty, uttered from that mouth by which a free citizen was so recently consigned to slavery, occasioned general silence. And, whilst they observe to each other, that "at length there are gods, and that they do not disregard human affairs; and that punishments await tyranny and cruelty, which, though late, are still by no means light; that he now appealed, who had abolished all right of appeal; and that he implored the protection of the people, who had trampled down all the rights of the people; and that he was dragged off to prison, destitute of the rights of liberty, who had doomed a free person to slavery." Amid the murmurs of the assembly, the voice of Appius was heard imploring the protection of the Roman people. He enumerated the services of his ancestors to the state, at home and abroad; his own unfortunate zeal towards the Roman commons; that he had resigned the consulship, to the great displeasure of the patricians, for the purpose of equalizing the laws; (he then mentioned) his laws; which, though they still remained in force, the framer of them was dragged to a prison. But the peculiar advantages and disadvantages of his case he would then make trial of, when an opportunity would be afforded him of stating his defence. At present, he, a Roman citizen, demanded, by the common right of citizenship, that he be allowed to speak on the day appointed, and to appeal to the judgment of the Roman people. That he did not dread popular rage so much as not to place any hope in the equity and compassion of his fellow citizens. But if he were led to prison without being heard, that he once more appealed to the tribunes of the people, and warned them not to imitate those whom they hated. But if the tribunes acknowledge themselves bound in the same confederacy for abolishing the right of appeal, which they charged the decemvirs with having formed, then he appealed to the people: he implored the benefit of the laws passed that very year, both by the consuls and tribunes, regarding the right of appeal. For who would appeal, if this were not allowed a person as yet uncondemned, whose case has not been heard? what plebeian and humble individual would find protection in the laws, if Appius Claudius could not? that he would afford a proof, whether tyranny or liberty was established by the new laws; and whether the right of appeal and of challenge against the injustice of magistrates was only held out in empty words, or effectually granted.

Virginius, on the other hand, affirmed that Appius Claudius was the only person not entitled to a participation in the laws, nor in civil or human society. That men should look to the tribunal, the fortress of all villanies; where that perpetual decemvir, venting his fury on the properties, backs, and blood of the citizens, threatening all with his rods and axes, a despiser of gods and men, attended with executioners, not lictors, changing his mind from rapine and murder to lust, before the eyes of the Roman people, tore a free-born maiden, as if a prisoner of war, from the embraces of her father, and gave her as a present to a dependant, the pander to his secret pleasures. Where by a cruel decree, and by a most villainous decision, he armed the right hand of the father against the daughter: where he ordered the spouse and uncle, on their raising the lifeless body of the girl, to be taken off to a prison; moved more at the interruption to his sensual gratification than at her untimely death. That the prison was built for him also, which he used to call the domicile of the Roman commons. Wherefore, though he may appeal again and oftener, he would as frequently refer him to a judge, on the charge of having sentenced a free person to slavery; if he would not go before a judge, that he ordered him to be taken to prison as one condemned. He was thrown into prison, and though without the disapprobation of any individual, yet not without considerable emotions of the public mind, when, in consequence of the punishment of so distinguished a man, their own liberty began to appear to the commons themselves as excessive. The tribune deferred the day of trial. Whilst these matters are going on, ambassadors from the Hernicians and Latins came to Rome to present their congratulations on the harmony subsisting between the patricians and commons; and as an offering on that account to Jupiter, the best and greatest, they brought into the Capitol a golden crown, of small weight, as riches at that time did not abound, and the duties of religion were performed rather with piety than magnificence. From the same source it was ascertained that the Æquans and Volscians were preparing for war with the utmost energy. The consuls were therefore ordered to divide the provinces between them. The Sabines fell to the lot of Horatius, the Æquans and Volscians to that of Valerius. On their proclaiming a levy for these wars, through the good wishes of the commons, not only the younger men, but of those who had served out their time, a considerable portion as volunteers, attended to give in their names: and hence the army was stronger not only by the number, but also by the kind of soldiers, veterans being mixed with them. Before they marched out of the city, they engraved on brass, and fixed up in public view, the decemviral laws, which have received the name of "the twelve tables." There are some who state that the ædiles discharged that office by order of the tribunes.

Caius Claudius, who, detesting the crimes of the decemvirs and, above all, incensed at the arrogant conduct of his brother's son, had retired to Regillum, the country of his forefathers, having returned, though now advanced in years, to deprecate the dangers impending over that man, whose vices he had shunned, now clad in a mourning garment, with the members of his family and his clients, went about the forum, and solicited the interest of the citizens individually, "That they would not cast such a stain on the Claudian family, as to consider them deserving of imprisonment and chains; that a man whose image would be most highly honoured with posterity, the framer of their laws and the founder of Roman jurisprudence, lay in chains amongst nightly thieves and robbers. (He begged) that they would turn away their minds from resentment for a while to examination and reflection; and rather pardon one at the intercession of so many members of the Claudian family, than through a hatred of one spurn the entreaties of many; that he himself also paid this tribute to the family and the name; nor had he been reconciled to him, whose unfortunate situation he wished to relieve; that by fortitude liberty had been recovered; by clemency the harmony of the several orders might be established." Some there were whom he influenced more by his warm attachment to his family than for the sake of him for whom he interceded. But Virginius begged that "they would rather pity him and his daughter; and that they would listen to the entreaties, not of the Claudian family, which had assumed a sort of sovereignty over the commons, but those of the near friends of Virginia and of the three tribunes; who having been created for the aid of the commons, were now themselves imploring the protection and aid of the commons." These tears appeared more just. Accordingly, all hope being cut off, Appius put a period to his life, before the day arrived appointed for his trial. Soon after, Spurius Oppius, the next object of public indignation, as having been in the city when the unjust decision was given by his colleague, was arraigned by Publius Numitorius. However, an act of injustice committed by Oppius brought more odium on him, than the not preventing one (in the case of Appius). A witness was brought forward, who, after reckoning up twenty campaigns, after having been particularly honoured eight different times, and wearing these honours in the sight of the Roman people, tore open his garment and exhibited his back torn with stripes, asking no other conditions but "that, if the accused could name any one guilty act of his, he might, though a private individual, once more repeat his severity on him." Oppius was also thrown into prison, where he put a period to his life before the day of trial. The tribunes confiscated the property of Appius and Oppius. Their colleagues left their homes to go into exile; their property was confiscated. Marcus Claudius, the claimant of Virginia, being condemned on the day of his trial, was discharged and went away into exile to Tibur, Virginius himself remitting the penalty as far as it affected his life; and the shade of Virginia, more fortunate after death than when living, after having roamed through so many families in quest of vengeance, at length rested in peace, no guilty person being left unpunished.

Great alarm seized the patricians, and the countenances of the tribunes were now the same as those of the decemvirs had been, when Marcus Duilius, tribune of the people, having put a salutary check to their immoderate power, says, "There has been both enough of liberty on our own part, and of vengeance on our enemies; wherefore for this year I will neither suffer a day of trial to be appointed for any one, nor any person to be thrown into prison. For it is neither pleasing to me that old crimes now forgotten should be again brought forward, seeing that the recent ones have been atoned for by the punishment of the decemvirs; and the unremitting care of both the consuls in defending your liberties, is ample security that nothing will be committed which will call for tribunitian interference." This moderation of the tribune first relieved the patricians from their fears, and at the same time increased their ill-will towards the consuls; for they had been so devoted to the commons, that even a plebeian magistrate took an earlier interest in the safety and liberty of the patricians, than one of patrician rank; and their enemies would have been surfeited with inflicting punishments on them, before the consuls, to all appearance, would have resisted their licentious career. And there were many who said that a want of firmness was shown, inasmuch as the fathers had given their approbation to the laws proposed; nor was there a doubt, but that in this troubled state of public affairs they had yielded to the times.

The business in the city being settled, and the rights of the commons being firmly established, the consuls departed to their respective provinces. Valerius prudently deferred all warlike operations against the armies of the Æquans and the Volscians, which had now formed a junction at Algidum. But if he had immediately committed the result to fortune, I know not but that, such were the feelings both of the Romans and of their enemies since the unfavourable auspices of the decemvirs, the contest would have stood them in a heavy loss. Having pitched his camp at the distance of a mile from the enemy, he kept his men quiet. The enemy filled the space lying between the two camps with their army in order of battle, and not a single Roman made them any answer when they challenged them to battle. At length, wearied from standing and from waiting in vain for a contest, the Æquans and Volscians, considering that the victory was in a manner conceded to them, go off, some to the Hernicians, some to the Latins, to commit depredations. There was left in the camp rather a garrison for its defence than sufficient force for a contest. When the consul perceived this, he retorted the terror previously occasioned to his men, and drawing up his troops in order of battle, he now in his turn provokes the enemy to fight. When they, from a feeling of the absence of their forces, declined battle, the courage of the Romans immediately increased, and they considered as vanquished those who stood panic-stricken within their rampart. After having stood for the entire day prepared for the contest, they retired at night. And the Romans, now full of hope, set about refreshing themselves. The enemy, in by no means equal spirits, being now in trepidation, despatch messengers in every direction to call back the plundering parties. Those in the nearest places return thence; those who were farther off were not found. When the day dawned, the Romans leave the camp, determining on assaulting the rampart unless an opportunity of fighting were afforded; and when the day was now far advanced, and no movement was made by the enemy, the consul orders them to advance; and the troops being put in motion, the Æquans and the Volscians became indignant, that victorious armies were to be defended by a rampart rather than by valour and arms. Wherefore they also earnestly demanded the signal for battle from their generals, and received it. And now half of them had got out of the gates, and the others in succession were observing order, marching down each to his own post, when the Roman consul, before the enemy's line could be drawn up, supported by their entire strength, advanced on them; and having attacked them before they were all as yet led forth, and when those who were so had not their ranks sufficiently arranged, he falls on the unsteady crowd of them, running in trepidation from one place to another, and throwing around their eyes on themselves and on their friends, a shout and violent onset adding to the already confused state of their minds. The enemy at first gave way; then, when they had rallied their spirits, and their generals on every side reprovingly asked them, whether they were about to yield to their vanquished foes, the battle was restored.

On the other side, the consul desired the Romans to remember that "on that day, for the first time, they fought as free men in defence of Rome, now a free city. That it was for themselves they were to conquer, and not that they should be the prize of the decemvirs, after conquering. That it was not under the command of Appius that the action was being conducted, but under their consul Valerius, descended from the liberators of the Roman people, himself too a liberator. That they should show that in former battles it had been the fault of the generals, and not of the soldiers, that they did not conquer. That it was shameful to have had more courage against their own countrymen than against their enemies, and to have dreaded slavery more at home than abroad. That Virginia was the only person whose chastity was in danger in time of peace: that Appius was the only citizen of dangerous lust. But if the fortune of war should turn against them, all their children would be in danger from so many thousands of enemies. That he would not, on account of the omen, mention things which may neither Jupiter nor their father Mars suffer to befall a city built under such auspices." He reminded them of the Aventine and the Sacred mount; and "that they should bring back dominion unimpaired to that spot, where their liberty had been established but a few months before: and that they should show that the Roman soldiers retained the same abilities after the expulsion of the decemvirs, which they had possessed before they were appointed; and that the valour of the Roman people was not deteriorated after the laws were equalized." After he uttered these words among the battalions of the infantry, he flies from them to the cavalry. "Come, young men, surpass in valour the infantry, as you already surpass them in honour and in rank. The infantry at the first onset have made the enemy give way: now that they have given way, do you give reins to your horses and drive them from the field. They will not stand your charge: even now they rather hesitate than resist." They spur on their horses, and drive in amongst the enemy who were already thrown into confusion by the attack of the infantry; and having broken through the ranks, and pushed on to the rear of their line, a part wheeling round in the open space, turn most of them away from the camp to which they were now flying from all sides, and by riding on before they deter them from that direction. The line of infantry, and the consul himself, and the main body of the army make for the camp, and having taken it with considerable slaughter, they get possession of a great quantity of booty. The fame of this battle was carried not only to the city, but to the other army also among the Sabines. In the city it was celebrated only with public rejoicing; in the camp it fired the courage of the soldiers to emulate such glory. Horatius, by training them in excursions, and making trial of them in slight skirmishes, had accustomed them to trust in themselves rather than to remember the ignominy incurred under the command of the decemvirs, and these little encounters had now gone so far as to insure to them the consummation of all their hopes. The Sabines, elated at their success on the preceding year, ceased not to provoke and urge them (to fight,) constantly asking them why they wasted time, sallying forth in small numbers and returning like marauders, and why they parcelled out the grand effort of a single war on a number of insignificant skirmishes? why did they not engage them in the field, and consign the result to fortune to be determined at once?

Besides that they had already of themselves recovered a sufficient degree of courage, the Romans were fired with exasperation "that the other army would soon return victorious to the city; that the enemy were now wantonly insulting them by contumelies; when would they be a match for the enemy, if they were not so then?" When the consul ascertained that the soldiers gave expression to these sentiments in the camp, having summoned an assembly: "How matters have gone on in Algidum," says he, "I suppose that you, soldiers, have already heard. As became the army of a free people to behave, so have they behaved: through the judicious conduct of my colleague and the valour of the soldiers, the victory has been gained. For my part, the plan and determination which I am to maintain, you yourselves shall suggest. The war may be both prolonged with advantage, and be brought to a speedy conclusion. If it is to be prolonged, I shall take care by the same discipline with which I have commenced, that your hopes and your valour may increase every day. If you have now sufficient courage, and it is your wish that the matter be decided, come on, raise here that shout such as you will raise in the field of battle, the index at once of your inclination and your valour." When the shout was raised with great alacrity, he assures them "that with the good favour of heaven, he would comply with their wishes and lead them next day to the field." The remainder of the day is spent in preparing their arms. On the following day, as soon as the Sabines saw the Roman army being drawn up in order of battle, they too, as being long since eager for the encounter, come forward. The battle was such a one as may be expected between two armies confident in themselves, the one animated by the glory of former and uninterrupted glory, the other lately so by an unusual instance of success. The Sabines aided their strength by stratagem also; for having formed a line equal (to that of the enemy,) they kept two thousand men in reserve, to make an attack on the left wing of the Romans in the heat of the battle. When these, by an attack in flank, were overpowering that wing, now almost surrounded, about six hundred of the cavalry of two legions leap down from their horses, and rush forward in front of their men, now giving way; and they at the same time both oppose the progress of the enemy, and incite the courage of the infantry, first sharing the danger equally with them, and then by arousing in them a sense of shame. It was a matter of shame that the cavalry should fight in their own proper character and in that of others; and that the infantry should not be equal to the cavalry even when dismounted.

They press forward therefore to the fight, which had been suspended on their part, and endeavour to regain the ground which they had lost, and in a moment not only is the battle restored, but one of the wings of the Sabines gives way. The cavalry, covered between the ranks of the foot, return to their horses; they then gallop across to the other division to announce their success to their party; at the same time also they make a charge on the enemy, now disheartened by the discomfiture of their stronger wing. The valour of none shone more conspicuous in that battle. The consul provided for all emergencies; he applauded the brave, rebuked wherever the battle seemed to slacken. When reproved, they displayed immediately the energy of brave men; and a sense of shame stimulated them as much as praises excited the others. The shout being raised anew, and making a united effort, they drive the enemy back; nor could the Roman power be any longer resisted. The Sabines, driven in every direction through the country, leave behind them their camp as plunder for the enemy. There the Roman recovers the effects not of the allies, as at Algidum, but his own property, which had been lost by the devastations of their lands. For this double victory, obtained in two battles, in two different places, the senate through jealousy decreed merely supplications in the name of the consuls for one day only. The people went, however, on the second day also in great numbers of their own accord to offer thanksgiving; and this unauthorized and popular supplication was even more zealously attended. The consuls by concert came to the city within the same two days, and called out the senate to the Campus Martius. Where, when they were relating the services performed by themselves, the chiefs of the patricians complained that the senate was convened among the soldiers designedly for the purpose of intimidation. The consuls therefore, lest there might be any foundation for such a charge, called away the senate to the Flaminian meadows, where the temple of Apollo now is (even then they called it Apollinaris). Where, when a triumph was refused by a large majority of the patricians, Lucius Icilius, tribune of the commons, proposed to the people regarding the triumph of the consuls, many persons coming forward to argue against the measure, but in particular Caius Claudius, exclaiming, "That it was over the senate, not over the enemy, the consuls wished to triumph; and that it was intended as a return for a private service to a tribune, and not as an honour due to valour. That never before was the matter of a triumph managed through the people; but that the consideration concerning the honour and the disposal of it, always lay with the senate; that not even the kings had infringed on the majesty of this highest order. That the tribunes should not thus occupy every department with their own authority, so as to allow the existence of no public council; that the state would be free, and the laws equalized by these means only, if each rank would retain its own rights, its own dignity." Though much had been said by the other senior patricians also to the same purpose, all the tribes approved that proposition. Then for the first time a triumph was celebrated by order of the people, without the authority of the senate.

This victory of the tribunes and people was well nigh terminating in an extravagance of a by no means salutary tendency, a conspiracy being formed among the tribunes to have the same tribunes re-elected, and in order that their ambition might be the less conspicuous, to continue their office to the consuls. They pleaded, as a cause, the combination of the patricians by which the privileges of the commons were attempted to be undermined by the affronts thrown upon the consuls. What would be the consequence, before the laws are yet firmly established, if consuls should through their factions attack the new tribunes. For that Horatii and Valerii would not always be consuls, who would postpone their own interest to the liberty of the people. By some concurrence of circumstances, useful at the time, it fell by lot to Marcus Duilius above any one else to preside at the elections, a man of prudence, and who perceived the storm of public odium that was hanging over them from the continuance of their office. And when he stated that he would take no notice of the former tribunes, and his colleagues strenuously insisted that he should allow the tribes to be at liberty to vote, or should give up the office of presiding at the elections to his colleagues, who would hold the election according to law rather than according to the pleasure of the patricians; a contention being now excited, when Duilius had sent for the consuls to his seat and asked them what they contemplated doing with respect to the consular elections, and they answered that they would appoint new consuls, having found popular supporters of a measure by no means popular, he proceeded with them into the assembly. Where, when the consuls, being brought forward before the people, and asked, whether if the Roman people, mindful of their liberty recovered at home through them, mindful also of their military services, should again elect them consuls, what they would do, made no change in their sentiments; he held the election, after eulogizing the consuls, because they persevered to the last in being unlike the decemvirs; and five tribunes of the people being elected, when, through the zealous exertions of the nine tribunes who openly pushed their canvass, the other candidates could not make up the required number of tribes, he dismissed the assembly; nor did he hold one after for the purpose of an election. He said that he had fulfilled the law, which without any where specifying the number of tribunes, only enacted that tribunes should be left; and recommended that colleagues be chosen by those who had been elected. And he recited the terms of the law, in which (it is said,) "If I shall propose ten tribunes of the commons, if you elect this day less than ten tribunes of the people, then that those whom they may have chosen as colleagues for themselves be legitimate tribunes of the people, by the same law as those whom you have this day elected tribunes of the people." When Duilius persevered to the last, stating that the republic could not have fifteen tribunes of the people, after baffling the ambition of his colleagues, he resigned his office, being equally approved by the patricians and people.

The new tribunes of the people in electing their colleagues evinced a disposition to gratify the wishes of the patricians; they even elected two who were patricians, and even consulars, Spurius Tarpeius and Aulus Aterius. The consuls then elected, Largius Herminius, Titus Virginius Cælimontanus not very much inclined to the cause either of the patricians or commons, had perfect tranquillity both at home and abroad. Lucius Trebonius, tribune of the commons, incensed against the patricians, because, as he said, he was imposed on by them in the affair of choosing colleagues, and betrayed by his colleagues, carried a proposal, "that whoever took the votes of the commons in electing tribunes of the people, he should go on taking the votes, until he elected ten tribunes of the people;" and he spent his tribuneship in worrying the patricians, whence the cognomen of Asper was given him. Next Marcus Geganius Macerinus, and Caius Julius, being elected consuls, quieted some combinations of the tribunes against the youth of the nobility, without any harsh proceeding against that power, and still preserving the dignity of the patricians; by proclaiming a levy for the war against the Volscians and Æquans, they kept the people from riots by keeping matters in abeyance; affirming, that every thing was quiet abroad, there being harmony in the city, and that through civil discord the enemies assumed new courage. Their anxiety for peace was also the cause of concord at home. But each of the orders ever took advantage of moderation in the other. Acts of injustice began to be committed by the younger patricians on the commons when perfectly quiet. When the tribunes would assist the weaker party, at first it was of little use; then not even themselves escaped being ill-treated; particularly in the latter months, when injustice was committed through the combinations among the more powerful, and the vigour of every magistracy becomes considerably more lax in the latter part of the year; and now the commons placed hopes in the tribuneship, only on the condition that they had tribunes like Icilius; that for the last two years they had had only mere names. On the other hand, the elder members of the patrician order, though they considered their young men to be too overbearing, yet would rather, if bounds were to be exceeded, that a redundancy of spirit should exist in their own order than in their adversaries. So difficult a thing is moderation in maintaining liberty, whilst by pretending to desire equalization, every person raises himself in such a manner as to depress another; and men, by their very precautions against fear, cause themselves to become objects of dread; and we saddle on others injustice thrown off from ourselves, as if it were actually necessary either to commit injustice or to submit to it.

Titus Quintius Capitolinus, for the fourth time, and Agrippa Furius being then elected consuls, found neither disturbance at home nor war abroad; both, however, were impending. The discord of the citizens could now no longer be checked, both tribunes and commons being exasperated against the patricians, when a day of trial being appointed for any of the nobility always embroiled the assemblies with new contests. On the first noise of which the Æquans and Volscians, as if they had received a signal, took up arms; at the same time because their leaders, desirous of plunder, had persuaded them that the levy proclaimed two years previously could not be proceeded with, the commons now refusing obedience; that on that account no armies were sent against them; that military discipline was subverted by licentiousness; and that Rome was no longer considered as their common country; that whatever resentment and animosity they may have entertained against foreigners, was now turned against each other; that now an occasion offered for destroying those wolves blinded by intestine rage. Having united their forces, they first laid waste the Latin territory: when no resistance was found there, then indeed, to the great exultation of the advisers of the war, they approached the very walls of Rome, carrying their depredations into the district around the Esquiline gate, pointing out to the city the devastation of the land by way of insult. Whence when they marched back to Corbio unmolested, and driving the prey before them, Quintius the consul summoned the people to an assembly.

There I find that he spoke to this purport: "Though I am conscious to myself of no fault, Romans, yet with the greatest shame I have come forward to your assembly. That you should know this; that this should be handed down on record to posterity, that the Æquans and Volscians, a short time since scarcely a match for the Hernicians, have with impunity come with arms in their hands to the walls of Rome, in the fourth consulate of Titus Quintius. Had I known that this ignominy was reserved for this particular year, (though we are now long living in such a manner, such is the state of affairs, that my mind could augur nothing good,) I would have avoided this honour either by exile or by death, if there were no other means of escaping it. Then if men of courage had those arms, which were at our gates, could Rome be taken in my consulate? I have had sufficient honours, enough and more than enough of life: I should have died in my third consulate. Whom did these most dastardly enemies despise? us, consuls, or you, citizens? If the fault is in us, take away the command from us as unworthy persons; and if that is insufficient, further inflict punishment on us. If in you, may there be none of gods or men who will punish your offences; do you only repent of them. It is not your cowardice they have despised, nor their own valour they have confided in; for having been so often routed and put to flight, stripped of their camp, amerced in their land, sent under the yoke, they know both themselves and you. The discord among the several orders is the bane of this city; the contests of the patricians and commons have raised their spirits; whilst we have neither bounds in the pursuit of power, nor you in that of liberty, whilst you are tired of patrician, these of plebeian magistrates. In the name of heaven, what would ye have? You coveted tribunes of the commons; we conceded them for the sake of concord. Ye longed for decemvirs; we suffered them to be created. Ye became weary of decemvirs; we compelled them to resign the office. Your resentment against these same persons when they became private citizens still continuing, we suffered men of the highest families and rank to die or go into exile. Ye wished again to create tribunes of the commons; ye created them. Though we saw that it was unjust to the patricians to create consuls in your own interest, we have even seen a patrician magistracy conceded as an offering to the people. The aid of tribunes, right of appeal to the people, the acts of the commons made binding on the patricians under the pretext of equalizing the laws, the subversion of our privileges, we have borne and still bear. What termination is there to be to our dissensions? when shall it be allowed us to have a united city? when to have one common country? When defeated we submit with more resignation than you when victorious. Is it enough for you, that you are objects of terror to us? The Aventine is taken against us; against us the Sacred mount is seized. When the Esquiliæ is almost taken by the enemy, and when the Volscian foe is scaling your rampart, there is no one to dislodge him: against us ye are men, against us ye take up arms.

"Come, when ye have blockaded the senate-house here, and have made the forum the seat of war, and filled the prison with the leading men of the state, march forth through the Esquiline gate, with that same determined spirit; or if ye do not even venture thus far, behold from your walls the lands laid waste with fire and sword, booty driven off, the houses set on fire in every direction and smoking. But (I may be told) it is the public weal that is in a worse condition through these results: the land is burned, the city is besieged, all the glory of the war is centred in the enemy. What in the name of heaven? in what state is your own private interest? just now his own private losses were announced to each of you from the lands. What, pray, is there at home, whence you may recruit them? Will the tribunes restore and compensate you for what ye have lost? Of sound and words they will heap on you as much as ye please, and of charges against the leading men, and laws one upon another, and of public meetings. But from these meetings never has one of you returned home more increased in substance or in fortune. Has any one ever brought back to his wife and children aught save hatred, quarrels, grudges public and private? from which (and their effects) you have been ever protected, not by your own valour and integrity, but by the aid of others. But, when you served under the guidance of us consuls, not under your tribunes, and the enemy trembled at your shout in the field of battle, not the Roman patricians in the assembly, booty being obtained, land taken from the enemy, with a plentiful stock of wealth and glory, both public and private, you used to return home to your household gods in triumph: now you allow the enemy to go off laden with your property. Continue immovably tied to your assemblies, live in the forum; the necessity of taking the field, which ye avoid, still follows you. Was it too hard on you to march against the Æquans and the Volscians? The war is at your gates: if it is not repelled from thence, it will soon be within your walls, and will scale the citadel and Capitol, and follow you into your very houses. Two years ago the senate ordered a levy to be held, and the army to march to Algidum; yet we sit down listless at home, quarrelling with each other like women; delighting in present peace, and not seeing that after that short-lived intermission complicated wars are sure to return. That there are other topics more pleasing than these, I well know; but even though my own mind did not prompt me to it, necessity obliges me to speak that which is true instead of that which is pleasing. I would indeed be anxious to please you, Romans; but I am much more anxious that ye should be preserved, whatever sentiments ye shall entertain towards me. It has been so ordained by nature, that he who addresses a multitude for his own private interest, is more pleasing than the man whose mind has nothing in view but the public interest. Unless perhaps you suppose that those public sycophants, those flatterers of the commons, who neither suffer you to take up arms nor to live in peace, incite and work you up for your own interests. When excited, you are to them sources either of honour or of profit: and because, during concord between the several orders, they see that themselves are of no importance on any side, they wish to be leaders of a bad cause rather than of no cause whatever, of tumults, and of sedition. Of which state of things, if a tedium can at length enter your minds, and if ye are willing to resume the modes of acting practised by your forefathers, and formerly by yourselves, I submit to any punishment, if I do not rout and put to flight, and strip of their camp, those ravagers of our lands, and transfer from our gates and walls to their cities this terror of war, by which you are now thrown into consternation."

Scarcely ever was the speech of a popular tribune more acceptable to the commons, than was this of a most strict consul on that occasion. The young men also, who during such alarming emergencies had been accustomed to employ the refusal to enlist as the sharpest weapon against the patricians, began to direct their thoughts to war and arms: and the flight of the rustics, and those who had been robbed on the lands and wounded, announcing matters more revolting even than what was exhibited to view, filled the whole city with a spirit of vengeance. When the senate assembled, these all turning to Quintius, looked on him as the only champion of Roman majesty; and the leading senators declared "his harangue to be worthy of the consular authority, worthy of so many consulships formerly borne by him, worthy of his whole life, which was full of honours frequently enjoyed, more frequently deserved. That other consuls had either flattered the commons by betraying the dignity of the patricians, or by harshly maintaining the rights of their order, had rendered the multitude more difficult to subdue: that Titus Quintius had delivered a speech mindful of the dignity of the patricians, of the concord of the different orders, and above all, of the times. They entreated him and his colleague to take up the interest of the commonwealth; they entreated the tribunes, that by acting in concert with the consuls they would join in repelling the war from the city and the walls, and that they would induce the commons to be obedient to the senate in so perilous a conjuncture: that, their lands being devastated, and their city in a manner besieged, their common country appealed to them as tribunes, and implored their aid." By universal consent the levy is decreed and held. When the consuls gave public notice "that there was no time for examining into excuses, that all the young men should attend on the following morning at the first dawn in the Campus Martius; that when the war was over, they should afford time for inquiring into the excuses of those who had not given in their names; that the man should be held as a deserter, with whose excuse they might not be satisfied;" the entire youth attended on the following day. The cohorts chose each their centurions: two senators were placed at the head of each cohort. We have heard that all these measures were perfected with such expedition, that the standards, having been brought forth from the treasury on that very day by the quæstors and conveyed to the Campus, began to move from thence at the fourth hour; and the newly raised army halted at the tenth stone, followed by a few cohorts of veteran soldiers as volunteers. The following day brought the enemy within view, and camp was joined to camp near Corbio. On the third day, when resentment urged on the Romans, a consciousness of guilt for having so often rebelled, and despair (of pardon) urged them on the other side, there was no delay made in coming to an engagement.

In the Roman army, though the two consuls were invested with equal authority, the supreme command was by the concession of Agrippa resigned to his colleague, a thing which is most salutary in the management of matters of great importance; and he who was preferred politely responded to the ready condescension of him who lowered himself, by communicating to him all his measures and sharing with him his honours, and by equalizing himself to him no longer his equal.

On the field of battle Quintius commanded the right, Agrippa the left wing; the command of the central line is intrusted to Spurius Postumius Albus, as lieutenant-general. Servius Sulpicius, the other lieutenant-general, they place over the cavalry. The infantry on the right wing fought with distinguished valour, with stout resistance from the Volscians. Servius Sulpicius broke with his cavalry through the centre of the enemy's line; whence though he might have returned in the same way to his own party, before the enemy could have restored their broken ranks, it seemed more advisable to attack the enemy's rear, and by attacking the rear he would in a moment have dispersed the enemy by the twofold attack, had not the cavalry of the Volscians and Æquans intercepted him and kept him engaged by a mode of fighting similar to his own. Then indeed Sulpicius asserted that "there was no time for delaying," crying out that "they were surrounded and cut off from their own friends, unless they united all their efforts and despatched the engagement with the cavalry. Nor was it enough to rout the enemy without disabling them; that they should slay horses and men, lest any might return to the fight or renew the battle; that they could not resist them, before whom a compact body of infantry had given way." His orders were addressed to by no means deaf ears; by one charge they routed the entire cavalry, dismounted great numbers, and killed with their javelins both the men and the horses. This put a termination to the battle with the cavalry. Then attacking the enemy's line, they send an account to the consuls of what they had done, where the enemy's line was now giving way. The news both gave new spirits to the Romans who were now conquering, and dismayed the Æquans as they were beginning to give way. They first began to be beaten in the centre, where the charge of the cavalry had broken their ranks. Then the left wing began to lose ground before the consul Quintius; there was most difficulty on the right. Then Agrippa, buoyed up by youth and vigour, on seeing matters going more favourably in every part of the battle than in his own quarter, took some of the standards from the standard-bearers and carried them on himself, some even he began to throw into the thick of the enemy. The soldiers, urged on by the fear of this disgrace, attacked the enemy; thus the victory was equalized in every quarter. News then came from Quintius that he, being now victorious, was about to attack the enemy's camp; that he was unwilling to break into it before he learned that they were beaten in the left wing also. If he had routed the enemy, that he should now join him, that all the army together might take possession of the booty. Agrippa being victorious came with mutual congratulations to his victorious colleague and to the enemy's camp. There being but few to defend it, and these being routed in a moment, they break into the fortifications without a struggle; and they march back the army after it obtained a large share of spoil, having recovered also their own effects, which had been lost by the devastation of the lands. I have not ascertained that either they themselves demanded a triumph, nor that such was conferred on them by the senate; nor is any cause assigned for the honour being either overlooked or not hoped for. As far as I can conjecture at so great a distance of time, when a triumph had been refused to the consuls Horatius and Valerius, who, in addition to the Æquans and Volscians, had gained the glory of finishing the Sabine war, the consuls were ashamed to demand a triumph for one half of the services done by them; lest if they even should obtain it, regard of persons rather than of merit might appear to have been entertained.

A disgraceful decision of the people regarding the boundaries of their allies disgraced the honourable victory obtained over their enemies. The states of Aricia and of Ardea, having frequently contended in arms concerning a disputed piece of land, and being wearied out by many mutual losses, appointed the Roman people as arbitrators. When they came to support their claims, an assembly of the people being granted them by the magistrates, a debate ensued conducted with great warmth. And the witnesses being now produced, when the tribes were to be called, and the people were to give their votes, Publius Scaptius, a plebeian advanced in years, rises up and says; "Consuls, if it is permitted me to speak on the public interest, I will not suffer the people to be led into a mistake in this matter." When the consuls said that he, as unworthy of attention, was not to be heard and, on his exclaiming "that the public interest was being betrayed," ordered him to be put aside, he appeals to the tribunes. The tribunes, as they are always directed by the multitude, rather than they direct them, indulged the people, who were anxious to hear him, in granting Scaptius leave to say what he pleased. He then commences: "That he was in his eighty-third year, and that he had served in that district which was now in dispute, not even then a young man as he was serving his twentieth campaign, when operations were going on at Corioli. He therefore adduced a fact forgotten by length of time, but one deeply fixed in his own memory: the district now in dispute had belonged to the territory of Corioli, and after the taking of Corioli, it became by right of war the public property of the Roman people. That he was surprised how the states of Ardea and Aricia should hope to intercept from the Roman people, whom from being the right owners they made arbitrators, a district the right to which they never claimed whilst the state of Corioli subsisted. That he for his part had but a short time to live; he could not however bring himself, old as he now was, to decline claiming by his voice, the only means he now had, a district which, as a soldier, he had contributed to acquire, as far as an individual could. That he strenuously advised the people not to damn their own interest by an improper feeling of delicacy."

The consuls, when they perceived that Scaptius was listened to not only in silence, but even with approbation, appealing to gods and men, that an enormous and disgraceful act was being committed, send for the principal senators: with these they went around to the tribunes; entreated, "that, as judges, they would not be guilty of a most heinous crime, with a still worse precedent, by converting the dispute to their own interest, more especially when, even though it may be lawful for a judge to protect his own emolument, so much would by no means be acquired by keeping the land, as would be lost by alienating the affections of their allies by injustice; for that the losses of character and of reputation were greater than could be estimated. Were the ambassadors to carry home this answer; was this to go out to the world; were their allies to hear this; were their enemies to hear it—with what sorrow the one—with what joy the other party? Could they suppose, that the neighbouring states would impute this proceeding to Scaptius, an old babbler at assemblies? that Scaptius would be rendered distinguished by this statue: that the Roman people would assume the character of a usurper and intercepter of the claims of others. For what judge in a private cause ever acted in this way, so as to adjudge to himself the property in dispute? That even Scaptius himself would not act so, though he has now outlived all sense of shame." Thus the consuls, thus the senators exclaimed; but covetousness, and Scaptius, the adviser of that covetousness, had more influence. The tribes, when convened, decided that the district was the public property of the Roman people. Nor is it denied that it might have been so, if they had gone to other judges; now the disgrace of the decision is certainly not at all diminished by the fairness of the title: nor did it appear more disgraceful or more hideous to the people of Aricia and of Ardea, than it did to the Roman senate. The remainder of the year continued free from either city or foreign commotions.

## Book IV.

*A law was passed concerning the intermarriage of the patricians and plebeians, after strong resistance on the part of the patricians. Military tribunes with consular power. Censors created. Restoration of the lands unjustly taken from the people of Ardea. Spurius Melius, suspected of aiming at regal power, is slain by C. Servilius Ahala by order of Quintius Cincinnatus, dictator. Cornelius Cossus, having killed Tolumnius, king of the Veientes, offers the second* spolia opima. *Duration of the censorship, originally five years, limited to one year and a half. Fidenæ reduced, and a colony settled there. The colonists destroyed by the Fidenatians, who are subsequently conquered by Mamercus Æmilius, dictator. A conspiracy of the slaves put down. Postumius, a military tribune, slain by the army for his cruelties. Pay from the treasury first given to the soldiers. Operations against the Volscians, Fidenatians, and Faliscians.*

Marcus Genucius and Caius Curtius followed these as consuls. The year was disturbed both at home and abroad. For at the commencement of the year Caius Canuleius, tribune of the people, proposed a law concerning the intermarriage of the patricians and commons; by which the patricians considered that their blood would be contaminated, and the privileges of birth would be confounded; and a hint at first lightly suggested by the tribunes, that it should be lawful that one of the consuls should be elected from the commons, afterwards proceeded so far, that the nine tribunes proposed a bill, "that the people should have the power of electing the consuls, whether they wished, from the commons or the patricians. But they thought that if that were done, the supreme authority would not only be shared with the lowest ranks, but be wholly transferred from the nobility to the commons. With joy therefore the patricians heard that the people of Ardea had revolted in consequence of the injustice of the taking away their land, and that the Veientians had laid waste the frontiers of the Roman territory, and that the Volscians and Æquans murmured on account of the fortifying of Verrugo; so much did they prefer an unsuccessful war to an ignominious peace." These tidings therefore being received and with exaggerations, in order that during the din of so many wars the tribunitian proceedings might be suspended, they order the levies to be held, preparations to be made for war and arms with the utmost activity; with more energy, if possible, than had been used in the consulship of Titus Quintius. Then Caius Canuleius declared aloud in brief terms in the senate, that "the consuls wished in vain to divert the commons from attention to the new laws; that they never should hold a levee while he lived, before the commons had first ratified the laws proposed by him and his colleagues;" and he instantly summoned them to an assembly.

Both the consuls incited the senate against the tribune, and the tribune the people against the consuls at one and the same time. The consuls denied "that tribunitian frenzies could any longer be endured; that they were now come to a crisis; that more hostilities were being stirred up at home than abroad. That this happened not more through the fault of the commons than of the patricians; nor more through that of the tribunes than of the consuls. That the matter for which there was a reward in the state thrived always with the greatest proficiency; that thus it was that men became meritorious in peace, thus in war. That at Rome the highest reward was for sedition; that had ever been the source of honour both to individuals and to collective bodies. They should remember in what condition they had received the majesty of the senate from their forefathers, in what condition they were about to transmit it to their children; that, like the commons, they should have it in their power to boast that it was improved in degree and in splendour. That there was no end, nor would there be, so long as the promoters of sedition were rewarded with honour in proportion as sedition was successful. What and how important schemes Caius Canuleius had set on foot! that he was introducing confounding of family rank, a disturbance of the auspices both public and private, that nothing may remain pure, nothing uncontaminated; that, all distinction being abolished, no one might know either himself or those he belonged to. For what other tendency had those promiscuous intermarriages, except that intercourse between commons and patricians might be made common after the manner of wild beasts; so that of the offspring each may be ignorant of what blood he may be, of what form of religion he was; that he may belong half to the patricians, half to the commons, not being homogeneous even with himself? That it appeared not enough, that all things divine and human should be confounded; that those disturbers of the common people were now preparing to (seize) the consulship; and first that they sounded people's sentiments in mere conversation on the project of having one consul appointed from the commons; that now the proposition was brought forward, that the people may appoint the consuls, whether they pleased from the patricians or from the people; and that they would appoint no doubt every most turbulent person. The Canuleii, therefore, and the Icilii would be consuls. (They expressed a hope) that Jupiter, the best and greatest, would not suffer the imperial majesty of the sovereign power to descend to that; and that they would certainly die a thousand deaths rather than such a disgrace should be incurred. They were certain that their ancestors, could they have divined that the commons would become not more placable to them, but more intractable, by making successive demands still more unreasonable, after they had obtained the first, would have rather submitted to any struggle, than have suffered such laws to be saddled on them. Because it was then conceded to them with respect to tribunes, the concession was made a second time. There was no end to it; tribunes of the commons and patricians could not subsist in the same state; either the one order or the other office must be abolished; and that a stop should be put to presumption and temerity rather late than never. (Was it right) that they, by sowing discord, should with impunity stir up the neighbouring states against us? and then prevent the state from arming and defending itself against those evils which they may have brought on us? and after they have almost sent for the enemy, not suffer the armies to be levied against the enemies? But Canuleius may have the audacity to declare openly in the senate that, unless the patrician suffer the laws proposed by himself as victorious, to be enacted, he would prevent the levy from being held. What else was this, but threatening that he would betray his country; that he would suffer it to be attacked and captured? What courage would that expression afford, not to the Roman commons, but to the Volscians, Æquans, and the Veientians! would they not hope that, under the generalship of Canuleius, they should be able to scale the Capitol and citadel, if with the deprivation of privilege and majesty, the tribunes should rob the patricians of their courage also? That the consuls were prepared to act against the wicked schemes of their countrymen, before they would act against the arms of the enemy."

Just when these matters were going on in the senate, Canuleius thus declaimed in favour of his laws and against the consuls: "Frequently even before now I think I have observed how much the patricians despised you, Romans, how unworthy they deemed you to dwell in the one city and within the same walls with them; but on the present occasion most clearly, in their having risen up so determinedly in opposition to those propositions of ours: in which what else do we do, but remind them that we are their fellow citizens, and that though we possess not the same power, we inhabit the same city? In the one we demand intermarriage, a thing which is usually granted to neighbours and foreigners: we have granted even to vanquished enemies the right of citizenship, which is more than the right of intermarriage. In the other we propose nothing new; we only reclaim and demand that which is the people's; that the Roman people may confer honours on whomsoever they may please. And what in the name of goodness is it for which they embroil heaven and earth? why was almost an attack made on me just now in the senate? why do they say that they will not restrain themselves from violence, and threaten that they will insult an office, sacred and inviolable? Shall this city no longer be able to stand, and is the empire at stake, if the right of free suffrage is granted to the Roman people, to confer the consulship on whomsoever they may please, and if a plebeian, though he may be worthy of the highest honour, is not precluded from the hope of attaining that honour? and is this of the same import, whether a plebeian be made a consul, as if any one were to propose a slave or the son of a slave to be consul? Do you perceive in what contempt you live? they would take from you a participation in this light, if it were permitted them. That you breathe, that you enjoy the faculty of speech, that you possess the forms of human beings, excites their indignation. Nay even, as I hope for mercy, they say that it is contrary to religion that a plebeian should be made consul. I pray, though we are not admitted to the annals, nor to the commentaries of the pontiffs, do we not know even those things which strangers know? that consuls have succeeded kings? and that they possess no privilege, no majesty which was not formerly inherent in kings? Do you suppose that we ever heard it mentioned that Numa Pompilius, who not only was not a patrician, but not even a citizen of Rome, was sent for from the country of the Sabines by order of the people, with the approbation of the senate, and that he was made king at Rome? that afterwards Lucius Tarquinius, who was not only not of Roman, but not even of Italian extraction, the son of Damaratus of Corinth, an emigrant from Tarquinii, was made king, even whilst the sons of Ancus still lived? that after him Servius Tullius, the son of a captive woman of Corniculum, with his father unknown, his mother a slave, attained the throne by his ability and merit? For what shall I say of Titus Tatius the Sabine, whom Romulus himself, the founder of our city, admitted into partnership of the throne? Accordingly, whilst no class of persons is disdained, in whom conspicuous merit may be found, the Roman dominion increased. You do well to be dissatisfied now with a plebeian consul, when your ancestors disdained not foreigners as kings, and when, even after the expulsion of kings, the city was not shut against foreign merit. After the expulsion of the kings, we certainly admitted the Claudian family from the Sabine country not only into citizenship, but even into the number of the patricians. Can a man from a foreigner be made a patrician, then a consul? shall a Roman citizen, if he belong to the commons, be precluded from all hope of the consulate? Do we then deem it impossible that a man of the commons can be a person of fortitude and activity, qualified to excel both in peace and war, tyke to Numa, Lucius Tarquinius, and Servius Tullius? Or, should such appear, shall we not suffer him to meddle with the helm of government? or shall we have consuls like the decemvirs, the most abandoned of mortals, who were, however, all patricians, rather than like the best of kings, though new men?

"But (I may be told) no commoner has been consul since the expulsion of the kings. What then? ought no innovation to be introduced? and what has not yet been practised, (and in a new state there are many things not yet practised,) ought not even such measures, even though they be useful, be adopted? During the reign of Romulus there were no pontiffs, nor augurs: they were appointed by Numa Pompilius. There was no census in the state, nor the distribution of centuries and classes; it was introduced by Servius Tullius: there never had been consuls; they were created after the expulsion of the kings. Of a dictator neither the office nor the name had existed; it commenced its existence among the senators. There were no tribunes of the people, ædiles, nor quæstors: it was resolved that those officers should be appointed. Within the last ten years we both created decemvirs for compiling laws, and we abolished them. Who can doubt but that in a city doomed for eternal duration, increasing to an immense magnitude, new civil offices, priesthoods, rights of families and of individuals, may be established? This very matter, that there should not be the right of intermarriage between patricians and commons, did not the decemvirs introduce within the last few years to the utmost injury of the commons, on a principle most detrimental to the public? Can there be a greater or more marked insult, than that one portion of the state, as if contaminated, should be deemed unworthy of intermarriage? What else is it than to suffer exile within the same walls, actual rustication? They wish to prevent our being mixed with them by affinity or consanguinity; that our blood be not mingled with theirs. What? if this cast a stain on that nobility of yours, which most of you, the progeny of Albans or Sabines, possess, not in right of birth or blood, but by co-optation into the patricians, having been elected either by the kings, or after the expulsion of kings, by order of the people, could ye not keep it pure by private regulations, by neither marrying into the commons, and by not suffering your daughters or sisters to marry out of the patricians. No one of the commons would offer violence to a patrician maiden; such lust as that belongs to the patricians. None of them would oblige any man against his will to enter into a marriage contract. But really that such a thing should be prevented by law, that the intermarriage of the patricians and plebeians should be interdicted, that it is which is insulting to the commons. Why do you not combine in enacting a law that there shall be no intermarriage between rich and poor? That which has in all places and always been the business of private regulations, that a woman might marry into whatever family she has been engaged to, and that each man might take a wife out of whatever family he had contracted with, that ye shackle with the restraints of a most tyrannical law, by which ye sever the bonds of civil society and split one state into two. Why do ye not enact a law that a plebeian shall not dwell in the neighbourhood of a patrician? that he shall not go the same road with him? that he shall not enter the same banquet with him? that he shall not stand in the same forum? For what else is there in the matter, if a patrician man wed a plebeian woman, or a plebeian a patrician? What right, pray, is thereby changed? the children surely go with the father. Nor is there any thing which we seek from intermarriage with you, except that we may be held in the number of human beings and fellow citizens; nor is there any reason why ye contest the point, except that it delights you to strive for insult and ignominy to us.

"In a word, whether is the supreme power belonging to the Roman people, or is it yours? Whether by the expulsion of kings has dominion been acquired for you or equal liberty for all? It is fitting that the Roman people should be allowed to enact a law, if it please. Or will ye decree a levy by way of punishment, according as each bill shall be proposed? and as soon as I, as tribune, shall begin to call the tribes to give their votes, will you, forthwith, as consul, force the younger men to take the military oath, and lead them out to camp? and will you threaten the commons? will you threaten the tribune? What, if you had not already twice experienced how little those threats availed against the united sense of the people? Of course it was because you wished to consult for our interest, that you abstained from force. Or was there no contest for this reason, that the party which was the stronger was also the more moderate? Nor will there be any contest now, Romans: they will try your spirit; your strength they will not make trial of. Wherefore, consuls, the commons are prepared to accompany you to these wars, whether real or fictitious, if, by restoring the right of intermarriage, you at length make this one state; if they can coalesce, be united and mixed with you by private ties; if the hope, if the access to honours be granted to men of ability and energy; if it is lawful to be in a partnership and share of the government; if, what is the result of equal freedom, it be allowed in the distribution of the annual offices to obey and to govern in their turns. If any one shall obstruct these measures, talk about wars, multiply them by report; no one will give in his name, no one will take up arms, no one will fight for haughty masters, with whom there is no participation of honours in public, nor of intermarriage in private."

When both the consuls came forward into the assembly, and the matter had changed from a long series of harangues to altercation, the tribune, on asking why it was not right that a plebeian should be made a consul, an answer was returned truly perhaps, though by no means expediently for the present contest, "that no plebeian could have the auspices, and for this reason the decemvirs had prohibited the intermarriage, lest from uncertainty of descent the auspices might be vitiated." The commons were fired with indignation at this above all, because, as if hateful to the immortal gods, they were denied to be qualified to take auspices. And now (as the commons both had a most energetic supporter in the tribune, and they themselves vied with him in perseverance) there was no end of the contentions, until the patricians, being at length overpowered, agreed that the law regarding intermarriage should be passed, judging that by these means most probably the tribunes would either give up altogether or postpone till after the war the question concerning the plebeian consuls; and that in the mean time the commons, content with the intermarriage-law (being passed,) would be ready to enlist. When Canuleius was now in high repute by his victory over the patricians and by the favour of the commons, the other tribunes being excited to contend for their bill, set to work with all their might, and, the accounts regarding the war augmenting daily, obstruct the levy. The consuls, when nothing could be transacted through the senate in consequence of the opposition of the tribunes, held meetings of the leading men at their own houses. It was becoming evident that they must concede the victory either to the enemies or to their countrymen. Valerius and Horatius alone of the consulars did not attend the meetings. The opinion of Caius Claudius was for arming the consuls against the tribunes. The sentiments of the Quintii, both Cincinnatus and Capitolinus, were averse to bloodshed, and to violating (persons) whom by the treaty concluded with the commons they had admitted to be sacred and inviolable. Through these meetings the matter was brought to this, that they suffered tribunes of the soldiers with consular authority to be elected from the patricians and commons without distinction; that with respect to the election of consuls no change should be made; and with this the tribunes were content, as were also the commons. An assembly is now proclaimed for electing three tribunes with consular power. This being proclaimed, forthwith whoever had contributed to promote sedition by word or deed, more particularly men who had been tribunes, began to solicit support and to bustle about the forum as candidates; so that despair, in the first instance, of obtaining the honour, by reason of the irritated state of the people's mind, then indignation at having to hold the office with such persons, deterred the patricians; at length however, being forced, they stood as candidates, lest they might appear to have relinquished all share in the government. The result of this election showed that the sentiments of persons in the struggle for liberty and dignity are different from those they feel when the contest is laid aside, the judgment being unbiassed; for the people elected all patricians as tribunes, content with this, that the plebeians had been taken into account. Where could you now find in an individual such moderation, disinterestedness, and elevation of mind, as was then displayed by the entire people?

In the three hundred and tenth year after the city of Rome was built, for the first time military tribunes in the room of consuls enter into office, Aulus Sempronius Atratinus, Lucius Atilius, Titus Clælius; in whose office the concord prevailing at home afforded peace also abroad. There are some who, without mentioning the proposal of the law concerning the election of consuls from among the commons, say that three military tribunes were elected on account of the Veientian war being added to the war of the Æquans and the Volscians and to the revolt of the Ardeates, because two consuls could not execute so many wars together, these tribunes being invested also with the authority and insignia of consuls. The jurisdiction of that office however did not stand on a firm footing, because the third month after they entered on the office, they resigned the honour, in pursuance of a decree of the augurs, as if unduly elected; because Caius Curtius, who had presided at the election, had not selected his tent with due regard to ceremony. Ambassadors came to Rome from Ardea complaining of the injustice in such a manner, that it appeared that, if it were redressed, they would continue in amity and the observance of the treaty, on the restitution of their land. The answer returned by the senate was: "that the judgment of the people could not be rescinded by the senate, besides such a measure could not be adopted on precedent or with justice;, as an additional reason also for the purpose of preserving concord between the several orders of the state. If the Ardeans were willing to abide a seasonable conjuncture, and leave to the senate the mode of redressing the injustice done to them, that the consequence would be that they would rejoice for having moderated their resentment, and that they should be convinced that the patricians were equally anxious that no injustice should arise against them, and that any which may have arisen should not be lasting." Thus the ambassadors, saying that they should lay the whole matter anew before their friends, were dismissed courteously. The patricians, now that the republic was without any curule magistrate, assembled together and elected an interrex. The contest whether consuls or military tribunes should be elected, kept the matter for several days in a state of interregnum. The interrex and senate strive that the elections of consuls be held; the tribunes of the people, and the people themselves, that elections of the military tribunes be held. The patricians succeeded, because both the commons, sure to confer the one or the other honour on patricians, gave up a needless contest, and the leaders of the commons preferred those elections at which no account was to be taken of them (as candidates) to those at which they should be passed by as unworthy. The tribunes of the commons also gave up the contest without a decision, as a compliment to the chiefs of the patricians. Titus Quintius Barbatus, the interrex, elects consuls Lucius Papirius Mugillanus, Lucius Sempronius Atratinus. During their consulship, the treaty was renewed with the Ardeans; and that is a record to prove, that they were consuls in that year, though they are not to be found among the ancient annals, nor in the books of the magistrates. I suppose because military tribunes existed at the commencement of the year, on that account, though these consuls were substituted, the names of the consuls were left out, just as if the military tribunes were the entire year in office. Licinius Macer states, that they were found both in the Ardean treaty and in the linen books at the temple of Moneta. There was tranquillity both at home and abroad, though so many alarms were held out by the neighbouring states.

This year (whether it had tribunes only, or consuls substituted in the room of tribunes) is followed by a year when there were undoubtedly consuls, scil. Marcus Geganius Macerinus a second time, Titus Quintius Capitolinus a fifth time. This same year was the commencement of the censorship, a thing which arose from an humble origin, which afterwards increased so much in importance, that in it was vested the regulation of the morals and discipline of Rome, the senate and the centuries of the knights, the distinction of honour and of ignominy were under the sway of that office, the legal right to public and private places, the revenues of the Roman people fell under their beck and jurisdiction. The institution of the thing originated in this, that the people not having been subjected to a survey for several years, the census could neither be deferred, nor had the consuls leisure to discharge their duty, when wars impended from so many states. An observation was made by the senate, "that an office laborious in itself, and one little suited to the consular office, required a magistrate for itself, to whose authority should be submitted the duties of the several scribes, the custody and care of the records, as well as the adjustment of the form to be adopted in the census." And inconsiderable though the proposal might be, still the senate received it with great pleasure, because it increased the number of patrician magistrates in the state, judging also that that would come to pass, which really did occur, viz. that the influence of those who should preside, and the honour of the office would derive on it additional authority and dignity. The tribunes also, considering the discharge of the duty (as was really the case) as necessary rather than the duty itself, as being attended with lustre, did not indeed offer opposition, lest they should through perverseness show a disposition to thwart them even in trifles. After the honour was rejected by the leading men of the state, the people by their suffrages appointed to the office of conducting the census Papirius and Sempronius, concerning whose consulate doubts are entertained, that in that magistracy they might have some recompence for the incompleteness of their consulate. They were called censors from the nature of their office.

Whilst these matters are transacting at Rome, ambassadors come from Ardea, imploring aid for their city, which was nearly destroyed, in consideration of their very ancient alliance, and of the treaty recently renewed. For by intestine wars they were not allowed to enjoy the peace with Rome, which they had by the soundest policy preserved; the cause and origin of which is said to have arisen from a struggle between factions; which have proved and ever will prove more a cause of destruction to several states, than foreign wars, famine, or disease, or any of the other evils which men refer to the anger of heaven, as the severest of public calamities. Two young men courted a maiden of a plebeian family, highly distinguished for beauty: one of them on a level with the maid in point of birth, and favoured by her guardians, who were themselves of the same rank; the other of noble birth, captivated by nothing but her beauty. The latter was aided by the good wishes of the nobles, through which party disputes made their way even into the girl's family. The nobleman was preferred in the judgment of the mother, who was anxious that her daughter should have the most splendid match possible: the guardians, mindful of party even in that transaction, strove for the person of their own order. As the matter could not be settled within the walls of the house, they proceeded to a court of justice. On hearing the claim of the mother and of the guardians, the magistrate decides the right of marriage in conformity with the wish of the mother. But violence was the more powerful. For the guardians, having harangued openly in the forum among persons of their own faction, on the injustice of the decree, collected a party and carry off the girl from her mother's house: against whom a body of nobles having arisen more incensed than before, attends the young man rendered furious by the outrage. A desperate battle takes place; the commons in no respect like to the Roman commons were worsted, and having set out from the city in arms, and taken possession of a hill, make excursions into the lands of the nobles with fire and sword. The city too, which had been previously free from all contest, they set about besieging, having induced, by the hope of plunder, a multitude of artisans to join them: nor was any appearance or calamity of war absent; as if the whole state were infested by the mad rage of the two young men, who sought the accomplishment of the fatal match through their country's ruin. The arms and war at home seemed insufficient to both parties. The nobles called in the Romans to the relief of their besieged city; the commons called upon the Volscians to join them in storming Ardea. The Volscians, under the command of Clælius, an Æquan, came first to Ardea, and drew a line of circumvallation around the enemy's walls. When news of this was brought to Rome, Marcus Geganius, the consul, having set out immediately at the head of an army, selected a place for his camp about three miles from the enemy; and the day being now fast declining, he orders his soldiers to refresh themselves; then at the fourth watch he puts his troops in motion; and the work, once commenced, was expedited in such a manner, that at sun-rise the Volscians found themselves enclosed by the Romans with stronger works than the city was by themselves. The consul had also at another place connected an arm to the wall of Ardea, through which his friends might pass to and from the town.

The Volscian general, who up to that period had maintained his army, not out of provisions which had been previously provided, but with corn brought in daily from the plunder of the country, when now encompassed by a rampart he perceives himself suddenly destitute of every thing, calling the consul to a conference, says, that "if the Roman came for the purpose of raising the siege, he would withdraw the Volscians from thence." To this the consul made answer, that "the vanquished had to accept terms, not to dictate them; and as the Volscians came at their own discretion to attack the allies of the Roman people, they should not go off in the same same way." He orders, "that their general be given up, their arms laid down, acknowledging themselves vanquished, and ready to submit to his further orders: otherwise, whether they went away or stayed, that he would prove a determined enemy, and would prefer to carry to Rome a victory over the Volscians than an insidious peace." The Volscians, determined on trying the slender hope they had in arms, all other being now cut off, besides many other disadvantages, having come to an engagement in a place unfavourable for fighting, and still more so for retreat, when they were being cut down on every side, from fighting have recourse to entreaties; having given up their general and surrendered their arms, they are sent under the yoke and dismissed full of disgrace and suffering, with one garment each. And when they halted not far from the city of Tusculum, in consequence of an old grudge of the Tusculans they were surprised, unarmed as they were, and suffered severe punishment, a messenger being scarcely left to bring an account of their defeat. The Roman general quieted the disturbed state of affairs at Ardea, beheading the principal authors of that commotion, and confiscating their effects to the public treasury of the Ardeans; the Ardeans considered the injustice of the decision completely repaired by such kindness on the part of the Roman people; it seemed to the senate, however, that something remained to be done to obliterate the remembrance of public avarice. The consul returns to the city in triumph, Clælius, the general of the Volscians, being led before his chariot, and the spoils being carried before him, of which he had stripped the enemy's army after he had sent them under the yoke. Quintius the consul, by his civil administration, equalled, which is no easy matter, the glory attained by his colleague in war; for he so regulated the domestic care of harmony and peace, by dispensing justice with moderation to the highest and the lowest, that both the patricians considered him a strict consul, and the commons, as one sufficiently lenient. Against the tribunes too he carried his measures more by his influence than by striving against them. Five consulships conducted with the same even tenor of conduct, and every part of his life being passed in a manner worthy of the consular dignity, rendered himself almost more venerable than the high office itself. On this account no mention was made of the military tribunes during this consulate.

They appoint as consuls Marcus Fabius Vibulanus, Publius

Æbutius Cornicen. Fabius and Æbutius, the consuls, inasmuch as they perceived that they succeeded to a greater glory of achievements performed at home and abroad, (the year was rendered particularly remarkable among the neighbouring states, both friendly and hostile, because relief had been afforded to the Ardeans in their perilous situation with so much zeal,) the more strenuously exerted themselves in obtaining a decree of the senate, that they might completely efface the infamy of the decision from the memory of men, to the effect that since the state of the Ardeans had been reduced to a few by intestine war, a colony should be sent thither as a protection against the Volscians. This is what was stated publicly on the tables, that the intention entertained of rescinding the decision might escape the knowledge of the commons and tribunes. But they had agreed that, a much greater number of Rutulian colonists being enrolled than of Romans, no land should be distributed, except that which had been intercepted by the infamous decision; and that not a sod of it should be assigned to any Roman, until all the Rutulians had had their share. In this way the land returned to the Ardeans. The commissioners appointed to transplant the colony to Ardea were Agrippa Menenius, Titus Clælius Siculus, and Marcus Æbutius Elva. When they, in the discharge of their by no means popular office, had given offence to the commons by assigning to the allies the land which the Roman people had decided to be their own, and were not even much supported by the patricians, because they had not deferred in any way to the influence of any one, a day having been appointed for them by the tribunes to appear before the people, they escaped all vexatious annoyance by enrolling themselves as settlers and remaining in the colony, which they now had as a testimony of their integrity and justice.

There was peace at home and abroad both this and the following year, Caius Furius Pacilus and Marcus Papirius Crassus being consuls. The games which had been vowed by the decemvirs, in pursuance of a decree of the senate on occasion of the secession of the commons from the patricians, were performed this year. An occasion for sedition was sought in vain by Pætelius, who, having been made a tribune of the commons a second time, by denouncing these same threats, could neither prevail on the consuls to submit to the senate the questions concerning the division of the lands among the people; and when, after a hard struggle, he had succeeded so far that the patricians should be consulted as to whether it was their pleasure that an election should be held of consuls or of tribunes, consuls were ordered to be elected; and the menaces of the tribune were now laughed at, when he threatened that he would stop the levy, inasmuch as the neighbouring states being now quiet, there was no occasion either for war or for preparations for war. This tranquil state of things is followed by a year, in which Proculus Geganius Macerinus, Lucius Menenius Lanatus were consuls, remarkable for a variety of disasters and dangers, also for disturbances, famine, for their having almost submitted their necks to the yoke of arbitrary power through the allurement of largesses. Foreign war alone was wanting, by which if matters had been aggravated, they could scarcely have stood out against them by the aid of all the gods. Their misfortunes began with famine; whether it was that the season was unfavourable to the crops, or that the cultivation of the land was relinquished for the allurements of the city, and of public harangues; for both causes are assigned. And the patricians accused the commons as being idle; the tribunes of the commons complained sometimes of the fraud, at other times of the negligence of the consuls. At length the commons prevailed, without opposition on the part of the senate, that Lucius Minutius should be appointed president of the market; doomed to be more successful in that office in preserving liberty than in the discharge of his own peculiar province: although in the end he bore away the well-earned gratitude of the people as well as the glory of having lowered the price of provisions. When he had made but slight advance in relieving the markets by sending embassies around the neighbouring states by land and sea to no purpose, except that an inconsiderable quantity of corn was imported from Etruria, and applying himself to the careful dispensations of their scanty stock, by obliging persons to show their supply, and to sell whatever was over and above a month's provision, and by depriving the slaves of one half of their daily allowance; then by censuring and holding up to the resentment of the people the corn-hoarders, he rather discovered the great scarcity of grain than relieved it by this rigorous inquisition. Many of the commons, all hope being lost, rather than be tortured by dragging out existence, muffled up their heads and precipitated themselves into the Tiber.

Then Spurius Mælius, of the equestrian order, extremely rich considering these times, set about a project useful in itself, but having a most pernicious tendency, and a still more pernicious motive. For having, by the assistance of his friends and clients, bought up corn from Etruria at his private expense, (which very circumstance, I think, had been an impediment in the endeavour to reduce the price of corn by the exertions of the state,) he set about giving out largesses of corn: and having won over the commons by this munificence, he drew them with him wherever he went, conspicuous and consequential beyond the rank of a private citizen, insuring to him as undoubted the consulship by the favour (they manifested towards him) and the hopes (they excited in him.) He himself, as the mind of man is not to be satiated with that which fortune holds out the hope of, began to aspire to things still higher, and altogether unwarrantable; and since even the consulship would have to be taken from the patricians against their will, he began to set his mind on kingly power;—that that would be the only prize worthy of such grand designs and of the struggle which would have to be endured. The consular elections were now coming on, which circumstance destroyed him completely, his plans being not yet arranged or sufficiently matured. Titus Quintius Capitolinus was elected consul for the sixth time, a man by no means well suited to answer the views of one meditating political innovations: Agrippa Menenius is attached to him as colleague, who bore the cognomen of Lanatus: and Lucius Minutius as president of the markets, whether he was re-elected, or created for an indefinite period, as long as circumstances should require; for there is nothing certain in the matter, except this, his name was entered as president in the linen books among the magistrates for both years. Here Minucius, conducting the same office in a public capacity which Mælius had undertaken to conduct in a private character, the same class of persons frequenting the houses of both, having ascertained the matter, lays it before the senate, "that arms were collecting in the house of Mælius, and that he held assemblies in his house: and that his designs were unquestionably bent on regal dominion: that the time for the execution of the project was not yet fixed: that all other matters were settled; and that the tribunes were bought over for hire to betray the public liberty, and that the several parts were assigned to the leaders of the multitude. That he laid these things before them almost later than was consistent with safety, lest he might be the reporter of any thing uncertain or ill-grounded." When these things were heard, the chiefs of the patricians both rebuked the consuls of the former year, for having suffered those largesses and meetings of the people to go on in a private house, as well as the new consuls for having waited until a matter of such importance should be reported to the senate by the president of the markets, which required the consul to be not only the reporter, but the punisher also; then Titus Quintius said, "that the consuls were unfairly censured, who being fettered by the laws concerning appeal, enacted to weaken their authority, by no means possessed as much power in their office as will, to punish that proceeding according to its atrocity. That there was wanting a man not only determined in himself, but one who was unshackled and freed from the fetters of those laws. That he would therefore appoint Lucius Quintius dictator; that in him there would be a determination suitable to so great a power." Whilst all approved, Quintius at first refused; and asked them what they meant, in exposing him in the extremity of age to such a contest. Then when they all said that in that aged mind there was not only more wisdom, but more energy also, than in all the rest, and went on loading him with deserved praises, whilst the consul relaxed not in his original determination; Cincinnatus at length having prayed to the immortal gods, that his old age might not prove a detriment or disgrace to the republic at so dangerous a juncture, is appointed dictator by the consul: he himself then appoints Caius Servilius Ahala his master of the horse.

On the next day, having stationed proper guards, when he had gone down to the forum, and the attention of the commons was attracted to him by the strangeness and extraordinary nature of the thing, and Mælius's friends and himself their leader perceived that the power of such high authority was directly aimed at them; when, moreover, those who were not aware of the designs on regal power, went on asking, "what tumult, what sudden war, had called for either the dictatorial authority, or Quintius, after his eightieth year, administrator of affairs," Servilius, master of the horse, being sent by the dictator to Mælius, says, "The dictator summons you." When he, being alarmed, asked what he meant, and Servilius stated that "he must stand a trial," and answer the charge brought against him before the senate by Minucius, Mælius drew back into the band of his adherents, and at first, looking around him, he began to skulk off: at length when the beadle, by order of the master of the horse, was bringing him off, being rescued by those present, and running away, he implored the protection of the Roman people, and alleged that he was persecuted by a conspiracy of the patricians because he had acted kindly towards the people: he besought them that they would assist him in this critical emergency, and not suffer him to be butchered before their eyes. Ahala Servilius overtook and slew him whilst exclaiming in this manner; and smeared with the blood of the person so slain, and surrounded by a body of young nobles, he carries back word to the dictator that Mælius having been summoned to him, and commencing to excite the multitude after he had repulsed the beadle, had received condign punishment. "Thou hast acted nobly, Caius Servilius," said the dictator, "in having saved the republic."

He then ordered the multitude, who were much agitated, not knowing what judgment to form of the deed, to be called to an assembly: and he openly declared, "that Mælius had been justly put to death, even though he may have been innocent of the charge of aiming at regal power, who, when summoned to attend the dictator by the master of the horse, had not come. That he himself had taken his seat to examine into the case; that, after it had been investigated, Mælius should have met a result corresponding to his deserts; that when employing force, in order that he might not commit himself to a trial, he had been checked by force. Nor should they proceed with him as with a citizen, who, born in a free state amid laws and rights, in a city from which he knew that kings had been expelled, and on the same year the sons of the king's sister and the children of the consul, the liberator of his country, had been put to death by their father, on a plot for readmitting the royal family into the city having been discovered, from which Collatinus Tarquinius the consul, through a hatred of his name, was ordered to resign his office and go into exile; in which capital punishment was inflicted on Spurius Cassius several years after for forming designs to assume the sovereignty; in which the decemvirs were recently punished with confiscation, exile, and death, in consequence of regal tyranny in that city, Spurius Mælius conceived a hope of attaining regal power. And who was this man? Although no nobility, no honours, no deserts should open to any man the road to domination, yet still the Claudii and Cassii, by reason of the consulates, the decemvirates, the honours of their own and those of their ancestors, and from the splendour of their families, had raised their aspiring minds to heights to which it was impious to raise them: that Spurius Mælius, to whom a tribuneship of the commons should rather be an object of wishes than of hope, a wealthy corn-merchant, had conceived the hope to purchase the liberty of his countrymen for two pounds of corn; had supposed that a people victorious over all their neighbours could be cajoled into servitude by throwing them a morsel of food; so that a person whom the state could scarcely digest as a senator, it should tolerate as king, possessing the ensigns and authority of Romulus their founder, who had descended from and had returned to the gods. This was to be considered not more criminal than it was monstrous: nor was it sufficiently expiated by his blood; unless the roof and walls within which so mad a project had been conceived, should be levelled to the ground, and his effects were confiscated, as being contaminated with the price of purchasing kingly domination. He ordered, therefore, that the quæstors should sell this property and deposit the proceeds in the treasury."

He then ordered his house to be immediately razed, that the vacant ground might serve as a monument of nefarious hopes destroyed. This was called Æquimælium. Lucius Minucius was presented with a gilded ox on the outside of the gate Trigemina, and this not even against the will of the commons, because he distributed Mælius's corn, after valuing it at one *as* per bushel. In some writers I find that this Minucius had changed sides from the patricians to the commons, and that having been chosen as eleventh tribune of the people, he quieted a commotion which arose on the death of Mælius. But it is scarcely credible that the patricians would have suffered the number of the tribunes to be increased, and that such a precedent should be introduced more particularly in the case of a man who was a patrician; or that the commons did not afterwards maintain, or at least attempt, that privilege once conceded to them. But the legal provision made a few years before, viz. that it should not be lawful for the tribunes to choose a colleague, refutes beyond every thing else the false inscription on the statue. Quintus Cæcilius, Quintus Junius, Sextus Titinius, were the only members of the college of tribunes who had not been concerned in passing the law for conferring honours on Minucius; nor did they cease both to throw out censures one time on Minucius, at another time on

Servilius, before the commons, and to complain of the unmerited death of Mælius. They succeeded, therefore, in having an election held for military tribunes rather than for consuls, not doubting but that in six places, for so many were now allowed to be elected, some plebeians also might be appointed, by their professing to be avengers of the death of Mælius. The commons, though they had been agitated that year by many and various commotions, neither elected more than three tribunes with consular power; and among them Lucius Quintius, son of Cincinnatus, from the unpopular nature of whose dictatorship an occasion for disturbance was sought. Mamercus Æmilius, a man of the highest dignity, was voted in, prior to Quintius. In the third place they appoint Lucius Julius.

During their office Fidenæ, a Roman colony, revolted to Lars Tolunmius, king of the Veientians, and to the Veientians. To the revolt a more heinous crime was added. By order of Tolumnius they put to death Caius Fulcinius, Clælius Tullus, Spurius Antius, Lucius Roscius, Roman ambassadors, who came to inquire into the reason of this new line of conduct. Some palliate the guilt of the king; that an ambiguous expression of his, during a lucky throw of dice, having been mistaken by the Fidenatians, as if it seemed to be an order for their execution, had been the cause of the ambassadors' death. An incredible tale; that his thoughts should not have been drawn away from the game on the arrival of the Fidenatians, his new allies, when consulting him on a murder tending to violate the law of nations; and that the act was not afterwards viewed by him with horror. It is more probable that he wished the state of the Fidenatians to be so compromised by their participation in so great a crime, that they might not afterwards look to any hope from the Romans. Statues of the ambassadors, who were slain at Fidenæ, were set up in the rostra at the public expense. A desperate struggle was coming on with the Veientians and Fidenatians, who, besides that they were neighbouring states, had commenced the war with so heinous a provocation. Therefore, the commons and their tribunes being now quiet, so as to attend to the general welfare, there was no dispute with respect to the electing of Marcus Geganius Macerinus a third time, and Lucius Sergius Fidenas, as consuls; so called, I suppose, from the war which he afterwards conducted. For he was the first who fought a successful battle with the king of the Veientians on this side of the Anio, nor did he obtain an unbloody victory. Greater grief was therefore felt from the loss of their countrymen, than joy from the defeat of the enemy: and the senate, as in an alarming crisis, ordered Mamercus Æmilius to be appointed dictator. He appointed as his master of the horse from the college of the preceding year, in which there had been tribunes of the soldiers with consular power, Lucius Quintius Cincinnatus, a youth worthy of his parent. To the levy held by the consuls were added the old centurions well versed in war, and the number of those lost in the late battle was made up. The dictator ordered Lucius Quintius Capitolinus and Marcus Fabius Vibulanus to attend him as his lieutenants-general. Both the higher powers, and the man suitable to such powers, caused the enemy to move from the Roman territory to the other side of the Anio, and continuing their retrograde movement, they took possession of the hills between Fidenæ and the Anio, nor did they descend into the plains until the troops of the Faliscians came to their aid; then at length the camp of the Etrurians was pitched before the walls of Fidenæ. The Roman dictator took his post at no great distance from thence at the conflux on the banks of both rivers, lines being run across between them, as far as he was able to follow by a fortification. Next day he marched out his army into the field.

Among the enemy there was a diversity of opinion. The Faliscians, impatient of the hardships of war at a distance from home, and sufficiently confident of their own strength, earnestly demanded battle; the Veientians and Fidenatians placed more hope in protracting the war. Tolumnius, though the measures of his own subjects were more agreeable to him, proclaims that he would give battle on the following day, lest the Faliscians might not brook the service at so great a distance from their home. The dictator and the Romans took additional courage from the fact of the enemy having declined giving battle: and on the following day, the soldiers exclaiming that they would attack the camp and the city, if an opportunity of fighting were not afforded them, the armies advance on both sides into the middle of a plain between the two camps. The Veientians, having the advantage in numbers, sent around a party behind the mountains to attack the Roman camp during the heat of the battle. The army of the three states stood drawn up in such a manner, that the Veientians occupied the right wing, the Faliscians the left, whilst the Fidenatians constituted the centre. The dictator charged on the right wing against the Faliscians, Quintius Capitolinus on the left against the Veientians, and the master of the horse with the cavalry advanced in the centre. For a short time all was silence and quiet, the Etrurians being determined not to engage unless they were compelled, and the dictator looking back towards a Roman fort, until a signal should be raised, as had been agreed on, by the augurs, as soon as the birds had given a favourable omen. As soon as he perceived this, he orders the cavalry first to charge the enemy, after raising a loud shout; the line of infantry following, engaged with great fury. In no quarter did the Etrurian legions withstand the shock of the Romans. The cavalry made the greatest resistance; and the king himself, far the bravest of the cavalry, charging the Romans whilst they were pursuing in disorder in every direction, prolonged the contest.

There was then among the cavalry, Aulus Cornelius Cossus, a tribune of the soldiers, distinguished for the beauty of his person, and equally so for courage and great strength of body, and mindful of his rank, which, having received in a state of the highest lustre, he left to his posterity still greater and more distinguished. He perceiving that the Roman troops gave way at the approach of Tolumnius, wherever he directed his charge, and knowing him as being remarkable by his royal apparel, as he flew through the entire line, exclaims, "Is this the infringer of human treaties and the violator of the law of nations? This victim I shall now slay, (provided the gods wish that there should be any thing sacred on earth,) and shall offer him up to the manes of the ambassadors." Having clapped spurs to his horse, he advances against this single foe with spear presented; and after having struck and unhorsed him, he immediately, by help of his lance, sprung on the ground. And as the king attempted to rise, he throws him back again with the boss of his shield, and with repeated thrusts pins him to the earth. He then stripped off the spoils from the lifeless body; and having cut off his head and carrying it on the point of his spear, he puts the enemy to rout through terror on seeing their king slain. Thus the line of cavalry, which alone had rendered the combat doubtful, was beaten. The dictator pursues closely the routed legions, and drove them to their camp with slaughter. The greater number of the Fidenatians, through their knowledge of the country, made their escape to the mountains. Cossus, having crossed the Tiber with the cavalry, carried off great plunder from the Veientian territory to the city. During the battle there was a fight also at the Roman camp against a party of the forces, which, as has been already mentioned, had been sent by Tolumnius to the camp. Fabius Vibulanus first defends his lines by a ring; then, whilst the enemy were wholly taken up with the entrenchment, sallying out from the principal gate on the right, he suddenly attacks them with the triarii: and a panic being thus struck into them there was less slaughter, because they were fewer, but their flight was no less disorderly than it had been on the field of battle.

Matters being managed successfully in every direction, the dictator, by a decree of the senate and order of the people, returned to the city in triumph. By far the most remarkable object in the triumph was Cossus, bearing the *spolia opima* of the king he had slain. The soldiers chaunted their uncouth verses on him, extolling him as equal to Romulus. With the usual form of dedication, he presented, as an offering, the spoils in the temple of Jupiter Feretrius, near the spoils of Romulus, which, having been the first called *opima*, were the only ones at that time; and he attracted the eyes of all the citizens from the dictator's chariot to himself, and enjoyed almost solely the honour of that day's solemnity. The dictator offered up to Jupiter in the Capitol a golden crown a pound in weight, at the public expense, by order of the people. Following all the Roman writers, I have represented Aulus Cornelius Cossus as a military tribune, when he carried the second *spolia opima* to the temple of Jupiter Feretrius. But besides that those spoils are rightly considered *opima*, which one general has taken from another; and we know no general but the person under whose auspices the war is conducted, the inscription itself written on the spoils proves, against both me and them, that Cossus was consul when he took them. Having once heard Augustus Cæsar, the founder or restorer of all our temples, on entering the temple of Jupiter Feretrius, which being dilapidated by time he rebuilt, aver that he himself had read the said inscription on the linen breastplate, I thought it would be next to sacrilege to rob Cossus of such a testimony respecting his spoils as that of Cæsar, the renovator of the temple itself. Whether the mistake is chargeable on the very ancient annals and the linen books of the magistrates, deposited in the temple of Moneta, and which Licinius Macer occasionally cites as authorities, which have Aulus Cornelius Cossus consul with Titus Quintius Pennus, in the ninth year after this, every person may form his own opinion. For there is this additional proof, that a battle so celebrated could not be transferred to that year; that the three years before and after the consulship of Aulus Cornelius were entirely free from war, in consequence of a pestilence and a scarcity of grain; so that some annals, as if in mourning, present nothing but the names of the consuls. The third year from the consulship of Cossus has him as military tribune with consular power; in the same year as master of the horse, in which office he fought another distinguished horse battle. Conjecture is open on the matter; but, as I think, idle surmises may be turned to support any opinion: when the hero of the fight, having placed the recent spoils in the sacred repository, having before him Jove himself, to whom they were consecrated, and Romulus, no contemptible witnesses in case of a false inscription, entitled himself Aulus Cornelius Cossus consul.

Marcus Cornelius Maluginensis and Lucius Papirius Crassus being consuls, the armies were led into the territories of the Veientians and Faliscians; numbers of men and cattle were driven off as spoil; the enemy was no where to be found on the land, and no opportunity of fighting was afforded; the cities however were not attacked, because a pestilential disorder ran through the people. Disturbances were also sought at home, but not actually excited, however, by Spurius Mælius, tribune of the people; who thinking that he might create some tumult through the popularity of his name, had both appointed a day of trial for Minucius, and had also proposed a law for confiscating the property of Servilius Ahala: alleging that Mælius had been circumvented through false impeachments by Minucius, charging Servilius with the killing of a citizen on whom no sentence had been passed; charges which, when brought before the people, proved to be more idle than the author himself. But the virulence of the disease now becoming worse, was more an object of concern to them, as also the terrors and prodigies, more especially because accounts were being brought, that houses were falling throughout the country, in consequence of frequent earthquakes. A supplication was therefore performed by the people, according to the form dictated by the decemvirs.[153] The year being still more pestilential, Caius Julius a second time and Lucius Virginius being consuls, occasioned such dread of desolation through the city and country, that not only no one left the Roman territory for the purpose of committing depredations, and not only did none of the patricians or commons entertain an idea of commencing any military aggressions; but the Fidenatians, who at first had shut themselves up either within their town, or mountains, or fortifications, now descended without provocation to commit depredations on the Roman territory. Then the army of the Veientians being called in to their aid, (for the Faliscians could be induced to renew the war neither by the distresses of the Romans, nor by the remonstrances of their allies,) the two states crossed the Anio; and displayed their ensigns at no great distance from the Colline gate. Great consternation arose therefore, not more in the country than in the city. Julius the consul draws up his troops on the rampart and walls; the senate is consulted by Virginius in the temple of Quirinus. It is determined that Aulus Servilius be appointed dictator, who some say had the cognomen of Priscus, others that of Structus. Virginius having delayed whilst he consulted his colleague, with his permission, named the dictator at night. He appoints Postumus Æbutius Elva his master of the horse.

The dictator orders all to attend at break of day outside the Colline gate. All whosoever had sufficient strength to bear arms, attended; the standards were quickly brought forth from the treasury and conveyed to the dictator. Whilst these matters were going on, the enemies retired to the higher grounds; thither the dictator follows them with a determined army; and having come to a general engagement not far from Nomentum, he routed the Etrurian legions; he then drove them into the city of Fidenæ, and surrounded it with a rampart. But neither could the city be taken by storm as being high and well fortified, nor was there any effect in a blockade, because corn was supplied to them in abundance not only for necessary consumption, but for plenty also, in consequence of that previously laid up. Thus all hope being lost of taking it by assault, or of forcing it to a surrender, the dictator determined on carrying a sap into the citadel in places which were well known to him on account of their near situation on the remote side of the city, as being most neglected because it was best protected by reason of its own nature; he himself by advancing up to the walls in

---

[153] In the performance of such rites, the slightest mistake of a word or syllable was deemed highly inauspicious; to prevent which, the regular form of words was pronounced by a priest, and repeated after him by the persons officiating.

places most remote, with his army divided into four sections, which were to succeed each other in the action, by continuing the fight day and night continuously he prevented the enemy from perceiving the work; until the mountain being dug through from the camp, a passage was opened up into the citadel; and the Etrurians being diverted from the real danger by the idle threats, the shouting of the enemy over their heads proved to them that their city was taken. On that year Caius Furius Pacilus and Marcus Geganius Macerinus, censors, approved of the public edifice[154] in the Campus Martius, and the census of the people was there performed for the first time.

That the same consuls were re-elected on the following year, Julius for the third time, Virginius for the second time, I find in Licinius Macer. Valerius Antias and Quintus Tubero state that Marcus Manlius and Quintus Sulpicius were, the consuls for that year. But in representations so different both Tubero and Macer cite the linen books as their authority; neither of them denies that it was said by ancient historians that there were military tribunes on that year. Licinius thinks that we should unhesitatingly follow the linen books; and Tubero is uncertain as to the truth. But this also is left unsettled among other points not ascertained from length of time. Alarm was raised in Etruria after the capture of Fidenæ, not only the Veientians being terrified by the apprehension of similar ruin, but the Faliscians also, from the recollection of the war having first commenced with them, although they had not joined with those who renewed hostilities. Accordingly when the two nations, having sent ambassadors around to the twelve states, succeeded so far that a general meeting was proclaimed for all Etruria at the temple of Voltumna; the senate, apprehending a great attack threatening from that quarter, ordered Mamercus Æmilius again to be appointed dictator. Aulus Postumius Tubertus was appointed by him as master of the horse; and preparations for war were made with so much the more energy than on the last occasion, in proportion as there was more danger from the whole body of Etruria than from two of its states.

That matter passed off much more quietly than any one expected. Therefore when word was brought by certain traders, that aid was refused to the Veientians, and that they were bid to prosecute with their own strength a war entered into on their own separate views, and not to seek out persons as sharers in their distresses, to whom they had not communicated their hopes when flourishing; the dictator, that his appointment might not be in vain, all opportunity of acquiring military glory being now taken from him, desirous of performing during peace some work which might serve as a memorial of his dictatorship, sets

---

[154] *Villa publica.* It was destined to public uses, such as holding the census, or survey of the people, the reception of ambassadors, &c.

about limiting the censorship, either judging its powers excessive, or disapproving of the duration rather than the extent of the office. Accordingly, having summoned a meeting, he says "that the immortal gods had taken on themselves that the public affairs should be managed externally, and that the general security should be insured; that with respect to what was to be done within the walls, he would provide for the liberty of the Roman people. But that the most effectual guarding of it was, that offices of great power should not be of long continuance; and that a limit of time should be set to those to which a limit of jurisdiction could not be set. That other offices were annual, that the censorship was quinquennial; that it was a grievance to be subject to the same individuals for such a number of years in a considerable part of the affairs of life. That he would propose a law, that the censorship should not last longer than a year and half." Amid the great approbation of the people he passed the law on the following day, and says, "that you may know, Romans, in reality, how little pleasing to me are offices of long duration, I resign the dictatorship." Having laid down his own office, and set a limit to the office of others, he was escorted home with the congratulation and great good will of the people. The censors resenting Mamercus' conduct for his having diminished the duration of one of the offices of the Roman people, degraded him from his tribe, and increasing his taxes eight-fold, disfranchised[155] him. They say that he bore this with great magnanimity, as he considered the cause of the disgrace, rather than the disgrace itself; that the principal patricians also, though they had been averse to the curtailing the privileges of the censorship, were much displeased at this instance of censorial severity; inasmuch as each saw that he would be longer and more frequently subjected to the censors, than he should hold the office of censor. Certain it is that such indignation is said to have arisen on the part of the people, that violence could not be kept off from the censors through the influence of any person except of Mamercus himself.

The tribunes of the people, by preventing the election of consuls by incessant harangues, succeeded at length, after the matter had been well nigh brought to an interregnum, in having tribunes of the soldiers elected with consular authority: as for the prize of their victory, which was the thing sought, *scil.* that a plebeian should be elected, there was none. All patricians were elected, Marcus Fabius Vibulanus, Marcus Foslius, Lucius Sergius Fidenas. The pestilence during that year afforded a quiet in other matters. A temple was vowed to Apollo for the health of the people. The duumvirs did much, by direction of the books, for the purpose of appeasing the wrath of heaven and averting the plague from the people; a great mortality however was sustained in the

---

[155] *ærarium facere*, signifies to strip a person of all the privileges of a citizen, on which he became *civis ærarius*, a citizen only so far as he paid taxes.

city and country, by the death of men and of cattle promiscuously. Apprehending a famine for the agriculturists, they sent into Etruria, and the Pomptine district, and to Cumæ, and at last to Sicily also to procure corn. No mention was made of electing consuls. Military tribunes with consular authority were appointed, all patricians, Lucius Pinarius Mamercinus, Lucius Furius Medullinus, Spurius Postumius Albus. In this year the violence of the distemper abated, nor was there any danger from a scarcity of corn, because provision had been previously made against it. Schemes for exciting wars were agitated in the meetings of the Æquans and Volscians, and in Etruria at the temple of Voltumna. Here the matter was postponed for a year, and by a decree it was enacted, that no meeting should be held before that time, the Veientian state in vain complaining that the same destiny hung over Veii, as that by which Fidenæ was destroyed. Meanwhile at Rome the chiefs of the commons, who had now for a long time been vainly pursuing the hope of higher dignity, whilst there was tranquillity abroad, appointed meetings to be held in the houses of the tribunes of the commons. There they concerted plans in secret: they complained "that they were so despised by the commons, that though tribunes of the soldiers, with consular authority, were now appointed for so many years, no plebeian ever obtained access to that honour. That their ancestors had shown much foresight in providing that plebeian offices should not be open to any patrician; otherwise they should be forced to have patricians as tribunes of the commons; so despicable were they even with their own party, and were not less despised by the commons than by the patricians." Others exculpated the commons, and threw the blame on the patricians,—"that by their intriguing and schemes it happened that the road to honour was barred against the commons. If the commons were allowed to breathe from their mixed entreaties and menaces, that they would enter on their suffrages with a due regard to men of their own party; and, assistance being already procured, that they would assume a share in the government also." It is determined that, for the purpose of doing away with all intriguing, the tribunes should propose a law, that no person be allowed to add white to his garment for the purposes of canvassing. The matter may now appear trivial and scarcely deserving serious consideration, which then enkindled such strife between the patricians and commons. The tribunes, however, prevailed in carrying the law; and it appeared evident, that in their present state of irritation, the commons would incline their support to men of their own party; and lest this should be optional with them, a decree of the senate is passed, that the election for consuls should be held.

The cause was the rising, which the Hernicians and Latins announced as about to take place on the part of the Æquans and Volscians. Titus Quintius Cincinnatus, son of Lucius, (to the same person the cognomen of Pennus also is annexed,) and Caius Julius Mento were elected consuls: nor was the terror of war longer deferred. A levy being held under the devoting law, which with them is the most powerful instrument of forcing men into service, powerful armies set out from thence, and met at Algidum; and there the Æquans and Volscians fortified their camps separately; and the general took greater care than ever before to fortify their posts and train their soldiers; so much the more terror did the messengers bring to Rome. The senate wished that a dictator should be appointed, because though these nations had been often conquered, yet they renewed hostilities with more vigorous efforts than ever before, and a considerable number of the Roman youth had been carried off by sickness. Above all, the perverseness of the consuls, and the disagreement between them, and their contentions in all the councils, terrified them. There are some who state that an unsuccessful battle was fought by these consuls at Algidum, and that such was the cause of appointing a dictator. This much is certain, that, though differing in other points, they perfectly agreed in one against the wishes of the patricians, not to nominate a dictator; until when accounts were brought, one more alarming than another, and the consuls would not be swayed by the authority of the senate, Quintus Servilius Priscus, who had passed through the highest honours with singular honour, says, "Tribunes of the people, since we are come to extremities, the senate calls on you, that you would, by virtue of your authority, compel the consuls to nominate a dictator in so critical a conjuncture of the state." On hearing this, the tribunes, conceiving that an opportunity was presented to them of extending their power, retire together, and declare for their college, that "it was their wish that the consuls should be obedient to the instruction of the senate; if they persisted further against the consent of that most illustrious order, that they would order them to be taken to prison." The consuls were better pleased to be overcome by the tribunes than by the senate, alleging that the prerogatives of the highest magistracy were betrayed by the patricians and the consulship subjugated to tribunitian power, inasmuch as the consuls were liable to be overruled by a tribune in any particular by virtue of his power, and (what greater hardship could a private man have to dread?) even to be carried off to prison. The lot to nominate the dictator (for the colleagues had not even agreed on that) fell on Titus Quintius. He appointed a dictator, Aulus Postumius Tubertus, his own father-in-law, a man of the utmost strictness in command: by him Lucius Julius was appointed master of the horse: a suspension of civil business is also proclaimed; and, that nothing else should be attended to throughout the city but preparations for war, the examination of the cases of those who claimed exemption from the military service is deferred till after the war. Thus even doubtful persons are induced to give in their names. Soldiers were also enjoined of the Hernicians and Latins: the most zealous obedience is shown to the dictator on both sides.

All these measures were executed with great despatch: and Caius Julius the consul being left to guard the city, and Lucius Julius master of the horse, for the sudden exigencies of the war, lest any thing which they might want in the camp should cause delay, the dictator, repeating the words after Aulus Cornelius the chief pontiff, vowed the great games on account of the sudden war; and having set out from the city, after dividing his army with the consul Quintius, he came up with the enemy. As they had observed two separate camps of the enemy at a small distance one from the other, they in like manner encamped separately about a mile from them, the dictator towards Tusculum, the consul towards Lanuvium. Thus they had their four armies, as many fortified posts, having between them a plain sufficiently extended not only for excursions to skirmish, but even for drawing up the armies on both sides in battle-array. From the time camp was brought close to camp, they ceased not from light skirmishing, the dictator readily allowing his soldiers, by comparing strength, to entertain beforehand the hope of a general victory, after they had gradually essayed the result of slight skirmishes. Wherefore the enemy, no hope being now left in a regular engagement, attacked the consuls' camp in the night, and bring the matter to the chance of a doubtful result. The shout which arose suddenly awoke not only the consuls' sentinels and then all the army, but the dictator also. When circumstances required instant exertion, the consul evinced no deficiency either in spirit or in judgment. One part of the troops reinforce the guards at the gates, another man the rampart around. In the other camp with the dictator, inasmuch as there is less of confusion, so much the more readily is it observed, what is required to be done. Despatching then forthwith a reinforcement to the consuls' camp, to which Spurius Postumius Albus is appointed lieutenant-general, he himself with a part of his forces, making a small circuit, proceeds to a place entirely sequestered from the bustle, whence he might suddenly attack the enemy's rear. Quintus Sulpicius, his lieutenant-general, he appoints to take charge of the camp; to Marcus Fabius as lieutenant he assigns the cavalry, and orders that those troops, which it would be difficult to manage amid a nightly conflict, should not stir before day-light. All the measures which any other prudent and active general could order and execute at such a juncture, he orders and executes with regularity; that was an extraordinary specimen of judgment and intrepidity, and one deserving of no ordinary praise, that he despatched Marcus Geganius with some chosen troops to attack the enemy's camp, whence it had been ascertained that they had departed with the greater part of their troops. When he fell on these men, wholly intent on the result of the danger of their friends, and incautious with respect to themselves, the watches and advanced guards being even neglected, he took their camp almost before the enemy were perfectly sure that it was attacked. Then when the signal given with smoke, as had been agreed on, was perceived by the dictator, he exclaims that the enemy's camp was taken, and orders it to be announced in every direction.

And now day was appearing, and every thing lay open to view; and Fabius had made an attack with his cavalry, and the consul had sallied from the camp on the enemy now disconcerted; when the dictator on the other side, having attacked their reserve and second line, threw his victorious troops, both horse and foot, in the way of the enemy as they turned themselves about to the dissonant shouts and the various sudden assaults. Thus surrounded on every side, they would to a man have suffered the punishment due to their reassumption of hostilities, had not Vectius Messius, a Volscian, a man more ennobled by his deeds than his extraction, upbraiding his men as they were forming a circle, called out with a loud voice, "Are ye about offering yourselves here to the weapons of the enemy, undefended, unavenged? why is it then ye have arms? or why have you undertaken an offensive war, ever turbulent in peace, and dastardly in war? What hopes have you in standing here? do you expect that some god will protect you and bear you hence? With the sword way must be opened. Come on ye, who wish to behold your homes, your parents, your wives, and your children, follow me in the way in which you shall see me lead you on. It is not a wall, not a rampart, but armed men that stand in your way with arms in your hands. In valour you are equal to them; in necessity, which is the ultimate and most effective weapon, superior." As he uttered these words and was putting them into execution, they, renewing the shout and following him, make a push in that quarter where Postumius Alba had opposed his troops to them: and they made the victor give ground, until the dictator came up, as his own men were now retreating. To that quarter the whole weight of the battle was now turned. On Messius alone the fortune of the enemy depends. Many wounds and great slaughter now took place on both sides. By this time not even the Roman generals themselves fight without receiving wounds, one of them, Postumius, retired from the field having his skull fractured by a stroke of a stone; neither the dictator could be removed by a wound in the shoulder, nor Fabius by having his thigh almost pinned to his horse, nor the consul by his arm being cut off, from the perilous conflict.

Messius, with a band of the bravest youths, by a furious charge through heaps of slaughtered foes, was carried on to the camp of the Volscians, which had not yet been taken: the same route the entire body of the army followed. The consul, pursuing them in their disordered flight to the very rampart, attacks both the camp and the rampart; in the same direction the dictator also brings up his forces on the other side. The assault was conducted with no less intrepidity than the battle had been. They say that the consul even threw a standard within the rampart, in order that the soldiers might push on the more briskly, and that the first impression was made in recovering the standard. The dictator also, having levelled the rampart, had now carried the fight into the camp. Then the enemy began in every direction to throw down their arms and to surrender: and their camp also being taken, all the enemy were set up to sale, except the senators.[156] Part of the plunder was restored to the Latins and Hernicians, when they demanded their property; the remainder the dictator sold by auction: and the consul, being invested with the command of the camp, he himself, entering the city in triumph, resigned his dictatorship. Some writers cast a gloom on the memory of this glorious dictatorship, when they state that his son, though victorious, was beheaded by Aulus Postumius, because, tempted by a favourable opportunity of fighting to advantage, he had left his post without orders. We are disposed to refuse our belief; and we are warranted by the variety of opinions on the matter. And it is an argument against it, that such orders have been entitled "Manlian," not "Postumian," since the person who first set on foot so barbarous a precedent, was likely to obtain the signal title of cruelty. Besides, the cognomen of "Imperiosus" was affixed to Manlius: Postumius has not been marked by any hateful brand. Caius Julius the consul, in the absence of his colleague, without casting lots, dedicated the temple of Apollo: Quintius resenting this, when, after disbanding his army, he returned into the city, made a complaint of it in the senate to no purpose.

To the year marked by great achievements is added an event which seemed to have no relation to the interest of Rome, viz. that the Carthaginians, destined to be such formidable enemies, then, for the first times on the occasion of some disturbances among the Sicilians, transported an army into Sicily in aid of one of the parties.

In the city efforts were made by the tribunes of the people that military tribunes with consular power should be elected; nor could the point be carried. Lucius Papirius Crassus and Lucius Junius were made consuls. When the ambassadors of the Æquans solicited a treaty from the senate, and instead of a treaty a surrender was pointed out to them, they obtained a truce for eight years. The affairs of the Volscians, in addition to the disaster sustained at Algidum, were involved in strifes and seditions by an obstinate contention between the advocates for peace and those for war. The Romans enjoyed tranquillity on all sides. The consuls, having ascertained through the information of one of the college, that a law regarding the appraising of the fines,[157] which was

---

[156] *Senators.* Niebuhr, ii. note 995, seems to doubt whether these belonged to single cities or were the senators of the entire Volscian nation.

[157] *Fines.* The fines imposed in early times were certain numbers of sheep or oxen; afterwards it was ordered by law that these fines should be appraised and the value paid

very acceptable to the people, was about to be introduced by the tribunes, took the lead themselves in proposing it. The new consuls were Lucius Sergius Fidenas a second time, and Hostus Lucretius Tricipitinus. During their consulate nothing worth mentioning occurred. The consuls who followed them were Aulus Cornelius Cossus and Titus Quintius Pennus a second time. The Veientians made excursions into the Roman territory. A report existed that some of the youth of the Fidenatians had been participators in that depredation; and the cognizance of that matter was left to Lucius Sergius, and Quintus Servilius and Mamercus Æmilius. Some of them were sent into banishment to Ostia, because it did not appear sufficiently clear why during these days they had been absent from Fidenæ. A number of new settlers was added, and the land of those who had fallen in war was assigned to them. There was very great distress that year in consequence of drought; there was not only a deficiency of rain; but the earth also destitute of its natural moisture, scarcely enabled the rivers to flow. In some places the want of water occasioned heaps of cattle, which had died of thirst, around the springs and rivulets which were dried up; others were carried off by the mange; and the distempers spread by infection to the human subject, and first assailed the husbandmen and slaves; soon after the city becomes filled with them; and not only were men's bodies afflicted by the contagion, but superstitions of various kinds, and most of them of foreign growth, took possession of their minds; persons, to whom minds enslaved by superstition were a source of gain, introducing by pretending to divination new modes of sacrificing; until a sense of public shame now reached the leading men of the state, seeing in all the streets and chapels extraneous and unaccustomed ceremonies of expiation for the purpose of obtaining the favour of the gods. A charge was then given to the ædiles, that they should see that no other than Roman gods should be worshipped, nor in any other manner, save that of the country. Their resentment against the Veientians was deferred till the following year, Caius Servilius Ahala and Lucius Papirius Mugillanus being consuls. Then also superstitious influences prevented the immediate declaration of war or the armies being sent; they deemed it necessary that heralds should be first sent to demand restitution. There had been battles fought lately with the Veientians at Nomentum and Fidenæ; and after that a truce, not a peace, had been concluded; of which both the time had expired and they had renewed hostilities before the expiration. Heralds however were sent; and when, according to ancient usage, they were sworn and demanded restitution, their application was not listened to. Then arose a dispute whether a war should be declared by order of the

---

in money. Another law fixed a certain rate at which the cattle should be estimated, 100 asses for an ox, 10 for a sheep.

people, or whether a decree of the senate would be sufficient. The tribunes, by threatening that they would stop the levy, so far prevailed that the consuls should take the sense of the people concerning the war. All the centuries voted for it. In this particular also the commons showed a superiority by gaining this point, that consuls should not be elected for the next year.

Four military tribunes with consular authority were elected—Titus Quintius Pennus, from the consulship, Caius Furius, Marcus Postumius, and Aulus Cornelius Cossus. Of these Cossus held the command in the city. The other three, after the levy was held, set out to Veii, and were an instance how mischievous in military affairs is a plurality of commanders. By insisting each on his own plans, whilst they severally entertained different views, they left an opportunity open to the enemy to take them at advantage. For the Veientians, taking an opportunity, attacked their line whilst still uncertain as to their movements, some ordering the signal to be given, others a retreat to be sounded: their camp, which was nigh at hand, received them in their confusion and turning their backs. There was more disgrace therefore than loss. The state, unaccustomed to defeat, was become melancholy; they hated the tribunes, they insisted on a dictator, the hopes of the state now seemed to rest on him. When a religious scruple interfered here also, lest a dictator could not be appointed except by a consul, the augurs on being consulted removed that scruple. Aulus Cornelius nominated Mamercus Æmilius, and he himself was nominated by him master of the horse. So little did censorial animadversion avail, so as to prevent them from seeking a regulator of their affairs from a family unmeritedly censured, as soon as the condition of the state stood in need of genuine merit. The Veientians elated with their success, having sent ambassadors around the states of Etruria, boasting that three Roman generals had been beaten by them in an engagement, though they could not effect a public co-operation in their designs, procured volunteers from all quarters allured by the hope of plunder. The state of the Fidenatians alone determined on renewing hostilities; and as if it would be an impiety to commence war unless with guilt, after staining their arms with the blood of the new settlers there, as they had on a former occasion with that of the ambassadors, they join the Veientians. After this the leading men of the two states consulted whether they should select Veii or Fidenæ as the seat of war. Fidenæ appeared the more convenient. Accordingly, having crossed the Tiber, the Veientians transferred the war thither. There was great consternation at Rome. The army being recalled from Veii, and that same army dispirited in consequence of their defeat, the camp is pitched before the Colline gate, and armed soldiers are posted along the walls, and a suspension of all civil business is proclaimed in the forum, and the shops were closed; and every place becomes more like to a camp than a city.

Then the dictator, having sent criers through the streets, and having summoned the alarmed citizens to an assembly, began to chide them "that they allowed their minds to depend on such slight impulses of fortune, that, on the receipt of a trifling loss, which itself was sustained not by the bravery of the enemy, nor by the cowardice of the Roman army, but by the disagreement of the generals, they now dreaded the Veientian enemy, six times vanquished, and Fidenæ, which was almost taken oftener than attacked. That both the Romans and the enemies were the same as they were for so many ages: that they retained the same spirits, the same bodily strength, the same arms. That he himself, Mamercus Æmilius, was also the same dictator, who formerly defeated the armies of the Veientians and Fidenatians, with the additional support of the Faliscians, at Nomentum. That his master of the horse, Aulus Cornelius, would be the same in the field, he who, as military tribune in a former war, slew Lar Tolumnius, king of the Veientians, in the sight of both armies, and brought the *spolia opima* into the temple of Jupiter Feretrius. Wherefore that they should take up arms, mindful that with them were triumphs, with them spoils, with them victory; with the enemy the guilt of murdering the ambassadors contrary to the law of nations, the massacre of the Fidenatian colonists in time of peace, the infraction of truces, a seventh unsuccessful revolt. As soon as they should bring their camp near them, he was fully confident that the joy of these most impious enemies at the disgrace of the Roman army would not be of long continuance, and that the Roman people would be convinced how much better those persons deserved of the republic, who nominated him dictator for the third time, than those who, in consequence of his abolishing the despotism of the censorship, would cast a slur on his second dictatorship." Having offered up his vows and set out on his march, he pitches his camp fifteen hundred paces on this side of Fidenæ, covered on his right by mountains, on his left by the river Tiber. He orders Titus Quintius Pennus to take possession of the mountains, and to post himself secretly on some eminence which might be in the enemy's rear. On the following day, when the Etrurians had marched out to the field, full of confidence in consequence of their accidental success of the preceding day, rather than of their good fighting, he himself, having delayed a little until the senate brought back word that Quintius had gained an eminence nigh to the citadel of Fidenæ, puts his troops into motion and led on his line of infantry in order of battle in their quickest pace against the enemy: the master of the horse he directs not to commence the fight without orders; that, when it would be necessary, he would give the signal for the aid of the cavalry; then that he would conduct the action, mindful of his fight with the king, mindful of the rich oblation, and of Romulus and Jupiter Feretrius. The legions begin the conflict with impetuosity. The Romans, fired with hatred, gratified that feeling both with deeds and words, calling the Fidenatian impious, the Veientian robbers, truce-breakers, stained with the horrid murder of ambassadors, sprinkled with the blood of their own brother-colonists, treacherous allies, and dastardly enemies.

In the very first onset they had made an impression on the enemy; when on a sudden, the gates of Fidenæ flying open, a strange sort of army sallies forth, unheard of and unseen before that time. An immense multitude armed with fire and all blazing with fire-brands, as if urged on by fanatical rage, rush on the enemy: and the form of this unusual mode of fighting frightened the Romans for the moment. Then the dictator, having called to him the master of the horse and the cavalry, and also Quintius from the mountains animating the fight, hastens himself to the left wing, which, more nearly resembling a conflagration than a battle, had from terror given way to the flames, and exclaims with a loud voice, "Vanquished by smoke, driven from your ground as if a swarm of bees, will ye yield to an unarmed enemy? will ye not extinguish the fires with the sword? or if it is with fire, not with weapons, we are to fight, will ye not, each in his post, snatch those brands, and hurl them on them? Come, mindful of the Roman name, of the valour of your fathers, and of your own, turn this conflagration against the city of your enemy, and destroy Fidenæ by its own flames, which ye could not reclaim by your kindness. The blood of your ambassadors and colonists and the desolation of your frontiers suggest this." At the command of the dictator the whole line advanced; the firebrands that were discharged are partly caught up; others are wrested by force: the armies on either side are now armed with fire. The master of the horse too, on his part, introduces among the cavalry a new mode of fighting; he commands his men to take the bridles off their horses: and he himself at their head, putting spurs to his own, dashing forward, is carried by the unbridled steed into the midst of the fires: the other horses also being urged on carry their riders with unrestrained speed against the enemy. The dust being raised and mixed with smoke excluded the light from the eyes of both men and horses. That appearance which had terrified the soldiers, no longer terrified the horses. The cavalry therefore, wherever they penetrated, produced a heap of bodies like a ruin. A new shout then assailed their ears; and when this attracted the attention of the two armies looking with amazement at each other, the dictator cries out "that his lieutenant-general and his men had attacked the enemy on the rear:" he himself, on the shout being renewed, advances against them with redoubled vigour. When two armies, two different battles pressed on the Etrurians, now surrounded, in front and rear, and there was now no means of flight back to their camp, nor to the mountains, where new enemies were ready to oppose them, and the horses, now freed from their bridles, had scattered their riders in every direction, the principal part of the Veientians make precipitately for the Tiber. Such of the Fidenatians as survived, bend their course to the city of Fidenæ. Their flight hurries them in their state of panic into the midst of slaughter; they are cut to pieces on the banks; others, when driven into the water, were carried off by the eddies; even those who could swim were weighed down by fatigue, by their wounds, and by fright; a few out of the many make their way across. The other party make their way through the camp into the city. In the same direction their impetuosity carries the Romans in pursuit; Quintius more especially, and with him those who had just come down from the mountain, being the soldiers who were freshest for labour, because they had come up towards the close of the engagement.

These, after they entered the gate mixed with the enemy, make their way to the walls, and raise from their summit a signal to their friends of the town being taken. When the dictator saw this, (for he had now made his way into the deserted camp of the enemy,) he leads on the soldiers, who were now anxious to disperse themselves in quest of booty, entertaining a hope of a greater spoil in the city, to the gate; and being admitted within the walls, he proceeds to the citadel, whither he saw the crowds of fugitives hurrying. Nor was the slaughter in the city less than in the battle; until, throwing down their arms, begging nothing but their life, they surrendered to the dictator. The city and camp are plundered. On the following day, one captive being allotted to each horseman and centurion, and two to those whose valour had been conspicuous, and the rest being sold by auction, the dictator in triumph led back to Rome his army victorious and enriched with spoil; and having ordered the master of the horse to resign his office, he immediately resigned his own on the sixteenth day (after he had obtained it); surrendering in peace that authority which he had received during war and trepidations. Some annals have reported that there was a naval engagement with the Veientians at Fidenæ, a thing as difficult as it was incredible, the river even now not being broad enough for such a purpose; and at that time, as we learn from old writers, being considerably narrower: except that perhaps in disputing the passage of the river, magnifying, as will happen, the scuffle of a few ships, they sought the empty honour of a naval victory.

The following year had as military tribunes with consular power Aulus Sempronius Atratinus, Lucius Quintius Cincinnatus, Lucius Furius Medullinus, Lucius Horatius Barbatus. To the Veientians a truce for twenty years was granted, and one for three years to the Æquans, though they had solicited one for a longer term. There was quiet also from city riots. The year following, though not distinguished either by war abroad or by disturbance at home, was rendered celebrated by the games which had been vowed during the war, both through the magnificence displayed in them by the military tribunes, and also through the concourse of the neighbouring states. The tribunes with consular power were Appius Claudius Crassus, Spurius Nautilus Rutilus, Lucius Sergius Fidenas, Sextus Julius Iulus. The exhibition, besides that they had come with the public concurrence of their states, was rendered still more grateful to the strangers by the courtesy of their hosts. After the games seditious harangues were delivered by the tribunes of the commons upbraiding the multitude; "that stupified with admiration of those persons whom they hated, they kept themselves in a state of eternal bondage; and they not only had not the courage to aspire to the recovery of their hopes of a share in the consulship, but even in the electing of military tribunes, which elections lay open to both patricians and commons, they neither thought of themselves nor of their party. That they must therefore cease feeling surprised why no one busied himself about the interests of the commons: that labour and danger would be expended on objects whence emolument and honour might be expected. That there was nothing men would not attempt if great rewards were proposed for those who make great attempts. That any tribune of the commons should rush blindly at great risk and with no advantage into contentions, in consequence of which he may rest satisfied that the patricians against whom he should strive, will persecute him with inexpiable war, whilst with the commons in whose behalf he may have contended he will not be one whit the more honoured, was a thing neither to be expected nor required. That by great honours minds became great. That no plebeian would think meanly of himself, when they ceased to be despised by others. That the experiment should be at length made in the case of one or two, whether there were any plebeian capable of sustaining a high dignity, or whether it were next to a miracle and a prodigy that any one sprung from the commons should be a brave and industrious man. That by the utmost energy the point had been gained, that military tribunes with consular power might be chosen from among the commons also. That men well approved both in the civil and military line had stood as candidates. That during the first years they were hooted at, rejected, and ridiculed by the patricians: that at length they had ceased to expose themselves to insult. Nor did he for his part see why the law itself might not be repealed; by which that was made lawful which never could take place; for that there would be less cause for blushing at the injustice of the law, than if they were to be passed over through their own want of merit."

Harangues of this kind, listened to with approbation, induced some persons to stand for the military tribuneship, each avowing that if in office he would propose something to the advantage of the commons. Hopes were held out of a distribution of the public land, of colonies to be planted, and of money to be raised for the pay of the soldiers, by a tax imposed on the proprietors of estates. Then an opportunity was laid hold of by the military tribunes, so that during the absence of most persons from the city, when the patricians who were to be recalled by a private intimation were to attend on a certain day, a decree of the senate might be passed in the absence of the tribunes of the commons; that a report existed that the Volscians had gone forth into the lands of Hernici to commit depredations, the military tribunes were to set out to examine into the matter, and that an assembly should be held for the election of consuls. Having set out, they leave Appius Claudius, son of the decemvir, as prefect of the city, a young man of great energy, and one who had ever from his cradle imbibed a hatred of the tribunes and the commons. The tribunes of the commons had nothing for which they should contend, either with those persons now absent, who had procured the decree of the senate, nor with Appius, the matter being now all over.

Caius Sempronius Atratinus, Quintus Fabius Vibulanus were elected consuls. An affair in a foreign country, but one deserving of record, is stated to have happened in that year. Vulturnum, a city of the Etrurians, which is now Capua, was taken by the Samnites; and was called Capua from their leader, Capys, or, what is more probable, from its champaign grounds. But they took possession of it, after having been admitted into a share of the city and its lands, when the Etrurians had been previously much harassed in war; afterwards the new-comers attacked and massacred during the night the old inhabitants, when on a festival day they had become heavy with wine and sleep. After those transactions the consuls whom we have mentioned entered on office on the ides of December. Now not only those who had been expressly sent, reported that a Volscian war was impending; but ambassadors also from the Latins and Hernicians brought word, "that never at any former period were the Volscians more intent either in selecting commanders, or in levying an army; that they commonly observed either that arms and war were to be for ever consigned to oblivion, and the yoke to be submitted to; or that they must not yield to those, with whom they contended for empire, either in valour, perseverance, or military discipline." The accounts they brought were not unfounded; but neither the senate were so much affected by the circumstance; and Caius Sempronius, to whom the province fell by lot, relying on fortune, as if a most constant object, because he was the leader of a victorious state against one frequently vanquished, executed all his measures carelessly and remissly; so that there was more of the Roman discipline in the Volscian than in the Roman army. Success therefore, as on many other occasions, attended merit. In the first battle, which was entered on by Sempronius without either prudence or caution, they met, without their lines being strengthened by reserves, or their cavalry being properly stationed. The shout was the first presage which way the victory would incline; that raised by the enemy was louder and more continued; that by the Romans, being dissonant, uneven, and frequently repeated in a lifeless manner, betrayed the prostration of their spirits. The enemy advancing the more boldly on this account, pushed with their shields, brandished their swords; on the other side the helmets drooped, as the men looked around, and disconcerted they waver, and keep close to the main body. The ensigns at one time standing their ground are deserted by their supporters, at another time they retreat between their respective companies. As yet there was no absolute flight, nor was there victory. The Romans rather covered themselves than fought. The Volscians advanced, pushed against their line, saw more of the enemy slain than running away.

They now give way in every direction, the consul Sempronius in vain chiding and exhorting them; neither his authority nor his dignity availed any thing; and they would presently have turned their backs to the enemy, had not Sextus Tempanius, a commander of a troop of horse, with great presence of mind brought them support, when matters were now desperate. When he called out aloud, "that the horsemen who wished for the safety of the commonwealth should leap from their horses," the horsemen of all the troops being moved, as if by the consul's orders, he says, "unless this cohort by its arms can stop the progress of the enemy, there is an end of the empire. Follow my spear as your standard. Show to the Romans and Volscians, that no cavalry are equal to you as cavalry, nor infantry to you as infantry." When this exhortation was approved by a loud shout, he advances, holding his spear aloft. Wherever they go, they open a passage for themselves; putting forward their targets they force on to the place where they saw the distress of their friends greatest. The fight is restored in every part, as far as their onset reached; nor was there a doubt but that if so few could, accomplish every thing at the same time, the enemy would have turned their backs.

And when they could now be withstood in no part, the Volscian commander gives a signal, that an opening should be made for the targeteers, the enemy's new cohort; until carried away by their impetuosity they should be cut off from their own party. When this was done, the horsemen were intercepted; nor were they able to force their way in the same direction as that through which they had passed; the enemy being thickest in that part through which they had made their way; and the consul and Roman legions, when they could no where see that party which had lately been a protection to the entire army, lest the enemy should cut down so many men of distinguished valour by cutting them off, push forward at all hazards. The Volscians, forming two fronts, sustained the attack of the consul and the legions on the one hand, with the other front pressed on Tempanius and the horsemen: and when they after repeated attempts were unable to force their way to their own party, they took possession of an eminence, and defended themselves by forming a circle, not without taking vengeance on their enemies. Nor was there an end of the battle before night. The consul also, never relaxing his efforts as long as any light remained, kept the enemy employed. The night at length separated them undecided as to victory; and such a panic seized both camps, from their uncertainty as to the issue, that, leaving behind their wounded and a great part of the baggage, both armies, as if vanquished, betook themselves to the adjoining mountains. The eminence, however, continued to be besieged till beyond midnight; but when word was brought to the besiegers that the camp was deserted, supposing that their own party had been defeated, they too fled, each whithersoever his fears carried him in the dark. Tempanius, through fear of an ambush, detained his men till daylight. Then having himself descended with a few men to look about, when he ascertained by inquiring from some of the wounded enemy that the camp of the Volscians was deserted, he joyously calls down his men from the eminence, and makes his way into the Roman camp: where, when he found every thing waste and deserted, and the same unsightliness as with the enemy, before the discovery of this mistake should bring back the Volscians, taking with him all the wounded he could, and not knowing what route the consul had taken, he proceeds by the shortest roads to the city.

The report of the unsuccessful battle and of the abandonment of the camp had already reached there; and, above all other objects, the horsemen were mourned not more with private than with public grief; and the consul Fabius, the city also being now alarmed, stationed guards before the gates; when the horsemen, seen at a distance, not without some degree of terror by those who doubted who they were, but soon being recognised, from a state of dread produced such joy, that a shout pervaded the city, of persons congratulating each other on the horsemen having returned safe and victorious; and from the houses a little before in mourning, as they had given up their friends for lost, persons were seen running into the street; and the affrighted mothers and wives, forgetful of all ceremony through joy, ran out to meet the band, each one rushing up to her own friends, and through extravagance of delight scarcely retaining power over body or mind. The tribunes of the people who had appointed a day of trial for Marcus Postumius and Titus Quintius, because of the unsuccessful battle fought near Veii by their means, thought that an opportunity now presented itself for renewing the public odium against them by reason of the recent displeasure felt against the consul Sempronius. Accordingly, a meeting being convened, when they exclaimed aloud that the commonwealth had been betrayed at Veii by the generals, that the army was afterwards betrayed by the consul in the country of the Volscians, because they had escaped with impunity, that the very brave horsemen were consigned to slaughter, that the camp was shamefully deserted;

Caius Julius, one of the tribunes, ordered the horseman Tempanius to be cited, and in presence of them he says, "Sextus Tempanius, I ask of you, whether do you think that Caius Sempronius the consul either commenced the battle at the proper time, or strengthened his line with reserves, or that he discharged any duty of a good consul? or did you yourself, when the Roman legions were beaten, of your own judgment dismount the cavalry and restore the fight? then when you and the horsemen with you were cut off from our army, did either the consul himself come to your relief, or did he send you succour? Then again, on the following day, had you any assistance any where? or did you and your cohort by your own bravery make your way into your camp? Did you find a consul or an army in the camp, or did you find the camp forsaken, the wounded soldiers left behind? These things are to be declared by you this day, as becomes your valour and honour, by which alone the republic has stood its ground on this day. In a word, where is Caius Sempronius, where are our legions? Have you been deserted, or have you deserted the consul and the army? In a word, have we been defeated, or have we gained the victory?"

In answer to these questions the language of Tempanius is said to have been entirely devoid of elegance, but firm as became a soldier, not vainly parading his own merits, nor exulting in the inculpation of others: "How much military skill Caius Sempronius possessed, that it was not his business as a soldier to judge with respect to his commander, but the business of the Roman people when they were choosing consuls at the election. Wherefore that they should not require from him a detail of the plans to be adopted by a general, nor of the qualifications to be looked for in a consul; which matters required to be considered by great minds and great capacities; but what he saw, that he could state. That before he was separated from his own party, he saw the consul fighting in the first line, encouraging his men, actively employed amid the Roman ensigns and the weapons of the enemy; that he was afterwards carried out of sight of his friends. That from the din and shouting he perceived that the contest was protracted till night; nor did he think it possible, from the great numbers of the enemy, that they could force their way to the eminence which he had seized on. Where the army might be, he did not know; he supposed that as he protected himself and his men, by advantage of situation when in danger, in the same way the consul, for the purpose of preserving his army, had selected a more secure place for his camp. Nor did he think that the affairs of the Volscians were in a better condition than those of the Roman people. That fortune and the night had occasioned a multitude of mistakes on both sides:" and then when he begged that they would not detain him, fatigued with toil and wounds, he was dismissed with high encomiums, not more on his bravery than his modesty. While these things were going on, the consul was at the temple of Rest on the road leading to Lavici. Waggons and other modes of conveyance were sent thither from the city, and took up the army, exhausted by the action and the travelling by night. Soon after the consul entered the city, not more anxious to remove the blame from himself, than to bestow on Tempanius the praises so well deserved. Whilst the citizens were still sorrowful in consequence of their ill success, and incensed against their leaders, Marcus Postumius, being arraigned and brought before them, he who had been military tribune with consular power at Veii, is condemned in a fine of ten thousand *asses* in weight, of brass. His colleague, Titus Quintius, who endeavoured to shift the entire blame of that period on his previously condemned colleague, was acquitted by all the tribes, because both in the country of the Volscians, when consul, he had conducted business successfully under the auspices of the dictator, Postumius Tubertus, and also at Fidenæ, as lieutenant-general of another dictator, Mamercus Æmilius. The memory of his father, Cincinnatus, a man highly deserving of veneration, is said to have been serviceable to him, as also Capitolinus Quintius, now advanced in years, humbly entreating that they would not suffer him who had so short a time to live to be the bearer of such dismal tidings to Cincinnatus.

The commons elected as tribunes of the people, though absent, Sextus Tempanius, Aulus Sellius, Sextus Antistius, and Spurius Icilius, whom the horsemen by the advice of Tempanius had appointed to command them as centurions. The senate, inasmuch as the name of consuls was now becoming displeasing through the hatred felt towards Sempronius, ordered that military tribunes with consular power should be elected. Those elected were Lucius Manlius Capitolinus, Quintus Antonius Merenda, Lucius Papirius Mugillanus. At the very commencement of the year, Lucius Hortensius, a tribune of the people, appointed a day of trial for Caius Sempronius, a consul of the preceding year, and when his four colleagues, in sight of the Roman people, entreated him that he would not involve in vexation their unoffending general, in whose case nothing but fortune could be blamed, Hortensius took offence, thinking it to be a trying of his perseverance, and that the accused depended not on the entreaties of the tribunes, which were merely used for show, but on their protection. Therefore now turning to him, he asked, "Where were those patrician airs, where the spirit supported and confiding in conscious innocence; that a man of consular dignity took shelter under the shade of the tribunes?" Another time to his colleagues, "What do you intend doing, if I go on with the prosecution; will you wrest their jurisdiction from the people and overturn the tribunitian authority?" When they said that, "both with respect to Sempronius and all others, the power of the Roman people was supreme; that they had neither the will nor the power to do away with the judgment of the people; but if their entreaties for their commander, who was to them in the light of a parent, were to prove of no avail, that they would change their apparel along with him:" then Hortensius says, "The commons of Rome shall not see their tribunes in the garb of culprits. To Caius Sempronius I have nothing more to say, since when in office he has attained this good fortune, to be so dear to his soldiers." Nor was the dutiful attachment of the four tribunes more grateful alike to the commons and patricians, than was the temper of Hortensius, which yielded so readily to their just entreaties. Fortune no longer indulged the Æquans, who had embraced the doubtful victory of the Volscians as their own.

In the year following, when Numerius Fabius Vibulanus and Titus Quintius Capitolinus, son of Capitolinus, were consuls, nothing worth mentioning was performed under the conduct of Fabius, to whom that province had fallen by lot. When the Æquans had merely showed their dastardly army, they were routed by a shameful flight, without any great honour to the consul; therefore a triumph is refused. However in consequence of having effaced the ignominy of Sempronius's defeat, he was allowed to enter the city with an ovation. As the war was terminated with less difficulty than they had apprehended, so in the city, from a state of tranquillity, an unexpected mass of dissensions arose between the commons and patricians, which commenced with doubling the number of quæstors. When the patricians approved most highly of this measure, (viz. that, besides the two city quæstors, two should attend the consuls to discharge some duties of the military service,) after it was moved by the consuls, the tribunes of the commons contended in opposition to the consuls, that half of the quæstors should be appointed from the commons; for up to that time all patricians were appointed. Against this proceeding both the consuls and patricians at first strove with all their might; then by making a concession that the will of the people should be equally free in the case of quæstors, as they enjoyed in the election of tribunes with consular power, when they produced but little effect, they gave up the entire matter about increasing the number of quæstors. When relinquished, the tribunes take it up, and other seditious schemes are continually started, among which is that of the agrarian law. On account of these disturbances the senate was desirous that consuls should be elected rather than tribunes, but no decree of the senate could be passed in consequence of the protests of the tribunes; the government from being consular came to an interregnum, and not even that without a great struggle (for the tribunes prevented the patricians from meeting). When the greater part of the following year was wasted in contentions by the new tribunes of the commons and some interreges, the tribunes at one time hindering the patricians from assembling to declare an interrex, at another time preventing the interrex from passing a decree regarding the election of consuls; at length Lucius Papirius Mugillanus, being nominated interrex, censuring now the patricians, now the tribunes of the people, asserted "that the state, deserted and forsaken by man, being taken up by the providence and care of the gods, subsisted by the Veientian truce and the dilatoriness of the Æquans. From which quarter if any alarm of danger be heard, did it please them that the state, left without a patrician magistrate, should be taken by surprise? that there should be no army, nor general to enlist one? Will they repel a foreign war by an intestine one? And if they both meet, the Roman state can scarcely be saved, even by the aid of the gods, from being overwhelmed. That they, by resigning each a portion of their strict right, should establish concord by a compromise; the patricians, by suffering military tribunes with consular authority to be elected; the tribunes of the commons, by ceasing to protest against the four quæstors being elected promiscuously from the commons and patricians by the free suffrage of the people."

The election of tribunes was first held. There were chosen tribunes with consular power, Lucius Quintius Cincinnatus a third time, Lucius Furius Medullinus a second time, Marcus Manlius, Aulus Sempronius Atratinus. On the last-named tribune presiding at the election of quæstors, and among several other plebeians a son of Antistius, a plebeian tribune, and a brother of Sextus Pompilius, also a tribune of the commons, becoming candidates, neither the power nor interest of the latter at all availed so as to prevent those, whose fathers and grandfathers they had seen consuls, from being preferred for their high birth. All the tribunes of the commons became enraged, above all Pompilius and Antistius were incensed at the rejection of their relatives. "What could this mean? that neither through their own kindnesses, nor in consequence of the injurious treatment of the patricians, nor even through the natural desire of making use of their new right, as that is now allowed which was not allowed before, was any individual of the commons elected if not a military tribune, not even a quæstor. That the prayers of a father in behalf of a son, those of one brother in behalf of another, had been of no avail, though proceeding from tribunes of the people, a sacrosanct power created for the support of liberty. There must have been some fraud in the matter, and Aulus Sempronius must have used more of artifice at the elections than was compatible with honour." They complained that by the unfairness of his conduct their friends had been kept out of office. Accordingly as no attack could be made on him, secured by his innocence and by the office he then held, they turned their resentment against Caius Sempronius, uncle to Atratinus; and, with the aid of their colleague Marcus Cornelius, they entered a prosecution against him on account of the disgrace sustained in the Volscian war. By the same tribunes mention was frequently made in the senate concerning the division of the lands, (which scheme Caius Sempronius had always most vigorously opposed,) they supposing, as was really the case, that the accused, should he give up the question, would become less valued among the patricians, or by persevering up to the period of trial he would give offence to the commons. He preferred to expose himself to the torrent of popular prejudice, and to injure his own cause, than to be wanting to the public cause; and he stood firm in the same sentiment, "that no largess should be made, which was sure to turn to the benefit of the three tribunes; that it was not land was sought for the people, but odium for him. That he too would undergo that storm with a determined mind; nor should either himself, nor any other citizen, be of so much consequence to the senate, that in showing tenderness to an individual, a public injury may be done." When the day of trial came, he, having pleaded his own cause with a spirit by no means subdued, is condemned in a fine of fifteen thousand *asses*, though the patricians tried every means to make the people relent. The same year Postumia, a Vestal virgin, is tried for a breach of chastity, though guiltless of the charge; having fallen under suspicion in consequence of her dress being too gay and her manners less reserved than becomes a virgin, not avoiding the imputation with sufficient care. The case was first deferred, she was afterwards acquitted; but the chief pontiff, by the instruction of the college, commanded her to refrain from indiscreet mirth, and to dress with more regard to sanctity than elegance. In the same year Cumæ, a city which the Greeks then occupied, was taken by the Campanians.

The following year had for military tribunes with consular power, Agrippa Menenius Lanatus, Publius Lucretius Tricipitinus, Spurius Nautius Rutilus: to the good fortune of the Roman people, the year was remarkable rather by great danger than by losses. The slaves conspire to set fire to the city in several quarters, and whilst the people should be intent in bearing assistance to the houses in every direction, to take up arms and seize the citadel and Capitol. Jupiter frustrated their horrid designs; and the offenders, being seized on the information of two (accomplices), were punished. Ten thousand *asses* in weight of brass paid out of the treasury, a sum which at that time was considered wealth, and their freedom, was the reward conferred on the parties who discovered. The Æquans then began to prepare for a renewal of hostilities; and an account was brought to Rome from good authority, that new enemies, the Lavicanians, were forming a coalition with the old ones. The state had now become habituated, as it were, to the anniversary arms of the Æquans. When ambassadors were sent to Lavici and brought back from thence an evasive answer, from which it became evident that neither war was intended there, nor would peace be of long continuance, instructions were given to the Tusculans, that they should observe attentively, lest any new commotion should arise at Lavici. To the military tribunes, with consular power, of the following year, Lucius Sergius Fidenas, Marcus Papirius Mugillanus, Caius

Servilius the son of Priscus, in whose dictatorship Fidenæ had been taken, ambassadors came from Tusculum, just as they entered on their office. The ambassadors brought word that the Lavicanians had taken arms, and having ravaged the Tusculan territory in conjunction with the army of the Æquans, that they had pitched their camp at Algidum. Then war was proclaimed against the Lavicanians; and a decree of the senate having been passed, that two of the tribunes should proceed to the war, and that one should manage affairs at Rome, a contest suddenly sprung up among the tribunes. Each represented himself as a fitter person to take the lead in the war, and scorned the management of the city as disagreeable and inglorious. When the senate beheld with surprise the indecent contention between the colleagues, Quintus Servilius says, "Since there is no respect either for this house, or for the commonwealth, parental authority shall set aside this altercation of yours. My son, without having recourse to lots, shall take charge of the city. I wish that those who are so desirous of managing the war, may conduct it with more consideration and harmony than they covet it."

It was determined that the levy should not be made out of the entire body of the people indiscriminately. Ten tribes were drawn by lot; the two tribunes enlisted the younger men out of these, and led them to the war. The contentions which commenced between them in the city, were, through the same eager ambition for command, carried to a much greater height in the camp: on no one point did they think alike; they contended strenuously for their own opinion; they desired their own plans, their own commands only to be ratified; they mutually despised each other, and were despised, until, on the remonstrances of the lieutenant-generals, it was at length so arranged, that they should hold the supreme command on alternate days. When an account of these proceedings was brought to Rome, Quintus Servilius, taught by years and experience, is said to have prayed to the immortal gods, that the discord of the tribunes might not prove more detrimental to the commonwealth than it had done at Veii: and, as if some certain disaster was impending over them, he pressed his son to enlist soldiers and prepare arms. Nor was he a false prophet. For under the conduct of Lucius Sergius, whose day of command it was, being suddenly attacked by the Æquans on disadvantageous ground near the enemy's camp, after having been decoyed thither by the vain hope of taking it, because the enemy had counterfeited fear and betaken themselves to their rampart, they were beaten down a declivity, and great numbers were overpowered and slaughtered by their tumbling one over the other rather than by flight: and the camp, retained with difficulty on that day, was, on the following day, deserted by a shameful flight through the opposite gate, the enemy having invested it in several directions. The generals, lieutenant-generals, and such of the main body of the army as kept near the colours, made their way to Tusculum; others, dispersed in every direction through the fields, hastened to Rome by different roads, announcing a heavier loss than had been sustained. There was less of consternation, because the result corresponded to the apprehensions of persons; and because the reinforcements, which they could look to in this distressing state of things, had been prepared by the military tribune: and by his orders, after the disturbance in the city was quieted by the inferior magistrates, scouts were instantly despatched, and brought intelligence that the generals and the army were at Tusculum; that the enemy had not removed their camp. And, what raised their spirits most, Quintus Servilius Priscus was created dictator in pursuance of a decree of the senate; a man whose judgment in public affairs the state had experienced as well on many previous occasions, as in the issue of that war, because he alone had expressed his apprehensions of the result of the disputes among the tribunes, before the occurrence of the misfortune; he having appointed for his master of the horse, by whom, as military tribune, he had been nominated dictator, his own son, as some have stated, (for others mention that Ahala Servilius was master of the horse that year;) and setting out to the war with his newly-raised army, after sending for those who were at Tusculum, chose ground for his camp at the distance of two miles from the enemy.

The arrogance and negligence arising from success, which had previously existed in the Roman generals, were now transferred to the Æquans. Accordingly, when in the very first engagement the dictator had thrown the enemy's van into disorder by a charge of his cavalry, he immediately ordered the infantry to advance, and slew one of his own standard-bearers who hesitated in so doing. So great was the ardour to fight, that the Æquans did not stand the shock; and when, vanquished in the field, they made for their camp in a precipitate flight, the taking of it was shorter in time and less in trouble than the battle had been. After the camp had been taken and plundered, and the dictator had given up the spoil to the soldiers, and the cavalry, who had pursued the enemy in their flight, brought back intelligence that all the Lavicanians were vanquished, and that a considerable number of the Æquans had fled to Lavici, the army was marched to Lavici on the following day; and the town, being invested on all sides, was taken by storm and plundered. The dictator, having marched back his victorious army to Rome, resigned his office on the eighth day after he had been appointed; and before agrarian disturbances could be raised by the tribunes of the commons, allusion having been made to a division of the Lavicanian land, the senate very opportunely voted in full assembly that a colony should be conducted to Lavici. One thousand five hundred colonists were sent from the city, and received each two acres. Lavici being taken, and subsequently Agrippa Menenius Lanatus, and Lucius Servilius Structus, and Publius Lucretius Tricipitinus, all these a second time, and Spurius Rutilius Crassus being military tribunes with consular authority, and on the following year Aulus Sempronius Atratinus a third time, and Marcus Papirius Mugillanus and Spurius Nautius Rutilus both a second time, affairs abroad were peaceable for two years, but at home there was dissension from the agrarian laws.

The disturbers of the commons were Spurius Mæcilius a fourth time, and Spurius Mætilius a third time, tribunes of the people, both elected during their absence. And after they had proposed a bill, that the land taken from the enemy should be divided man by man, and the property of a considerable part of the nobles would be confiscated by such a measure; for there was scarcely any of the land, considering the city itself was built on a strange soil, that had not been acquired by arms; nor had any other persons except the commons possession of that which had been sold or publicly assigned, a violent contest between the commons and patricians seemed to be at hand; nor did the military tribunes discover either in the senate, or in the private meetings of the nobles, any line of conduct to pursue; when Appius Claudius, the grandson of him who had been decemvir for compiling the laws, being the youngest senator of the meeting, is stated to have said; "that he brought from home an old and a family scheme, for that his great-grandfather, Appius Claudius, had shown the patricians one method of baffling tribunitian power by the protests of their colleagues; that men of low rank were easily led away from their opinions by the influence of men of distinction, if language were addressed to them suitable to the times, rather than to the dignity of the speakers. That their sentiments were regulated by their circumstances. When they should see that their colleagues, having the start in introducing the measure, had engrossed to themselves the whole credit of it with the commons, and that no room was left for them, that they would without reluctance incline to the interest of the senate, through which they may conciliate the favour not only of the principal senators, but of the whole body." All expressing their approbation, and above all, Quintius Servilius Priscus eulogizing the youth, because he had not degenerated from the Claudian race, a charge is given, that they should gain over as many of the college of the tribunes as they could, to enter protests. On the breaking up of the senate the tribunes are applied to by the leading patricians: by persuading, admonishing, and assuring them "that it would be gratefully felt by them individually, and gratefully by the entire senate, they prevailed on six to give in their protests." And on the following day, when the proposition was submitted to the senate, as had been preconcerted, concerning the sedition which Mæcilius and Mætilius were exciting by urging a largess of a most mischievous precedent, such speeches were delivered by the leading senators, that each declared "that for his part he had no measure to advise, nor did he see any other resource in any thing, except in the aid of the tribunes.

That to the protection of that power the republic, embarrassed as it was, fled for succour, just as a private individual in distress. That it was highly honourable to themselves and to their office that there resided not in the tribuneship more strength to harass the senate and to excite disunion among the several orders, than to resist their perverse colleagues." Then a shout arose throughout the entire senate, when the tribunes were appealed to from all parts of the house: then silence being established, those who had been prepared through the interest of the leading men, declare that they will protest against the measure which had been proposed by their colleagues, and which the senate considers to tend to the dissolution of the state. Thanks were returned to the protestors by the senate. The movers of the law, having convened a meeting, and styling their colleagues traitors to the interests of the commons and the slaves of the consulars, and after inveighing against them in other abusive language, relinquished the measure.

The following year, on which Publius Cornelius Cossus, Caius Valerius Potitus, Quintus Quintius Cincinnatus, Numerius Fabius Vibulanus were military tribunes with consular power, would have brought with it two continual wars, had not the Veientian campaign been deferred by the religious scruples of the leaders, whose lands were destroyed, chiefly by the ruin of the country-seats, in consequence of the Tiber having overflowed its banks. At the same time the loss sustained three years before prevented the Æquans from affording assistance to the Bolani, a state belonging to their own nation. Excursions had been made from thence on the contiguous territory of Lavici, and hostilities were committed on the new colony. As they had expected to be able to defend this act of aggression by the concurrent support of all the Æquans, when deserted by their friends they lost both their town and lands, after a war not even worth mentioning, through a siege and one slight battle. An attempt made by Lucius Sextius, tribune of the people, to move a law by which colonists might be sent to Bolæ also, in like manner as to Lavici, was defeated by the protests of his colleagues, who declared openly that they would suffer no order of the commons to be passed, unless with the approbation of the senate. On the following year the Æquans, having recovered Bolæ, and sent a colony thither, strengthened the town with additional fortifications, the military tribunes with consular power at Rome being Cneius Cornelius Cossus, Lucius Valerius Potitus, Quintus Fabius Vibulanus a second time, Marcus Postumius Regillensis. The war against the Æquans was intrusted to the latter, a man of depraved mind, which victory manifested more effectually than war. For having with great activity levied an army and marched it to Bolæ, after breaking down the spirits of the Æquans in slight engagements, he at length forced his way into the town. He then turned the contest from the enemy to his countrymen; and when during the assault he had proclaimed, that the plunder should belong to the soldiers, after the town was taken he broke his word. I am more inclined to believe that this was the cause of the displeasure of the army, than that in a city lately sacked and in a colony still young there was less booty found than the tribune had represented. An expression of his heard in the assembly, which was very silly and almost insane, after he returned into the city on being sent for on account of some tribunitian disturbances, increased this bad feeling; on Sextus, a tribune of the commons, proposing an agrarian law, and at the same time declaring that he would also propose that colonists should be sent to Bolæ; for that those who had taken them by their arms were deserving that the city and lands of Bolæ should belong to them, he exclaimed, "Woe to my soldiers, if they are not quiet;" which words, when heard, gave not greater offence to the assembly, than they did soon after to the patricians. And the plebeian tribune being a sharp man and by no means devoid of eloquence, having found among his adversaries this haughty temper and unbridled tongue, which by irritating and exciting he could urge into such expressions as might prove a source of odium not only to himself, but to his cause and to the entire body, he strove to draw Postumius into discussion more frequently than any of the college of military tribunes. Then indeed, after so brutal and inhuman an expression, "Romans," says he, "do ye hear him threatening woe to his soldiers as to slaves? Yet this brute will appear to you more deserving of so high an honour than those who send you into colonies, after having granted to you cities and lands; who provide a settlement for your old age, who fight against such cruel and arrogant adversaries in defence of your interests. Begin then to wonder why few persons now undertake your cause. What are they to expect from you? is it honours which you give to your adversaries rather than to the champions of the Roman people. You felt indignant just now, on hearing an expression of this man? What matters that, if you will prefer this man who threatens woe to you, to those who are desirous to secure for you lands, settlements, and property?"

This expression of Postumius being conveyed to the soldiers, excited in the camp much greater indignation. "Did the embezzler of the spoils and the defrauder threaten woe also to the soldiers?" Accordingly, when the murmur of indignation now became avowed, and the quæstor, Publius Sestius, thought that the mutiny might be quashed by the same violence by which it had been excited; on his sending a lictor to one of the soldiers who was clamorous, when a tumult and scuffle arose from the circumstance, being struck with a stone he retired from the crowd; the person who had given the blow, further observing with a sneer, "That the quæstor got what the general had threatened to the soldiers." Postumius being sent for in consequence of the disturbance, exasperated every thing by the severity of his inquiries and the cruelty of his punishment. At last, when he set no bounds to his resentment, a crowd collecting at the cries of those whom he had ordered to be put to death under a hurdle, he himself madly ran down from his tribunal to those who were interrupting the execution. There, when the lictors, endeavouring to disperse them, as also the centurions, irritated the crowd, their indignation burst forth to such a degree, that the military tribune was overwhelmed with stones by his own army. When an account was brought to Rome of so heinous a deed, the military tribunes endeavouring to procure a decree of the senate for an inquiry into the death of their colleague, the tribunes of the people entered their protest. But that contention branched out of another subject of dispute; because the patricians had become uneasy lest the commons, through dread of the inquiries and through resentment, might elect military tribunes from their own body: and they strove with all their might that consuls should be elected. When the plebeian tribunes did not suffer the decree of the senate to pass, and when they also protested against the election of consuls, the affair was brought to an interregnum. The victory was then on the side of the patricians.

Quintus Fabius Vibulanus, interrex, presiding in the assembly, Aulus Cornelius Cossus, Lucius Furius Medullinus were elected consuls. During their office, at the commencement of the year, a decree of the senate was passed that the tribunes should, at the earliest opportunity, propose to the commons an inquiry into the murder of Postumius, and that the commons should appoint whomsoever they thought proper to conduct the inquiry. The office is intrusted to the consuls by the commons with the consent of the people at large, who, after having executed the task with the utmost moderation and lenity by punishing only a few, who there are sufficient grounds for believing put a period to their own lives, still could not succeed so as to prevent the people from feeling the utmost displeasure. "That constitutions, which were enacted for their advantages, lay so long unexecuted; while a law passed in the mean time regarding their blood and punishment was instantly put into execution and possessed full force." This was a most seasonable time, after the punishment of the mutiny, that the division of the territory of Bolæ should be presented as a soother to their minds; by which proceeding they would have diminished their eagerness for an agrarian law, which tended to expel the patricians from the public land unjustly possessed by them. Then this very indignity exasperated their minds, that the nobility persisted not only in retaining the public lands, which they got possession of by force, but would not even distribute to the commons the unoccupied land lately taken from the enemy, and which would, like the rest, soon become the prey of a few. The same year the legions were led out by the consul Furius against the Volscians, who were ravaging the country of the Hernicians, and finding no enemy there, they took Ferentinum, whither a great multitude of the Volscians had betaken themselves. There was less plunder than they had expected; because the Volscians, seeing small hopes of keeping it, carried off their effects and abandoned the town. It was taken on the following day, being nearly deserted. The land itself was given to the Hernicians.

The year, tranquil through the moderation of the tribunes, was succeeded by one in which Lucius Icilius was plebeian tribune, Quintus Fabius Ambustus, Caius Furius Pacilus being consuls. When this man, at the very commencement of the year, began to excite disturbances by the publication of agrarian laws, as if such was the task of his name and family, a pestilence broke out, more alarming however than deadly, which diverted men's thoughts from the forum and political disputes to their domestic concerns and the care of their personal health; and persons think that it was less mischievous than the disturbance would have proved. The state being freed from this (which was attended) with a very general spread of illness, though very few deaths, the year of pestilence was followed by a scarcity of grain, the cultivation of the land having been neglected, as usually happens, Marcus Papirius Atratinus, Caius Nautius Rutilus being consuls. The famine would now have proved more dismal than the pestilence, had not the scarcity been relieved by sending envoys around all the states, which border on the Tuscan Sea and the Tiber, to purchase the corn. The envoys were prevented from trading in an insolent manner by the Samnitians, who were in possession of Capua and Cumæ; on the contrary, they were kindly assisted by the tyrants of Sicily. The Tiber brought down the greatest supplies, through the very active zeal of the Etrurians. In consequence of the sickness, the consuls laboured under a paucity of hands in conducting the government; when not finding more than one senator for each embassy, they were obliged to attach to it two knights. Except from the pestilence and the scarcity, there was no internal or external annoyance during those two years. But as soon as these causes of anxiety disappeared, all those evils by which the state had hitherto been distressed, started up, discord at home, war abroad.

In the consulship of Mamercus Æmilius and Caius Valerius Potitus, the Æquans made preparations for war; the Volscians, though not by public authority, taking up arms, and entering the service as volunteers for pay. When on the report of these enemies having started up, (for they had now passed into the Latin and Hernican land,) Marcus Mænius, a proposer of an agrarian law, would obstruct Valerius the consul when holding a levy, and when no one took the military oath against his own will under the protection of the tribune; an account is suddenly brought that the citadel of Carventa had been seized by the enemy. The disgrace incurred by this event was both a source of odium to Mænius in the hands of the fathers, and it moreover afforded to the other tribunes, already pre-engaged as protestors against an agrarian law, a more justifiable pretext for resisting their colleague. Wherefore after the matter had been protracted for a long time by wrangling, the consuls calling gods and men to witness, that whatever disgrace or loss had either been already sustained or hung over them from the enemy, the blame of it would be imputed to Mænius, who hindered the levy; Mænius, on the other hand, exclaiming "that if the unjust occupiers would yield up possession of the public land, he would cause no delay to the levy:" the nine tribunes interposing a decree, put an end to the contest; and they proclaimed as the determination of their college, "that they would, for the purposes of the levy, in opposition to the protest of their colleague, afford their aid to Caius Valerius the consul in inflicting fines and other penalties on those who refused to enlist." When the consul, armed with this decree, ordered into prison a few who appealed to the tribune, the rest took the military oath from fear. The army was marched to the citadel of Carventa, and though hated by and disliking the consul, they on their first arrival recovered the citadel in a spirited manner, having dislodged those who were protecting it; some in quest of plunder having straggled away through carelessness from the garrison, afforded an opportunity for attacking them. There was considerable booty from the constant devastations, because all had been collected into a safe place. This the consul ordered the quæstors to sell by auction and carry it into the treasury, declaring that the army should then participate in the booty, when they had not declined the service. The exasperation of the commons and soldiers against the consul was then augmented. Accordingly, when by a decree of the senate the consul entered the city in an ovation, rude verses in couplets were thrown out with military licence; in which the consul was severely handled, whilst the name of Mænius was cried up with encomiums, when at every mention of the tribune the attachment of the surrounding people vied by their applause and commendation with the loud praises of the soldiers. And that circumstance occasioned more anxiety to the patricians, than the wanton raillery of the soldiers against the consul, which was in a manner a usual thing; and the election of Mænius among the military tribunes being deemed as no longer questionable, if he should become a candidate, he was kept out of it by an election for consuls being appointed.

Cneius Cornelius Cossus and Lucius Furius Medullinus were elected consuls. The commons were not on any other occasion more dissatisfied at the election of tribunes not being conceded to them. This sense of annoyance they both manifested at the nomination of quæstors, and avenged by then electing plebeians for the first time as quæstors; so that in electing four, room was left for only one patrician; whilst three plebeians, Quintus Silius, Publius Aelius, and Publius Pupius, were preferred to young men of the most illustrious families. I learn that the principal advisers of the people, in this so independent a bestowing of their suffrage, were the Icilii, three out of this family most hostile to the patricians having been elected tribunes of the commons for that year, by their holding out the grand prospect of many and great achievements to the people, who became consequently most ardent; after they had affirmed that they would not stir a step, if the people would not, even at the election of quæstors, the only one which the senate had left open to the commons and patricians, evince sufficient spirit to accomplish that which they had so long wished for, and which was allowed by the laws. This therefore the people considered an important victory; and that quæstorship they estimated not by the extent of the honour itself; but an access seemed opened to new men to the consulship and the honours of a triumph. The patricians, on the other hand, expressed their indignation not so much at the honours of the state being shared, but at their being lost; they said that, "if matters be so, children need no longer be educated; who being driven from the station of their ancestors, and seeing others in the possession of their dignity, would be left without command or power, as mere salii and flamens, with no other employment than to offer sacrifices for the people." The minds of both parties being irritated, since the commons had both assumed new courage, and had now three leaders of the most distinguished reputation for the popular side; the patricians seeing that the result of all the elections would be similar to that for quæstors, wherever the people had the choice from both sides, strove vigorously for the election of consuls, which was not yet open to them. The Icilii, on the contrary, said that military tribunes should be elected, and that posts of honour should be at length imparted to the commons.

But the consuls had no proceeding on hand, by opposing which they could extort that which they desired; when by an extraordinary and favourable occurrence an account is brought that the Volscians and Æquans had proceeded beyond their frontiers into the Latin and Hernican territory to commit depredations. For which war when the consuls commence to hold a levy in pursuance of a decree of the senate, the tribunes then strenuously opposed them, affirming that such a fortunate opportunity was presented to them and to the commons. There were three, and all very active men, and of respectable families, considering they were plebeians. Two of them choose each a consul, to be watched by them with unremitting assiduity; to one is assigned the charge sometimes of restraining, sometimes of exciting, the commons by his harangues. Neither the consuls effected the levy, nor the tribunes the election which they desired. Then fortune inclining to the cause of the people, expresses arrive that the Æquans had attacked the citadel of Carventa, the soldiers who were in garrison having straggled away in quest of plunder, and had put to death the few left to guard it; that others were slain as they were returning to the citadel, and others who were dispersed through the country. This circumstance, prejudicial to the state, added force to the project of the tribunes. For, assailed by every argument to no purpose that they would then at length desist from obstructing the war, when they yielded neither to the public storm, nor to the odium themselves, they succeed so far as to have a decree of the senate passed for the election of military tribunes; with an express stipulation, however, that no candidate should be considered, who was tribune of the people that year, and that no one should be re-elected plebeian tribune for the year following; the senate undoubtedly pointing at the Icilians, whom they suspected of aiming at the consular tribuneship as the reward of their turbulent tribuneship of the commons. Then the levy began to proceed, and preparations for war began to be made with the concurrence of all ranks. The diversity of the statements of writers leaves it uncertain whether both the consuls set out for the citadel of Carventa, or whether one remained behind to hold the elections; those facts in which they do not disagree are to be received as certain, that they retired from the citadel of Carventa, after having carried on the attack for a long time to no purpose: that Verrugo in the Volscian country was taken by the same army, and that great devastation had been made, and considerable booty captured both amongst the Æquans and in the Volscian territory.

At Rome, as the commons gained the victory so far as to have the kind of elections which they preferred, so in the issue of the elections the patricians were victorious; for, contrary to the expectation of all, three patricians were elected military tribunes with consular power, Caius Julius Julus, Publius Cornelius Cossus, Caius Servilius Ahala. They say that an artifice was employed by the patricians (with which the Icilii charged them even at the time); that by intermixing a crowd of unworthy candidates with the deserving, they turned away the thoughts of the people from the plebeian through the disgust excited by the remarkable meanness of some. Then tidings are brought that the Volscians and Æquans, whether the retention of the citadel of Carventa raised their hopes, or the loss of the garrison at Verrugo excited their resentment, united in making preparations for war with the utmost energy: that the Antians were the chief promoters of the project; that their ambassadors had gone about the states of both these nations, upbraiding their dastardly conduct; that shut up within their walls, they had on the preceding year suffered the Romans to carry their depredations throughout their country, and the garrison of Verrugo to be overpowered. That now not only armed troops but colonies also were sent into their territories; and that not only the Romans distributed among themselves and kept their property, but that they had made a present to the Hernici of Ferentinum what had been taken from them. After their minds were inflamed by these remonstrances, according as they made applications to each, a great number of young men were enlisted. Thus the youth of all the states were drawn together to

Antium: there they pitched their camp and awaited the enemy. When these accounts are reported at Rome with much greater alarm than the circumstance warranted, the senate instantly ordered a dictator to be nominated, which was their last resource in perilous circumstances. They say that Julius and Cornelius were much offended at this proceeding, and that the matter was accomplished with great warmth of temper: when the leading men of the patricians, complaining fruitlessly that the military tribunes would not conform to the judgment of the senate, at last appealed even to the tribunes of the commons, and stated that force had been used even with the consuls by that body on a similar occasion. The plebeian tribunes, overjoyed at the dissension among the patricians, said, "that there was no support in persons who were not held in the rank of citizens, nor even of human beings; if ever the posts of honour were open, and the administration of government were shared, that they should then see that the decrees of the senate should not be invalidated by the arrogance of magistrates; that in the mean while, the patricians, unrestrained as they were by respect for laws or magistrates, must manage the tribunitian office also by themselves."

This contention occupied men's thoughts at a most unseasonable time, when a war of such importance was on hand: until when Julius and Cornelius descanted for a long time by turns, on "how unjust it was that a post of honour conferred on them by the people was now to be wrested from them, since they were generals sufficiently qualified to conduct that war." Then Ahala Servilius, military tribune, says, "that he had remained silent for so long a time, not because he was uncertain as to his opinion, (for what good citizen can separate his own interests from those of the public,) but because he wished that his colleagues should of their own accord yield to the authority of the senate, rather than suffer the tribunitian power to be suppliantly appealed to against them. That even then, if circumstances permitted, he would still give them time to retract an opinion too pertinaciously adhered to. But since the exigences of war do not await the counsels of men, that the public weal was of deeper importance to him than the good will of his colleagues, and if the senate continued in the same sentiments, he would, on the following night, nominate a dictator; and if any one protested against a decree of the senate being passed, that he would be content with its authority."[158] When by this conduct he bore away the well-merited praises and good will of all, having named Publius Cornelius dictator, he himself being appointed by him as master of the horse, served as an instance to those who considered his case and that

[158] The passing of a *senatus-consultum*, or decree of the senate, might be prevented in several ways; as, for instance, by the want of a sufficiently full meeting, &c.; in such cases the judgment of the majority was recorded, and that was called *auctoritas senatûs*.

of his colleagues, how much more attainable public favour and honour sometimes were to those who evinced no desire for them. The war was in no respect a memorable one. The enemy were beaten at Antium in one, and that an easy battle; the victorious army laid waste the Volscian territory; their fort at the lake Fucinus was taken by storm, and in it three thousand men made prisoners; the rest of the Volscians being driven within the walls, and not defending the lands. The dictator having conducted the war in such a manner as to show that he was not negligent of fortune's favours, returned to the city with a greater share of success than of glory, and resigned his office. The military tribunes, without making any mention of an election of consuls, (through pique, I suppose, for the appointment of a dictator,) issued a proclamation for the election of military tribunes. Then indeed the perplexity of the patricians became still greater, as seeing their cause betrayed by their own party. Wherefore, as on the year before, by bringing forward as candidates the most unworthy individuals from amongst the plebeians, they produced a disgust against all, even those who were deserving; so then by engaging such of the patricians as were most distinguished by the splendour of their character and by their influence to stand as candidates, they secured all the places; so that no plebeian could get in. Four were elected, all of them men who had already served the office, Lucius Furius Medullinus, Caius Valerius Potitus, Numerius Fabius Vibulanus, Caius Servilius Ahala. The last had the honour continued to him by re-election, as well in consequence of his other deserts, as on account of his recent popularity, acquired by his singular moderation.

In that year, because the term of the truce with the Veientian nation was expired, restitution began to be demanded through ambassadors and heralds, who on coming to the frontiers were met by an embassy from the Veientians. They requested that they would not proceed to Veii, until they should first have access to the Roman senate. They obtained from the senate, that, because the Veientians were distressed by intestine dissension, restitution would not be demanded from them; so far were they from seeking, in the troubles of others, an opportunity for advancing their own interest. In the Volscian territory also a disaster was sustained in the loss of the garrison at Verrugo; where so much depended on time, that when the soldiers who were besieged there, and were calling for succour, might have been relieved, if expedition had been used, the army sent to their aid only came in time to surprise the enemy, who were straggling in quest of plunder, just after their putting [the garrison] to the sword. The cause of the dilatoriness was less referrible to the tribunes than to the senate, who, because word was brought that they were holding out with the most vigorous resistance, did not duly reflect that there is a limit to human strength, which no bravery can exceed. These very gallant soldiers, however, were not without revenge, both before and after their death. In the following year, Publius and Cneius Cornelius Cossus, Numerius Fabius Ambustus, and Lucius Valerius Potitus, being military tribunes with consular power, the Veientian war was commenced on account of an insolent answer of the Veientian senate, who, when the ambassadors demanded restitution, ordered them to be told, that if they did not speedily quit the city and the territories, they should give them what Lars Tolumnius had given them. The senate, indignant at this, decreed that the military tribunes should, on as early a day as possible, propose to the people the proclaiming war against the Veientians. When this was first made public, the young men expressed their dissatisfaction. "That the war with the Volscians was not yet over; that a little time ago two garrisons were utterly destroyed, and that [one of the forts] was with great risk retained. That there was not a year in which they had not to fight in the field: and, as if they were dissatisfied at the insufficiency of these toils, a new war was now set on foot with a neighbouring and most powerful nation, who were likely to rouse all Etruria." These discontents, first discussed among themselves, were further aggravated by the plebeian tribunes. These constantly affirm that the war of the greatest moment was that between the patricians and commons. That the latter was designedly harassed by military service, and exposed to be butchered by the enemy; that they were kept at a distance from the enemy, and as it were banished, lest during the enjoyment of rest at home, mindful of liberty and of establishing colonies, they may form plans for obtaining some of the public land, or for giving their suffrages freely; and taking hold of the veterans, they recounted the campaigns of each, and their wounds and scars, frequently asking what sound spot was there on their body for the reception of new wounds? what blood had they remaining which could be shed for the commonwealth? When by discussing these subjects in private conversations, and also in public harangues, they produced in the people an aversion to undertaking a war, the time for proposing the law was adjourned; which would obviously have been rejected, if it had been subjected to the feeling of discontent then prevailing.

In the mean time it was determined that the military tribunes should lead an army into the Volscian territory. Cneius Cornelius alone was left at Rome. The three tribunes, when it became evident that the Volscians had not established a camp any where, and that they would not venture an engagement, separated into three different parties to lay waste the country. Valerius makes for Antium, Cornelius for Ecetræ. Wherever they came, they committed extensive devastations on the houses and lands, so as to separate the Volscians: Fabius, without committing any devastation, proceeded to attack Auxur, which was a principal object in view. Auxur is the town now called Tarracinæ; a city built on a declivity leading to a morass: Fabius made a feint of attacking it on that side. When four cohorts sent round under Caius

Servilius Ahala took possession of a hill which commanded the city, they attacked the walls with a loud shout and tumult, from the higher ground where there was no guard of defence. Those who were defending the lower parts of the city against Fabius, astounded at this tumult, afforded him an opportunity of applying the scaling ladders, and every place soon became filled with the enemy, and a dreadful slaughter continued for a long time, indiscriminately of those who fled and those who resisted, of the armed or unarmed. The vanquished were therefore obliged to fight, there being no hope for those who gave way, when a proclamation suddenly issued, that no persons except those with arms in their hands should be injured, induced all the remaining multitude voluntarily to lay down their arms; of whom two thousand five hundred are taken alive. Fabius kept his soldiers from the spoil, until his colleagues should come; affirming that Auxur had been taken by these armies also, who had diverted the other Volscian troops from the defence of that place. When they came, the three armies plundered the town, which was enriched with wealth of many years' accumulation; and this generosity of the commanders first reconciled the commons to the patricians. It was afterwards added, by a liberality towards the people on the part of the leading men the most seasonable ever shown, that before any mention should be made of it by the commons or tribunes, the senate should decree that the soldiers should receive pay out of the public treasury, whereas up to that period every one had discharged that duty at his own expense.

It is recorded that nothing was ever received by the commons with so much joy; that they ran in crowds to the senate-house, and caught the hands of those coming out, and called them fathers indeed; acknowledging that the result of such conduct was that no one would spare his person or his blood, whilst he had any strength remaining, in defence of a country so liberal. Whilst the prospect of advantage pleased them, that their private property should remain unimpaired at the time during which their bodies should be devoted and employed for the interest of the commonwealth, it further increased their joy very much, and rendered their gratitude for the favour more complete, because it had been offered to them voluntarily, without ever having been agitated by the tribunes of the commons, or made the subject of a demand in their own conversations. The tribunes of the commons, the only parties who did not participate in the general joy and harmony prevailing through the different ranks, denied "that this measure would prove so much a matter of joy, or so honourable to the patricians,[159] as they themselves might imagine. That the measure at first sight was better than it would prove by experience. For from what source was

---

[159] The reading of the original here is decidedly incorrect. Various emendations have been attempted, but none can be deemed satisfactory.

that money to be raised, except by levying a tax on the people. That they were generous to some therefore at the expense of others; and even though others may endure it, those who had already served out their time in the service, would never endure that others should serve on better terms than they themselves had served; and that these same individuals should have to bear the expense of their own service, and then that of others." By these arguments they influenced a part of the commons. At last, when the tax was now announced, the tribunes publicly declared, that they would afford protection to any one who should refuse to contribute his proportion for the pay of the soldiers. The patricians persisted in supporting a matter so happily commenced. They themselves were the first to contribute; and because there was as yet no coined silver, some of them conveying their weighed brass to the treasury in waggons, rendered their contribution very showy. After the senate had contributed with the utmost punctuality according to their rated properties, the principal plebeians, friends of the nobility, according to a concerted plan, began to contribute. And when the populace saw these men highly applauded by the patricians, and also looked up to as good citizens by men of the military age, scorning the support of the tribunes, an emulation commenced at once about paying the tax. And the law being passed about declaring war against the Veientians, the new military tribunes with consular power marched to Veii an army consisting in a great measure of volunteers.

The tribunes were Titus Quintius Capitolinus, Publius Quintius Cincinnatus, Caius Julius Julus a second time, Aulus Manlius, Lucius Furius Medullinus a second time, and Manius Æmilius Mamercinus. By these Veii was first invested. A little before the commencement of this siege, when a full meeting of the Etrurians was held at the temple of Voltumna, it was not finally determined whether the Veientians were to be supported by the public concurrence of the whole confederacy. The siege was less vigorous in the following year, some of the tribunes and their army being called off to the Volscian war. The military tribunes with consular power in this year were Caius Valerius Potitus a third time, Manius Largius Fidenas, Publius Cornelius Maluginensis, Cneius Cornelius Cossus, Kæso Fabius Ambustus, Spurius Nautius Rutilus a second time. A pitched battle was fought with the Volscians between Ferentinum and Ecetra; the result of the battle was favourable to the Romans. Artena then, a town of the Volscians, began to be besieged by the tribunes. Thence during an attempt at a sally, the enemy being driven back into the town, an opportunity was afforded to the Romans of forcing in; and every place was taken except the citadel. Into the fortress, well protected by nature, a body of armed men retired. Beneath the fortress many were slain and made prisoners. The citadel was then besieged; nor could it either be taken by storm, because it had a garrison sufficient for the size of the place, nor did it hold out any hope of surrender, all the public corn having been conveyed to the citadel before the city was taken; and they would have retired from it, being wearied out, had not a slave betrayed the fortress to the Romans: the soldiers being admitted by him through a place difficult of access, took it; by whom when the guards were being killed, the rest of the multitude, overpowered with sudden panic, surrendered. After demolishing both the citadel and city of Artena, the legions were led back from the Volscian territory; and the whole Roman power was turned against Veii. To the traitor, besides his freedom, the property of two families was given as a reward. His name was Servius Romanus. There are some who think that Artena belonged to the Veientians, not to the Volscians. What occasions the mistake is that there was a city of the same name between Cære and Veii. But the Roman kings destroyed it; and it belonged to the Cæretians, not to the Veientians. The other of the same name, the demolition of which has been mentioned, was in the Volscian territory.

## Book V.

*During the siege of Veii winter dwellings erected for the soldiers. This being a novelty, affords the tribunes of the people a pretext for exciting discontent. The cavalry for the first time serve on horses of their own. Furius Camillus, dictator, takes Veii after a siege of ten years. In the character of military tribune, whilst laying siege to Falisci, he sends back the children of the enemy, who were betrayed into his hands. Furius Camillus, on a day being appointed for his trial, goes into exile. The Senonian Gauls lay siege to Clusium. Roman ambassadors, sent to mediate peace between the Clusians and Gauls, are found to take part with the former; in consequence of which the Gauls march directly against Rome, and after defeating the Romans at Allia take possession of the city with the exception of the Capitol. They scaled the Capitol by night, but are discovered by the cackling of geese, and repulsed, chiefly by the exertions of Marcus Manlius. The Romans, compelled by famine, agree to ransom themselves. Whilst the gold is being weighed to them, Camillus, who had been appointed dictator, arrives with an army, expels the Gauls, and destroys their army. He successfully opposes the design of removing to Veii.*

Peace being established in every other quarter, the Romans and Veientians were still in arms with such rancour and animosity, that it was evident that ruin awaited the vanquished party. The elections in the two states were conducted in very different methods. The Romans augmented the number of military tribunes with consular power. Eight, a number greater than on any previous occasion, were appointed, Manius Æmilius Mamercinus a second time, Lucius Valerius Potitus a third time, Appius Claudius Crassus, Marcus Quintilius Varus, Lucius Julius Iulus, Marcus Postumius, Marcus Furius Camillus, Marcus Postumius Albinus. The Veientians, on the contrary, through disgust at the annual intriguing which was sometimes the cause of dissensions, elected a king. That step gave offence to the feelings of the states of Etruria, not more from their hatred of kingly government than of the king himself. He had before this become obnoxious to the nation by reason of his wealth and arrogance, because he had violently broken off the performance of some annual games, the omission of which was deemed an impiety: when through resentment of a repulse, because another had been preferred to him as a priest by the suffrages of the twelve states, he suddenly carried off, in the middle of the performance, the performers, of whom a great part were his own slaves. The nation, therefore, devoted beyond all others to religious performances, because they excelled in the method of conducting them, passed a decree that aid should be refused to the Veientians, as long as they should be subject to a king. All allusion to this decree was suppressed at Veii through fear of the king, who would have considered the person by whom any such matter might be mentioned as a leader of sedition, not as the author of an idle rumour. Although matters were announced to the Romans as being quiet in Etruria, yet because it was stated that this matter was being agitated in all their meetings, they so managed their fortifications, that there should be security on both sides; some were directed towards the city and the sallies of the townsmen; by means of others a front looking towards Etruria was opposed to such auxiliaries as might happen to come from thence.

When the Roman generals conceived greater hopes from a blockade than from an assault, winter huts also, a thing quite new to the Roman soldier, began to be built; and their determination was to continue the war by wintering there. After an account of this was brought to Rome to the tribunes of the people, who for a long time past had found no pretext for exciting disturbances, they run forward into the assembly, stir up the minds of the commons, saying that "this was the motive for which pay had been established for the soldiers, nor had it escaped their knowledge, that such a present from the enemies was tainted with poison. That the liberty of the commons had been sold; that their youth removed for ever, and exiled from the city and the republic, did not now even yield to the winter and to the season of the year, and visit their homes and private affairs. What could they suppose was the cause for continuing the service without intermission? That undoubtedly they should find none other than [the fear] lest any thing might be done in furtherance of their interests by the attendance of those youths in whom the entire strength of the commons lay. Besides that they were harassed and worked much more severely than the Veientians. For the latter spent the winter beneath their own roofs, defending their city by strong walls and its natural situation, whilst the Roman soldier, in the midst of toil and hardship, continued beneath the covering of skins, overwhelmed with snow and frost, not laying aside his arms even during the period of winter, which is a respite from all wars by land and sea. Neither kings, nor those consuls, tyrannical as they were before the institution of the tribunitian office, nor the stern authority of the dictator, nor the overbearing decemvirs, ever imposed such slavery as that they should perform unremitting military service, which degree of regal power the military tribunes now exercised over the Roman commons. What would these men have done as consuls or dictators, who have exhibited the picture of the proconsular office so implacable and menacing? but that all this happened justly. Among eight military tribunes there was no room even for one plebeian. Formerly the patricians filled up three places with the utmost difficulty; now they went in file eight deep to take possession of the various offices; and not even in such a crowd is any plebeian intermixed; who, if he did no other good, might remind his colleagues, that it was freemen and fellow citizens, and not slaves, that constituted the army, who ought to be brought back during winter at least to their homes and roofs; and to come and see at some part of the year their parents, children, and wives, and to exercise the rights of freedom, and to take part in electing magistrates." While they exclaimed in these and such terms, they found in Appius Claudius an opponent not unequal to them, who had been left behind by his colleagues to check the turbulence of the tribunes; a man trained even from his youth in contests with the plebeians; who several years before, as has been mentioned, recommended the dissolution of the tribunitian power by means of the protests of their colleagues.

He, not only endowed with good natural powers, but well trained also by experience, on that particular occasion, delivered the following address: "If, Romans, there was ever reason to doubt, whether the tribunes of the people have ever promoted sedition for your sake or their own, I am certain that in the course of this year that doubt must have ceased to exist; and while I rejoice that an end has at length come of a mistake of such long continuance, I in the next place congratulate you, and on your account the republic, that this delusion has been removed during a course of prosperous events. Is there any person who can feel a doubt that the tribunes of the commons were never so highly displeased and provoked by any wrongs done to you, if ever such did happen, as by the munificence of the patricians to the commons, when pay was established for those serving in the army. What else do you suppose that they either then dreaded, or now wish to disturb, except the union between the orders, which they think contributes most to the dissolution of the tribunitian power? Thus, by Jove, like workers in iniquity, they are seeking for work, who also wish that there should be always some diseased part in the republic, that there may be something for the cure of which they may be employed by you. For, [tribunes,] whether do you defend or attack the commons? whether are you the enemies of those in the service, or do you plead their cause? Unless perhaps you say, whatever the patricians do, displeases us; whether it is for the commons, or against the commons; and just as masters forbid their slaves to have any dealing with those belonging to others, and deem it right that they should equally refrain from having any commerce with them, either for kindness or unkindness; ye, in like manner, interdict us the patricians from all intercourse with the people, lest by our courteousness and munificence we may challenge their regard, and they become tractable and obedient to our direction. And if there were in you any thing of the feeling, I say not of fellow-citizens, but of human beings, how much more ought you to favour, and, as far as in you lay, to promote rather the kindly demeanour of the patricians and the tractability of the commons! And if such concord were once permanent, who would not venture to engage, that this empire would in a short time become the highest among the neighbouring states?

"I shall hereafter explain to you how not only expedient, but even necessary has been this plan of my colleagues, according to which they would not draw off the army from Veii until the business has been completed. For the present I am disposed to speak concerning the condition of the soldiers. Which observations of mine I think would appear reasonable not only before you, but even, if they were delivered in the camp, in the opinion of the soldiers themselves; on which subject if nothing could suggest itself to my own mind to say, I certainly should be satisfied with that which is suggested by the arguments of my adversaries. They lately said, that pay should not be given to the soldiers because it had never been given. How then can they now feel displeased, that additional labour should be imposed in due proportion on those to whom some addition of profit has been added? In no case is there either labour without emolument, nor emolument in general without the expense of labour. Toil and pleasure, in their natures most unlike, are yet linked together by a sort of natural connexion. Formerly the soldier thought it a hardship that he gave his labour to the commonwealth at his own expense; at the same time he was glad for a part of the year to till his own ground; to acquire that means whence he might support himself and family at home and in war. Now he feels a pleasure that the republic is a source of advantage to him, and gladly receives his pay. Let him therefore bear with patience that he is a little longer absent from home and his family affairs, to which no heavy expense is now attached. Whether if the commonwealth should call him to a settlement of accounts, would it not justly say, You have pay by the year, perform labour by the year? do you think it just to receive a whole year's pay for six months' service? Romans, with reluctance do I dwell on this topic; for so ought those persons proceed who employ mercenary troops. But we wish to treat as with fellow-citizens, and we think it only just that you treat with us as with the country. Either the war should not have been undertaken, or it ought to be conducted suitably to the dignity of the Roman people, and brought to a close as soon as possible. But it will be brought to a conclusion if we press on the besieged; if we do not retire until we have consummated our hopes by the capture of Veii. In truth, if there were no other motive, the very discredit of the thing should impose on us perseverance. In former times a city was kept besieged for ten years, on account of one woman, by all Greece. At what a distance from their homes! how many lands, how many seas distant! We grumble at enduring a siege of a year's duration within twenty miles of us, almost within sight of our own city; because, I suppose, the cause of the war is trifling, nor is there resentment sufficiently just to stimulate us to persevere. Seven times they have rebelled: in peace they never acted faithfully. They have laid waste our lands a thousand times: the Fidenatians they forced to revolt from us: they have put to death our colonists there: contrary to the law of nations, they have been the instigators of the impious murder of our ambassadors: they wished to excite all Etruria against us, and are at this day busily employed at it; and they scarcely refrained from violating our ambassadors when demanding restitution. With such people ought war to be conducted in a remiss and dilatory manner?

"If such just resentment have no influence with us, will not, I entreat you, the following considerations influence you? Their city has been enclosed with immense works, by which the enemy is confined within their walls. They have not tilled their land, and what was previously tilled has been laid waste in the war. If we withdraw our army, who is there who can doubt that they will invade our territory not only from a desire of revenge, but from the necessity also imposed on them of plundering from the property of others, since they have lost their own? By such measures then we do not put off the war, but admit it within our own frontiers. What shall I say of that which properly interests the soldiers, for whose interests those worthy tribunes of the commons, all on a sudden, are now so anxious to provide, after they have endeavoured to wrest their pay from them? How does it stand? They have formed a rampart and a trench, both works of great labour, through so great an extent of ground; they have erected forts, at first only a few, afterwards very many, when the army became increased; they have raised defenders not only towards the city, but towards Etruria also, against any succours which may come from thence. What need I mention towers, vineæ, and testudines, and the other apparatus used in attacking towns? When so much labour has been expended, and they have now at length reached the end of the work, do you think that all these preparations should be abandoned that, next summer, the same course of toil may have to be undergone again in forming them anew? How much less trouble to support the works already done, and to press on and persevere, and to get rid of our task! For certainly the matter is of short duration, if it be conducted with a uniform course of exertions; nor do we by these intermissions and interruptions expedite the attainment of our hopes. I am now speaking of labour and of loss of time. What? do these such frequent meetings in Etruria on the subject of sending aid to Veii suffer us to disregard the danger which we encounter by procrastinating the war? As matters stand now, they are incensed, they dislike them, they refuse to send any; as far as they are concerned, we are at liberty to take Veii. Who can promise that their temper will be the same hereafter, if the war is suspended? when, if you suffer any relaxation, more respectable and more frequent embassies will go; when that which now displeases the Etrurians, the establishment of a king at Veii, may, after an interval, be done away with, either by the joint determination of the state that they may recover the good will of the Etrurians, or by a voluntary act of the king, who may be unwilling that his reign should stand in the way of the welfare of his countrymen. See how many circumstances, and how detrimental, follow that line of conduct: the loss of works formed with so great labour; the threatening devastation of our frontiers; an Etruscan excited instead of a Veientian war. These, tribunes, are your measures, pretty much the same, in truth, as if a person should render a disease tedious, and perhaps incurable, for the sake of present meat or drink, in a patient who, by resolutely suffering himself to be treated, might soon recover his health.

"If, by Jove, it were of no consequence with respect to the present war, yet it certainly would be of the utmost importance to military discipline, that our soldiers should be accustomed not only to enjoy the victory obtained by them; but even though matters should proceed more slowly than was anticipated, to brook the tediousness and await the issue of their hopes, however tardy; and if the war be not finished in the summer, to wait for the winter, and not, like summer birds, in the very commencement of autumn look out for shelter and a retreat. I pray you, the eagerness and pleasure of hunting hurries men into snow and frost, over mountains and woods; shall we not employ that patience on the exigencies of war, which even sport and pleasure are wont to call forth? Are we to suppose that the bodies of our soldiers are so effeminate, their minds so feeble, that they cannot hold out for one winter in a camp, and be absent from home? that, like persons who wage a naval war, by taking advantage of the weather, and observing the season of the year, they are able to endure neither heat nor cold? They would certainly blush, should any one lay these things to their charge; and would maintain that both their minds and their bodies were possessed of manly endurance, and that they were able to conduct war equally well in winter and in summer; and that they had not consigned to the tribunes the patronage of indolence and sloth, and that they remembered that their ancestors had created this very power, neither in the shade nor beneath their roofs. Such sentiments are worthy of the valour of your soldiers, such sentiments are worthy of the Roman name, not to consider merely Veii, nor this war which is now pressing us, but to seek a reputation for hereafter for other wars and for other states. Do you consider the difference of opinion likely to result from this matter as trivial? Whether, pray, are the neighbouring states to suppose that the Roman people is such, that if any one shall sustain their first assault, and that of very short continuance, they have nothing afterwards to fear? or whether such should be the terror of our name, that neither the tediousness of a distant siege, nor the inclemency of winter, can dislodge the Roman army from a city once invested, and that they know no other termination of war than victory, and that they carry on wars not more by briskness than by perseverance; which is necessary no doubt in every kind of war, but more especially in besieging cities; most of which, impregnable both by their works and by natural situation, time itself overpowers and reduces by famine and thirst; as it will reduce Veii, unless the tribunes of the commons shall afford aid to the enemy, and the Veientians find in Rome reinforcements which they seek in vain in Etruria. Is there any thing which can happen so much in accordance with the wishes of the Veientians, as that first the Roman city, then the camp, as it were by contagion, should be filled with sedition? But, by Jove, among the enemy so forbearing a state of mind prevails, that not a single change has taken place among them, either through disgust at the length of the siege nor even of the kingly form of government; nor has the refusal of aid by the Etrurians aroused their tempers. For whoever will be the abettor of sedition, will be instantly put to death; nor will it be permitted to any one to utter those sentiments which amongst you are expressed with impunity. He is sure to receive the bastinade, who forsakes his colours or quits his post. Persons advising not one or two soldiers, but whole armies to relinquish their colours or to forsake their camp, are openly listened to in your public assemblies. Accordingly whatever a tribune of the people says, although it tends to the ruin of the country or the dissolution of the commonwealth, you are accustomed to listen to with partiality; and captivated with the charms of that authority, you suffer all sorts of crimes to lie concealed beneath it. The only thing that remains is, that what they vociferate here, the same projects do they realize in the camp and among the soldiers, and seduce the armies, and not suffer them to obey their officers; since that and that only is liberty in Rome, to show no deference to the senate, nor to magistrates, nor laws, nor the usages of ancestors, nor the institutions of our fathers, nor military discipline."

Even already Appius was a match for the tribunes of the people in the popular assemblies; when suddenly a misfortune sustained before Veii, from a quarter whence no one could expect it, both gave Appius the superiority in the dispute, produced also a greater harmony between the different orders, and greater ardour to carry on the siege of Veii with more pertinacity. For when the trenches were now advanced to the very city, and the machines were almost about to be applied to the walls, whilst the works are carried on with greater assiduity by day, than they are guarded by night, a gate was thrown open on a sudden, and a vast multitude, armed chiefly with torches, cast fire about on all sides; and after the lapse of an hour the flames destroyed both the rampart and the machines, the work of so long a time, and great numbers of men, bearing assistance in vain, were destroyed by the sword and by fire. When the account of this circumstance was brought to Rome, it inspired sadness into all ranks; into the senate anxiety and apprehension, lest the sedition could no longer be withstood either in the city or in the camp, and lest the tribunes of the commons should insult over the commonwealth, as if vanquished by them; when on a sudden, those who possessed an equestrian fortune, but to whom horses had not been assigned by the public, having previously held a meeting together, went to the senate; and having obtained permission to speak, promise that they will serve on their own horses. And when thanks were returned to them by the senate in the most complimentary terms, and the report of this proceeding spread through the forum and the city, there suddenly ensues a concourse of the commons to the senate-house. They say that "they are now of the pedestrian order, and they preferred their services to the commonwealth, though not compelled to serve, whether they wished to march them to Veii, or to any other place. If they were led to Veii, they affirm, that they would not return from thence, until the city of the enemy was taken." Then indeed they with difficulty set bounds to the joy which now poured in upon them; for they were not ordered, as in the case of the horsemen, to be publicly eulogized, the order for so doing being consigned to the magistrates, nor were they summoned into the senate-house to receive an answer; nor did the senate confine themselves within the threshold of their house, but every one of them individually with their voice and hands testified from the elevated ground the public joy to the multitude standing in the assembly; they declared that by that unanimity the Roman city would be happy, and invincible and eternal; praised the horsemen, praised the commons; extolled the day itself by their praises; they acknowledged that the courtesy and kindness of the senate was outdone. Tears flowed in abundance through joy both from the patricians and commons; until the senators being called back into the house, a decree of the senate was passed, "that the military tribunes, summoning an assembly, should return thanks to the infantry and cavalry; and should state that the senate would be mindful of their affectionate attachment to their country. But that it was their wish that their pay should go on for those who had, out of their turn, undertaken voluntary service." To the horsemen also a certain stipend was assigned. Then for the first time the cavalry began to serve on their own horses. This army of volunteers being led to Veii, not only restored the works which had been lost, but also erected new ones. Supplies were conveyed from the city with greater care than before; lest any thing should be wanting for the accommodation of an army who deserved so well.

The following year had military tribunes with consular authority, Caius Servilius Ahala a third time, Quintus Servilius, Lucius Virginius, Quintus Sulpicius, Aulus Manlius a second time, Manius Sergius a second time. During their tribuneship, whilst the solicitude of all was directed to the Veientian war, the garrison at Anxur was neglected in consequence of the absence of the soldiers on leave, and from the indiscriminate admission of Volscian traders was overpowered, the guards at the gates being suddenly betrayed. Less of the soldiers perished, because they were all trafficking through the country and city like suttlers. Nor were matters conducted more successfully at Veii, which was then the chief object of all public solicitude. For both the Roman commanders had more quarrels among themselves, than spirit against the enemy; and the severity of the war was exaggerated by the sudden arrival of the Capenatians and the Faliscians. These two states of Etruria, because they were contiguous in situation, judging that in case Veii was conquered, they should be next to the attacks of the Romans in war; the Faliscians also, incensed from a cause affecting themselves, because they had already on a former occasion mixed themselves up in a Fidenatian war, being bound together by an oath by reciprocal embassies, marched unexpectedly with their armies to Veii. It so happened, they attacked the camp in that quarter where Manius Sergius, military tribune, commanded, and occasioned great alarm; because the Romans imagined that all Etruria was aroused and were advancing in a great mass. The same opinion aroused the Veientians in the city. Thus the Roman camp was attacked on both sides; and crowding together, whilst they wheeled round their battalions from one post to another, they were unable either to confine the Veientians within their fortifications, or repel the assault from their own works, and to defend themselves from the enemy on the outside. The only hope was, if succour could be brought from the greater camp, that the different legions should fight, some against the Capenatians and Faliscians, others against the sallies of the townsmen. But Virginius had the command of that camp, who, from personal grounds, was hateful to and incensed against Sergius. This man, when word was brought that most of the forts were attacked, the fortifications scaled, and that the enemy were pouring in on both sides, kept his men under arms, saying that if there was need of assistance, his colleague would send to him. His arrogance was equalled by the obstinacy of the other; who, that he might not appear to have sought any aid from an adversary, preferred being defeated by an enemy to conquering through a fellow-citizen. His men were for a long time cut down between both: at length, abandoning their works, a very small number made their way to the principal camp; the greater number, with Sergius himself, made their way to Rome. Where, when he threw the entire blame on his colleague, it was resolved that Virginius should be sent for from the camp, and that lieutenant-generals should take the command in the mean time. The affair was then discussed in the senate, and the dispute was carried on between the colleagues with (mutual) recriminations. But few took up the interests of the republic, (the greater number) favoured the one or the other, according as private regard or interest prejudiced each.

The principal senators were of opinion, that whether so ignominious a defeat had been sustained through the misconduct or the misfortune of the commanders, "the regular time of the elections should not be waited for, but that new military tribunes should be created immediately, who should enter into office on the calends of October." Whilst they were proceeding to intimate their assent to this opinion, the other military tribunes offered no opposition. But Sergius and Virginius, on whose account it was evident that the senate were dissatisfied with the magistrates of that year, at first deprecated the ignominy, then protested against the decree of the senate; they declared that they would not retire from office before the ides of December, the usual day for persons entering on magisterial duties. Upon this the tribunes of the plebeians, whilst in the general harmony and in the prosperous state of public affairs they had unwillingly kept silence, suddenly becoming confident, began to threaten the military tribunes, that unless they conformed to the order of the senate, they would order them to be thrown into prison. Then Caius Servilius Ahala, a military tribune, observed, "With respect to you, tribunes of the commons, and your threats, I would with pleasure put it to the test, how there is not more of authority in the latter than of spirit in yourselves. But it is impious to strive against the authority of the senate. Wherefore do you cease to seek amid our quarrels for an opportunity of doing mischief; and my colleagues will either do that which the senate thinks fit, or if they shall persist with too much pertinacity, I will immediately nominate a dictator, who will oblige them to retire from office." When this speech was approved with general consent, and the patricians rejoiced, that without the terrors of the tribunitian office, another and a superior power had been discovered to coerce the magistrates, overcome by the universal consent, they held the elections of military tribunes, who were to commence their office on the calends of October, and before that day they retired from office.

During the military tribuneship of Lucius Valerius Potitus for the fourth time, Marcus Furius Camillus for the second time, Manius Æmilius Mamercinus a third time, Cneius Cornelius Cossus a second time, Kæso Fabius Ambustus, Lucius Julius Iulus, much business was transacted at home and abroad. For there was both a complex war at the same time, at Veii, at Capena, at Falerii, and among the Volscians, that Anxur might be recovered from the enemy; and at the same time there was some difficulty experienced both in consequence of the levy, and of the contribution of the tax: there was also a contention about the appointment of plebeian tribunes; and the two trials of those, who a little before had been invested with consular authority, excited no trifling commotion. First of all the tribunes of the soldiers took care that the levy should be held; and not only the juniors were enlisted, but the seniors also were compelled to give in their names, to serve as a garrison to the city. But in proportion as the number of the soldiers was augmented, so much the greater sum of money was required for pay; and this was collected by a tax, those who remained at home contributing against their will, because those who guarded the city had to perform military service also, and to serve the commonwealth. The tribunes of the commons, by their seditious harangues, caused these things, grievous in themselves, to seem more exasperating, by their asserting, "that pay was established for the soldiers with this view, that they might wear out one half of the commons by military service, the other half by the tax. That a single war was being waged now for the third year, on purpose that they may have a longer time to wage it. That armies had been raised at one levy for four different wars, and that boys even and old men were dragged from home. That neither summer nor winter now made any difference, so that there may never be any respite for the unfortunate commons, who were now even at last made to pay a tax; so that after they brought home their bodies wasted by hardship, wounds, and eventually by age, and found their properties at home neglected by the absence of the proprietors, had to pay a tax out of their impaired fortunes, and to refund to the state in a manifold proportion the military pay which had been as it were received on interest." Between the levy and the tax, and their minds being taken up by more important concerns, the number of plebeian tribunes could not be filled up at the elections. A struggle was afterwards made that patricians should be elected into the vacant places. When this could not be carried, still, for the purpose of weakening the Trebonian law, it was managed that Caius Lacerius and Marcus Acutius should be admitted as tribunes of the commons, no doubt through the influence of the patricians.

Chance so directed it, that this year Cneius Trebonius was tribune of the commons, and he considered that he undertook the patronage of the Trebonian law as a debt due to his name and family. He crying out aloud, "that a point which some patricians had aimed at, though baffled in their first attempt, had yet been carried by the military tribunes; that the Trebonian law had been subverted, and tribunes of the commons had been elected not by the suffrages of the people but by the mandate of the patricians; and that the thing was now come to this, that either patricians or dependants of patricians were to be had for tribunes of the commons; that the devoting laws were taken away, the tribunitian power wrested from them; he alleged that this was effected by some artifice of the patricians, by the villany and treachery of his colleagues." While not only the patricians, but the tribunes of the commons also became objects of public resentment; as well those who were elected, as those who had elected them; then three of the college, Publius Curiatius, Marcus Metilius, and Marcus Minucius, alarmed for their interests, make an attack on Sergius and Virginius, military tribunes of the former year; they turn away the resentment of the commons, and public odium from themselves on them, by appointing a day of trial for them. They observe that "those persons by whom the levy, the tribute, the long service, and the distant seat of the war was felt as a grievance, those who lamented the calamity sustained at Veii; such as had their houses in mourning through the loss of children, brothers, relatives, and kinsmen, had now through their means the right and power of avenging the public and private sorrow on the two guilty causes. For that the sources of all their sufferings were centred in Sergius and Virginius: nor did the prosecutor advance that charge more satisfactorily than the accused acknowledged it; who, both guilty, threw the blame from one to the other, Virginius charging Sergius with running away, Sergius charging Virginius with treachery. The folly of whose conduct was so incredible, that it is much more probable that the affair had been contrived by concert, and by the common artifice of the patricians. That by them also an opportunity was formerly given to the Veientians to burn the works for the sake of protracting the war; and that now the army was betrayed, and the Roman camp delivered up to the Faliscians. That every thing was done that the young men should grow old before Veii, and that the tribunes should not be able to consult the people either regarding the lands or the other interests of the commons, and to give weight to their measures by a numerous attendance [of citizens], and to make head against the conspiracy of the patricians. That a previous judgment had been already passed on the accused both by the senate and the Roman people and by their own colleagues. For that by a decree of the senate they had been removed from the administration of affairs, and when they refused to resign their office they had been forced into it by their colleagues; and that the Roman people had elected tribunes, who were to enter on their office not on the ides of December, the usual day, but instantly on the calends of October, because the republic could no longer subsist, these persons remaining in office. And yet these individuals, overwhelmed and already condemned by so many decisions against them, presented themselves for trial before the people; and thought that they were done with the matter, and had suffered sufficient punishment, because they were reduced to the state of private citizens two months sooner [than ordinary] : and did not consider that the power of doing mischief any longer was then taken from them, that punishment was not inflicted; for that the official power of their colleagues also had been taken from them who certainly had committed no fault. That the Roman citizens should resume those sentiments which they had when the recent disaster was sustained, when they beheld the army flying in consternation, covered with wounds, and in dismay pouring into the gates, accusing not fortune nor any of the gods, but these their commanders. They were certain, that there was not a man present in the assembly who did not execrate and detest the persons, families, and fortunes of Lucius Virginius and Manius Sergius. That it was by no means consistent that now, when it was lawful and their duty, they should not exert their power against persons, on whom they had severally imprecated the vengeance of the gods. That the gods themselves never laid hands on the guilty; it was enough if they armed the injured with the means of taking revenge."

Urged on by these discourses the commons condemn the accused [in a fine] of ten thousand *asses* in weight, Sergius in vain throwing the blame on fortune and the common chance of war, Virginius entreating that he might not be more unfortunate at home than he had been in the field. The resentment of the people being turned against them, obliterated the remembrance of the assumption of the tribunes and of the fraud committed against the Trebonian law. The victorious tribunes, in order that the people might reap an immediate benefit from the trial, publish a form of an agrarian law, and prevent the tax from being contributed, since there was need of pay for so great a number of troops, and the enterprises of the service were conducted with success in such a manner, that in none of the wars did they reach the consummation of their hope. At Veii the camp which had been lost was recovered and strengthened with forts and a garrison. Here M. Æmilius and Kæso Fabius, military tribunes, commanded. None of the enemy were found outside the walls by Marcus Furius in the Falisean territory, and Cneius Cornelius in the Capenatian district: spoil was driven off, and the country laid waste by burning of the houses and the fruits of the earth: the towns were neither assaulted nor besieged. But among the Volscians, their territory being depopulated, Anxur, which was situate on an eminence, was assaulted, but to no purpose; and when force was ineffectual, they commenced to surround it with a rampart and a trench. The province of the Volscians had fallen [to the lot of] Valerius Potitus. In this state of military affairs an intestine disturbance broke out with greater violence than the wars were proceeded with. And when it was rendered impossible by the tribunes to have the tax paid, and the payment [of the army] was not remitted to the generals, and the soldiers became importunate for their pay, the camp also was well nigh being involved in the contagion of the sedition in the city. Amid this resentment of the commons against the patricians, though the tribunes asserted that now was the time for establishing liberty, and transferring the sovereign dignity from the Sergii and Virginii to plebeians, men of fortitude and energy, still they proceeded no further than the election of one of the commons, Publius Licinius Calvus, military tribune with consular power for the purpose of establishing their right by precedent: the others elected were patricians, Publius Mænius, Lucius Titinius, Publius Mælius, Lucius Furius Medullinus, Lucius Publius Volscus. The commons themselves were surprised at having gained so important a point, and not merely he who had been elected, being a person who had filled no post of honour before, being only a senator of long standing, and now weighed down with years. Nor does it sufficiently appear, why he was elected first and in preference to any one else to taste the sweets of the new dignity. Some think that he was raised to so high a dignity through the influence of his brother, Cneius Cornelius, who had been military tribune on the preceding year, and had given triple pay to the cavalry. Others [say] that he had himself delivered a seasonable address equally acceptable to the patricians and commons, concerning the harmony of the several orders [of the state] . The tribunes of the commons, exulting in this victory at the election, relaxed in their opposition regarding the tax, a matter which very much impeded the progress of public business. It was paid in with submission, and sent to the army.

In the country of the Volscians Anxur was soon retaken, the guarding of the city having been neglected during a festival day. This year was remarkable for a cold and snowy winter, so that the roads were impassable, and the Tiber not navigable. The price of provisions underwent no change, in consequence of the abundance previously laid in. And because Publius Licinius, as he obtained his office without any rioting, to the greater joy of the commons than annoyance of the patricians, so also did he administer it; a rapturous desire of electing plebeians at the next election took possession of them. Of the patricians Marcus Veturius alone obtained a place: almost all the centuries appointed the other plebeian candidates as military tribunes with consular authority. Marcus Pomponius, Caius Duilius, Volero Publilius, Cneius Genucius, Lucius Atilius. The severe winter, whether from the ill temperature of the air [arising] from the abrupt transition to the contrary state, or from whatsoever other cause, was followed by an unhealthy summer, destructive to all species of animals; and when neither the cause nor termination of this intractable pestilence could be discovered, the Sibylline books were consulted according to a decree of the senate. The duumvirs for the direction of religious matters, the lectisternium being then for the first time introduced into the city of Rome, for eight days implored the favour of Apollo and Latona, Diana and Hercules, Mercury and Neptune, three couches being laid out with the greatest magnificence that was then possible. The same solemn rite was observed also by private individuals. The doors lying open throughout the entire city, and the use of every thing lying out in common, they say that all passengers, both those known and those unknown indiscriminately, were invited to lodgings, and that conversation was adopted between persons at variance with complaisance and kindness, and that they refrained from disputes and quarrels; their chains were also taken off those who were in confinement during those days; that afterward a scruple was felt in imprisoning those to whom the gods had brought such aid. In the mean while the alarm was multiplied at Veii, three wars being concentred in the one place. For as the Capenatians and Faliscians had suddenly come with succour [to the Veientians], they had to fight against three armies on different sides in the same manner as formerly, through the whole extent of their works. The recollection of the sentence passed on Sergius and Virginius aided them above every thing else. Accordingly some forces being led around in a short time from the principal camp, where some delay had been made on the former occasion, attack the Capenatians on their rear, whilst they were engaged in front against the Roman rampart. The fight commencing in this quarter struck terror into the Faliscians also, and a sally from the camp opportunely made put them to flight, thrown into disorder as they now were. The victors, having then pursued them in their retreat, made great slaughter amongst them. And soon after those who had been devastating the territory of Capena, having met them as it were by chance, entirely cut off the survivors of the fight as they were straggling through the country: and many of the Veientians in their retreat to the city were slain before the gates; whilst, through fear lest the Romans should force in along with them, they excluded the hindmost of their men by closing the gates.

These were the transactions of that year. And now the election of military tribunes approached; about which the patricians felt more intense solicitude than about the war, inasmuch as they saw that the supreme authority was not only shared with the commons, but almost lost to themselves. Wherefore the most distinguished individuals being, by concert, prepared to stand candidates, whom they thought [the people] would feel ashamed to pass by, they themselves, nevertheless, as if they were all candidates, trying every expedient, strove to gain over not only men, but the gods also, raising religious scruples about the elections held the two preceding years; that, in the former of those years, a winter set in intolerably severe, and like to a prodigy from the gods; on the next year [they had] not prodigies, but events, a pestilence inflicted on both city and country through the manifest resentment of the gods: whom, as was discovered in the books of the fates, it was necessary to appease, for the purpose of warding off that plague. That it seemed to the gods an affront that honours should be prostituted, and the distinctions of birth confounded, in an election which was held under proper auspices. The people, overawed as well by the dignity of the candidates as by a sense of religion, elected all the military tribunes with consular power from among the patricians, the greater part being men who had been most highly distinguished by honour; Lucius Valerius Potitus a fifth time, Marcus Valerius Maximus, Marcus Furius Camillus a third time, Lucius Furius Medullinus a third time, Quintus Servilius Fidenas a second time, Quintus Sulpicius Camerinus a second time. During this tribunate, nothing very memorable was performed at

Veii. All their force was employed in depopulating the country. Two consummate commanders, Potitus from Falerii, Camillus from Capena, carried off great booty, nothing being left undestroyed which could be injured by sword or by fire.

In the mean time many prodigies were announced; the greater part of which were little credited or even slighted, because individuals were the reporters of them, and also because, the Etrurians being now at war with them, they had no aruspices through whom they might attend to them. The attention of all was turned to a particular one: the lake in the Alban grove swelled to an unusual height without any rain, or any other cause which could account for the matter independently of a miracle. Commissioners were sent to the Delphic oracle to inquire what the gods portended by this prodigy; but an interpreter of the fates was presented to them nearer home in a certain aged Veientian, who, amid the scoffs thrown out by the Roman and Etrurian soldiers from the out-posts and guards, declared, after the manner of one delivering a prophecy, that until the water should be discharged from the Alban lake, the Romans should never become masters of Veii. This was disregarded at first as having been thrown out at random, afterwards it began to be canvassed in conversation; until one of the Roman soldiers on guard asked one of the townsmen who was nearest him (a conversational intercourse having now taken place in consequence of the long continuance of the war) who he was, who threw out those dark expressions concerning the Alban lake? After he heard that he was an aruspex, being a man whose mind was not without a tincture of religion, pretending that he wished to consult him on the expiation of a private portent, if he could aid him, he enticed the prophet to a conference. And when, being unarmed, they had proceeded a considerable distance from their respective parties without any apprehension, the Roman youth having the advantage in strength, took up the feeble old man in the sight of all, and amid the ineffectual bustle made by the Etrurians, carried him away to his own party. When he was conducted before the general, and sent from thence to Rome to the senate, to those who asked him what that was which he had stated concerning the Alban lake, he replied, "that undoubtedly the gods were angry with the Veientian people on that day, on which they had inspired him with the resolve to disclose the ruin of his country as destined by the fates. Wherefore what he then declared urged by divine inspiration, he neither could recall so that it may be unsaid; and perhaps by concealing what the immortal gods wished to be published, no less guilt was contracted than by openly declaring what ought to be concealed. Thus therefore it was recorded in the books of the fates, thus in the Etrurian doctrine, that whensoever the Alban water should rise to a great height, then, if the Romans should discharge it in a proper manner, victory was granted them over the Veientians: before that occurred, that the gods would not desert the walls of Veii." He then detailed what would be the legitimate method of draining. But the senate deeming his authority as but of little weight, and not to be entirely depended on in so important a matter, determined to wait for the deputies and the responses of the Pythian oracle.

Before the commissioners returned from Delphos, or an expiation of the Alban prodigy was discovered, the new military tribunes with consular power entered on their office, Lucius Julius Iulus, Lucius Furius Medullinus for the fourth time, Lucius Sergius Fidenas, Aulus Postumius Regillensis, Publius Cornelius Maluginensis, and Aulus Manlius. This year a new enemy, the Tarquinians, started up. Because they saw the Romans engaged in many wars together, that of the Volscians at Anxur, where the garrison was besieged, that of the Æquans at Lavici, who were attacking the Roman colony there, moreover in the Veientian, Faliscan, and Capenatian war, and that matters were not more tranquil within the walls, by reason of the dissensions between the patricians and commons; considering that amid these [troubles] there was an opportunity for an attack, they send their light-armed cohorts to commit depredations on the Roman territory. For [they concluded] either that the Romans would suffer that injury to pass off unavenged, that they might not encumber themselves with an additional war, or that they would resent it with a scanty army, and one by no means strong. The Romans [felt] greater indignation, than alarm, at the inroads of the Tarquinians. On this account the matter was neither taken up with great preparation, nor was it delayed for any length of time. Aulus Postumius and Lucius Julius, having raised a body of men, not by a regular levy, (for they were prevented by the tribunes of the commons,) but [a body consisting] mostly of volunteers, whom they had aroused by exhortations, having proceeded by cross marches through the territory of Cære, fell unexpectedly on the Tarquinians, as they were returning from their depredations and laden with booty; they slew great numbers, stripped them all of their baggage, and, having recovered the spoils of their own lands, they return to Rome. Two days were allowed to the owners to reclaim their effects. On the third day, that portion not owned (for most of it belonged to the enemies themselves) was sold by public auction; and what was produced from thence, was distributed among the soldiers. The other wars, and more especially the Veientian, were of doubtful issue. And now the Romans, despairing of human aid, began to look to the fates and the gods, when the deputies returned from Delphos, bringing with them an answer of the oracle, corresponding with the response of the captive prophet: "Roman, beware lest the Alban water be confined in the lake, beware of suffering it to flow into the sea in its own stream. Thou shalt let it out and form a passage for it through the fields, and by dispersing it in channels thou shalt consume it. Then press boldly on the walls of the enemy, mindful that the victory is granted to you by these fates which are now revealed over that city which thou art besieging for so many years. The war being ended, do thou, as victorious, bring ample offerings to my temples, and having renewed the religious institutions of your country, the care of which has been given up, perform them in the usual manner."

Upon this the captive prophet began to be held in high esteem, and Cornelius and Postumius, the military tribunes, began to employ him for the expiation of the Alban prodigy, and to appease the gods in due form. And it was at length discovered wherein the gods found fault with the neglect of the ceremonies and the omission of the customary rites; that it was undoubtedly nothing else, than that the magistrates, having been appointed under some defect [in their election], had not directed the Latin festival and the solemnities on the Alban mount with due regularity. The only mode of expiation in the case was, that the military tribunes should resign their office, the auspices be taken anew, and an interregnum be adopted. All these things were performed according to a decree of the senate. There were three interreges in succession, Lucius Valerius, Quintus Servilius Fidenas, Marcus Furius Camillus. In the mean time disturbances never ceased to exist, the tribunes of the commons impeding the elections until it was previously stipulated, that the greater number of the military tribunes should be elected out of the commons. Whilst these things are going on, assemblies of Etruria were held at the temple of Voltumna, and the Capenatians and Faliscians demanding that all the states of Etruria should by common consent and resolve aid in raising the siege of Veii, the answer given was: "that on a former occasion they had refused that to the Veientians, because they had no right to demand aid from those from whom they had not solicited advice on so important a matter. That for the present their own condition instead of themselves[160] denied it to them, more especially in that part of Etruria. That a strange nation, the Gauls, were become new neighbours, with whom they neither had a sufficiently secure peace, nor a certainty of war: to the blood, however, and the name and the present dangers of their kinsmen this [mark of respect] was paid, that if any of their youth were disposed to go to that war, they would not prevent them." Hence there was a report at Rome, that a great number of enemies had arrived, and in consequence the intestine dissensions began to subside, as is usual, through alarm for the general safety.

Without opposition on the part of the patricians, the prerogative tribe elect Publius Licinius Calvus military tribune without his suing for it, a man of tried moderation in his former tribunate, but now of extreme old age; and it was observed that all were re-elected in regular

---

[160] So I have rendered *pro se*—or it may be rendered, "considering their circumstances," scil. the external circumstances in which they were placed.

succession out of the college of the same year, Lucius Titinius, Publius Mænius, Publius Mælius, Cneius Genucius, Lucius Atilius: before these were proclaimed, the tribes being summoned in the ordinary course, Publius Licinius Calvus, by permission of the interrex, spoke as follows: "Romans, I perceive that from the recollection of our administration you are seeking an omen of concord, a thing most important at the present time, for the ensuing year. If you re-elect the same colleagues, improved also by experience, in me you no longer behold the same person, but the shadow and name of Publius Licinius now left. The powers of my body are decayed, my senses of sight and hearing are grown dull, my memory falters, the vigour of my mind is blunted. Behold here a youth," says he, holding his son, "the representation and image of him whom ye formerly made a military tribune, the first from among the commons. This youth, formed under my own discipline, I present and dedicate to the commonwealth as a substitute for myself. And I beseech you, Romans, that the honour readily offered by yourselves to me, you would grant to his suit, and to my prayers added in his behalf." The favour was granted to the request of the father, and his son, Publius Licinius, was declared military tribune with consular power along with those whom I have mentioned above. Titinius and Genucius, military tribunes, proceeded against the Faliscians and Capenatians, and whilst they conduct the war with more courage than conduct, they fall into an ambush. Genucius, atoning for his temerity by an honourable death, fell among the foremost in front of the standards. Titinius, having collected his men from the great confusion [into which they were thrown] on a rising ground, restored their order of battle; nor did he, however, venture to engage the enemy on even ground. More of disgrace than of loss was sustained; which was well nigh proving a great calamity; so much alarm was excited not only at Rome, whither an exaggerated account of it had reached, but in the camp also at Veii. There the soldiers were with difficulty restrained from flight, as a report had spread through the camp that, the generals and army having been cut to pieces, the victorious Capenatians and Faliscians and all the youth of Etruria were not far off. At Rome they gave credit to accounts still more alarming than these, that the camp at Veii was now attacked, that a part of the enemy was now advancing to the city prepared for an attack: they crowded to the walls, and supplications of the matrons, which the public panic had called forth from their houses, were offered up in the temples; and the gods were petitioned by prayers, that they would repel destruction from the houses and temples of the city and from the walls of Rome, and that they would avert that terror to Veii, if the sacred rites had been duly renewed, if the prodigies had been expiated.

The games and the Latin festival had now been performed anew; now the water from the Alban lake had been discharged upon the fields, and the fates were demanding [the ruin of] Veii. Accordingly a general destined for the destruction of that city and the preservation of his country, Marcus Furius Camillus, being nominated dictator, appointed Publius Cornelius Scipio his master of the horse. The change of the general suddenly produced a change in every thing. Their hopes seemed different, the spirits of the people were different, the fortune also of the city seemed changed. First of all, he punished according to military discipline those who had fled from Veii in that panic, and took measures that the enemy should not be the most formidable object to the soldier. Then a levy being proclaimed for a certain day, he himself in the mean while makes an excursion to Veii to strengthen the spirits of the soldiers: thence he returns to Rome to enlist the new army, not a single man declining the service. Youth from foreign states also, Latins and Hernicians, came, promising their service for the war: after the dictator returned them thanks in the senate, all preparations being now completed for the war, he vowed, according to a decree of the senate, that he would, on the capture of Veii, celebrate the great games, and that he would repair and dedicate the temple of Mother Matuta, which had been formerly consecrated by King Servius Tullius. Having set out from the city with his army amid the high expectation[161] rather than mere hopes of persons, he first encountered the Faliscians and Capenatians in the district of Nepote. Every thing there being managed with consummate prudence and skill, was attended, as is usual, with success. He not only routed the enemy in battle, but he stripped them also of their camp, and obtained a great quantity of spoil, the principal part of which was handed over to the quæstor; not much was given to the soldiers. From thence the army was marched to Veii, and additional forts close to each other were erected; and by a proclamation being issued, that no one should fight without orders, the soldiers were taken off from those skirmishes, which frequently took place at random between the wall and rampart, [so as to apply] to the work. Of all the works, far the greatest and more laborious was a mine which they commenced to carry into the enemies' citadel. And that the work might not be interrupted, and that the continued labour under ground might not exhaust the same individuals, he divided the number of pioneers into six companies; six hours were allotted for the work in rotation; nor by night or day did they give up, until they made a passage into the citadel.

When the dictator now saw that the victory was in his hands, that a most opulent city was on the point of being taken, and that there would be more spoil than had been obtained in all previous wars taken together, that he might not incur either the resentment of the soldiers

---

[161] *Expectatione*, &c. With confident expectations on the part of his countrymen, rather than simple hope.

from a parsimonious partition of the plunder, or displeasure among the patricians from a prodigal lavishing of it, he sent a letter to the senate, "that by the kindness of the immortal gods, his own measures, and the perseverance of the soldiers, Veii would be soon in the power of the Roman people." What did they think should be done with respect to the spoil? Two opinions divided the senate; the one that of the elder Publius Licinius, who on being first asked by his son, as they say, proposed it as his opinion, that a proclamation should be openly sent forth to the people, that whoever wished to share in the plunder, should proceed to the camp before Veii; the other that of Appius Claudius,[162] who, censuring such profusion as unprecedented, extravagant, partial, and one that was unadvisable, if they should once judge it criminal, that money taken from the enemy should be [deposited] in the treasury when exhausted by wars, advised their pay to be paid to the soldiers out of that money, so that the commons might thereby have to pay less tax. For that "the families of all would feel their share of such a bounty in equal proportion; that the hands of the idlers in the city, ever greedy for plunder, would not then carry off the prizes due to brave warriors, as it generally so happens that according as each individual is wont to seek the principal part of the toil and danger, so is he the least active as a plunderer." Licinius, on the other hand, argued that the money in that case would ever prove the source of jealousy and animosity, and that it would afford grounds for charges before the commons, and thence for seditions and new laws. "That it was more advisable therefore that the feelings of the commons should be conciliated by that bounty; that succour should be afforded them, exhausted and drained by a tax of so many years, and that they should feel the fruits arising from a war, in which they had in a manner grown old. What each took from the enemy with his own hand and brought home with him would be more gratifying and delightful, than if he were to receive a much larger share at the will of another." That the dictator himself wished to shun the odium and recriminations arising from the matter; for that reason he transferred it to the senate. The senate, too, ought to hand the matter thus referred to them over to the commons, and suffer every man to have what the fortune of war gave to him. This proposition appeared to

---

[162] According to Niebuhr, (vol. ii. p. 233,) this fear put into the mouth of Claudius, is attributable to ignorance or forgetfulness on the part of Livy, of the early usage in the dividing of spoils, which had ceased to be observed in the time of Augustus. According to former Roman usage, half of the conquering army was employed, under the sanction of a solemn oath, to subtract nothing, in collecting the spoil, which was then partly divided by lot, partly sold, and the proceeds, if promised to the soldiers, disbursed to them man by man, if otherwise, it was brought into the treasury. Both schemes mentioned here by Livy, it will be observed, contemplated compensation to the people for the war-tax which they had so long paid; but that of Licinius was more favourable, especially to the poor, as the ordinary citizens would receive equal shares, and the compensation would be direct and immediate.—*Gunne*.

be the safer, as it would make the senate popular. A proclamation was therefore issued, that those who chose should proceed to the camp to the dictator for the plunder of Veii.

The vast multitude who went filled the camp. Then the dictator, going forth after taking the auspices, having issued orders that the soldiers should take arms, says, "Under thy guidance, O Pythian Apollo, and inspired by thy divinity, I proceed to destroy the city of Veii, and I vow to thee the tenth part of the spoil.[163] Thee also, queen Juno, who inhabitest Veii, I beseech, that thou wilt accompany us, when victors, into our city, soon to be thine, where a temple worthy of thy majesty shall receive thee."[164] Having offered up these prayers, there being more than a sufficient number of men, he assaults the city on every quarter, in order that the perception of the danger threatening them from the mine might be diminished. The Veientians, ignorant that they had already been doomed by their own prophets, already by foreign oracles, that the gods had been already invited to a share in their plunder, that some, called out by vows from their city, were looking towards the temple of the enemy and new habitations, and that they were spending that the last day [of their existence], fearing nothing less than that, their walls being undermined, the citadel was now filled with enemies, briskly run to the walls in arms, wondering what could be the reason that, when no one had stirred from the Roman posts for so many days, then, as if struck with sudden fury, they should run heedlessly to the walls. A fabulous narrative is introduced here, that, when the king of the Veientians was offering sacrifice, the voice of the aruspex, declaring that the victory was given to him who should cut up the entrails of that victim, having been heard in the mine, incited the Roman soldiers to burst open the mine, carry off the entrails, and bring them to the dictator. But in matters of such remote antiquity, I should deem it sufficient, if matters bearing a resemblance to truth be admitted as true. Such stories as this, more suited to display on the stage, which delights in the marvellous, than to historic authenticity, it is not worth while either to affirm or refute. The mine, at this time full of chosen men, suddenly discharged the armed troops in the temple of Juno which was in the citadel of Veii.[165] Some of them attack the rear of the enemy on the walls; some tore open the bars of the gates; some set fire to the

---

[163] "This vow frequently occurs in Grecian history, like that made of the Persian booty, but this is the only instance in the history of Rome."—*Niebuhr*, vol. ii. 239.

[164] *Evocatos.* When the Romans besieged a town, and thought themselves sure of taking it, they used solemnly to call out of it the gods in whose protection the place was supposed to be.

[165] The idea of the Romans working a mine, even through the soil of Veii, so as to be sure of reaching not only the town and the citadel, and even the temple, is considered by Niebuhr as extremely ridiculous. He deems the circumstance a clear proof of the fiction that attaches to the entire story of the capture of Veii. The whole seems to be an imitation of the siege of Troy.—*Gunne.*

houses, while stones and tiles were thrown down from the roofs by the women and slaves. Clamour, consisting of the various voices of the assailants and the terrified, mixed with the crying of women and children, fills every place. The soldiers being in an instant beaten off from the walls, and the gates being thrown open, some entering in bodies, others scaling the deserted walls, the city become filled with enemies, fighting takes place in every quarter. Then, much slaughter being now made, the ardour of the fight abates; and the dictator commands the heralds to proclaim that the unarmed should be spared. This put an end to bloodshed. Then laying down their arms, they commenced to surrender; and, by permission of the dictator, the soldiers disperse in quest of plunder. And when this was collected before his eyes, greater in quantity and in the value of the effects than he had hoped or expected, the dictator, raising his hands to heaven, is said to have prayed, "that, if his success and that of the Roman people seemed excessive to any of the gods and men, it might be permitted to the Roman people to appease that jealousy with as little detriment as possible to himself and the Roman people."[166] It is recorded that, when turning about during this prayer, he stumbled and fell; and to persons judging of the matter by subsequent events, that seemed to refer as an omen to Camillus' own condemnation, and the disaster of the city of Rome being akin, which happened a few years after. And that day was consumed in slaughtering the enemy and in the plunder of this most opulent city.

On the following day the dictator sold the inhabitants of free condition by auction: that was the only money applied to public use, not without resentment on the part of the people: and for the spoil they brought home with them, they felt no obligation either to their commander, who, in his search for abettors of his own parsimony, had

---

[166] The passage in the original, in the generality of editions, is read as follows: *ut eam invidium lenire, quàm minimo suo privato incommodo publicoque, populo Romano liceret*: i. e. that both himself and the Roman people may get over the evil consequences of the jealousy of the gods with as little detriment as possible to either: *populi Romani* seems preferable here: i. e. "that it might be allowed to lighten that jealousy, by the least possible injury to his own private interest, and to the public interests of the Roman people." There were certainly two persons concerned in the *invidia* and *incommodum* here, Camillus himself, and the Roman people; to whom respectively the *damnatio*, and *elades captæ urbis*, afterwards mentioned, obviously refer. Some editions read, *invidiam lenire suo privato incommodo, quàm minimo publico populi Romani liceret*. This is the reading adopted by Crevier; i. e. "to appease the jealousy by his own private loss, rather than the least public loss." This is more in accordance with the account given of Camillus by Plutarch, and contains a sentiment certainly more worthy both of Livy and of Camillus. Sentiments ascribed by Plutarch to Camillus, will have suo privato incommodo, quam minimo publico P. R., giving him the patriotic wish to render light the odium by his own private loss, *rather than* the least public loss; or, by his own private loss, but if not, by as small a public loss as possible. Pop-*li* R-*i*, better than o, o, as *liceret* would, in the latter case, apply only to one of the parties; in the former both are understood.

referred to the senate a matter within his own jurisdiction, or to the senate, but to the Licinian family, of which the son had laid the matter before the senate, and the father had been the proposer of so popular a resolution. When all human wealth had been carried away from Veii, they then began to remove the offerings to their gods and the gods themselves, but more after the manner of worshippers than of plunderers. For youths selected from the entire army, to whom the charge of conveying queen Juno to Rome was assigned, after having thoroughly washed their bodies and arrayed themselves in white garments, entered her temple with profound adoration, applying their hands at first with religious awe, because, according to the Etrurian usage, no one but a priest of a certain family had been accustomed to touch that statue. Then when some one, moved either by divine inspiration, or in youthful jocularity, said, "Juno, art thou willing to go to Rome," the rest joined in shouting that the goddess had nodded assent. To the story an addition was afterwards made, that her voice was heard, declaring that "she was willing." Certain it is, we are informed that, having been raised from her place by machines of trifling power, she was light and easily removed, like as if she [willingly] followed; and that she was conveyed safe to the Aventine, her eternal seat, whither the vows of the dictator had invited her; where the same Camillus who had vowed it, afterwards dedicated a temple to her. Such was the fall of Veii, the wealthiest city of the Etrurian nation, which even in its final overthrow demonstrated its greatness; for having been besieged for ten summers and winters without intermission, after it had inflicted considerably greater losses than it had sustained, eventually, fate now at length urging [its destruction], it was carried after all by the contrivances of art, not by force.

When news was brought to Rome that Veii was taken, although both the prodigies had been expiated, and the answers of the prophets and the Pythian responses were well known, and though they had selected as their commander Marcus Furius, the greatest general of the day, which was doing as much to promote success as could be done by human prudence; yet because the war had been carried on there for so many years with various success, and many losses had been sustained, their joy was unbounded, as if for an event not expected; and before the senate could pass any decree, all the temples were crowded with Roman matrons returning thanks to the gods. The senate decrees supplications for the space of four days, a number of days greater than [was prescribed] in any former war. The dictator's arrival also, all ranks pouring out to meet him, was better attended than that of any general before, and his triumph considerably surpassed all the ordinary style of honouring such a day. The most conspicuous of all was himself, riding through the city in a chariot drawn by white horses; and that appeared unbecoming, not to say a citizen, but even a human being. The people considered it an outrage on religion that the dictator's equipage should emulate that of Jupiter and Apollo; and for that single reason his triumph was rather splendid than pleasing. He then contracted for a temple for queen Juno on Mount Aventine, and consecrated that of Mother Matuta: and, after having performed these services to the gods and to mankind, he laid down his dictatorship. They then began to consider regarding the offering to Apollo; and when Camillus stated that he had vowed the tenth part of the spoil to him, and the pontiff declared that the people ought to discharge their own obligation, a plan was not readily struck out of ordering the people to refund the spoil, so that the due proportion might be set aside out of it for sacred purposes. At length they had recourse to this which seemed the easiest course, that, whoever wished to acquit himself and his family of the religious obligation, after he had made his own estimate of his portion of the plunder, should pay into the treasury the value of the tenth part, so that out of it a golden offering worthy of the grandeur of the temple and the divinity of the god might be made, suitable to the dignity of the Roman people. This contribution also tended to alienate the affections of the commons from Camillus. During these transactions ambassadors came from the Volscians and Æquans to sue for peace; and peace was obtained, rather that the state wearied by so tedious a war might obtain repose, than that the petitioners were deserving of it.

After the capture of Veii, the following year had six military tribunes with consular power, the two Publii Cornelii, Cossus and Scipio, Marcus Valerius Maximus a second time, Kæso Fabius Ambustus a third time, Lucius Furius Medullinus a fifth time, Quintus Servilius a third time. To the Cornelii the Faliscian war, to Valerius and Servilius the Capenatian war, fell by lot. By them no cities were attempted by storm or by siege, but the country was laid waste, and the plunder of the effects on the lands was driven off; not a single fruit tree, not a vegetable was left on the land. These losses reduced the people of Capena; peace was granted to them on their suing for it. The war among the Faliscians still continued. At Rome in the mean time sedition became multiplied; and for the purpose of assuaging this they resolved that a colony should be sent off to the Volscian country, for which three thousand Roman citizens should be enrolled; and the triumvirs appointed for the purpose, distributed three acres and seven-twelfths to each man. This donation began to be scorned, because they thought that it was offered as a solace for the disappointment of higher hopes. For why were the commons to be sent into exile to the Volscians, when the magnificent city of Veii was still in view, and the Veientian territory, more fertile and extensive than the Roman territory? The city also they extolled as preferable to the city of Rome, both in situation, in the grandeur of its enclosures, and buildings, both public and private. Nay, even that scheme was proposed, which after the taking of Rome by the Gauls was still more strongly urged, of removing to Veii. But they destined Veii to be inhabited by half the commons and half the senate; and that two cities of one common republic might be inhabited by the Roman people.[167] When the nobles strove against these measures so strenuously, as to declare "that they would sooner die in the sight of the Roman people, than that any of these things should be put to the vote; for that now in one city there were so many dissensions; what would there be in two? Would any one prefer a vanquished to a victorious city; and suffer Veii now after being captured to enjoy greater prosperity than it had before its capture? Lastly, that they may be forsaken in their country by their fellow-citizens; that no power should ever oblige them to forsake their country and fellow-citizens, and follow Titus Licinius (for he was the tribune of the commons who proposed the measure) as a founder to Veii, abandoning the divine Romulus, the son of a god, the parent and founder of the city of Rome." When these proceedings were going on with shameful contentions, (for the patricians had drawn over, one half of the tribunes of the commons to their sentiments,) nothing else obliged the commons to refrain from violence, but that whenever a clamour was set up for the purpose of commencing a riot, the principal members of the senate, presenting themselves among the foremost to the crowd, ordered that they themselves should be attacked, struck, and put to death. Whilst they abstained from violating their age, dignity, and honourable station, their respect for them checked their rage even with respect to similar attempts on others.

Camillus, at every opportunity and in all places, stated publicly, "that this was not at all surprising; that the state was gone mad; which, though bound by a vow, yet felt greater concern in all other matters than in acquitting itself of its religious obligations. He would say nothing of the contribution of an alms more strictly speaking than of a tenth; since each man bound himself in his private capacity by it, the public was set free. However, that his conscience would not permit him to pass this over in silence, that out of that spoil only which consisted of movable effects, a tenth was set apart; that no mention was made of the city and captured land, which were also included in the vow." As the discussion of this point seemed difficult to the senate, it was referred to the pontiffs; Camillus being invited [to the council], the college decided, that whatever had belonged to the Veientians before the uttering of the vow, and had come into the power of the Roman people after the vow was made, of that a tenth part was sacred to

---

[167] "A proposal so absurd would have justified the most vehement opposition of the senate. But it is much more probable, that the scope of the proposition was, that on this occasion the whole of the conquered land should be divided, but amongst the whole nation, so that the patricians also and their clients should receive a share as absolute property."—*Neibuhr*, vol. ii. p. 248.

Apollo. Thus the city and land were brought into the estimate. The money was issued from the treasury, and the consular tribunes of the soldiers were commissioned to purchase gold with it. And when there was not a sufficient quantity of this [metal], the matrons having held meetings to deliberate on the subject, and by a general resolution having promised the military tribunes their gold and all their ornaments, brought them into the treasury. This circumstance was peculiarly grateful to the senate, and they say that in return for this generosity the honour was conferred on the matrons, that they might use covered chariots [when going] to public worship and the games, and open chaises on festival and common days. A certain weight of gold being received from each and valued, in order that the price might be paid for it, it was resolved that a golden bowl should be made of it, which was to be carried to Delphos as an offering to Apollo. As soon as they disengaged their minds from the religious obligation, the tribunes of the commons renew their seditious practices; the populace are excited against all the nobles, but above all against Camillus: that "he by confiscating and consecrating the plunder of Veii had reduced it to nothing." The absent [nobles] they abuse in violent terms: they evince a respect for them in their presence, when they voluntarily presented themselves to their fury. As soon as they perceived that the business would be protracted beyond that year, they re-elect as tribunes of the commons for the following year the same abettors of the law; and the patricians strove to accomplish the same thing with respect to those who were opponents of the law. Thus the same persons in a great measure were re-elected tribunes of the commons.

At the election of military tribunes the patricians succeeded by their utmost exertions in having Marcus Furius Camillus elected. They pretended that he was wanted as a commander on account of the wars; but he was intended as an opponent to the tribunes in their profusion. The military tribunes with consular authority elected with Camillus were, Lucius Furius Medullinus a sixth time, Caius Æmilius, Lucius Valerius Publicola, Spurius Postumius, Publius Cornelius a second time. At the commencement of the year the tribunes of the commons took not a step until Marcus Furius Camillus should set out to the Faliscians, as that war had been assigned to him. Then by delaying the project cooled; and Camillus, whom they chiefly dreaded as an antagonist, acquired an increase of glory among the Faliscians. For when the enemy at first confined themselves within the walls, considering it the safest plan, by laying waste their lands and burning their houses, he compelled them to come forth from the city; but their fears prevented them from proceeding to any considerable length. At about a mile from the town they pitch their camp; trusting that it was sufficiently secure from no other cause, than the difficulty of the approaches, the roads around being rough and craggy, in some parts narrow, in others steep. But Camillus having followed the direction of a prisoner belonging to the country as his guide, decamping at an advanced hour of the night, at break of day shows himself on ground considerably higher [than theirs] . The Romans worked at the fortifications in three divisions: the rest of the army stood prepared for battle. There he routs and puts to flight the enemy when they attempted to interrupt his works; and such terror was struck into the Faliscans in consequence, that, in their precipitate flight passing by their own camp which lay in their way, they made for the city. Many were slain and wounded, before that in their panic they could make their way through the gates. Their camp was taken; the spoil was given up to the quæstors, to the great dissatisfaction of the soldiers; but overcome by the strictness of his authority, they both hated and admired the same firmness of conduct. Then a regular siege of the city took place, and the lines of circumvallation were carried on, and sometimes occasional attacks were made by the townsmen on the Roman posts, and slight skirmishes took place: and the time was spent, no hope [of success] inclining to either side, whilst corn and other provisions were possessed in much greater abundance by the besieged than the besiegers from [the store] which had been previously laid in. And their toil appeared likely to prove just as tedious as it had at Veii, had not fortune presented to the Roman general at once both an opportunity for displaying his virtuous firmness of mind already tested in warlike affairs, and a speedy victory.

It was the custom among the Faliscans to employ the same person as preceptor and private tutor for their children; and, as continues the usage to this day in Greece, several youths were intrusted to the care of one man. The person who appeared to excel in knowledge, instructed, as it is natural to suppose, the children of the leading men. As he had established it as a custom during peace to carry the boys out beyond the city for the sake of play and of exercise; that custom not having been discontinued during the existence of the war; then drawing them away from the gate, sometimes in shorter, sometimes in longer excursions, advancing farther than usual, when an opportunity offered, by varying their play and conversation, he led them on between the enemy's guards, and thence to the Roman camp into his tent to Camillus. There to the atrocious act he added a still more atrocious speech: that "he had delivered Falerii into the hands of the Romans, when he put into their power those children, whose parents are there at the head of affairs." When Camillus heard this, he says, "Wicked as thou art, thou hast come with thy villanous offering neither to a people nor a commander like thyself. Between us and the Faliscans there exists not that form of society which is established by human compact; but between both there does exist, and ever will exist, that which nature has implanted. There are laws of war as well of peace; and we have learned to wage them justly not less than bravely. We carry arms not against that age which is spared even when towns are taken, but against men who are themselves armed, and who, not having been injured or provoked by us, attacked the Roman camp at Veii. Those thou hast surpassed, as far as lay in you, by an unprecedented act of villany: I shall conquer them, as I did Veii, by Roman arts, by bravery, labour, and by arms." Then having stripped him naked, and tied his hands behind his back, he delivered him up to the boys to be brought back to Falerii; and supplied them with rods to scourge the traitor and drive him into the city. At which spectacle, a crowd of people being assembled, afterwards the senate being convened by the magistrates on the extraordinary circumstance, so great a change was produced in their sentiments, that the entire state earnestly demanded peace at the hands of those, who lately, outrageous by hatred and anger, almost preferred the fate of the Veientians to the peace of the Capenatians. The Roman faith, the justice of the commander, are cried up in the forum and in the senate-house; and by universal consent ambassadors set out to the camp to Camillus, and thence by permission of Camillus to Rome to the senate, in order to deliver up Falerii. When introduced before the senate, they are represented as having spoken thus: "Conscript fathers, overcome by you and your commander by a victory at which neither god nor man can feel displeasure, we surrender ourselves to you, considering that we shall live more happily under your rule than under our own law, than which nothing can be more glorious for a conqueror. In the result of this war, two salutary examples have been exhibited to mankind. You preferred faith in war to present victory: we, challenged by your good faith, have voluntarily given up to you the victory. We are under your sovereignty. Send men to receive our arms, our hostages, our city with its gates thrown open. You shall never have to repent of our fidelity, nor we of your dominion." Thanks were returned to Camillus both by the enemy and by his own countrymen. Money was required of the Faliscians to pay off the soldiers for that year, that the Roman people might be relieved from the tribute. Peace being granted, the army was led back to Rome.

When Camillus returned home, signalized by much more solid glory than when white horses had drawn him through the city, having vanquished the enemy by justice and good faith, the senate did not conceal their sense of respect for him, but immediately set about acquitting him of his vow; and Lucius Valerius, Lucius Sergius, Aulus Manlius, being sent in a ship of war as ambassadors to carry the golden bowl to Delphos as an offering to Apollo, were intercepted by the pirates of the Liparenses not far from the Sicilian Strait, and carried to Liparæ. It was the custom of the state to make a division of all booty which was acquired, as it were, by public piracy. On that year it so happened that one Timasitheus filled the office of chief magistrate, a man more like the Romans than his own countrymen. Who, himself reverencing the name of ambassadors, and the offering, and the god to whom it was sent, and the cause of the offering, impressed the multitude also, who almost on all occasions resemble their ruler, with [a sense] of religious justice; and after having brought the ambassadors to a public entertainment, escorted them with the protection of some ships to Delphos, and from thence brought them back in safety to Rome. By a decree of the senate a league of hospitality was formed with him, and presents were conferred on him by the state. During the same year the war with the Æquans was conducted with varying success; so that it was a matter of doubt both among the troops themselves and at Rome, whether they had been victorious or were vanquished. The Roman commanders were Caius Æmilius and Spurius Postumius, two of the military tribunes. At first they acted in conjunction; then, after the enemy were routed in the field, it was agreed that Æmilius should take possession of Verrugo with a certain force, and that Postumius should devastate the country. There, as the latter proceeded rather negligently, and with his troops irregularly drawn up, he was attacked by the Æquans, and an alarm being occasioned, he was driven to the nearest hill; and the panic spread from thence to Verrugo to the other detachment of the army. When Postumius, having withdrawn his men to a place of safety, summoned an assembly and upbraided them with their fright and flight; with having been beaten by a most cowardly and dastardly enemy; the entire army shout aloud that they deserved to hear all this, and admitted the disgrace they had incurred; but [they promised] that they would make amends, and that the enemy's joy should not be of long duration. Demanding that he would instantly lead them from thence to the camp of the enemy, (this lay in the plain within their view,) they submitted to any punishment, if they did not take it before night. Having praised them, he orders them to take refreshment, and to be in readiness at the fourth watch. And the enemy, in order to prevent the flight of the Romans from the hill through the road which led to Verrugo, were posted to meet them; and the battle commenced before daylight, (but the moon was up all the night,) and was not more confused than a battle fought by day. But the shout having reached Verrugo, when they thought that the Roman camp was attacked, occasioned such a panic, that in spite of the entreaties of Æmilius and his efforts to stop them, they fled to Tusculum in great disorder. From thence a report was carried to Rome that "Postumius and his army were cut to pieces." When the dawn of day had removed all apprehension of an ambuscade in case of a hasty pursuit, after riding through the ranks, by demanding [the performance of] their promises he infused such ardour into them, that the Æquans could no longer withstand their impetuosity. Then the slaughter of them in their flight, such as takes place when matters are conducted more under the influence of anger than of courage, was continued even to the total destruction of the enemy, and the melancholy news from Tusculum, the state having been alarmed without cause, was followed by a letter from Postumius decked with laurel, (announcing) that "the victory belonged to the Roman people; that the army of the Æquans was destroyed."

As the proceedings of the plebeian tribunes had not yet attained a termination, both the commons exerted themselves to continue their office for the promoters of the law, and the patricians to re-elect the opponents of the law; but the commons were more successful in the election of their own magistrates. Which annoyance the patricians avenged by passing a decree of the senate that consuls should be elected, magistrates detested by the commons. After an interval of fifteen years, Lucius Lucretius Flavus and Servius Sulpicius Camerinus were appointed consuls. In the beginning of this year, whilst the tribunes of the commons united their efforts to pass the law, because none of their college were likely to oppose them, and the consuls resisted them with no less energy, the Æquans storm Vitellia, a Roman colony in their territory. The chief part of the colonists made their way in safety to Rome, because the town, having been taken by treachery in the night, afforded an unimpeded mode of escape by the remote side of the city. That province fell to the lot of Lucius Lucretius the consul. He having set out with his army, vanquished the enemy in the field; and returned victorious to Rome to a much more serious contest. A day of trial had been appointed for Aulus Virginius and Quintus Pomponius, plebeian tribunes of the two preceding years, in whose defence by the combined power of the patricians, the honour of the senate was involved. For no one laid against them any other impeachment, either of their mode of life or of their conduct in office, save that, to gratify the patricians, they had protested against the tribunitian law. The resentment of the commons, however, prevailed over the influence of the senate; and by a most pernicious precedent these men, though innocent, were condemned [to pay a fine of] ten thousand *asses* in weight. At this the patricians were very much incensed. Camillus openly charged the commons with gross violation of duty, "who, now turning their venom against their own body, did not feel that by their iniquitous sentence on the tribune they abolished the right of protesting; that abolishing this right of protesting, they had upset the tribunitian authority. For they were mistaken in expecting that the patricians would tolerate the unbridled licentiousness of that office. If tribunitian violence could not be repelled by tribunitian aid, that the patricians would find out some other weapon." The consuls he also blamed, because they had in silence suffered those tribunes who had followed the authority of the senate to be deceived by [their reliance] on the public faith. By openly expressing these sentiments, he every day still further exasperated the angry feelings of the people.

But he ceased not to urge the senate to oppose the law; "that when the day for proposing the law had arrived they should go down to the forum with no other feeling than as men who remembered that they had to contend for their altars and homes, and the temples of the gods, and the soil in which they had been born. For that as far as he himself individually was concerned, if during this contest [to be sustained] by his country it were allowable for him to think of his own glory, it would even reflect honour on himself, that a city captured by him should be densely inhabited, that he would daily enjoy the monument of his glory, and that he would have before his eyes a city borne by him in his triumph, that all would tread in the footsteps of his renown. But that he deemed it an impiety that a city deserted and forsaken by the immortal gods should be inhabited; that the Roman people should reside in a captive soil, and that a vanquished should be taken in exchange for a victorious country." Stimulated by these exhortations of their leader, the patricians, both young and old, entered the forum in a body, when the law was about to be proposed: and dispersing themselves through the tribes, each earnestly appealing to the members of their own tribe, began to entreat them with tears "not to desert that country for which they themselves and their fathers had fought most valiantly and successfully," pointing to the Capitol, the temple of Vesta, and the other temples of the gods around; "not to drive the Roman people, exiles and outcasts, from their native soil and household gods into the city of the enemy; and not to bring matters to such a state, that it was better that Veii were not taken, lest Rome should be deserted." Because they proceeded not by violence, but by entreaties, and in the midst of these entreaties frequent mention was [made] of the gods, the greatest part [of the people] were influenced by religious scruples: and more tribes by one rejected the law than voted for it. And so gratifying was this victory to the patricians, that on the following day, on a motion made by the consuls, a decree of the senate was passed, that seven acres a man of Veientian territory should be distributed to the commons; and not only to the fathers of families, but so that all persons in their house in a state of freedom should be considered, and that they might be willing to rear up their children with that prospect.

The commons being won over by such a boon, no opposition was made to holding the elections for consuls. Lucius Valerius Potitus, and Marcus Manlius, who afterwards obtained the surname of Capitolinus, were elected consuls. These consuls celebrated the great games which Marcus Furius, when dictator, had vowed in the Veientian war. In the same year the temple of imperial Juno, vowed by the same dictator and during the same war, is dedicated; and they state that the dedication was attended with great zeal by the matrons. A war scarcely worth mentioning was waged with the Æquans at Algidum, the enemies taking to flight almost before they commenced the fight. To Valerius, because he was more persevering in slaughtering them in their flight, a triumph was granted; it was decreed that Manlius should enter the city with an ovation. The same year a new war broke out with the Volsinians; whither an army could not be led, on account of a famine and pestilence in the Roman territories, which arose from drought and excessive heat; on account of which the Volsinians forming a junction with the Salpinians, being elated with pride, made an unprovoked incursion into the Roman territories. War was then proclaimed against the two states. Caius Julius died during his censorship; Marcus Cornelius was substituted in his room; a proceeding which was afterwards considered as offensive to religion; because during that lustrum Rome was taken. Nor since that time has a censor ever been substituted in the room of one deceased. And the consuls being seized by the distemper, it was determined that the auspices should be taken anew during an interregnum.

Therefore when in pursuance of a decree of the senate the consuls resigned their office, Marcus Furius Camillus is created interrex, who appointed Publius Cornelius Scipio interrex, and he afterwards Lucius Valerius Potitus. By him were appointed six military tribunes with consular power; so that, though any one of them should be incommoded by bad health, the state might have a sufficient number of magistrates. On the calends of July, the following entered on their office, Lucius Lucretius, Servius Sulpicius, Marcus Æmilius, Lucius Furius Medullinus a seventh time, Agrippa Furius, Caius Æmilius a second time. Of these, Lucius Lucretius and Caius Æmilius got the Volsinians as their province; the Salpinians fell to the lot of Agrippa Furius and Servius Sulpicius. The first engagement was with the Volsinians. The war, important from the number of the enemy, was without difficulty brought to a close. At the first onset, their army was put to flight. Eight thousand soldiers, hemmed in by the cavalry, laid down their arms and surrendered. The account received of that war had the effect of preventing the Salpinians from hazarding an engagement; the troops secured themselves within their towns. The Romans drove spoil in every direction, both from the Salpinian and Volsinian territory, there being no one to repel that aggression; until a truce for twenty years was granted to the Volsinians, exhausted by the war, on this condition, that they should make restitution to the Roman people, and furnish the pay of the army for that year. During the same year, Marcus Cædicius, a plebeian, announced to the tribunes that in the New Street, where the chapel now stands, above the temple of Vesta, he had heard in the silence of the night a voice louder than that of a human being, which ordered the magistrates to be told, that the Gauls were approaching. This, as is usual, was disregarded, on account of the humble station of the author, and also because the nation was a remote one, and therefore the less known. And not only were the warnings of the gods disregarded, fate now impending; but further, the only human aid which was left them, Marcus Furius, they drove away from the city; who, on a day [of trial] being appointed for him by Lucius Appuleius, a tribune of the people, in reference to the Veientian spoil, he having also lost his son, a young man, about the same time, when he summoned to his house the members of his tribe and his dependents, (they constituted a considerable portion of the commons,) and having sounded their sentiments, he received for answer, "that they would contribute whatever fine he should be condemned to pay; that to acquit him they were unable,"[168] retired into exile; after praying to the immortal gods, "that if that outrage was done to him without his deserving it, they would at the earliest opportunity give cause to his ungrateful country to regret his absence." In his absence he was fined fifteen thousand *asses* in weight.

That citizen being driven away, who being present, Rome could not be captured, if any thing is certain regarding human affairs; the destined ruin now approaching the city, ambassadors came from the Clusinians, soliciting aid against the Gauls. A report is current that that nation, allured by the delightfulness of the crops, and more especially of the wine, an enjoyment then new to them, crossed the Alps, and took possession of the lands formerly cultivated by the Etrurians; and that Aruns, a native of Clusium, introduced wine into Gaul for the purpose of enticing the nation, through resentment for his wife's having been debauched by Lucumo, whose guardian he himself had been, a very influential young man, and on whom vengeance could not be taken, unless foreign aid were resorted to; that this person served as a guide to them when crossing the Alps, and advised them to lay siege to Clusium. I would not indeed deny that the Gauls were brought to Clusium by Aruns or any other native of Clusium; but that those persons who laid siege to Clusium were not they who first crossed the Alps, is sufficiently certain. For two hundred years before they laid siege to Clusium and captured the city of Rome, the Gauls passed over into Italy. Nor were these the first of the Etrurians with whom the Gauls fought, but long before that they frequently fought with those who dwelt between the Apennines and the Alps. Before the Roman empire the sway of the Tuscans was much extended by land and by sea; how very powerful they were in the upper and lower seas, by which Italy is encompassed like an island, the names [of these seas] is a proof;

---

[168] Niebuhr and Arnold understand these words to signify, that these persons had already made up their minds not to acquit him, or assist him by voting in favour of him—in fact, that they could not conscientiously do so. It may, however, signify simply, that the people were so incensed against him, that there existed not a rational prospect of acquittal for him.

the one of which the Italian nations have called the Tuscan sea, the general appellation of the people; the other the Hadriatic, from Hadria, a colony of Tuscans. The Greeks call these same seas the Tyrrhenian and Hadriatic. This people inhabited the country extending to both seas in twelve cities, colonies equal in number to the mother cities having been sent, first on this side the Apennines towards the lower sea, afterwards to the other side of the Apennines; who obtained possession of all the district beyond the Po, even as far as the Alps, except the corner of the Venetians, who dwell round the extreme point of the [Hadriatic] sea. The Alpine nations also have this origin, more especially the Rhætians; whom their very situation has rendered savage, so as to retain nothing of their original, except the accent of their language, and not even that without corruption.

Concerning the passage of the Gauls into Italy we have heard as follows. In the reign of Tarquinius Priscus at Rome, the supreme government of the Celts, who compose the third part of Gaul, was in the hands of the Biturigians: they gave a king to the Celtic nation. This was Ambigatus, one very much distinguished by his merit, and both his great prosperity in his own concerns and in those of the public; for under his administration Gaul was so fruitful and so well peopled, that so very great a population appeared scarcely capable of being restrained by any government. He being now advanced in years, and anxious to relieve his kingdom of so oppressive a crowd, declares his intention to send his sister's sons, Bellovesus and Sigovesus, two enterprising youths, into whatever settlements the gods should grant them by augury: that they should take out with them as great a number of men as they pleased, so that no nation might be able to obstruct them in their progress. Then to Sigovesus the Hercynian forest was assigned by the oracle: to Bellovesus the gods marked out a much more cheering route into Italy. He carried out with him from the Biturigians, the Arvernians, the Senonians, the Æduans, the Ambarrians, the Carnutians, and the Aulercians, all that was superfluous in their population. Having set out with an immense force of horse and foot, he arrived in the country of the Tricastinians. Next the Alps were opposed [to their progress], and I am not surprised that they should seem impassable, as they had never been climbed over through any path as yet, as far at least as tradition can extend, unless we are disposed to believe the stories regarding Hercules. When the height of the mountains kept the Gauls there penned up as it were, and they were looking around [to discover] by what path they might pass into another world between the summits, which joined the sky, a religious scruple detained them, it having been announced to them that strangers in search of lands were attacked by the nation of the Salyans. These were the Massilians, who had come by sea from Phocæa. The Gauls considering this an omen of their own fortune, assisted them in fortifying the ground which they had taken possession of on their first landing, covered with spacious woods. They themselves crossed the Alps through the Taurinian and pathless forests; and having defeated the Etrurians not far from the Ticinus, on hearing that the land in which they had posted themselves was called Insubria, the same name as the Insubres, a canton of the Ædui: embracing the omen of the place, they built a city there, and called it Mediolanum.

Some time after another body, consisting of Cenomanians, having followed the tracks of the former under the conduct of Elitovius, crossed the Alps through the same forest, with the aid of Bellovesus, and settle themselves where the cities of Brixia and Verona now stand (the Libuans then possessed these places). After these came the Salluvians, who fix themselves near the ancient canton of the Ligurians called Lævi, inhabiting the banks of the Ticinus. Next the Boians and Lingonians, having made their way over through the Penine pass, all the tract between the Po and the Alps being occupied, crossed the Po on rafts, and drove out of the country not only the Etrurians, but the Umbrians also: they confined themselves however within the Apennines. Then the Senonians, the latest of these emigrants, took possession of the track [extending] from the Utens to the Æsis. I find that it was this nation that came to Clusium, and thence to Rome; whether alone, or aided by all the nations of the Cisalpine Gauls, is not duly ascertained. The Clusians, terrified at their strange enemy, on beholding their great numbers, the forms of the men such as they had never seen, and the kind of arms [they carried], and on hearing that the troops of the Etrurians had been frequently defeated by them on both sides of the Po, sent ambassadors to Rome to solicit aid from the senate, though they had no claim on the Roman people, in respect either of alliance or friendship, except that they had not defended their relations the Veientians against the Roman people. No aid was obtained: three ambassadors were sent, sons of Marcus Fabius Ambustus, to treat with the Gauls in the name of the senate and Roman people; that they should not attack the allies and friends of the Roman people from whom they had received no wrong. That they should be supported by the Romans even by force of arms, if circumstances obliged them; but it seemed better that war itself should be kept aloof, if possible; and that the Gauls, a nation strangers to them, should be known by peace, rather than by arms.

The embassy was a mild one, had it not been consigned to ambassadors too hot in temper, and who resembled Gauls more than Romans. To whom, after they delivered their commission in the assembly of the Gauls, the following answer is returned: Though the name of the Romans was new to their ears, yet they believed them to be brave men, whose aid was implored by the Clusians in their perilous conjuncture. And since they chose to defend their allies against them by negociation rather than by arms, that they on their part would not reject the pacific terms which they propose, if the Clusians would give up to the Gauls in want of land, a portion of their territories which they possessed to a greater extent than they could cultivate; otherwise peace could not be obtained: that they wished to receive an answer in presence of the Romans; and if the land were refused them, that they would decide the matter with the sword in presence of the same Romans; that they might have an opportunity of carrying home an account how much the Gauls excelled all other mortals in bravery. On the Romans asking what right they had to demand land from the possessors, or to threaten war [in case of refusal], and what business the Gauls had in Etruria, and on their fiercely replying, that they carried their right in their swords, that all things were the property of the brave, with minds inflamed on both sides they severally have recourse to arms, and the battle is commenced. Here, fate now pressing hard on the Roman city, the ambassadors, contrary to the law of nations, take up arms; nor could this be done in secret, as three of the noblest and bravest of the Roman youth fought in the van of the Etrurians; so conspicuous was the valour of the foreigners. Moreover Quintus Fabius, riding out beyond the line, slew a general of the Gauls who was furiously charging the very standards of the Etrurians, having run him through the side with his spear: and the Gauls recognised him when stripping him of his spoils; and a signal was given throughout the entire line that he was a Roman ambassador. Giving up therefore their resentment against the Clusians, they sound a retreat, threatening the Romans. Some gave it as their opinion that they should proceed forthwith to Rome. The seniors prevailed, that ambassadors should be sent to complain of the injuries done them, and to demand that the Fabii should be given up to them in satisfaction for having violated the law of nations. When the ambassadors had stated matters, according to the instructions given to them, the conduct of the Fabii was neither approved by the senate, and the barbarians seemed to them to demand what was just: but in the case of men of such station party favour prevented them from decreeing that which they felt to be right. Wherefore lest the blame of any misfortune, which might happen to be received in a war with the Gauls, should lie with them, they refer the consideration of the demands of the Gauls to the people, where influence and wealth were so predominant, that those persons, whose punishment was under consideration, were elected military tribunes with consular power for the ensuing year. At which proceeding the Gauls being enraged, as was very natural, openly menacing war, return to their own party. With the three Fabii the military tribunes elected were Quintus Sulpicius Longus, Quintus Servilius a fourth time, Servius Cornelius Maluginensis.

Though danger of such magnitude was impending (so completely does Fortune blind the minds of men when she wishes not her threatening stroke to be foiled) a state, which against the Fidenatian and Veientian enemies, and other neighbouring states, had recourse to aid even from the most extreme quarters, and had appointed a dictator on many trying occasions, that same state now, when an enemy, never before seen or heard of, from the ocean and remotest regions of the earth, was advancing in arms against them, looked not for any extraordinary command or aid. Tribunes, by whose temerity the war had been brought on them, were appointed to the chief direction of affairs, and even making less of the war than fame had represented it, held the levy with no greater diligence than used to be exercised for ordinary wars. In the mean while the Gauls, on hearing that honour was even conferred on the violators of human law, and that their embassy was slighted, inflamed with resentment, over which that nation has no control, immediately snatched up their standards, and enter on their march with the utmost expedition. When the cities, alarmed at the tumult occasioned by them as they passed precipitately along, began to run to arms, and the peasants took to flight, they indicated by a loud shout that they were proceeding to Rome, taking up an immense space of ground, wherever they passed, with their horses and men, their troops spreading widely in every direction. But fame and the messengers of the Clusians, and then of the other states one after another, preceding them, the rapid advance of the enemy brought the greatest consternation to Rome; for, with their tumultuary troops hastily led on, they met them within the distance of the eleventh mile-stone, where the river Allia, descending from the Crustuminian mountains in a very deep channel, joins the river Tiber not far below the road. Already all places in front and on each side were crowded with the enemy, and this nation, which has a natural turn for causeless confusion, by their harsh music and discordant clamours, filled all places with a horrible din.

There the military tribunes, without having previously selected a place for their camp, without having previously raised a rampart to which they might have a retreat, unmindful of their duty to the gods, to say nothing of that to man, without taking auspices or offering sacrifices, draw up their line, which was extended towards the flanks, lest they should be surrounded by the great numbers of the enemy. Still their front could not be made equal to that of the enemy, though by thinning their line they rendered their centre weak and scarcely connected. There was on the right a small eminence, which it was determined to fill with bodies of reserve; and that circumstance, as it was the first cause of their dismay and flight, so it proved their only means of safety in their flight. For Brennus, the chieftain of the Gauls, being chiefly apprehensive of some design[169] being intended in the small number of the enemy, thinking that the high ground had been seized for this purpose, that, when the Gauls had been engaged in front with the line of the legions, the reserve was to make an attack on their rear and flank, directed his troops against the reserve; certain, that if he had dislodged them from their ground, the victory would be easy in the plain for a force which had so much the advantage in point of numbers: thus not only fortune, but judgment also stood on the side of the barbarians. In the opposite army there appeared nothing like Romans, either in the commanders, or in the soldiers. Terror and dismay had taken possession of their minds, and such a forgetfulness of every thing, that a far greater number of them fled to Veii, a city of their enemy, though the Tiber stood in their way, than by the direct road to Rome, to their wives and children. Their situation defended the reserve for some time; throughout the remainder of the line as soon as the shout was heard, by those who stood nearest on their flank, and by those at a distance on their rear, almost before they could look at the enemy as yet untried, not only without attempting to fight, but without even returning the shout, fresh and unhurt they took to flight. Nor was there any slaughter of them in the act of fighting; but their rear was cut to pieces, whilst they obstructed their flight by their struggling one with another. Great slaughter was made on the bank of the Tiber, whither the entire left wing, having thrown down their arms, directed their flight; and many who did not know how to swim, or were exhausted, being weighed down by their coats of mail and other defensive armour, were swallowed up in the current. The greatest part however escaped safe to Veii; whence not only no reinforcement, but not even an account of their defeat, was forwarded to Rome. Those on the right wing which had been posted at a distance from the river, and rather near the foot of the mountain, all made for Rome, and, without even shutting the gates, fled into the citadel.

The miraculous attainment of so sudden a victory held even the Gauls in a state of stupefaction. And at first they stood motionless with panic, as if not knowing what had happened; then they apprehended a stratagem; at length they began to collect the spoils of the slain, and to pile up the arms in heaps, as is their custom. Then, at length, when no appearance of any thing hostile was any where observed, having proceeded on their journey, they reach the city of Rome not long before sun-set: where when some horsemen, who had advanced before, brought back word that the gates were not shut, that no guard was posted before the gates, no armed troops on the walls, another cause of

---

[169] In my translation of this passage I have differed from Baker, who thus renders: "thinking, that as his enemies were few in number, their skill was what he had chiefly to guard against." Dureau De Lamalle thus translates: "supposant de la ruse aux ennemis, a raison de leur petit nombre." This is obviously the correct version.

amazement similar to the former made them halt; and dreading the night and ignorance of the situation of the city, they posted themselves between Rome and the Anio, after sending scouts about the walls and the several gates to ascertain what plans the enemy would adopt in their desperate circumstances. With respect to the Romans, as the greater part had gone to Veii from the field of battle, and no one supposed that any survived except those who had fled back to Rome, being all lamented as lost, both those living and those dead, they caused the entire city to be filled with wailings. The alarm for the public interest stifled private sorrow, as soon as it was announced that the enemy were at hand. Presently the barbarians patrolling around the walls in troops, they heard their yells and the dissonant clangour of their arms. All the interval up to the next day kept their minds in such a state of suspense, that an assault seemed every moment about to be made on the city: on their first approach, when they arrived at the city, [it was expected;] for if this were not their design, that they would have remained at the Allia; then towards sunset, because there was not much of the day remaining, they imagined that they would attack them before night; then that the design was deferred until night, in order to strike the greater terror. At length the approach of light struck them with dismay; and the calamity itself followed closely upon their continued apprehension of it, when the troops entered the gates in hostile array. During that night, however, and the following day, the state by no means bore any resemblance to that which which had fled in so dastardly a manner at the Allia. For as there was not a hope that the city could be defended, so small a number of troops now remaining, it was determined that the youth fit for military service, and the abler part of the senate with their wives and children, should retire into the citadel and Capitol; and having collected stores of arms and corn, and thence from a fortified post, that they should defend the deities, and the inhabitants, and the Roman name: that the flamen [Quirinalis] and the vestal priestesses should carry away far from slaughter and conflagration the objects appertaining to the religion of the state: and that their worship should not be intermitted, until there remained no one who should continue it. If the citadel and Capitol, the mansion of the gods, if the senate, the source of public counsel, if the youth of military age, should survive the impending ruin of the city, the loss would be light of the aged, the crowd left behind in the city, and who were sure to perish[170] under any circumstances. And in order that the plebeian portion of the multitude might bear the thing with greater resignation, the aged men, who had enjoyed triumphs and consulships, openly declared that they would die along with them, and

---

[170] The aged were doomed to perish under any circumstances, (*utique,*) from scarcity of provisions, whether they retired into the Capitol with the military youth, or were left behind in the city.

that they would not burden the scanty stores of the armed men with those bodies, with which they were now unable to bear arms, or to defend their country. Such was the consolation addressed to each other by the aged now destined to death.

Their exhortations were then turned to the band of young men, whom they escorted to the Capitol and citadel, commending to their valour and youth whatever might be the remaining fortune of a city, which for three hundred and sixty years had been victorious in all its wars. When those who carried with them all their hope and resources, parted with the others, who had determined not to survive the ruin of their captured city; both the circumstance itself and the appearance [it exhibited] was really distressing, and also the weeping of the women, and their undecided running together, following now these, now those, and asking their husbands and children what was to become of them, [all together] left nothing that could be added to human misery. A great many of them, however, escorted their friends into the citadel, no one either preventing or inviting them; because the measure which was advantageous to the besieged, that of reducing the number of useless persons, was but little in accordance with humanity. The rest of the crowd, chiefly plebeians, whom so small a hill could not contain, nor could they be supported amid such a scarcity of corn, pouring out of the city as if in one continued train, repaired to the Janiculum. From thence some were dispersed through the country, some made for the neighbouring cities, without any leader or concert, following each his own hopes, his own plans, those of the public being given up as lost. In the mean time the Flamen Quirinalis and the vestal virgins, laying aside all concern for their own affairs, consulting which of the sacred deposits should be carried with them, which should be left behind, for they had not strength to carry them all, or what place would best preserve them in safe custody, consider it best to put them into casks and to bury them in the chapel adjoining to the residence of the Flamen Quirinalis, where now it is profane to spit out. The rest they carry away with them, after dividing the burden among themselves, by the road which leads by the Sublician bridge to the Janiculum. When Lucius Albinius, a Roman plebeian, who was conveying his wife and children in a waggon, beheld them on that ascent among the rest of the crowd which was leaving the city as unfit to carry arms; even then the distinction of things divine and human being preserved, considering it an outrage on religion, that the public priests and sacred utensils of the Roman people should go on foot and be carried, that he and his family should be seen in a carriage, he commanded his wife and children to alight, placed the virgins and sacred utensils in the vehicle, and carried them on to Cære, whither the priests had intended to go.

Meanwhile at Rome all arrangements being now made, as far as was possible in such an emergency, for the defence of the citadel, the

crowd of aged persons having returned to their houses, awaited the
enemy's coming with minds firmly prepared for death. Such of them as
had borne curule offices, in order that they may die in the insignia of
their former station, honours, and merit, arraying themselves in the
most magnificent garments worn by those drawing the chariots of the
gods in procession, or by persons riding in triumph, seated themselves
in their ivory chairs, in the middle of their halls. Some say that they
devoted themselves for their country and the citizens of Rome, Marcus
Fabius, the chief pontiff, dictating the form of words. The Gauls, both
because by the intervention of the night they had abated all angry
feelings arising from the irritation of battle, and because they had on no
occasion fought a well-disputed fight, and were then not taking the city
by storm or violence, entering the city the next day, free from
resentment or heat of passion, through the Colline gate which lay open,
advance into the forum, casting their eyes around on the temples of the
gods, and on the citadel, which alone exhibited any appearance of war.
From thence, after leaving a small guard, lest any attack should be
made on them whilst scattered, from the citadel or Capitol, they
dispersed in quest of plunder; the streets being entirely desolate, rush
some of them in a body into the houses that were nearest; some repair
to those which were most distant, considering these to be untouched
and abounding with spoil. Afterwards being terrified by the very
solitude, lest any stratagem of the enemy should surprise them whilst
being dispersed, they returned in bodies into the forum and the parts
adjoining to the forum, where the houses of the commons being shut,
and the halls of the leading men lying open, almost greater
backwardness was felt to attack the open than the shut houses; so
completely did they behold with a sort of veneration men sitting in the
porches of the palaces, who besides their ornaments and apparel more
august than human, bore a striking resemblance to gods, in the majesty
which their looks and the gravity of their countenance displayed.
Whilst they stood gazing on these as on statues, it is said that Marcus
Papirius, one of them, roused the anger of a Gaul by striking him on the
head with his ivory, while he was stroking his beard, which was then
universally worn long; and that the commencement of the bloodshed
began with him, that the rest were slain in their seats. After the
slaughter of the nobles, no person whatever was spared; the houses
were plundered, and when emptied were set on fire.

But whether it was that all were not possessed with a desire of
destroying the city, or it had been so determined by the leading men of
the Gauls, both that some fires should be presented to their view, [to
see] if the besieged could be forced into a surrender through affection
for their dwellings, and that all the houses should not be burned down,
so that whatever portion should remain of the city, they might hold as a
pledge to work upon the minds of the enemy; the fire by no means

spread either indiscriminately or extensively on the first day, as is usual in a captured city. The Romans beholding from the citadel the city filled with the enemy, and their running to and fro through all the streets, some new calamity presenting itself in every different quarter, were neither able to preserve their presence of mind, nor even to have perfect command of their ears and eyes. To whatever direction the shouts of the enemy, the cries of women and children, the crackling of the flames, and the crash of falling houses, had called their attention, thither, terrified at every incident, they turned their thoughts, faces, and eyes, as if placed by fortune to be spectators of their falling country, and as if left as protectors of no other of their effects, except their own persons: so much more to be commiserated than any others who were ever besieged, because, shut out from their country, they were besieged, beholding all their effects in the power of the enemy. Nor was the night, which succeeded so shockingly spent a day, more tranquil; daylight then followed a restless night; nor was there any time which failed to produce the sight of some new disaster. Loaded and overwhelmed by so many evils, they did not at all abate their determination, [resolved,] though they should see every thing in flames and levelled to the dust, to defend by their bravery the hill which they occupied, small and ill provided as it was, being left [as a refuge] for liberty. And now, as the same events recurred every day, as if habituated to misfortunes, they abstracted their thoughts from all feeling of their circumstances, regarding their arms only, and the swords in their right hands, as the sole remnants of their hopes.

The Gauls also, after having for several days waged an ineffectual war against the buildings of the city, when they saw that among the fires and ruins of the captured city nothing now remained except armed enemies, neither terrified by so many disasters, nor likely to turn their thoughts to a surrender, unless force were employed, determine to have recourse to extremities, and to make an attack on the citadel. A signal being given at break of day, their entire multitude is marshalled in the forum; thence, after raising the shout and forming a testudo, they advance to the attack. Against whom the Romans, acting neither rashly nor precipitately, having strengthened the guards at every approach, and opposing the main strength of their men in that quarter where they saw the battalions advancing, suffer the enemy to ascend, judging that the higher they ascended, the more easily would they be driven back down the steep. About the middle of the ascent they met them: and making a charge thence from the higher ground, which of itself bore them against the enemy, they routed the Gauls with slaughter and destruction, so that never after, either in parties or with their whole force, did they try that kind of fighting. Laying aside all hope of succeeding by force of arms, they prepare for a blockade; of which having had no idea up to that time, they had, whilst burning the city, destroyed whatever corn had been therein, and during those very days all the provisions had been carried off from the land to Veii. Accordingly, dividing their army, they resolved that one part should plunder through the neighbouring states, that the other part should carry on the siege of the citadel, so that the ravagers of the country might supply the besiegers with corn.

The Gauls, who marched from the city, were led by fortune herself, to make trial of Roman valour, to Ardea, where Camillus was in exile: who, more distressed by the fortune of the public than his own, whilst he now pined away arraigning gods and men, fired with indignation, and wondering where were now those men who with him had taken Veii and Falerii, who had conducted other wars rather by their own valour than by the favour of fortune, hears on a sudden that the army of the Gauls was approaching, and that the people of Ardea in consternation were met in council on the subject. And as if moved by divine inspiration, after he advanced into the midst of the assembly, having hitherto been accustomed to absent himself from such meetings, he says, "People of Ardea, my friends of old, of late my fellow-citizens also, since your kindness so ordered it, and my good fortune achieved it, let no one of you suppose that I have come forward here forgetful of my condition; but the [present] case and the common danger obliges every one to contribute to the common good whatever service he can in our present alarming situation. And when shall I repay you for your so very important services to me, if I now be remiss? or where will you derive benefit from me, if not in war? By this accomplishment I maintained my rank in my native country: and, unconquered in war, I was banished during peace by my ungrateful fellow-citizens. To you, men of Ardea, a favourable opportunity has been presented of making a return for all the former favours conferred by the Roman people, such as you yourselves remember, (for which reason, as being mindful of them, you are not to be upbraided with them,) and of obtaining great military renown for this your city over the common enemy. The nation, which now approaches in disorderly march, is one to which nature has given great spirits and bodies rather huge than firm. Let the disaster of Rome serve as a proof. They captured the city when lying open to them; a small handful of men from the citadel and Capitol withstand them. Already tired out by the slow process of a siege, they retire and spread themselves through the country. Gorged with food and wine hastily swallowed, when night comes on they stretch themselves indiscriminately, like brutes, near streams of water, without entrenchment, without guards or advanced posts; more incautious even now than usual in consequence of success. If you then are disposed to defend your own walls, and not to suffer all these places to become Gaul, take up arms in a full body at the first watch: follow me to slaughter, not to battle. If I do not deliver them up to you fettered by sleep, to be butchered like cattle, I decline not the same issue of my affairs at Ardea as I had at Rome."

Both friends and enemies were satisfied that there existed no where at that time a man of equal military talent. The assembly being dismissed, they refresh themselves, carefully watching the moment the signal should be given; which being given, during the silence of the beginning of the night they attended Camillus at the gates. Having gone forth to no great distance from the city, they found the camp of the Gauls, as had been foretold, unprotected and neglected on every side, and attack it with a shout. No fight any where, but slaughter every where; their bodies, naked and relaxed with sleep, are cut to pieces. Those most remote, however, being roused from their beds, not knowing what the tumult was, or whence it came, were directed to flight, and some of them, without perceiving it, into the midst of the enemy. A great number flying into the territory of Antium, an attack being made on them in their straggling march by the townspeople, were surrounded and cut off. A like carnage was made of the Tuscans in the Veientian territory; who were so far from compassionating the city which had now been its neighbour for nearly four hundred years, overpowered as it now was by a strange and unheard-of enemy, that at that very time they made incursions on the Roman territory; and laden with plunder, had it in contemplation to lay siege to Veii, the bulwark and last hope of the Roman race. The Roman soldiers had seen them straggling over the country, and collected in a body, driving the spoil before them, and they perceived their camp pitched at no great distance from Veii. Upon this, first self-commiseration, then indignation, and after that resentment, took possession of their minds: "Were their calamities to be a subject of mockery to the Etrurians, from whom they had turned off the Gallic war on themselves?" Scarce could they curb their passions, so as to refrain from attacking them at the moment; and being restrained by Quintus Cædicius, the centurion, whom they had appointed their commander, they deferred the matter until night. A leader equal to Camillus was all that was wanted; in other respects matters were conducted in the same order and with the same fortunate result. And further, under the guidance of some prisoners, who had survived the nightly slaughter, they set out to Salinæ against another body of Tuscans, they suddenly made on the following night still greater havoc, and returned to Veii exulting in their double victory.

Meanwhile, at Rome, the siege, in general, was slow, and there was quiet on both sides, the Gauls being intent only on this, that none of the enemy should escape from between their posts; when, on a sudden, a Roman youth drew on himself the admiration both of his countrymen and the enemy. There was a sacrifice solemnized at stated times by the Fabian family on the Quirinal hill. To perform this Caius Fabius Dorso having descended from the Capitol, in the Gabine cincture, carrying in his hands the sacred utensils, passed out through the midst of the enemy's post, without being at all moved by the calls or threats of any of them, and reached the Quirinal hill; and after duly performing there the solemn rites, coming back by the same way with the same firm countenance and gait, confident that the gods were propitious, whose worship he had not even neglected when prohibited by the fear of death, he returned to the Capitol to his friends, the Gauls being either astounded at such an extraordinary manifestation of boldness, or moved even by religious considerations, of which the nation is by no means regardless. In the mean time, not only the courage, but the strength of those at Veii increased daily, not only those Romans repairing thither from the country who had strayed away after the unsuccessful battle, or the disaster of the city being taken, but volunteers also flowing in from Latium, to come in for share of the spoil. It now seemed high time that their country should be recovered and rescued from the hands of the enemy. But a head was wanting to this strong body. The very spot put them in mind of Camillus, and a considerable part consisted of soldiers who had fought successfully under his guidance and auspices: and Cædicius declared that he would not give occasion that any one, whether god or man, should terminate his command rather than that, mindful of his own rank, he would himself call (for the appointment of) a general. With universal consent it was resolved that Camillus should be sent for from Ardea, but not until the senate at Rome were first consulted: so far did a sense of propriety regulate every proceeding, and so carefully did they observe the distinctions of things in their almost desperate circumstances. They had to pass at great risk through the enemy's guards. For this purpose a spirited youth, Pontius Cominius, offered his services, and supporting himself on cork was carried down the Tiber to the city. From thence, where the distance from the bank was shortest, he makes his way into the Capitol over a portion of the rock that was craggy, and therefore neglected by the enemy's guard: and being conducted to the magistrates, he delivers the instructions received from the army. Then having received a decree of the senate, both that Camillus should be recalled from exile at the comitia curiata, and be forthwith appointed dictator by order of the people, and that the soldiers should have the general whom they wished, he passed out the same way and proceeded with his despatches to Veii; and deputies being sent to Camillus to Ardea, conducted him to Veii: or else the law was passed by the curiæ, and he was nominated dictator in his absence; for I am more inclined to believe that he did not set out from Ardea until he found that the law was passed; because he could neither change his residence without an order of the people, nor hold the privilege of the auspices in the army until he was nominated dictator.

Whilst these things were going on at Veii, in the mean while the citadel and Capitol of Rome were in great danger. For the Gauls either having perceived the track of a human foot where the messenger from Veii had passed, or having of themselves remarked the easy ascent by the rock at the temple of Carmentis, on a moonlight night, after they had at first sent forward an unarmed person, to make trial of the way, delivering their arms, whenever any difficulty occurred, alternately supported and supporting each other, and drawing each other up, according as the ground required, they reached the summit in such silence, that they not only escaped the notice of the sentinels, but of the dogs also, an animal extremely wakeful with respect to noises by night. The notice of the geese they did not escape, which, as being sacred to Juno, were spared though they were in the greatest scarcity of food. Which circumstance was the cause of their preservation. For Marcus Manlius, who three years before had been consul, a man distinguished in war, being aroused from sleep by their cackling and the clapping of their wings, snatched up his arms, and at the same time calling the others to do the same, proceeds to the spot; and whilst the others are thrown into confusion, he struck with the boss of his shield and tumbles down a Gaul, who had already got footing on the summit; and when the fall of this man as he tumbled threw down those who were next him, he slew others, who in their consternation had thrown away their arms, and caught hold of the rocks to which they clung. And now the others also having assembled beat down the enemy by javelins and stones, and the entire band, having lost their footing, were hurled down the precipice in promiscuous ruin. The alarm then subsiding, the remainder of the night was given up to repose, (as far as could be done considering the disturbed state of their minds,) when the danger, even though past, still kept them in a state of anxiety. Day having appeared, the soldiers were summoned by sound of trumpet to attend the tribunes in assembly, when recompence was to be made both to merit and to demerit; Manlius was first of all commended for his bravery and presented with gifts, not only by the military tribunes, but with the consent of the soldiers, for they all carried to his house, which was in the citadel, a contribution of half a pound of corn and half a pint of wine: a matter trifling in the relation, but the [prevailing] scarcity had rendered it a strong proof of esteem, when each man, depriving himself of his own food, contributed in honour of one man a portion subtracted from his body and from his necessary requirements. Then the guards of that place where the enemy had climbed up unobserved, were summoned; and when Quintus Sulpicius declared openly that he would punish all according to the usage of military discipline, being deterred by the consentient shout of the soldiers who threw the blame on one sentinel, he spared the rest. The man, who was manifestly guilty of the crime, he threw down from the rock, with the approbation of all. From this time forth the guards on both sides became more vigilant; on the part of the Gauls, because a rumour spread that messengers passed between Veii and Rome, and on that of the Romans, from the recollection of the danger which occurred during the night.

But beyond all the evils of siege and war, famine distressed both armies; pestilence, moreover, [oppressed] the Gauls, both as being encamped in a place lying between hills, as well as heated by the burning of the houses, and full of exhalations, and sending up not only ashes but embers also, whenever the wind rose to any degree; and as the nation, accustomed to moisture and cold, is most intolerant of these annoyances, and, suffering severely from the heat and suffocation, they were dying, the diseases spreading as among cattle, now becoming weary of burying separately, they heaped up the bodies promiscuously and burned them; and rendered the place remarkable by the name of Gallic piles. A truce was now made with the Romans, and conferences were held with the permission of the commanders; in which when the Gauls frequently alluded to the famine, and referred to the urgency of that as a further motive for their surrendering, for the purpose of removing that opinion, bread is said to have been thrown in many places from the Capitol, into the advanced posts of the enemy. But the famine could neither be dissembled nor endured any longer. Accordingly, whilst the dictator is engaged in person in holding a levy, in ordering his master of the horse, Lucius Valerius, to bring up the troops from Veii, in making preparations and arrangements, so that he may attack the enemy on equal terms, in the mean time the army of the Capitol, wearied out with keeping guard and with watches, having surmounted all human sufferings, whilst nature would not suffer famine alone to be overcome, looking forward from day to day, to see whether any succour would come from the dictator, at length not only food but hope also failing, and their arms weighing down their debilitated bodies, whilst the guards were being relieved, insisted that there should be either a surrender, or that they should be bought off, on whatever terms were possible, the Gauls intimating in rather plain terms, that they could be induced for no very great compensation to relinquish the siege. Then the senate was held and instructions were given to the military tribunes to capitulate. Upon this the matter was settled between Quintus Sulpicius, a military tribune, and Brennus, the chieftain of the Gauls, and one thousand pounds' weight of gold was agreed on as the ransom of a people, who were soon after to be the rulers of the world. To a transaction very humiliating in itself, insult was added. False weights were brought by the Gauls, and on the tribune objecting, his sword was thrown in in addition to the weight by the insolent Gaul, and an expression was heard intolerable to the Romans, "Woe to the vanquished!"

But both gods and men interfered to prevent the Romans from living on the condition of being ransomed; for by some chance, before the execrable price was completed, all the gold being not yet weighed in consequence of the altercation, the dictator comes up, and orders the gold to be removed, and the Gauls to clear away. When they, holding out against him, affirmed that they had concluded a bargain, he denied that the agreement was a valid one, which had been entered into with a magistrate of inferior authority without his orders, after he had been nominated dictator; and he gives notice to the Gauls to get ready for battle. He orders his men to throw their baggage in a heap, and to get ready their arms, and to recover their country with steel, not with gold, having before their eyes the temples of the gods, and their wives and children, and the soil of their country disfigured by the calamities of war, and all those objects which they were solemnly bound to defend, to recover, and to revenge. He then draws up his army, as the nature of the place admitted, on the site of the half-demolished city, and which was uneven by nature, and he secured all those advantages for his own men, which could be prepared or selected by military skill. The Gauls, thrown into confusion by the unexpected event, take up arms, and with rage, rather than good judgment, rushed upon the Romans. Fortune had now changed; now the aid of the gods and human prudence assisted the Roman cause. At the first encounter, therefore, the Gauls were routed with no greater difficulty than they had found in gaining the victory at Allia. They were afterwards beaten under the conduct and auspices of the same Camillus, in a more regular engagement, at the eighth stone on the Gabine road, whither they had betaken themselves after their defeat. There the slaughter was universal: their camp was taken, and not even one person was left to carry news of the defeat. The dictator, after having recovered his country from the enemy, returns into the city in triumph; and among the rough military jests which they throw out [on such occasions] he is styled, with praises by no means undeserved, Romulus, and parent of his country, and a second founder of the city. His country, thus preserved by arms, he unquestionably saved a second time in peace, when he hindered the people from removing to Veii, both the tribunes pressing the matter with greater earnestness after the burning of the city, and the commons of themselves being more inclined to that measure; and that was the cause of his not resigning his dictatorship after the triumph, the senate entreating him not to leave the commonwealth in so unsettled a state.

First of all, he proposed matters appertaining to the immortal gods; for he was a most scrupulous observer of religious duties; and he procures a decree of the senate, "that all the temples, as the enemy had possessed them, should be restored, their bounds traced, and expiations made for them, and that the form of expiation should be sought in the books by the decemvirs; that a league of hospitality should be entered into by public authority with the people of Cære, because they had afforded a reception to the sacred utensils of the Roman people and to their priests; and because, by the kindness of that people, the worship of the immortal gods had not been intermitted; that Capitoline games should be exhibited, for that Jupiter, supremely good and great, had protected his own mansion and the citadel of the Roman people when in danger; and that Marcus Furius, the dictator, should establish a college for that purpose, out of those who should inhabit the Capitol and citadel." Mention was also introduced of expiating the voice heard by night, which had been heard announcing the calamity before the Gallic war, and neglected, and a temple was ordered in the New Street to Aius Locutius. The gold, which had been rescued from the Gauls, and that also which during the alarm had been collected from the other temples into the recess of Jupiter's temple, the recollection being confused as to the temples to which it should be carried back, was all judged to be sacred, and ordered to be placed under the throne of Jupiter. Already the religious scruples of the state had appeared in this, that when gold was wanting for public uses, to make up for the Gauls the amount of the ransom agreed upon, they had accepted that which was contributed by the matrons, so that they might not touch the sacred gold. Thanks were returned to the matrons, and to this was added the honour of their having funeral orations pronounced on them after death, in the same manner as the men. Those things being finished which appertained to the gods, and such measures as could be transacted through the senate, then, at length, as the tribunes were teasing the commons by their unceasing harangues, to leave the ruins, to remove to Veii, a city ready prepared for them, being escorted by the entire senate, he ascends the tribunal, and spoke as follows:

"Romans, so disagreeable to me are contentions with the tribunes of the people, that in my most melancholy exile, whilst I resided at Ardea, I had no other consolation than that I was removed from these contests; and for this same reason I would never have returned, even though you recalled me by a decree of the senate, and by order of the people. Nor has it been any change in my own sentiments, but in your fortune, that has persuaded me to return now. For the question was that my country should remain in its own established seat, not that I should reside in my country. And on the present occasion I would gladly remain quiet and silent, were not the present struggle also appertaining to my country's interests, to be wanting to which, as long as life lasts, were base in others, in Camillus impious. For why have we recovered it? Why have we rescued it when besieged out of the hands of the enemy, if we ourselves desert it when recovered? And when, the Gauls being victorious, the entire city captured, both the gods and the natives of Rome still retained and inhabited the Capitol and citadel, shall even the citadel and the Capitol be deserted, now when the Romans are victorious and the city has been recovered? And shall our prosperous fortune cause more desolation to this city than our adverse caused?

Truly if we had no religious institutions established together with the city, and regularly transmitted down to us, still the divine power has so manifestly interested itself in behalf of the Roman state on the present trying occasion, that I should think that all neglect of the divine worship was removed from the minds of men. For consider the events of these latter years one after the other, whether prosperous or adverse; you will find that all things succeeded favourably with us whilst we followed the gods, and unfavourably when we neglected them. Now, first of all the Veientian war—of how many years' duration, with what immense labour waged!—was not brought to a termination, until the water was discharged from the Alban lake by the admonition of the gods. What, in the name of heaven, regarding this recent calamity of our city? did it arise, until the voice sent from heaven concerning the approach of the Gauls was treated with slight? until the law of nations was violated by our ambassadors, and until such violation was passed over by us with the same indifference towards the gods, when it should have been punished by us? Accordingly vanquished, made captives and ransomed, we have suffered such punishments at the hands of gods and men, as that we are now a warning to the whole world. Afterwards our misfortunes reminded us of our religious duties. We fled for refuge to the gods, to the seat of Jupiter supremely good and great; amid the ruin of all our effects our sacred utensils we partly concealed in the earth; part of them we carried away to the neighbouring cities and removed from the eyes of the enemy. Though deserted by gods and men, still we intermitted not the worship of the gods. Accordingly they have restored to us our country, and victory, our ancient renown in war which had been lost, and on our enemies, who, blinded by avarice, have violated the faith of a treaty with respect to the weight of gold, they have turned dismay, and flight, and slaughter.

"When you behold such striking instances of the effects of honouring or neglecting the deity, do you perceive what an act of impiety we are about to perpetrate, scarcely emerging from the wreck of our former misconduct and calamity? We possess a city founded under auspices and auguries; not a spot is there in it that is not full of religious rites and of the gods: the days for the anniversary sacrifices are not more definitely stated, than are the places in which they are to be performed. All these gods, both public and private, do ye, Romans, pretend to forsake. What similarity does your conduct bear [to that] which lately during the siege was beheld with no less admiration by the enemy than by yourselves in that excellent Caius Fabius, when he descended from the citadel amid the Gallic weapons, and performed on the Quirinal hill the solemn rites of the Fabian family? Is it your wish that the family religious rites should not be intermitted even during war, but that the public rites and the Roman gods should be deserted even in time of peace, and that the pontiffs and flamens should be more negligent of public religious ceremonies, than a private individual in the anniversary rite of a particular family? Perhaps some one may say, that we will either perform these duties at Veii, or that we will send our priests hither from thence in order to perform them; neither of which can be done, without infringing on the established forms. For not to enumerate all the sacred rites severally and all the gods, whether in the banquet of Jupiter can the lectisternium be performed in any other place, save in the Capitol? What shall I say of the eternal fire of Vesta, and of the statue, which, as the pledge of empire, is kept under the safeguard of her temple? What, O Mars Gradivus, and you, father Quirinus, of your Ancilia? Is it right that these sacred things, coeval with the city, some of them more ancient than the origin of the city, should be abandoned to profanation? And, observe the difference existing between us and our ancestors. They handed down to us certain sacred rites to be performed by us on the Alban and on the Lavinian mounts. Was it in conformity with religion that these sacred rites were transferred to us to Rome from the cities of our enemies? shall we transfer them hence to Veii, an enemy's city, without impiety? Come, recollect how often sacred rites are performed anew, because some ceremony of our country had been omitted through negligence or accident. On a late occasion, what circumstance, after the prodigy of the Alban lake, proved a remedy to the state distressed by the Veientian war, but the repetition of the sacred rites and the renewal of the auspices? But further, as if duly mindful of ancient religious usages, we have both transferred foreign deities to Rome, and have established new ones. Very recently, imperial Juno was transferred from Veii, and had her dedication performed on a day how distinguished for the extraordinary zeal of the matrons, and with what a full attendance! We have directed a temple to be erected to Aius Locutius, in consequence of the heavenly voice heard in the New Street. To our other solemnities we have added the Capitoline games, and, by direction of the senate, we have founded a new college for that purpose. Which of these things need we have done, if we were to leave the Roman city together with the Gauls? if it was not voluntarily we remained in the Capitol for so many months of siege; if we were retained by the enemy through motives of fear? We are speaking of the sacred rites and of the temples; what, pray, of the priests? Does it not occur to you, what a degree of profaneness would be committed in respect of them. The Vestals, forsooth, have but that one settlement, from which nothing ever disturbed them, except the capture of the city. It is an act of impiety for the flamen Dialis to remain for a single night without the city. Do ye mean to make them Veientian instead of Roman priests? And shall the virgins forsake thee, O Vesta? And shall the flamen by living abroad draw on himself and on his country such a weight of guilt every night? What of the other things, all of which we transact under auspices within the Pomærium, to what oblivion, to what neglect do we consign them? The assemblies of the Curias, which comprise military affairs; the assemblies of the Centuries, at which you elect consuls and military tribunes, when can they be held under auspices, unless where they are wont [to be held]? Shall we transfer them to Veii? or whether for the purpose of holding their elections shall the people assemble at so great inconvenience into a city deserted by gods and men?

"But the case itself forces us to leave a city desolated by fire and ruin, and remove to Veii, where all things are entire, and not to distress the needy commons by building here. But that this is only held out as a pretext, rather than that it is the real motive, I think is evident to you, though I should say nothing on the subject; for you remember that before the arrival of the Gauls, when the buildings, both public and private, were still unhurt, and the city still stood in safety, this same question was agitated, that we should remove to Veii. Observe then, tribunes, what a difference there is between my way of thinking and yours. Ye think that though it may not have been advisable to do it then, still that now it ought certainly to be done; I, on the contrary, (and be not surprised until you shall have heard the state of the case,) admitting it were advisable to remove when the entire city was safe, would not vote for relinquishing these ruins now. For then victory would be the cause of our removing into a captured city, one that would be glorious to ourselves and our posterity; whilst now this same removal would be wretched and disgraceful to us, and glorious to the Gauls. For we shall appear not to have left our country as conquerors, but to have lost it from having been vanquished; the flight at Allia, the capture of the city, the blockading of the Capitol, [will seem] to have imposed this necessity on us of forsaking our household gods, of having recourse to exile and flight from that place which we were unable to defend. And have the Gauls been able to demolish Rome, which the Romans shall be deemed to have been unable to restore? What remains, but that if they should now come with new forces, (for it is evident that their number is scarcely credible,) and should they feel disposed to dwell in this city, captured by them, and deserted by you, would you suffer them? What, if not the Gauls, but your old enemies, the Æquans and Volscians, should form the design of removing to Rome; would you be willing that they should become Romans, you Veientians? Would ye prefer that this should be a desert in your possession, or a city of the enemy? For my part I can see nothing more impious. Is it because ye are averse to building, ye are prepared to incur this guilt, this disgrace? Even though no better, no more ample structure could be erected throughout the entire city than that cottage of our founder, is it not better to dwell in cottages, like shepherds and rustics, amid your sacred places and your household gods, than to go publicly into exile? Our forefathers, strangers and shepherds, when there was nothing in these places but woods and marshes, erected a new city in a very short time; do we, with a Capitol and citadel safe, and the temples of the gods still standing, feel it irksome to build up what has been burnt? and what we individually would have done, if our private residence had been burned down, shall we as a body refuse to do in the case of a public conflagration?

"What, if by some evil design of accident a fire should break out at Veii, and the flames spread by the wind, as may happen, should consume a considerable portion of the city; are we then to seek Fidenæ, or Gabii, or any other city to remove to? Has our native soil so slight a hold on us, or this earth which we call mother; or does our love of country lie merely in the surface and in the timber of the houses? For my part, I will acknowledge to you, whilst I was absent, though I am less disposed to remember this as the effect of your injustice than of my own misfortune, as often as my country came into my mind, all these circumstances occurred to me, the hills, the plains, the Tiber, the face of the country familiar to my eyes, and this sky, beneath which I had been born and educated; may these now induce you, by their endearing hold on you, to remain in your present settlement, rather than they should cause you to pine away through regret, after having left them. Not without good reason did gods and men select this place for founding a city: these most healthful hills; a commodious river, by means of which the produce of the soil may be conveyed from the inland countries, by which maritime supplies may be obtained; close enough to the sea for all purposes of convenience, and not exposed by too much proximity to the dangers of foreign fleets; a situation in the centre of the regions of Italy, singularly adapted by nature for the increase of a city. The very size of so new a city is a proof. Romans, the present year is the three hundred and sixty-fifth year of the city; for so long a time are you waging war amid nations of such long standing; yet not to mention single cities, neither the Volscians combined with the Æquans, so many and such strong towns, nor all Etruria, so potent by land and sea, occupying the breadth of Italy between the two seas, can cope with you in war. And as the case is so, where, in the name of goodness, is the wisdom in you who have tried [this situation] to make trial now of some other, when, though your own valour may be removed elsewhere, the fortune of this place certainly cannot be transferred? Here is the Capitol, where, a human head being found, it was foretold that in that place would be the head of the world, and the chief seat of empire. Here, when the Capitol was to be freed by the rites of augury, Juventas and Terminus, to the very great joy of our fathers, suffered not themselves to be moved. Here is the fire of Vesta, here the Ancilia sent down from heaven, here are all the gods propitious to you if you stay."

Camillus is said to have moved them as well by other parts of his speech, but chiefly by that which related to religious matters. But an expression seasonably uttered determined the matter whilst still undecided; for when a meeting of the senate, a little after this, was being held in the Curia Hostilia regarding these questions, and some troops returning from relieving guard passed through the forum in their march, a centurion in the comitium cried out, "Standard-bearer, fix your standard! it is best for us to remain here." Which expression being heard, both the senate came out from the senate-house, and all cried out that "they embraced the omen," and the commons, who were collected around, joined their approbation. The law [under discussion] being rejected, the building of the city commenced in several parts at once. Tiles were supplied at the public expense. The privilege of hewing stone and felling timber wherever each person wished was granted, security being taken that they would finish the buildings on that year. Their haste took away all attention to the regulating the course of the streets, whilst, setting aside all distinction of property, they build on any part that was vacant. That is the reason why the ancient sewers, at first conducted through the public streets, now in many places pass under private houses, and why the form of the city appears more like one taken up by individuals, than regularly portioned out [by commissioners].

THE END

Made in the USA
Coppell, TX
04 January 2023

10385567R00184